Governing Extractive Industries

Governing Extractive Industries

Politics, Histories, Ideas

Anthony Bebbington, Abdul-Gafaru Abdulai,
Denise Humphreys Bebbington, Marja Hinfelaar,
and Cynthia A. Sanborn

with

Jessica Achberger, Celina Grisi Huber,
Verónica Hurtado, Tania Ramírez,
and Scott D. Odell

OXFORD
UNIVERSITY PRESS

OXFORD
UNIVERSITY PRESS

Great Clarendon Street, Oxford, OX2 6DP,
United Kingdom

Oxford University Press is a department of the University of Oxford.
It furthers the University's objective of excellence in research, scholarship,
and education by publishing worldwide. Oxford is a registered trade mark of
Oxford University Press in the UK and in certain other countries

First Edition published in 2018

Published in the United States of America by Oxford University Press
198 Madison Avenue, New York, NY 10016, United States of America

British Library Cataloguing in Publication Data
Data available

Library of Congress Control Number: 2018937073

ISBN 978–0–19–882093–2

UK Aid Acknowledgement

This book is an output from a project funded by UK Aid from the UK government for the benefit of developing countries. However, the views expressed and information contained therein are not necessarily those of, or endorsed by, the UK Government, which can accept no responsibility for such views or information, or for any reliance placed on them.

Preface and Acknowledgements

This book has been several years in the making. Ideas for the research project on which it is based slowly began cooking in 2012 as part of wider discussions within the Effective States and Inclusive Development (ESID) Research Centre, an international collaboration of research centres coordinated by the Global Development Institute at the University of Manchester. ESID's unifying question is: 'What kinds of politics can help to secure inclusive development, and how can these be promoted?' Our research project asked how one might understand the interactions between political settlements, extractive industry governance, and patterns of inclusion over the long haul. We had each worked on extractive industries for a number of years, and for each of us it was more than obvious that politics is central to how the sector is governed. However, the challenge of finding a formal language for talking about this political dimension, and of doing so in a way that would allow for systematic comparison and synthesis across different country contexts, piqued our interest. And so began the initiative that has culminated in this manuscript.

In keeping with the general orientation of the broader ESID programme, we worked from literature on political settlements. This generated its own challenges—sometimes it seemed to help our analyses, while at other times it felt as if the language got in the way. We debated the usefulness or not of the concept, and in the end made our own settlement with political settlements. In part, this was because of the challenge at hand. It is completely reasonable to have to talk about 125 years of a country's political and natural resource governance history in forty pages: in political debate and general conversation, citizens are frequently in the business of making such concise interpretations of history and then mobilizing them as part of a broader debate. Yet, the actual challenge of writing these forty-page interpretations was brutal: on the one hand, it felt we were leaving so much out, while on the other, details were always getting in the way of the flow of our arguments. After very many iterations and discussions of the four country cases that constitute the basis of this book, we cycled back to the view that the political settlements framework became the most productive and integrative way to talk about these long-term dynamics in ways that allow comparisons over time and across space. We also concluded that the language of political settlements was especially useful because it allowed us to discuss through one framework quite different forms of resource extraction: large-scale mining, large-scale hydrocarbons, artisanal and small-scale mining (ASM), and mining cooperatives. This is important because in the literature, these different forms of extraction are most often discussed separately, notwithstanding the clear political, economic, and geographical relationships that exist among them.

As we have proceeded along this analytical and theoretical road trip (complete with flat tyres, breakdowns, and speeding tickets), we have received sterling intellectual guidance from Sam Hickey at Manchester. Sam has offered comment and criticism with great generosity, and has also been our project's most loyal supporter and cheerleader, especially when we felt we were treading water. Also in the core ESID team, the comments and thinking of Pablo Yanguas, Kunal Sen, and Matthias vom Hau have been very helpful. This project was linked to two others—one investigating corporate social responsibility (CSR) in mining, led by Tomas Frederiksen; the other addressing the relationships between natural resource taxation and redistributive social policy, led by Paul Mosley. Tomas and Paul were part of many of our team debates and we owe them an intellectual debt of gratitude also. In Peru, Tania Ramírez and Verónica Hurtado made considerable and important contributions to the research and writing, Alvaro Cano's work on the evolution of public policies towards ASM was fundamental to our understanding thereof, Alejandra Villanueva's research provided new insights into the mining sector, and Alvaro Paredes provided research assistance. For research on Bolivia, Celina Grisi Huber played a vital role in field research, Laura Riddering and Scott Odell each supported with invaluable assistance. In Zambia, Jessica Achberger and Justine Sichone each helped greatly in the preparation of research materials.

At Manchester and at our respective home institutions, many people have assisted with the management of this project. They have facilitated our meetings, organized workshops, handled budgets, and done all the other administrative work without which research—especially international collaborative and comparative research—would not be possible. In particular, we are grateful to Kat Bethell, Julia Brunt, Clare Degenhardt, Pamela Dunkle, Sophie King, Susan Puryear, Julie Rafferty, Zuleyka Ramos, Ingrid Vega, and Anna Webster. We are especially grateful to Scott Odell of Clark University, who did a remarkable job editing the chapters, teasing out their messages, clarifying and correcting syntax and grammar, and preparing the manuscript for Oxford University Press (OUP). At Melbourne, Chandra Jayasuriya was an enormous help in preparing all the maps for this book. At OUP, we thank Adam Swallow for his guidance and support of the project, and Catherine Owen and Katie Bishop for guiding it through contracting and production.

Many people have commented on this work as it has progressed, and their observations and criticisms have improved our arguments in many ways.

In particular, we are grateful to Martin Abregú, Javier Arellano-Yanguas, Kojo Asante, José Alejandro Peres Cajías, Alvaro Cano, John Crabtree, Gerardo Damonte, Eduardo Dargent, Sam Hickey, David Hulme, David Kaimowitz, Terry Karl, Carlos Monge, Alvaro Paredes, Maritza Paredes, Martin Scurrah, and Alejandra Villanueva. We are also grateful for the various anonymous reviews that we received on the book proposal and the different chapters of the manuscript. Our arguments and interpretations have also been presented in workshops, discussion fora, and panels at the Latin American Studies Association annual meetings in New York (2016) and Lima (2017); the Universidad del Pacífico in Lima; the ESID Research Dissemination workshop at the Ghana Centre for Democratic Development, Accra; the Southern African Institute for Policy Analysis and Research, Lusaka; the Centre for Regional Studies and Development of Tarija, Tarija; and the Bolivian Centre for Documentation and Information, Cochabamba. We thank participants at all these events for their feedback.

The project has received financial support from the ESID Research Centre, as well as many financial subsidies from our host institutions: Clark University, University of Melbourne, Universidad del Pacífico, the Southern African Institute for Policy and Research, and the University of Ghana Business School. Tony Bebbington also acknowledges with much gratitude the support of a John Simon Guggenheim Memorial Foundation Fellowship and an Australian Research Council funded Australian Laureate Fellowship.

Anthony Bebbington, Abdul-Gafaru Abdulai,
Denise Humphreys Bebbington, Marja Hinfelaar
and Cynthia Sanborn

Melbourne, Accra, Worcester, Lusaka, Lima
October 2017

Table of Contents

List of Figures

List of Maps

List of Tables

List of Abbreviations

AAC	Anglo-American Company
ADEX	National Exporters' Association (*Asociación de Exportadores,* Peru)
ADN	Nationalist Democratic Action (*Acción Democrática Nacionalista,* Bolivia)
ANC	African National Congress
ANMM	National Association of Medium-Scale Miners (*Asociación Nacional de Mineros Medianos,* Bolivia)
AP	Popular Action (*Acción Popular,* Peru)
APRA	American Popular Revolutionary Alliance (*Alianza Popular Revolucionaria Americana,* Peru)
ARPS	Aborigines Rights Protection Society (Ghana)
ASM	artisanal and small-scale mining
AU	African Union
BCRP	Central Reserve Bank of Peru (*Banco Central de Reserva del Perú*)
BHP	Broken Hill Proprietary
BSAC	British South Africa Company
CAF	Central African Federation
CEDIB	Bolivian Centre for Documentation and Information (*Centro de Documentación e Información Bolivia*)
CEO	chief executive officer
CIPEC	Intergovernmental Council of Copper Exporting Countries
CIUP	Research Center of the University of the Pacific (*Centro de Investigación de la Universidad del Pacífico,* Peru)
CNTCB	National Confederation of Peasant Workers of Bolivia (*Confederación Nacional de Trabajadores Campesinos de Bolivia*)
COB	Confederation of Bolivian Workers (*Central Obrera Boliviana*)
CODEPANAL	Committee for the Defence of National Patrimony (*Comité de Defensa del Patrimonio Nacional,* Bolivia)
COMIBOL	Bolivian Mining Corporation (*Corporación Minera de Bolivia*)
COMSUR	Mining Company of the South (*Compañía Minera del Sur*)

CONFIEP	National Confederation of Private Business Institutions (*Confederación Nacional de Instituciones Empresariales Privadas*, Peru)
CPMC	Cerro de Pasco Mining Company
CPP	Convention People's Party (Ghana)
CSR	corporate social responsibility
CSUTCB	Unified Confederation of Unionized Peasant Workers of Bolivia (*Confederación Sindical Única de Trabajadores Campesinos de Bolivia*)
DA	development agreement
DGAAM	General Direction of Environmental Issues in Mining (*Dirección General de Asuntos Ambientales Mineros*, Peru)
ECLAC	United Nations Economic Commission for Latin America and the Caribbean
EI	extractive industry
EIA	environmental impact assessment
EITI	Extractive Industries Transparency Initiative
ERP	Economic Recovery Programme (Ghana)
ESID	Effective States and Inclusive Development (Research Centre)
FDI	foreign direct investment
FENCOMIN	National Federation of Mining Cooperatives of Bolivia (*Federación Nacional de Cooperativas Mineras de Bolivia*, Bolivia)
FISP	Farmer Input Support Programme (Zambia)
FPIC	free, prior, and informed consent
FSTMB	Union Federation of Bolivian Mine Workers (*Federación Sindical de Trabajadores Mineros de Bolivia*)
FTA	free trade agreement
GDP	gross domestic product
GH	Ghana
GHEITI	Ghana Extractive Industry Transparency Initiative
GRA	Ghana Revenue Authority
GRFA	Revolutionary Government of the Armed Forces (*Gobierno Revolucionario de las Fuerzas Armadas*, Peru)
HIPC	heavily indebted poor countries initiative
ICMM	International Council on Mining and Metals
IFC	International Finance Corporation
IFI	international financial institution
IGV	General Consumption Tax (*Impuesto General a las Ventas*, Peru)
ILO	International Labour Organization

ILO 169	1989 Indigenous and Tribal Peoples Convention of the International Labour Organization
IMF	International Monetary Fund
INEI	National Institute for Statistics and Informatics (*Instituto Nacional de Estadística e Informática*, Peru)
INGEMMET	Geological, Mining, and Metallurgical Institute (*Instituto Geológico, Minero, y Metalúrgico*, Peru)
IPC	International Petroleum Company
IRAC	Institute for Land Reform and Colonization (*Instituto de Reforma Agraria y Colonización*, IRAC)
IRS	Internal Revenue Services (Ghana)
ISI	import substitution industrialization
IVA	value added tax
LAZ	Law Association of Zambia
LEAP	Livelihood Empowerment Against Poverty (Ghana)
MAS	Movement to Socialism (*Movimiento al Socialismo*, Bolivia)
MC	Ministry of Culture (*Ministerio de Cultura*, Peru)
MDF	Mineral Development Fund (Ghana)
MEF	Ministry of Economy and Finance (*Ministerio de Economía y Finanzas*, Peru)
MFEZ	multi-facility export zone (Zambia)
MINAM	Ministry of the Environment (*Ministerio del Ambiente*, Peru)
MINEM	Ministry of Energy and Mines (*Ministerio de Energía y Minas*, Peru)
MIR	Revolutionary Left Movement (*Movimiento de la Izquierda Revolucionaria*, Bolivia)
MMC	Marcona Mining Company
MMD	Movement for Multi-Party Democracy (Zambia)
MNR	National Revolutionary Movement (*Movimiento Nacionalista Revolucionario*, Bolivia)
MP	Member of Parliament
NCCM	Nchanga Consolidated Copper Mines
NCOM	National Coalition of NGOs in Mining (Ghana)
NDC	National Democratic Congress (Ghana)
NDPC	National Development Planning Commission (Ghana)
NFR	New Republican Force (*Nueva Fuerza Republicana*, Bolivia)
NGO	non-governmental organization
NLM	National Liberation Movement (Ghana)

NPP	New Patriotic Party (Ghana)
NRC	National Redemption Council (Ghana)
NT	Northern Territories (Ghana)
OAS	Organization of American States
OASL	Office of Administration of Stool Lands (Ghana)
OECD	Organization for Economic Co-operation and Development
OEFA	Organism for Environmental Evaluation and Fiscalization (*Organismo de Evaluación y Fiscalización Ambiental*, Peru)
OPEC	Organization of the Petroleum Exporting Countries
OVC	orphans and vulnerable children
PAMA	Environmental Adjustment and Management Plan (*Programa de Adecuación y Manejo Ambiental*, Peru)
PCP-Shining Path	Communist Party of Peru-Shining Path (*Partido Comunista del Perú-Sendero Luminoso*)
PEMEX	Mexican Petroleums (*Petróleos Mexicanos*)
PF	Patriotic Front (Zambia)
PMMC	Precious Minerals Marketing Company
PMSP	Mining Programme in Solidarity with the People (*Programa Minero de Solidaridad con el Pueblo*, Peru)
PNDC	Provisional National Defence Council (Ghana)
PPC	Christian People's Party (*Partido Popular Cristiano*, Peru)
PRMA	Petroleum Revenue Management Act (Ghana)
PRODUCE	Ministry of Production (*Ministerio de Producción*, Peru)
RCM	Roan Consolidated Copper Mines
RST	American Roan Selection Trust
SADA	Savannah Accelerated Development Authority (Ghana)
SAIPAR	Southern African Institute for Policy and Research
SAP	Structural Adjustment Programme
SENACE	National Service of Environmental Certification of Sustainable Investments (*Servicio Nacional de Certificación Ambiental para las Inversiones Sostenibles*, Peru)
SGMC	State Gold Mining Corporation (Ghana)
SMC	Supreme Military Council (Ghana)
SNMPE	National Society of Mining, Oil, and Energy (*Sociedad Nacional de Minería, Petróleo y Energía*, Peru)
SPCC	Southern Peru Copper Corporation
SUNAT	National Superintendency of Tax Administration (*Superintendencia Nacional de Administración Tributaria*, Peru)

TIPNIS	Isiboro-Sécure Indigenous Territory and National Park (*Territorio Indígena y Parque Nacional Isiboro-Sécure*, Bolivia)
UDI	Unilateral Declaration of Independence (Zambia)
UGCC	United Gold Convention Party (Ghana)
UNIP	United National Independence Party (Zambia)
UNO	Odriíst National Union (*Unión Nacional Odriísta*, Peru)
UPND	United Party for National Development (Zambia)
UPP	United Progressive Party (Zambia)
USAID	United States Agency for International Development
VAT	value added tax
WB	World Bank
WWII	World War II
YPFB	Bolivian National Oilfields (*Yacimientos Petrolíferos Fiscales de Bolivia*)
ZCCM	Zambia Consolidated Copper Mines
ZCCM-IH	Zambia Consolidated Copper Mines Investment Holdings
ZCTU	Zambia Congress of Trade Unions
ZIMCO	Zambia Industrial and Mining Corporation

1

Resource Extraction and Inclusive Development

Extending the Bases of the Political Settlements Approach

The large-scale extraction of minerals, hydrocarbons, and other natural resources[1] has long been central to national economies and the global economy. This has been the case in colonial and post-colonial economies alike, and the harnessing of such resources continues to feature prominently in the economic development strategies of many countries. The economic significance of resource extraction can be quantified through data on percentage contribution of oil, gas, and mining to GDP, exports, foreign direct investment, and the public budget (Mosley, 2017). In contrast, the contributions of extractive industries to 'development' and 'inclusive development' are more uncertain, not least because definitions of these terms differ based on the degree to which analysts emphasize goals of poverty and income inequality, environmental justice, gender equity, or human and citizenship rights. Even those advocating for the role of extractives in economic development and poverty reduction recognize that results have often been ambiguous (Davis, 2009). These observations have inspired much discussion of the factors explaining such disappointments, a series of policy recommendations regarding how to improve the contributions of resource extraction to development, and significant advocacy and social conflict surrounding the extractive economy across the globe (see Ross, 2015).

Much of the discussion regarding how to manage resource extraction more effectively has emphasized the importance of institutions and governance (Karl, 1997, 2007; Humphreys et al., 2007). Disappointing development outcomes in economies with substantial extractive activity have been explained in terms of the 'poor quality' or 'weakness' of institutions existing prior to and during the growth of investment in mining and hydrocarbons, as well as the adverse impacts of a growing extractive economy on institutional quality (Weber-Fahr, 2002; Robinson et al., 2006; Humphreys et al., 2007; Davis, 2009; Ross, 2015). Such centring of institutions in explanations of poor performance has also meant that many proposals for change have emphasized the need for new, improved, and strengthened institutions. The sorts of institutions proposed are diverse, often depending on the most pressing concerns of the commentator. These can include: institutions and processes for free, prior and informed consent (FPIC); sovereign wealth funds to manage resource rents without distorting incentives; transparency institutions ranging from subnational government oversight to the global Extractive Industries Transparency Initiative (EITI); and tax codes to reallocate benefits along the value chain and among stakeholders.[2] While such proposals each have their logic, they tend to say less about the conditions that would need to exist for such institutional changes to come into being, be sustained over time, and be effective.

Of course, there is only so much that any particular act of analysis or advocacy can achieve, but it remains important to explore the conditions under which institutions affecting natural resource governance have emerged. The literature on institutional change suggests that political, ideational, and bureaucratic factors are all likely to matter (Mahoney and Thelen, 2010). While much of this literature invokes exogenous drivers of change, drivers can also be endogenous to the institution and the geographical and social units that it governs (Bebbington et al., 2008; Mahoney and Thelen, 2010; Berdegué et al., 2015; Ospina et al., 2015). Regardless of whether drivers are primarily exogenous or endogenous, historical precursors are likely to affect the possibility of, and form taken by, such processes of emergence (Mahoney and Thelen, 2010; Thorp et al., 2012; Bebbington, 2013b).

This book synthesizes lessons from research enquiring into the drivers of institutional change in extractive industry governance over time and in different geographical contexts, and the implications of these governance arrangements for patterns of social, political, and economic inclusion. The project paid special attention to the political drivers of institutional change. We are certainly not the first to step into this terrain, and there is already a strong scholarly literature addressing the political dimensions of extractive industry governance (e.g. Karl, 1997; Leith, 2003; Le Billon, 2005; Robinson et al., 2006; Rajan, 2011; Mitchell, 2012; Ross, 2012; D'Argent et al., 2017). Our intended contribution is to take insights from such authors and explore what might be gained by reading the politics of resource extraction through a theoretical framework that grows out of the literature on political settlements and national developmental trajectories (Hickey, 2013; Hickey et al., 2015). In the remainder of this introduction, we discuss how we made use of these literatures, introduce the questions that the book addresses, describe the methodology underlying our research, and briefly introduce the remaining chapters.

1 Mapping the Conceptual Terrain

1.1 *The 'Resource Curse' and the Politics of Extractive Industry Governance*

In the words of Ross (2015), 'The resource curse might be defined as the adverse effects of a country's natural resource wealth on its economic, social, or political well-being' (2015: 240). Since the early 1990s, debates over the nature and existence of this 'curse' have been the dominant frame for discussions of extractive industry governance. These debates emerged around the claim that growth indicators for countries that are dependent on natural resource extraction (especially minerals, oil, gas, and timber) do not compare well with those of countries whose economies are more diversified and demonstrate more substantial manufacturing and service sectors (Gelb, 1988; Auty, 1993; Sachs and Warner, 1995). It was also argued that extractive industry-dependent economies were less effective in reducing poverty than more diversified economies (Ross, 2001b) and that 'natural resource wealth tends to adversely affect a country's governance' (Ross, 2015: 239). Claims regarding the existence of a 'resource curse' quickly stimulated a counter-literature arguing the converse, or at least asserting that there was no clear pattern to the relationship between resource dependence and national economic and social performance (Davis, 1995; Davis and Tilton, 2005; ICMM, 2007; Brunnschweiler and Bulte, 2008; Davis, 2009). At stake in much of this debate are arguments about statistical methods, choice of indicators, time horizons, and more. Discussions have made clear just how difficult it is to define and then measure appropriate indicators of 'resource dependence' or 'institutional quality', which then makes it challenging to build causal arguments about the effects of one of these on the other. Similar problems of indicator definition and measurement apply to other terms that circulate in discussions of the resource curse.

As debates progressed, they moved away from making strong statements on whether hydrocarbons and minerals were 'good' or 'bad' for development, towards recognition of the diverse outcomes associated with extractive industry wealth, and efforts to account for this diversity (Bebbington et al., 2008; Thorp et al., 2012; Ross, 2015). Most frequently, institutional quality became identified as the primary determinant of these diverse outcomes, and 'getting the institutions right' became a central objective in efforts at 'escaping the resource curse' (Humphreys et al., 2007). As authors, we take it as a given that the relationship between extractive industries and the quality of development is indeterminate and has much to do with the nature of dominant institutions. However, we would also argue that more often than not, resource-dependent development has delivered disappointing results and been plagued by a range of pathologies, and that the balance of political power has a significant influence on the qualities of the institutions that influence the effects of natural resources on development. Our primary concern is to understand how the interactions among politics, natural resources, and institutional form play out over time and across countries with a view to identifying convergences that might help us theorize these relationships.

There is already a literature on the political drivers of resource-dependent development on which we build; some of this precedes the 'resource curse' literature, while some of it has emerged as part of that literature. Of particular importance is the early work of Terry Karl (1987, 1997) that used a political economy lens to understand how oil exporting affects the relationships between politics, democracy, and development. In *The Paradox of Plenty,* Karl drew inspiration from her long-term empirical work on Venezuela, as well as the experiences of other oil and mineral-dependent nations, to move beyond generic assertions that 'politics matter'. Instead, she argued that the pacts and bargains made by elites in one phase of history, including the decisions they make about whether and how to sow revenue from resource extraction, deeply affect the space and options for development thereafter. She examined the decision to exploit oil revenues in the second half of the twentieth century in Venezuela, and showed how it affected the country's ability to create democratic institutions over time. In particular, she demonstrated the 'paradoxical' relationship between the abundance of oil and the existence of institutions that were deeply corrupt and fragile. This work showed the weight of external factors and actors in the politics of oil exporters, and how bonanza rents from such resources can 'grease the wheel' of domestic pact-making, keeping dissidents quiet by buying them off. When that no longer works, however, the revenues are often used to build up militaries that use force to exclude and suppress opponents. Yet her analysis also showed how such pact-making can unravel, as more people become excluded from the original deals and are negatively affected by the dependency of the state on extraction. When the structural inequalities are no longer masked by redistributive politics, things fall apart. In many regards, Karl's work was not just analytical—it was sadly prophetic, certainly for Venezuela.

The political significance of oil has also been at the core of the contributions of Michael Ross (2001a, 2012) and Timothy Mitchell (2012). Ross (2001a, 2012, 2015) argues that resource curse-like outcomes are much more systematically associated with oil dependence than with the extraction of other mineral resources. There are various reasons for this, including the price volatility of oil. However, Ross places particular explanatory emphasis on whether oil resources are in private or state hands. He suggests that oil began to have more systematically adverse impacts on the depth and quality of democracy following the creation of state-owned oil companies in the 1970s. State ownership offered elites privileged instruments with which to politicize oil—whether through using revenue for purposes of political patronage, pact-making, or private gain, or through instrumentalizing the control of oil as a metaphor for talking about imperial dependence and resource sovereignty. In either instance, the developmental effects are adverse, he argues. For Mitchell (2012), whose focus was more broadly on the relationships between the control of carbon and democracy, oil has also had nefarious political effects. These have derived from the capital intensity of oil extraction and transportation, which means that oil tends to strengthen economic and political elites rather than organized labour. In addition, oil has attracted the attention of powerful transnational companies with close ties to their host states, who together undermine national sovereignty and regulatory institutions in the countries whose oil deposits they have sought out. The adverse political consequences of oil also figure prominently in Michael Watts's sustained work on the Niger Delta (Watts, 2004a, 2004b; Watts with Kashi, 2008). Watts insists that any effort to understand the relationships between oil, politics, violence, and development must attend 'to the ways in which oil becomes an idiom for doing politics as it is inserted into an already existing political landscape of forces, identities and forms of power' (Watts, 2004b: 76). He demonstrates that this political landscape is one characterized by longer histories of colonialism, post-independence state-making, subnational power, and identity formation around locality and indigeneity. The politics driving oil governance thus have deep historical and cultural roots.

While also pointing to the centrality of politics in determining the relationships between natural resource wealth and development, Robinson et al. (2006) pursue a completely distinct analytical line from that of Watts, one that attends to political incentives rather than history. They do this through formal modelling of the ways in which leaders calculate how they will use the revenues from extractive industries if their goal is to stay in power. They argue that these calculations lead political authorities to over-extract resources in order to finance strategies for retaining power. While the incentive to over-extract declines in contexts of resource boom, the tendency to use resources to purchase political support increases, leading to further inefficiencies in how public resources are allocated across the economy. In either instance, the development consequences are adverse, as financial resources are not invested in those sectors where they would have the most economic and social impact. The authors argue, however, that the extent to which this is so depends on the quality of institutions and the extent to which they constrain leaders' proclivity to misallocate state revenue. What their framework does not offer is a means of accounting for the quality of such institutions in the first place.

Other parts of the literature on the politics of natural resource extraction explore the political strategies of activist groups and social movements (Kirsch, 2012; Bebbington and Bury, 2013; Li, 2015), the emergence of civil conflict (Le Billon, 2005; Collier et al., 2009), and the politics of scholarly engagement (Coumans, 2011), among others. The precursors laid out by Karl, Ross, Watts, and Robinson et al., however, help define the base from which we work in this study. Together, their insights make clear that elite strategies of political pact-making are deeply affected by the presence of natural resource revenues in ways that then structure subsequent room for manoeuvre in politics and policy. Watts and Karl show in different ways how history matters, and Watts draws attention to the importance of ideas and the cultural realm in affecting political action around resource revenues. Each of them—though particularly Ross and Robinson et al.—also emphasize that whoever owns resources (the state or private actors) influences the impact of resource extraction on politics. Like much of the broader literature in which their work is situated, each author shows that institutions matter to the relationships between extractive industry and development. Karl and Watts also imply (albeit with quite distinct languages) that the nature of such institutions must be explained from within the same concepts that are used to explain the broader relationships between politics and natural resources. Put another way, one cannot build a framework to analyse the relationships between politics, extractive industry, and development, and then introduce 'institutions' as an independent mediating variable. Such institutions are themselves a product of the same relationships that they mediate and have to be accounted for historically.

In the following sections, we develop a framework for addressing these relationships by drawing upon the literature on political settlements. We suggest that this framework extends earlier work on the politics of natural resource governance. It centres the focus on power and elite relationships, analyses institutions in terms of these political relationships, and accounts for drivers of institutional and political change that can derive from within national elite pacts, as well as from the strategies of subaltern and transnational actors. In this way, the framework converges with other recent work that seeks more explicitly to go beyond the focus on 'institutions' within the resource curse literature to focus on the political coalitions and ideas that shape the emergence of institutions and how they actually function in practice (e.g. Poteete, 2009; Hickey and Izama, 2017; Mohan et al., 2017).

1.2 *Political Settlements as Stable Orders*

Khan (2010) defines a political settlement as '... a combination of power and institutions that is mutually compatible and also sustainable in terms of economic and political viability' (2010: 4). The concept describes the agreements among powerful actors that enable social order in a given country (North et al., 2009; Khan, 2010). Framed slightly more broadly, for di John and Putzel (2009), a political settlement 'refers to the balance or distribution of power between contending social groups and social classes, on which any state is based' (2009: 4).

In these overlapping formulations, a focus on political settlements draws attention to the ways in which governing relations are negotiated among economic and political elites. Such negotiations produce distributions of economic and political opportunity that reflect the bargaining power of these different elites. Elite status is not necessarily understood in terms of long-standing historical privilege based on race, ethnicity, kinship, or inherited wealth, but more specifically refers to that minority of individuals or groups that hold resources which allow them to exercise control over the state and the overall distribution of assets and rights in society. Such resources can be economic (land and financial or industrial capital, held nationally or transnationally), intellectual (technocrats, think tanks, mainstream media), or coercive (in the case of military elites, control over the organized use of force) (di John and Putzel, 2009: 15; Hickey, 2013: 3, 4).

In maintaining these orders and distributions, elites who are party to the settlement—who are 'on the inside', if you will—have to manage relationships with actors who are not 'on the inside'—actors often referred to as 'excluded factions'. In the sometimes dichotomizing language of political settlements, these factions are referred to as 'horizontally' excluded and 'vertically' excluded. Horizontally excluded factions are those who are opposed to the coalition of elites controlling the state and social order; vertically excluded factions are those groups who are supportive of controlling elites but who are not themselves party to any of the negotiations through which mechanisms of control and order are determined. In a strict sense, these vertically 'lower' factions are not 'excluded' because they feel an affinity with governing elites, but they are in no way 'on the inside'. Elites have to manage relationships with these different factions in order to ensure that they do not threaten the settlement. Such relationships can be managed through the exercise or credible threat of force, through the framing of legitimate discourses (e.g. ideas around what constitutes legitimate forms of power and credible models of national development), or through clientelism and the manipulation of incentives (e.g. through distribution of benefits, entitlements, and subsidies).

How these relationships among elites, and between elites and excluded factions, are managed depends, in Khan's terms, on the distribution of 'holding power' among different actors (i.e. their power to exercise a hold over others). The settlement is what holds these different relationships of power together in stable form. In this sense, the nature of the settlement (the balances of power and how they are managed) drives the nature of institutions and policies. These institutions and policies are the formalization of the practices and rules governing the distributions that lead all parties (included and excluded) to stay on board with the settlement rather than to openly contest and seek to overturn it.

Various authors have taken these ideas and converted them into typologies that seek to relate 'types' of settlements to 'types' of policy regimes or forms of development (Khan, 2010; Hickey, 2013; Levy and Walton, 2013; Levy, 2014; Booth, 2015; Levy and Kelsall, 2016). Levy and Walton (2013) and Levy (2014) argue that how elites within a dominant coalition manage these relationships and approach development depends on whether the broader political system is characterized by competition among leaders and parties or by the dominance of a particular leader or party. Political competition would lead elites to recruit clients into the coalition as a means of holding on to power (a form of political settlement they refer to as 'competitive clientelism'), and would therefore tend to operate with shorter-term time horizons oriented towards recruitment of clients ahead of electoral cycles. The notion of clientelism here is not in the traditional sense of patron–client relationships of dominance and dependence, but rather of elites who, in competing for political power, need to recruit and sustain supporters both to assume power and then to remain in power. Conversely, dominant leaders and parties worry less about client recruitment and so use resources for longer-term political projects based on particular ideas of development or personal gain, a form of settlement referred to as a dominant leader/dominant party settlement. Dominant party/leader settlements can range from those underlying the authoritarian modernization project of a developmental state through to personalized forms of dominance, with or without corruption and theft. Forms of leadership may be autocratic or elected, but in either instance are dominant.

1.3 *Change in Political Settlements*

Political settlements frameworks are helpful in different ways: in thinking about the dynamics underlying bargains; in conceptualizing the relationships among states, actors within ruling coalitions, and other actors; and in elaborating typologies for classifying forms of rule. However, they are less powerful in other regards. Perhaps most importantly, they have no obvious theory for why and how groups emerge, decline, and become more or less powerful.

Second, and in some regard related to the first point, the frameworks have no clear theory of the relationship between time, power, and the nature of settlements. While political settlements frameworks clearly presume time, talking of different settlements as preceding or following each other, they say little about how this movement happens, and, more importantly, about the ways in which time 't' affects time 't+1'. Yet to the extent that human agents learn, that memories affect action, that formative discourses are framed and then continue to circulate and affect future action, and that prior institutional forms affect the nature and emergence of subsequent institutions, then these questions of time are critical (cf. Watts, 2004b; Hall, 2010; Mahoney and Thelen, 2010).

Such processes of change in political settlements demand theorization and empirical demonstration. Within the language of the settlements framework, such change would primarily be explained as a result of excluded actors becoming more powerful, which requires theorizing how such power might accrue. However, it might also be explained in terms of changing ideas regarding what are deemed to be legitimate and acceptable distributions of political and economic opportunity. As such ideas change, the strategies of incorporation, clientelism, and/or repression that have been used to sustain a settlement may become less effective at quelling unrest and resistance. Finally, change may also occur because factions within elites begin to shift their calculations of the settlements that suit them best and so begin to realign alliances.

The sorts of empirical phenomena that might drive such change can also vary widely.

One driver of change may be the emergence of national or subnational actors who steadily develop the capacity to challenge the dominant settlement. Such capacity may develop for different reasons: the increasing value of the income streams controlled by excluded factions; the increasing ability of these factions to mobilize a broad base of citizens; changes in their proclivity to use violence; or their ability to reframe debates and challenge ideas that have historically legitimated particular distributions of opportunity and power. In this sense, conflict can be a mechanism of change in the national settlement. Across much of Latin America, the example of indigenous movements comes to mind as a clear case of such emergence of new actors. For while indigenous people are still disadvantaged, their presence within national debates and within the nature of national settlements has expanded enormously over a fifty year period in ways that have shifted the terms of national debates (Yashar, 2005; van Cott, 2007). Another source of change may be the arrival or increasing leverage of transnational actors who for one or another reason have the capacity and legitimacy to affect arrangements in any given country. Such transnational actors might drive changes in dominant ideas, contribute to the increase in 'holding power' of certain actors, or present new opportunities and incentives that lead elite parties to the settlement to reconsider alliances. Of many possible examples, the joint arrival of Newmont Mining Corporation and the International Finance Corporation to Peru in the early 1990s would be a case in point, as it increased the leverage of national mining elites, helped craft the idea that Peru could be a 'mining country' once again, and helped endorse the idea that opportunities should be distributed in Peru so as to favour mining investment (Bury, 2005).

1.4 *Natural Resource Governance and Political Settlements*

The logic of the political settlements literature implies that the ways in which natural resources (or in our case, extractive industries) are governed would be a function of the political settlement. This approach to extractive industry governance is important and useful in that it keeps hold of a focus on the relationships between institutions and development, while decentring the primacy of institutions as causal factors and instead placing power and politics at the core of any analysis. This framing suggests that efforts to seek significant change in sector governance without important changes in the balance of power within a settlement are unlikely to prosper. A related implication would be that a starting point for reform efforts should be to analyse the existing settlement and identify room for manoeuvre, or 'cracks' (Holloway, 2010; Bornschlegl, 2017) within that settlement and work from there to identify politically feasible changes. This would be quite distinct from classic reform strategies that identify technocratically desirable changes, try to implement them, and then end up banging up against the nature of existing power relations and inter-elite pacts. Similarly, it would be distinct from those classic oppositional approaches to resource extraction that focus on direct resistance and advocacy but frequently lack a language and a strategy for operating among, and negotiating with, elites, or for shifting the overall balance of political power in any way that might be sustained.

A political settlements approach to extractive industry governance is also helpful because it provides a set of concepts and typologies that enable comparative discussion of the politics surrounding diverse forms of resource extraction. It is one thing to argue that institutional change is central to any improvement in the relationships between extractive industry, environment, and development, and to recognize that the drivers of institutional change are primarily political (Karl, 2007). It is quite another thing to theorize those political drivers in a way that allows them to be analysed systematically and comparatively and on the basis of shared typological frameworks. The political settlements framing offers such a comparative analytical framework. Importantly, in contrast to the bulk of research on extractive industries that treats large-scale mining, artisanal and small-scale mining (ASM), and hydrocarbon extraction as distinct objects of study, a political settlements approach permits discussion of these different sectors all within the same framework. It could also allow for incorporating ancillary sectors such as hydropower and large-scale infrastructure into the same analysis.[3] This is because the primary organizing language is not one that is related to the sector, but rather one that describes the relationships between power, institutions, and order.

Just as the political settlements lens is helpful for analysing extractive industry governance, we would also argue that engaging with the question of natural resource extraction and its implications for development brings new insights to the political settlements literature. In particular, a focus on natural resources raises issues of place, scalar relations, and time in ways that also help explain how new actors emerge and accrue holding power, while other actors wane and cease to be parts of governing coalitions. We will elaborate these ideas in more detail in Chapter 6 in the light of the four country studies. Here we simply outline why the weakness (or in many instances, complete absence) of a sensibility to place/space, scale and time/memory is a serious limitation of the political settlements literature.

Our starting point for this part of our argument is the concept of 'territorializing projects' (Wainwright and Robertson, 2003; Wilson, 2004; Humphreys Bebbington and Bebbington, 2010). Territorial projects are efforts to construct and govern space in ways that accord with a given actor's or coalition's political and ideological concerns. Though rarely framed as such, political settlements are themselves territorial projects. If a political settlement is about securing social order through an elite agreement over the state and institutions, this order always refers to how a particular geographical space should be governed. By extension, if a political settlement involves negotiations among elites and the management of relationships with excluded factions, then the territorial project underlying the settlement reflects an accommodation among the distinct territorial projects of the parties to the settlement as well as coexistence with (and likely domination over) the territorial projects of excluded factions. In this sense, the organization of space is an outcome of political settlements. But the converse is also the case: conditions set by the contradictions and synergies among these diverse territorial projects set limits on the settlement. This is reflected in the different ways in which the tensions between centralization/decentralization, unitary state/federal state, single nation/plurination, and centralized control/territorial autonomy are resolved across different country contexts.

The spatiality of natural resources is often a factor in the constitution of actors and their territorializing projects. For example, the emergence of cooperative miners as a political actor that has pursued its own projects of territorial control in the highlands of Bolivia is itself a consequence of prior geographies of state-led mining and of existing mineral deposits (because many cooperatives emerged from the ashes of these mines). In Zambia, the constitution of miners as an organized group emerged as part of the same process that produced the Copperbelt as a mining area, and that group continues a (more implicit than explicit) territorial project that revolves around the Copperbelt. Meanwhile in Ghana, the inherited spatial–administrative structure of chieftaincies, stools, and local authorities influences how actors organize politically and make spatial and identity-based claims around mining and oil development.

In each of these examples, we have subnational actors pursuing projects of territorial control that are in some way related to the geography of natural resources. Also in each instance, these subnational actors have made their presence felt in national politics, and have been involved in ongoing negotiations with national elites over who should have access to subsoil resources and/or how the rents from extractive industry should be shared between the territory and 'the centre'. Such examples help illustrate the notion that any given settlement is also a settlement over the distribution of powers and opportunities between the centre and the subnational, and that this distribution (coupled with the strength of ideas about the relative importance of unity and devolved autonomy) is an important factor in the constitution of political actors. For example, in the Peruvian mining sector since the 1990s, some of the most important players have been subnational political leaders who have emerged as powerful in part because of the ways in which the geography of subsoil resources, ideas about decentralization, and the structure of subnational government intersect with each other (cf. Watts, 2004b). This does not mean that the political and territorial projects of these subnational leaders are of a kind. For instance, in the north of the country, one regional government's president (himself a product of social mobilization in the region) was a key player in stopping the expansion of mineral investment. In contrast, a different regional government president in the south of the country played a critical role in securing greater protections and benefits for the region as a means of brokering conflicts over resource extraction in such a way that allowed a large copper mining project to proceed. In both instances, these leaders became important because of the existence of subnational administrative powers (otherwise they would not have become regional presidents) and because of the political resonance of the territorial projects that they articulated and the ways in which these have intersected with the geography of mining.

Examples such as these are also significant because they point to individual and collective actors emerging subnationally through the contentious politics surrounding natural resource extraction, and then becoming 'national' actors by virtue of being able to exercise power on the national stage. This in turn is a reminder that there is nothing inherently 'national' about 'national' elites. Such elites are not born 'national', nor are they necessarily defined by being based in the principal urban centres of the country. Rather, they are defined by an ability to exercise power over decisions that affect much or all of a national territory. They become 'national' elites because they have accrued resources which allow them to exercise influence over the state and the overall distribution of assets and rights in society. Put another way, all actors are place-based but differ in their ability to exercise influences over other actors in other places. Certain places are more apt to produce actors with such national projection, and capital cities are indeed one such place. What these two Peruvian examples illustrate is that territories with significant mineral resources and the potential to produce very substantial rents are also apt to produce such actors. The types of political project these actors pursue, and thus their implications for the political settlement, are influenced by these and other qualities of the places from which they emerge.

This does not mean that all place-based actors who become able to influence—or force themselves into the core of—national settlements emerge on the back of natural resources, but many have. In this sense, a natural resource lens draws particular attention to the importance in any political analysis of understanding the place- and resource-based processes through which parties to (or strong excluded factions from) the national settlement emerge. Something similar occurs with transnational actors. Indeed, just as the 'national' character of certain actors should be understood historically, so too should the transnational character of other actors. That is, actors *become* transnational just as actors *become* national. That certain actors are 'transnational' reflects the fact that they have acquired the power to exercise influence beyond the borders of the national spaces from which they originated and in which they have their primary locations. In turn, this acquisition of global power grows out of prior processes of becoming powerful within the domains of their original national states. Once again, the geography of natural resources becomes important here. Mining and hydrocarbon companies like Vale, Petrobras (Brazil), or Chinalco (China), for instance, only became influential in Africa or Latin America because of their prior emergence as nationally important companies and political actors within their countries of origin. Newmont (the principal owners of Yanacocha gold mine in Peru) grew out of mining in the western United States; Broken Hill Proprietary (BHP) grew out of Broken Hill, Australia; and so on.

While these issues are not unique to the natural resources sector, a focus on extractive industries does help bring themes of place, territory, and scalar relations into the forefront of thinking about how political settlements are contested and stabilized, and how certain elites have emerged to become party to elite settlements. A focus on natural resources also brings one more important contribution to political settlements discussions. The history of political contention surrounding extractive industries makes palpable that it is not just abstract ideas (of efficiency, national unity, development, etc.) that help constitute settlements (Hickey et al., 2015), but also memories. Of course, much is remembered in national politics; but minerals, and over the last century oil, are often remembered in particularly resonant ways. It is not accidental that in the opening of Eduardo Galeano's *Open Veins of Latin America* (Galeano, 1971), the book chronicling centuries of extraction in the region that Hugo Chávez gave to Barack Obama, Spanish mining in the Andes features prominently. Myrna Santiago (2006) has argued that oil is central to Mexican identity, and memories of its nationalization still loom large in debates over how the sector should be governed. Memories of copper in Zambia, and its extraction by colonial powers, still impinge on political alliances and proposals for mining governance. In Ghana, contestations between chiefs and traditional authorities over the distribution of mineral rents are often based on historical memories that go back to the precolonial period. In Bolivia, silver and gold speak both of pre-Hispanic greatness as well as colonial and imperial subjugation and dependency, while tin invokes memories of a small number of early twentieth-century families who become phenomenally rich and powerful while delivering very little by way of development. The politics surrounding these resources can never be separated from those meanings. More generally, ideas of resource nationalism—that help drive the extension of state control over mining and hydrocarbons—are more often than not imbued with memories of other powers which have taken advantage of national resources in times past.

1.5 *Extractive Industries and Inclusive Development*

Extractive industry faces particular challenges around inclusion, in large measure because—except in the case of ASM—the activity of extracting minerals, oil, and gas depends upon the existence of significant asymmetries of power, resources, and technical expertise. The capital intensity of extraction requires elites with control over or access to investment funds measured in the billions, or at least hundreds of millions of dollars. The technologies associated with the investment generate fewer and fewer jobs—and show trends towards increased use of robotics to operate mine sites in the spirit of increasing occupational safety (by reducing the number of human jobs where there is risk). The environmental and social impacts of extraction are concentrated in space, leading to spatial inequalities in exposure to these impacts. The rents generated by extractive industry can be very large, and are controlled in the first instance by just two sets of actors: the company, and government tax authorities. For these different reasons, any model of development based on resource extraction is a compensatory model (Gudynas, 2012; Bebbington et al., 2014). That is, it is a model that compensates for these original, inherent inequalities, and that uses compensation in the form of transfers to offset these inequalities and asymmetries and to seek development. These transfers can take the form of corporate social responsibility (CSR) programmes, public social protection programmes, payments for losses, indigenous and local development funds, fiscal transfers to subnational governments or chiefs in areas affected by extraction, and so on. A large part of inclusion linked to resource extraction, if there is inclusion, therefore occurs through compensation (Humphreys Bebbington and Bebbington, 2010).

It merits note that the very idea of inclusion itself implies another asymmetry: namely the incorporation of other worlds into the world defined by development. For most people working in development this would be a non-issue, on the presumption that, of course, the rural poor would want greater inclusion in a world defined by the desirability of increased income, consumption, and access to basic services, as well as of enhanced participation in the political systems of the dominant order. This is not a position shared by all. Indeed, some authors writing critically about the extractive economy would argue that this notion of inclusion is another form of violence, one that refuses to acknowledge—or at least grant validity to—alternative ontologies (Blaser, 2010; Yampara, 2011; Gudynas, 2014; de la Cadena, 2015). Such authors might argue that any notion of inclusive development should be considered through, and superseded by, concepts such as *buen vivir, vivir bien*, and *sumak kawsay*, which emphasize the importance of living well, in harmony with other humans and with nature, rather than the inherent desirability of income, consumption, and economic growth. In the Andean countries, at least, such authors would argue that extractivism and any development based upon it should be viewed as destructively colonial because it requires the despoliation and disappearing of worlds in order to gain access to the subsoil (whether these are mountain worlds, or forest worlds: Descola, 1996; de la Cadena, 2015). In these readings, enhanced inclusion is less the goal than the search for modes of joint existence between different worlds that connect but simultaneously diverge (de la Cadena, 2015).

This is not the approach we take here. This is not because we necessarily reject the arguments of such authors. Rather it is a matter of consistency: the language of political settlements is an inherently modernist one, and so it is only consistent on our part to proceed with a notion of inclusive development informed by the commitments of modernism. As we seek to assess the ways in which political settlements interact with extractive industry governance and the extent to which this interaction fosters development that enhances or diminishes inclusion, we have focused on process indicators of this inclusion. That is, our primary approach has not been to measure the impacts of extractive industry on inclusion through evidence on increased incomes and consumption, or increased access to services, for instance (though we include some of this data). Instead, we have assessed inclusion through the extent to which extractive industry has affected opportunities for political participation, has been used to increase budgets for social spending, has led to increased budget for subnational authorities, has created new labour markets that expand quality employment, and has enhanced the status of poor peoples' rights. In keeping with the focus on institutions, then, our emphasis has been on the extent to which extractive industry has enhanced or weakened institutions that foster social, economic, and political inclusion. In this sense, we work from what might be termed a 'critical modernist' view on inclusion that values notions of emancipation, progress, and rights, while also allowing for popular reinterpretations of the forms that such aspirations should take (c.f. Peet and Watts, 1996; Peet and Hartwick, 2015).

1.6 *Summary*

To summarize, then, the basic conceptual framework running through our argument takes its core ideas from political settlements theory, as well as from earlier work on the politics of extractive industries, namely: the importance of pacts, bargains, and elites; the significance of relationships among elites, excluded horizontal factions, and lower level vertical factions; the political drivers of institutional form and performance; and the sources of stability and instability in settlements. To these, we add an emphasis on: the significance of relationships across time; the importance of political and cultural ideas tied to natural resources; the interacting influences of transnational, national, and subnational actors, especially those living in areas where natural resources become rapidly valorized; and the factors driving the emergence and decline of powerful actors. In particular, we associate much of this emergence and decline with the ways in which national and local political economies of minerals and hydrocarbons interact with transnational (f)actors. New actors emerge and decline as part of changes in the economic structure (cf. Boix, 2008), which are themselves often related to articulation with external markets. In addition, actors can emerge because of articulations with transnational ideas and activists that give new resources and legitimacy to those local and national actors in ways that are themselves often linked to natural resources.

The framework pursued here also suggests the value of making natural resources central to political settlements thinking. This is because in many countries access to and control over resources and resource rents are central to elite bargains; the transnational valorization of resources serves to bring political actors into being and into demise; and the economic and cultural values apportioned to natural resources become critical elements of state and nation-building.

2 Research Concerns and Approaches Taken

2.1 *Our Research Concerns*

Overall, our intent is to use a political settlements approach in a way that captures the key insights of and builds on existing literature on the politics and institutions of natural resource governance, while proposing a more explicit typological and analytical framework that helps establish power and politics, rather than institutions, as the central focus. At the same time, the book seeks to deepen the political settlements framework in several ways. First, as just noted, we believe that the task at hand should not be one of only applying a political settlements lens to understand natural resources, but also exploring the ways in which the very qualities of these natural resources have implications for how they are governed and the forms of politics that surround and drive this governance. In this sense, we bring a natural resources lens to political settlements as much as the other way around, and work from the presumption that the materiality of mineral and hydrocarbon resources matters (Bakker and Bridge, 2006; Bebbington, 2013b). This materiality is important both because the qualities of deposits affect their potential for commodification and profitability, and because these resources have geographically specific locations. These locations interact with other geographies and histories (of populations, territorial claims, drainage basins, land use, urban–rural and centre–periphery relations, etc.) in ways that affect incentives, ideas, and interests surrounding resource extraction and the emergence of political actors.

Second, the book brings an explicit attention to scale and space in understanding political settlements. While we are in no doubt that the sorts of national-level relationships that dominate political settlements analysis are indeed key to understanding the nature of these settlements and the ways in which they interact with natural resources, we will argue that political settlements need to be understood as a product of scaled processes, running from the subnational to the transnational. We will argue that the materiality and political economy of natural resources make subnational and transnational actors particularly powerful players in the constitution of settlements.

Third, the book recovers the importance of history and historical sensibility in political approaches to resource governance. Most work on political settlements—especially that which is also concerned to speak to policy and/or questions of inclusion and development—has tended to focus on recent time periods.[4] This stands in some contrast to some of the formative texts underlying political settlements thinking, which address processes over longer historical periods (North et al., 2009; Khan, 2010; Acemoglu and Robinson, 2012),[5] as also does Karl's work on comparative oil states and regime change (1997). The reason for addressing history is not merely to give a 'fuller account' of processes, but to show how this history is important in understanding contemporary arrangements and policy options. A longer-term historical analysis helps understand more fully: the conditions under which resource governance arrangements change, or do not change; the nature and origins of contemporary elites and excluded factions; the relative resilience of their holding power; and how history is remembered (Bebbington, 2013b).

2.2 *Our Approach to the Research*

There were two points of departure in building a methodology to speak to these research concerns. First was a deeply held belief that Latin American and African experience have much to contribute to each other, and that comparative work across the two continents is both valuable and valid. Team members had fruitful prior experience with such cross-regional comparison. When similarities emerge in the context of apparently large differences in political economic and post-colonial context, then this implies something fundamental about the phenomenon in question. When there are differences, then the challenge to the analyst is to use systematic comparison to tease out the causal relations at work in the relationships between political economy and the issue being studied and why these relations work out differently across space. Given that the Effective States and Inclusive Development (ESID) initiative, of which this book is a part, has been funded by the UK Department for International Development, the overwhelming tendency has been for the programme to focus on African and Asian countries. However, we assert that Latin America's long-standing and troubled history with natural resource governance make it an important case for the research topic at hand. Further, we believe that comparative analysis between it and Africa yields crucial insights for both regions and the topics of natural resource governance and political settlements more broadly. We began this project committed to the value of learning across regions, and ended only further convinced of the validity of this conviction.

The second point of departure was a focus on countries as a unit of analysis. As we have discussed in Subsection 2.1, the project was motivated to go beyond the methodological nationalism of political settlements research and to recognize the causal importance of other scales of political action and bargaining. However, if we were to challenge methodological nationalism, it would be important to explore the significance of these other scales from *within* a focus on the country level. Furthermore, notwithstanding our multi-scalar approach to the relationship between settlements and the governance of resource extraction, we remained convinced of the importance of the national scale. Country-level analysis was, therefore, clearly the appropriate entry point for this enterprise.

The challenge was then to identify countries that it made some sense to compare. This brought us to a focus on Bolivia, Ghana, Peru, and Zambia. These four countries were selected because they share certain overall similarities with respect to politics and natural resources, while manifesting specific differences that allow for pairwise comparisons. All four are low- to middle-income countries, though their relative status has changed over time. None of the four countries has experienced extreme levels of autocratic rule characterized by sustained forms of kleptocratic natural resource extraction.[6] Each has a long history of hard-rock mining, and three of them have more recent histories of hydrocarbon extraction (Zambia is the exception). In each case, these histories are both colonial and post-colonial, and have meant that each of these economies has long been substantially dependent on commodity extraction, although the degree of dependence varies among the countries and also over time. In addition, each country has experienced shifts over time in the ways in which the extractive sector is governed, allowing for an analysis of how far these shifts can be explained by global trends and ideas, international commodity prices, or national and subnational political relationships. Likewise, each of the four has experienced similar national political changes, including periods when single leaders, institutions, or parties have been dominant and others that have been characterized by greater degrees of inter-elite and democratic competition. This allowed us to address the effects of these political changes on the governance of extractive industries, and to compare forms of extractive industry governance under dominant party/leader regimes and under regimes characterized by competition among contending elites.

In designing our approach to these country studies, our belief in the importance of history in political settlements also had implications for how we defined our primary unit of analysis. We opted for what we called a concern for the *longue durée,* and so decided that in each of Bolivia, Ghana, Peru, and Zambia, we would begin our analysis at the end of the nineteenth century or beginning of the twentieth.[7] While our time horizon is not as expansive as that often adopted by the French Annales School, from which the term *longue durée* originates, it is motivated by the same conviction that many ideas, structures, and relationships change only very slowly, and that it is important to capture these slow histories if one is to understand the governance of extractive industries in four countries with centuries-long histories of mining but disappointing development outcomes. This concern for the slowness of change also seemed to us consistent with the very notion of political settlements. Indeed, as will become clear in the chapters, we ended up identifying elements of these settlements that have proven highly resistant to change over the long term.

In this sense, then, our unit of analysis was a century or so of national history. In order to analyse the relationship between political settlements and extractive industries over this time frame, and to keep the country analyses comparative, our approach combined the following elements. Literature review was critical as a mode of building the historical narrative on political settlements. In this sense, our country level research builds upon, and from, other research literature on social, political, and economic history in each of the four countries. Second, we conducted rounds of interviews with key informants. These informants were a combination of participants in and observers of the relationships between politics and extractive industry governance that we were studying. Interviewees ranged from former ministers and elected officials to social movement leaders and miners.[8] In each country, we also made use of recent field research in sites of resource extraction in which we had been involved in the context of other studies. Third, workshops were conducted in each country with a mix of researchers, members of civil society, mining company representatives, and public sector actors working on extractive industry governance.[9] These workshops were important in refining our interpretations and arguments. Research was also presented for feedback at conferences and seminars. Fourth, drafts of the country analyses were shared widely with experts[10] for critical commentary, and these reviews helped us to refine our arguments and address crucial themes we may otherwise have missed or misunderstood. Fifth, the five of us were spread across three continents during the conduct of the research. Keeping the research comparative and allowing for each of us to feed into the analysis in each country required fluid communication. At different stages of the project, we convened to workshop versions of the country studies and attempts at synthesis of emerging findings. Workshops were held among all five of us on two occasions, and among subgroups of us on three other occasions. In the final chapter, we return to these methodological choices and reflect on some of their implications for the book as a whole.

3 Outline of Book

Following this introduction, the core of our book is made up of four chapters, each based on one of the four countries in which we worked. The chapters follow similar—though not identical—forms. They first trace the history of national political settlements, beginning from the late nineteenth century through to the second decade of the twenty-first century. They then relate these settlements to the changing ways in which mining—and in the case of Bolivia, mining and natural gas—have been governed and regulated over a period of approximately 125 years. They trace relationships between these forms of natural resource governance and the nature of political settlements and political conflict. The chapters also relate this changing governance of natural resources to the changing policies for, and patterns of, socio-economic and political inclusion. While history weighs heavily in each chapter, the bulk of the analysis focuses on the period since 1990.

At one point, we debated whether, rather than country analyses, the book would be better organized around key elements in the relationships between political settlements, resource extraction, and inclusion, marshalling evidence from all four countries to explore those elements in turn. Ultimately, however, we concluded that country level dynamics and the influence of national history and memory are central to understanding the relationships between politics and resource extraction. A thematic organization of our data would displace the centrality of both country and history in the relationships we are exploring. Opting for the focus on the country, however, makes for some quite long chapters: in some sense, each chapter is a mini-monograph. Moreover, while the country chapters each engage with the political settlements literature, and have been in conversation with each other over the course of this research, we have opted to write each of them as a relatively free-standing piece, recognizing that some readers will only dip into those country analyses of most interest to them. As a consequence, each country chapter opens with a short engagement with the political settlements framework, and ends with conclusions regarding that framework from the perspective of that particular country experience.

The risk of this extended country-based approach is that the reader may get immersed in country details, but lose a sense of convergences and differences across Bolivia, Ghana, Peru, and Zambia. Our final chapter therefore offers this comparative and synthetic reading of the four country essays, relating that comparison back to our conceptual framework and our guiding research concerns. In that chapter, we lay out the ways in which we think a focus on extractive industries and natural resource governance makes specific, conceptual contributions to political settlements theory around issues of space, scale, time, and memory.

Endnotes

1. Some of these other resources are also mined, as in the case of guano, the extraction of which was central to the Peruvian economy of the nineteenth century (e.g. Thorp et al., 2012).
2. For just a few examples of such proposals, see the websites and policy documents of organizations such as the Natural Resource Governance Institute, Oxfam, the International Council of Mining and Metals, or the World Bank.
3. Investment in hydropower is often closely related to large-scale mining as a source of energy for mine and processing sites, while infrastructure such as waterways,

railways, and electricity transmission is linked for energy supply and commodity transport. National and transnational elites involved in investments in these different sectors are also frequently linked.

4. See, for instance, the long list of Working Papers in the Effective States and Inclusive Development Research Consortium, here: http://www.effective-states.org/publications/, accessed 3 February 2018. These are almost entirely focused on periods of the last two to three decades.
5. While North et al. and Acemoglu and Robinson do not directly employ the concept of political settlement, their work is very much in line with political settlement thinking.
6. Of course, there have been periods of particularly nefarious rule, such as that of the Fujimori government in Peru and the governments of Banzer and Garcia-Mesa in Bolivia. Nonetheless, these still seem substantially different from the long and sustained commodity-funded machineries of centralized, repressive power that have characterized some other mining and hydrocarbon-dependent economies and societies.
7. Precise periods varied depending on the periodization of settlements in each country.
8. Because of potential risks to interviewees in some of the countries analysed in this study, and for consistency across the book as a whole, in general, we decided to cite information derived from interviews by referring only to the professional title and/or affiliation of the informant. The only exceptions are of visible public officials.
9. Of these different types of invitees, more researchers and civil society actors tended to accept invitations. That said, government and private sector representatives did also attend, and in one instance, after the workshop in Peru, one company representative asked for a follow-up meeting and gave us several more hours of his time and views.
10. These are noted in the Preface and Acknowledgements.

2

Mining, Political Settlements, and Inclusive Development in Peru

When one examines the history of Peru, the last thing that comes to mind is a stable order or settlement. 'Pendulum', 'labyrinth', and 'kaleidoscope' are among the terms used by scholars to characterize Peru's volatile political and social dynamics.[1] Since gaining independence from Spain in 1821, the country has had twelve constitutions and over 100 governments, while its economic system has run the gamut from extreme liberalism to statism and back again. A colonial legacy of violence, racism, and corruption, combined with erratic primary export-led development, high concentration of wealth, and narrow domestic markets, generated patterns of economic inequality and social exclusion that were also reflected in the political sphere. Democracy with universal suffrage was not achieved until 1980, and successive popularly elected governments have only been in place since 2001.

The relationship between these negative outcomes and Peru's historical reliance on natural resource-based exports, particularly large-scale mining, has been the subject of considerable debate. For years, scholars tended to blame Peru's erratic development on the perils of such dependency, and on the external economic shocks often associated with it (Thorp and Bertram, 2013). More recently, some analysts have shifted attention to the country's weak institutions, and to the lack of effective, broad-based political pacts behind them (Sanborn, 1991; Moron and Sanborn, 2007). Historically, Peruvian elites have been reluctant to construct stable alliances with broader sectors of the population, and have been unable or unwilling to build institutions that can govern the national territory, buffer external shocks, regulate natural resource extraction, and invest in the delivery of collective goods (Schmidt, 2004; Paredes, 2013).

Within this history, however, there have been periods of conflict and realignment, in which new leaders or coalitions have promoted significant changes in the state, and in its relation to natural resource extraction and governance. This was the case in 1968, and again in 1992 when authoritarian rulers emerged in the midst of crisis to concentrate power, construct alliances with key actors, and change the prevailing economic models and institutions and their relationship to key export sectors. This has also been partially the case since 2001, as the return to democracy was accompanied by new forms of political decentralization and innovations in the governance of Peru's abundant mineral resources, in line with global trends. At the same time, this period is also marked by continuity of the liberal economic reforms undertaken during the previous decade (Sanborn, 2008; Muñoz, 2010).

As we examine this case within the comparative framework laid out in Chapter 1, we pose the following questions:

- When have there been periods of political realignment and 'settlement', with a relatively stable balance of power between contending social groups or classes, as reflected in the institutions and policies of the state?
- How have such political settlements shaped the governance and exploitation of Peru's natural resources—and more specifically, its minerals—and in turn, how has this shaped the prospects for future settlements?
- How have the relationships between dominant elites, mineral extraction, and the state affected patterns of inclusive development over time?

These questions are addressed in Sections 1–5 of this chapter. In Section 1, we discuss the relevance to the Peruvian case of recent literature on political settlements, institutions, and inclusive development, as well as long-standing work on political pacts, regime transitions, and the so-called resource curse. We also define key concepts used in the rest of the chapter. In Section 2, we present an analysis of Peruvian history in terms of these concepts, and address the first question above, identifying the main periods of settlement and change. Our second question is addressed in Section 3, which examines the evolution of mining and the main forms of governance thereof, focused primarily on large-scale mining for export, but also mentioning the presence of artisanal and small-scale mining (ASM) operations. Section 4 discusses the interactions of political settlements and mining governance, drawing out the cross-cutting factors that emerge in this case and examining the outcomes of these interactions for inclusive development in contemporary Peru. The chapter ends with a summary of our answers to these questions and final reflections on this case.

In addressing these questions, the chapter adopts both an historical and transnational perspective. We stress how the legacies of dominant elites and prevailing ideologies have weighed heavily in the nature of the state, yet also point to moments of opportunity in which shifting political alliances and agency aimed to alter such legacies and introduce institutional changes. For most of this history, the mining sector has been dominated by foreign firms. Hence our study also points to the power of transnational actors, especially multinational corporations and banks, but also other states and, more recently, transnational social movements.

This chapter is based on the analysis of both primary and secondary sources. Given the historical scope of the study, we draw on extensive historical literature covering Peruvian politics and governance in the late nineteenth and twentieth centuries, and analyse a broad array of published sources on issues related to mining governance and policies. For more recent periods, we draw on data produced by numerous government agencies as well as private industry associations,[2] and on major print media and specialized economics and mining publications. A series of intensive, semi-structured interviews with experts and policymakers were also critical to understanding more recent events.

1 How Politics Shapes Development: A Conceptual Discussion with Reference to Peru

'Inclusive development' is a broad term, but generally refers to an equitable distribution of social and material benefits across the diverse groups within a given society. As Hickey puts it, 'such benefits necessarily comprise not only material and economic gains but enhanced wellbeing and capabilities, as well as social and political empowerment' (2013: 3). This moves beyond a primarily economic definition of development to one that includes the achievement of equity and citizenship rights, and moves beyond an exclusive focus on poverty to one with broader goals of social justice.

What does inclusive development look like in a country like Peru? Clearly, it involves sustaining economic growth, accompanied by state capacity to tax private wealth and spend public revenues effectively. It also involves diversifying the economy to decrease dependence on a few primary export sectors, reducing poverty and inequality, expanding access to basic services for the majority of the population, and also expanding labour rights and social security. Politically, this means guaranteeing human and civil rights to all citizens, strengthening democratic institutions, and expanding participation at all levels of government. Furthermore, for development to be inclusive in a country with a large indigenous population, as in Peru, it should be multicultural, including by granting collective rights to communal lands and other resources, and respecting ethnic and cultural differences.[3] And in a country with such diverse but fragile ecosystems, it should also involve the rational use of natural resources, with effective regulation of the extractive industries and measures to protect the environment for future generations.

How might these outcomes be achieved? The framework driving this research proposes to track the conditions under which state capacity and elite commitment to development are achieved and sustained, considering multiple variables such as intra-elite relations, coalitions and pacts, development ideologies, popular mobilization, and the role of transnational actors (see Chapter 1, this volume; Bebbington, 2013a; Hickey, 2013). This requires a fundamental understanding of the political dynamics that have affected the creation of institutions that might advance inclusive development. In addition, it involves not only the horizontal negotiations and bargains between elites, but also vertical relations between elites and their followers (Laws, 2012: 9).

For the purposes of this chapter, when we refer to 'elites', we mean the minority of individuals or groups that hold resources which allow them to exercise control over the state, and, more generally, to influence the establishment of political settlements and the corresponding distribution of assets and rights in society. Such resources are often economic (land and financial or industrial capital, held nationally or transnationally), but may also be intellectual (technocrats, think tanks, mainstream media) or coercive (in the case of military elites, control over the organized use of force) (di John and Putzel, 2009: 15; Hickey, 2013: 3, 4). Such elites and the sources of their power change over time. Within the framework of this project, it is important to identify periods when certain actors accumulate enough power from outside the dominant coalition to either provoke its breakdown or force a transition and analyse to what extent this leads to new agreements and policies that affect inclusive development.

The earlier work of authors such as Terry Karl (1997, 1986) and Michael L. Ross (1999), among others, reminds us that in countries highly dependent on natural resource extraction, the role of this activity per se must be taken into account when examining the evolution of politics and the prospects for inclusive development (Bebbington, 2013a). However, while extraction may distort the incentives of political and economic elites in various ways, it is also through politics that the revenues resulting from such activity can be channelled towards more desirable results. How can this be done? Some recent 'institutionalist' literature argues that if countries like Peru did not create inclusive politics and effective states early, it may be extremely difficult to avoid erratic and inequitable development outcomes (Slater and Soifer, 2010; Acemoglu and Robinson, 2012). Yet research and debate on democratic consolidation (Schmitter and Karl, 1991; Schmitter, 1992; Munck and Snyder, 2007), as well as that of authors such as Bebbington (2013a) and Orihuela (2013)—who look specifically at mining countries—argue that a country can also build such institutions at later stages under certain conditions.

This work indicates that there are at least two routes to alter the balance of power: (1) social mobilization, which can drive those in power to make positive institutional innovations, or can change the very balance of power (Tilly, 1978; Mahoney and Thelen, 2010; Bebbington, 2013a); or (2) linking to transnational actors and 'epistemic communities', which transmit new ideas and incentives for institutional reform (Haas, 1992; Bebbington et al., 2008; Orihuela, 2013). These routes may be related, but it is important to disaggregate them analytically. In the case of transnational actors, some may exert more coercive power over national elites, even pushing in a way to undermine prevailing settlements. Others work through peer networks and voluntary forms of engagement, and still others by informing and empowering local grassroots activists. In the case of social mobilization, which has expanded in Peru since 2000 when compared to the 1990s, transnational activists and donors have supported a number of environmental and social policy reforms. Yet this support has not helped to overcome the fundamentally fragmented and localized nature of much social movement and protest in Peru, and the inability to forge a movement or alliance capable of significantly changing the country's current development path (Remy, 2005; Panfichi, 2011).

When we refer to 'political settlements' in this chapter, we have in mind what Parks and Cole (2010: viii) call 'rolling agreements between powerful actors', which usually refer to informal power pacts, rather than formal and public ones. Such arrangements do not guarantee a stable social order, but do help to resolve or reduce high levels of political conflict and violence, and attain a minimum of political stability and economic performance (ibid.; also Khan, 2010; Laws, 2012; Schünemann and Lucey, 2015). Yet, because they involve managing the uneasy relationships between elite interests and the broader array of interests and needs in society, there are ongoing processes of conflict, negotiation, and compromise, which the ruling coalition attempts to shape and control (Parks and Cole, 2010: 5). A political settlement remains operative to the extent that it is 'underpinned by a viable combination of institutions and a distribution of power between organizationally powerful groups in society' (Khan, 2010: 20).

Within this framework, the argument in this chapter can be summarized as follows. There are three broad periods that we identify in the Peruvian case as 'settled', in terms of having relatively stable institutional arrangements that have been crucial for the development of economic policy models and the distribution of holding power among key actors—this being defined as 'the capability of an individual or group to engage and survive in conflicts' (Khan, 2010: 6). These are the very long period of oligarchic predominance (1895–1968), a second period we call statist (1968–90), and the neoliberal period which dates from the early 1990s. Each of these periods is reflected in particular patterns of state building and economic models, as well as governance of mining and related extractive industries. However, in the face of global market forces, and with pressure from new ideological trends and mobilization from excluded actors, each settlement lost strength and eventually became radically altered.

Transnational actors have been influential across this history, but as we will see, their roles have also changed over time. They have limited what parties to the settlement can do within national institutions, and they have also at certain times helped to undermine a settlement. Local and regional actors, including mayors and other community-based leaders, have not been part of the ruling coalition in the three settlements identified, or have played a marginal role. They have not forged stable alliances with the national political elite, and have encountered resistance to the projects they desire to roll out or to their efforts to modify investment priorities that come from the capital city, Lima. The power of these subnational elites lies in their protest capacity, rather than their ability to influence the prior definition of state priorities. This scenario is exacerbated by the fractured character of competitive politics, meaning local leaders have few party channels through which to express voice, allowing Lima-based technocrats operating in the state to define institutional arrangements.

2 A History of Political Settlements and Change

As noted above, we have identified three 'settlements'—understood as periods defined by a relative balance of power between contending social groups that influence the reproduction of institutions, including those associated with mining governance: the oligarchical, statist, and neoliberal settlements. In each case, realignments eventually occurred as a result of social conflict and mobilization, the changing composition of political elites, or both. We will discuss each settlement in turn.

2.1 *Oligarchical Rule and Foreign Capital Domination (1895–1968)*

Upon gaining its independence from Spain in 1821, Peru was characterized by a weak central state and limited capacity to control its national territory and sustain economic development. The early years of independence were marked by enormous instability, with powerful leaders (*caudillos*) and their associated 'client-groups' divided among themselves, and fearing that the indigenous people would stage a rebellion in reaction to their dispossession from native lands, subjection to forced labour, and heavy tax burdens (Paredes, 2013). In addition, new political authorities were often willing to cede economic power to foreign interests, including British commercial houses, bondholders, and foreign contractors competing over access to lucrative deposits of nitrates in the form of guano, or accumulated excrement of seabirds on islands off the Peruvian coast, which was widely used for fertilizer (Slater and Soifer, 2010; Hunt, 2011; Paredes, 2013; Thorp and Bertram, 2013).

The lack of a unified nation and strong ruling coalition is associated with Peru's loss of major southern territory, rich in these nitrates, to neighbouring Chile in the War of the Pacific (1879–83). It was in the wake of the crisis following this war that Peru attained the first semblance of a stable order: the 'Aristocratic Republic' (1895–1919). This period was characterized by a dominant oligarchy with a liberal economic orientation and elected civilian governments, although with highly restricted suffrage and personalist elite parties. In this period, we see an expansion and diversification of exports, including oil, copper, and silver, with significant presence of foreign investors, especially from Britain, Germany, and the United States.

In 1919, the Aristocratic Republic gave way to a long period of authoritarian rule under President Augusto Leguía (1919–30). Here there were important efforts to strengthen the state bureaucracy, including the creation of the Central Bank and the Bank of Agricultural Credit, and the construction of large irrigation and transportation infrastructure, mainly on the coast. Leguía also gave legal recognition to indigenous communities in the constitution of 1920, and created a central government agency for indigenous affairs (*Dirección de Asuntos Indigenas*). However, the land-based oligarchy retained enormous holding power over the state and continued to control large expanses of national territory. Hence, despite its pro-indigenous discourse, this administration adopted laws that forced thousands of indigenous men into mandatory unpaid labour in road building, while semi-feudal working conditions under large landowners in the highlands persisted.[4]

This regime also accelerated Peru's opening to foreign capital and control. Leguía incurred huge debts to US banks to cover the costs of his public works, and engaged US advisors in strategic areas, while allowing widespread corruption to persist. British owners of the Peruvian Corporation were given control over the railroads in perpetuity. The Great Depression of 1929, however, affected the economy significantly. Workers and emerging urban middle classes were hit hardest by the increased cost of living and a scarcity of basic goods, leading to an increase in labour protests. In 1930, Leguía was forced to resign by a military coalition led by Commander Luis Sánchez Cerro, who subsequently won election to the presidency in 1931 by a narrow margin that was challenged by the main opposition party, the American Popular Revolutionary Alliance (*Alianza Popular Revolucionaria Americana*, APRA).

During its first 100 years as an independent nation, therefore, Peru had an economy that was primarily liberal in orientation and, after recovery from the War of the Pacific, was oriented towards a variety of primary commodity exports. National power was largely in the hands of a coastal oligarchy, supported through a prevailing consensus with highland landowners, or *gamonales*, and acting as intermediaries for foreign capital (Burga and Flores Galindo, 1979; Klarén, 2004). Large sectors of the population continued to be excluded from full civil rights, as well as from the benefits of export booms, including the indigenous people and expanding urban working classes.

Because of the development of cities, from the 1930s onwards Peru saw the expansion of modern trades unions and of two mass-based political parties that operated more or less clandestinely: APRA and the Socialist Party. As the political and economic power of the United States expanded significantly in Latin America after the 1930s, both parties were critical of US imperialism and of the presence of foreign corporations operating largely as enclaves in Peru. However, the APRA would eventually ally with a sector of the economic elite and US interests in the context of the Cold War, while the Socialist Party would become the pro-Soviet Communist Party after the death of its founder, José Carlos Mariátegui.

During the Depression years, the international context was less favourable for large-scale foreign investment in Peru. The contraction of external demand led governments to offer greater stimulation to national industry, in the context of expanding middle classes and an internal market, and expansion of public services such as health and education (Contreras and Cueto, 2009; Thorp and Bertram, 2013). In this period, small- and medium-sized mining companies with national capital began to develop more projects. However, progress towards economic diversification was limited, and foreign capitalists remained in control of large-scale mineral operations. Mass-based politics were also largely repressed or controlled, except for a brief 'democratic spring' (1945–48), in which a civilian president was elected in alliance with the APRA, but quickly deposed by a military coup and a new coalition, led by General Manuel Odría, that gave strong emphasis to foreign investment, especially in mining (Portocarrero, 1983).

By the end of the 1950s, however, the elite consensus for economic liberalism with foreign domination of leading export sectors began to face greater challenges. The APRA and the above-mentioned Communist Party would be joined by other nationalist and reform-oriented parties, and by more radical Left groups and guerrilla movements inspired by increasing peasant demands for land reform, as well as by the Cuban revolution and other Third World experiences. The 1963 election of Fernando Belaúnde Terry of the moderate Popular Action (*Acción Popular*, AP) party appeared to signal a new political realignment in favour of democratic reform and economic modernization within a capitalist economy. However, this promise failed in the face of strong opposition from a pragmatic alliance between right-wing, pro-oligarchic forces grouped in the Odriíst National Union (*Unión Nacional Odriísta*,

UNO)[5] and the APRA party leadership in congress. By exercising veto power over public spending, the APRA–UNO alliance tied the executive's hands. Meanwhile, peasant organizations impatient with the slow pace of land reform began to forcibly take over lands in the Andean highlands, with support from leftist guerrillas, and the army was sent to brutally repress them (Klarén, 2004).

In a global context marked by increasing demand for energy and the creation of the Organization of the Petroleum Exporting Countries (OPEC), Peru's oil reserves remained in the hands of US corporations, and became the object of considerable popular demand for more national control. Belaúnde's modernizing project included an historical agreement to take back control of the country's northern oil fields from the US-owned International Petroleum Company (IPC), known as 'The Act of Talara', which was signed in 1968. However, the lack of transparency in negotiating the deal became the breaking point for this administration. In 1968, a group within the military led by General Juan Velasco Alvarado distanced itself from oligarchic interests and took power into its own hands, installing the Revolutionary Government of the Armed Forces (*Gobierno Revolucionario de la Fuerza Armada*, GRFA) (Stepan, 1978; Collier, 1979).

Although this section covers a very long period of time, from 1895 to 1968, we have opted to consider it as one overall political settlement—in terms of the prolonged economic and especially political power of the landed oligarchy, its hold on key institutions, and its ability to block social and political reforms. It is also a period in which the prevailing ideas about development, held by the elites in power, largely prioritized primary exports, including minerals, and largely in the hands of transnational firms. Yet we do also point to changes in this period, in terms of the growth of a state apparatus and emergence of new political and social actors contesting for power, especially during the 1960s, with alternative ideas focusing on strengthening internal markets and greater national control over key export sectors. Such actors would become dominant after 1968.

2.2 *Statism and Accelerated Social Change (1968–90)*

The GRFA initiated a dramatically distinct political settlement. It differed from previous military regimes in Peru, in that its leaders enjoyed a high level of autonomy from oligarchic interests and espoused a developmentalist agenda and a desire to dramatically reduce Peru's dependency on foreign states and capital (Cleaves and Scurrah, 1980). Most contending political elites were ousted from power and the regime's major reforms were imposed from the top down by military leaders and a new team of associated technocrats (McClintock and Lowenthal, 1983: 246–8; Dargent, 2015).

Ruling out elections and political parties, they proposed instead a corporatist model of political inclusion with organized participation along class lines, involving peasant communities, trades unions, progressive Catholics, and former members of the APRA and the Marxist Left who had been excluded from national politics. As various authors have pointed out, the GRFA eliminated the landed oligarchy as a political force, reduced the political and economic weight of foreign capital, and made enormous efforts to strengthen the state apparatus as well as its role in the economy (McClintock and Lowenthal, 1983; Sanborn, 1991; Cotler, 1995). Mining, hydrocarbons, and other productive sectors were nationalized; import substitution industrialization (ISI) policies were pursued by encouraging domestic banking and industrial groups to expand their presence in the economy while restricting foreign ownership; and Peru sought leadership in diverse Third World and non-aligned fora.

The global context for this 'Peruvian experiment' was initially favourable, given the rise of other progressive and radical regimes in the region and the emergence of numerous South–South efforts to empower developing country commodity exporters. Peru was active in OPEC in the 1960s, and was a co-founder of the Intergovernmental Council of Copper Exporting Countries (CIPEC), along with Zambia, Zaire, and Chile (see Chapter 4, Section 5.2, this volume). The Cold War and the global flow of 'petrodollars' gave Peru bargaining power vis-à-vis international financial institutions (IFI), and the banks made large loans against projected oil revenues, despite the authoritarian nature of the regime (Guasti, 1985; Stallings, 1992).

Ultimately, however, the military's pursuit of social inclusion through an autocratic regime failed to meet its own objectives. It did not eliminate poverty or social inequality, and instead of eliminating social conflict, it fostered new and more powerful mobilized forms of opposition. Furthermore, as in Ghana, Zambia, and Bolivia (see Chapters 3, 4, and 5), the global economic crisis of the 1970s placed an enormous strain on the country as it faced rapidly falling revenues from the mining and hydrocarbons sectors, and growing foreign debt. This situation was aggravated because of mismanagement and corruption in diverse sectors, and people expressed their disenchantment with the austerity measures that the regime began to introduce.

In 1975, an internal coup replaced Velasco with the more conservative General Francisco Morales-Bermúdez, and harsher repression of labour and popular protests ensued. Important social actors who were considered part of the political settlement under Velasco were eventually excluded by the generals under the new ruling junta (Sulmont, 1980). Strikes and protests in opposition to the junta culminated in a major national strike in July 1977 and the decision by the military to retreat from power (Sanborn, 1991). This retreat was negotiated from the top down, between the generals, leaders of APRA, and moderate right-wing parties. Although the Peruvian state emerged from this period larger in scope and less dependent on the United States and other foreign powers, it was also deeply in debt, and as a result the International Monetary Fund (IMF) and Peru's numerous creditors would continue gaining power over the country throughout the 1970s and 1980s (Stallings, 1992).

The political legacy of the military regime was a shift towards the Left in the political spectrum, with a renovation of the APRA as a centrist force and the emergence of a host of new Marxist parties. Having failed to establish a stable form of authoritarian rule, however, the military opted to initiate a process of transition to democracy. This included an elected constituent assembly, in which leftist parties held nearly a third of the seats, which in turn produced a new constitution in 1979. The constitution reflected considerable agreement among military and civilian elites in favour of a stronger state and executive branch than in the 1960s, but also contained a broader array of rights and freedoms than the military desired.

In 1980, former President Fernando Belaúnde and his AP party were elected back into power, forging an alliance with the more conservative Christian People's Party (*Partido Popular Cristiano*, PPC) to have a majority in congress and share cabinet posts. Yet the popularity of this centre-right alliance was transitory and plummeted as the economy slid into a worsening crisis. Continued efforts to impose austerity measures designed by the IMF and implemented by a group of liberal technocrats produced widespread protests (Dargent, 2015: 91). Despite their international ties, these technocrats (dubbed the *'Grupo Dynamo'*) faced the constant challenge of negotiating with President Belaúnde and the more populist wing of his party. As a result, the fundamentally statist nature of the national economy remained through the 1980s (ibid.).

Why did the transition to democracy after 1980 not result in a new and stable political settlement? Part of the answer can be attributed to external economic constraints, coupled with policy incoherence resulting from internal pressures between neoliberals and populists (Dargent, 2015). Yet the explanation also lies in the process of political negotiation that took place as the military withdrew from government. The new democracy was challenged on one hand by military leaders, who retained an enormous degree of power and impunity, and on the other by new leftist parties that continued to denounce 'bourgeois democracy'—some of them leaving open the option for armed struggle until well into the decade. The new regime was also challenged from the start by the Maoist splinter group, the Communist Party of Peru (*Partido Comunista del Peru,* PCP), also known as Shining Path (*Sendero Luminoso*)—insurgents who operated through force and terror, building power in territories and spaces (such as universities and public schools) where the central state had long neglected the population (CVR, 2003).

In 1985, the country elected a young reformist president, Alan García Pérez of APRA, who proposed to lead Peru out of crisis, restore peace, and construct a 'more social form of democracy' with support from European socialists and other allies (Sanborn, 1991). The Marxist United Left front was the second most powerful political force in the country by this time and leaders of the two parties shared similar views on various policy goals. García's initial strategy was to defy the international banks, with a moratorium on debt repayments, while negotiating with a handful of top business leaders for an economic recovery plan that involved their commitment to new investments in the country. When these leaders did not respond as expected, he turned on them and attempted to nationalize the private banks, provoking a schism in his own party and a new neoliberal protest movement, the Liberty Movement (*Movimiento Libertad*), led by writer Mario Vargas Llosa and joined by some business leaders and young urban professionals. In this period, foreign investment fell to minimal levels, the country entered a dual spiral of political violence and hyperinflation, and Peru became largely isolated from the global financial system.

2.3 *Neoliberalism in Two Stages (1990–2016)*

2.3.1 FIRST STAGE: NEOLIBERALISM AND COMPETITIVE AUTHORITARIANISM

In 1990, political outsider Alberto Fujimori Fujimori was elected president of Peru. Running against Vargas Llosa's strongly neoliberal platform, Fujimori initially marked a difference by promising *not* to privatize state enterprises or undertake other market liberalization measures, and his first cabinet included prominent figures from the moderate Left. Yet, within six months in office, he ditched his leftist allies and brought on a team of neoliberal advisors, drawn from and funded by the World Bank and other IFIs, as well as sectors of the Peruvian business community and the ranks of *Movimiento Libertad* (Wise, 2003). Being close to the president, these 'técnicos' progressively gained significant autonomy from congress and the competitive political system, and focused on the creation of a stronger Ministry of Economy and Finance and other market-friendly institutions (Orihuela, 2013; Dargent, 2015).

Throughout the 1980s, the Shining Path gained presence in remote areas of the Peruvian Andes and the Amazon, where poverty was widespread, public services and infrastructure were minimal, and the state had little presence or authority. Through a combination of political mobilizing, coercion, and terror, the group gained control in large parts of the country, and by 1990 much of the country was under states of emergency, with restricted civil liberties and shared political–military commandos.

In order to pursue structural adjustment and combat the Shining Path more aggressively, and without any significant opposition, Fujimori opted to forge an authoritarian coalition with military officers and key leaders of private business, staging a 'self-coup' in 1992 that included temporarily shutting down congress, intervening in the judiciary, and censoring the major media. These measures were accepted by a majority of Peruvians living in a context of political violence and extreme economic instability. Pressure from the Organization of American States (OAS) and international human rights organizations led Fujimori to maintain spaces of political competition, however, including a constituent congress that produced a significantly more liberal constitution in 1993, in which the state was limited to a subsidiary role in the economy.[6]

The dramatic realignment instigated by Fujimori led to what we consider a new political settlement in Peru, in which powerful elites coalesced around pro-market economics and the radical reopening of the economy to international competition. Two and a half decades later, there are still few political contenders who question the decision to return the most productive sectors of the economy to private hands, and virtually none with real power that propose re-establishing state-owned enterprises in mining or other key export sectors.

Another important characteristic of the settlement that emerged in the 1990s is the centrality and political power of technocrats, who acted as ideologues and agenda setters as they drafted and implemented public policy. Although both the military and prior civilian governments had employed technical advisors, they tended to have diverse partisan loyalties, and ultimately it was the generals or the politicians who remained at the forefront of policymaking. Success with stabilization in the 1990s, however, allowed technocrats without strong party ties to expand their influence in cabinet-level positions (Abusada et al., 2000; Wise, 2003) and to '[launch] more ambitious market reforms that transformed the state and structure of the economy' (Dargent, 2015: 98). Concentrated in the Ministry of the Presidency and the Ministry of Economy and Finance, they tended to come from a small group of private universities, and were supported by a network of new think tanks and consulting firms (Wise, 2003: 238–9), created by private business interests with funding from the World Bank and the United States Agency for International Development (USAID) (Dargent, 2015: 139).

Neoliberal reformers argued that deregulation of labour markets would encourage employers to join or remain in the formal sector, by lowering the costs of hiring and firing workers (Chong, Galdo, and Saavedra, 2007: 11–12). However, the share of informal sector labour actually expanded during this period, while trades unions were broken or discouraged. Privatization and deregulation also created sustained problems with quality and safety in such vital sectors as public transportation and basic and higher education, and did little to expand access to social security for the majority of Peruvians (Bielich, 2009: 29; Pasco-Font and Torero, 2001).

2.3.2 SECOND STAGE: NEOLIBERALISM, DEMOCRACY, AND DECENTRALIZATION

In 2000 President Fujimori fled the country and resigned from Japan after revelations of major corruption in his administration and the military reached the independent media. Yet the pattern of technocratic governance instigated during the Fujimori years survived his downfall and the return to a more democratic regime, thanks to a seriously weak and fragmented party system, debilitated trades unions and popular organizations, and a lack of strong ideological leadership. This power vacuum served to further empower the new class of technocrats, who ironically shared a hostility to the state with administrative knowledge thereof (Vergara and Encinas, 2016). Hence, we argue that the return to democracy did not represent a totally new political settlement.

The post-Fujimori period has been characterized by sustained economic growth fostered in part by strong mineral prices and production. Yet it has also been characterized by high levels of social conflict and a limited legitimacy of the so-called 'political class' and democratic institutions (Crabtree, 2011; Panfichi, 2011). Peru's elected presidents since 2001—centrist Alejandro Toledo Manrique (2001–06), centre-right Alan García (in his second term, 2006–11) and centre-left Ollanta Humala Tasso (2011–16)—have had no real social support bases to rely on and have been unable to build them from above, despite expanding budgets and social programmes. This is reflected in public opinion polls and in the inability of their parties to run credible successors or retain an important congressional base (Dargent and Muñoz, 2012).

In this period, the power of private corporations—notably those related to extractive industries, telecommunications, and banking—has been exhibited not only at the level of national policy, but across society. During the 2000s, business leadership associations and lobbies continued to be outspoken in their demands on government, and for the most part in their support for continuing with an economically liberal policy direction with priority placed on primary commodity exports. Successive Peruvian governments have strongly encouraged the movement towards corporate social responsibility (CSR) and have given incentives to private companies to provide essential public goods and services in their areas of operation (Sanborn, 2008). This has been questioned by critics, who point to the risks of giving private actors greater responsibilities for public functions and potentially undermining, rather than reinforcing, government capacity (Arellano-Yanguas, 2011; Perla, 2012).

This description suggests continuity in the long-standing history of concentration on primary commodity exports to drive economic growth and generate rents for the state. This creates asymmetries of power in favour of the world's most powerful corporations and their national partners in Peru.

Yet in other ways, the post-2000 period represents a new stage in Peruvian politics—the longest uninterrupted period of democratic government to date. In this context, a wider variety of domestic and international actors are vying for power and new channels for local participation and contention, placing new claims on the political agenda, including environmental regulation and respect for indigenous rights. This is undeniable, even if official discourse and policies have not been consistent. The extent of change and continuity in this period is discussed further in Section 4, in regard to the role of mineral extraction and governance, and in Section 5 in regard to the state and political dynamics.

3 Mineral Extraction and Governance over Time

As we have seen, Peru's economy has been fundamentally tied to the export of primary commodities as generators of revenue for the state, and minerals have been the leading sector for much of this history. As shown in Figure 2.1, the importance of mining to the economy has increased over the time period covered by this chapter. Figure 2.2 also shows that Peru's overall GDP tends to track closely with mining GDP. Peru is one of the world's leading mineral producers, with major deposits in copper, gold, silver, zinc, and lead, as well as other resources. Since 1960, mining products have accounted for over half of total export value and up to a quarter of total tax revenues. Figures 2.3 and 2.4 show data on mineral exports and tax revenues from mining which began in the twenty-first century. For most of this history, large-scale mining operations have been privately owned and dominated by foreign capital, with the exception of two decades under state-owned enterprises, in the 1970s and 1980s.

In this section, we shift from an analysis of Peru's overall history of political settlements and change, to a discussion of the changing nature of mineral governance and extraction in each of these periods. The objective is to discuss how or to what extent the political settlements shape the governance of mining, and how this in turn shapes the prospects for future settlements.

3.1 *Foreign Capital Domination (1895–1968)*

At the end of the nineteenth century, silver mining in the central and northern highlands of Peru was mainly in the hands of national owners, and this activity helped Peru recover from the impact of the War of the Pacific. Nevertheless, fluctuating international prices and the change of currency pattern from silver to gold eliminated the principal domestic market for national silver producers (Thorp and Bertram, 2013). Thereafter began a process

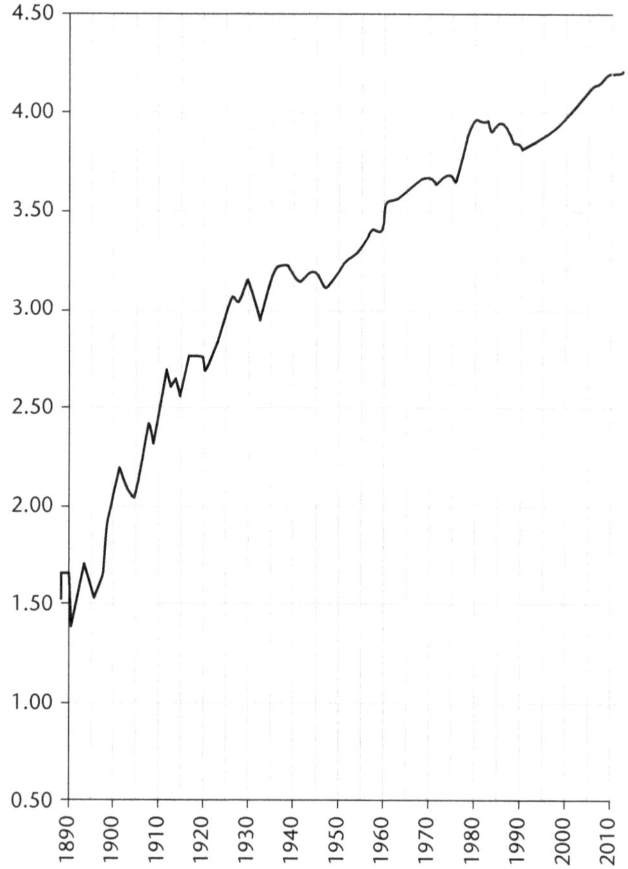

Figure 2.1. Mining share of GDP, Peru, 1890–2012 (millions of nuevos soles 2007, in logarithms)
Source: Seminario (2015: 937).

of denationalization, which coincided with the emergence of copper as an internationally demanded mineral, the production of which required major injections of capital and technology, which neither local entrepreneurs nor the state could provide (Deustua, 1995; Portocarrero, 2013).

Denationalization was also encouraged by direct government policies and liberal-oriented national elites, and facilitated by innovations in intercontinental sea transport and the construction of railroads to the most important mining centres of the central highlands (Miller, 2011). A new liberal mining code in 1901 equalized conditions for foreign and national investors, gave investors property rights over land and subsoil resources (eliminating a 350-year-old Spanish colonial tradition of state ownership of the subsoil), and ratified a tax freeze for all export-oriented activities (Becker, 1983).

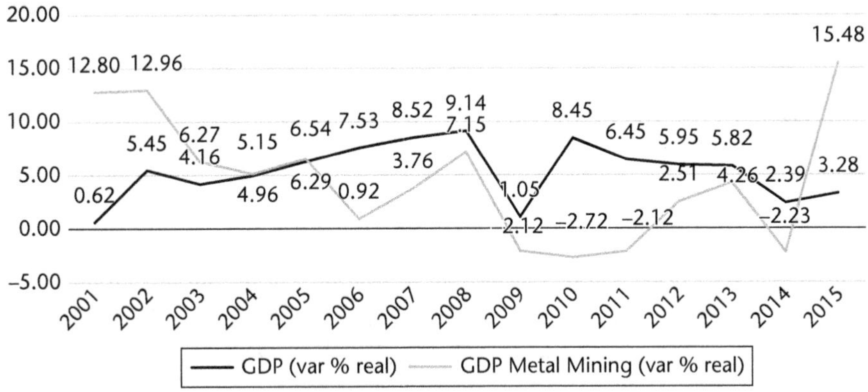

Figure 2.2. GDP and mining GDP variation, Peru, 2001–15

Source: Authors' elaboration with data from BCRP (2017).

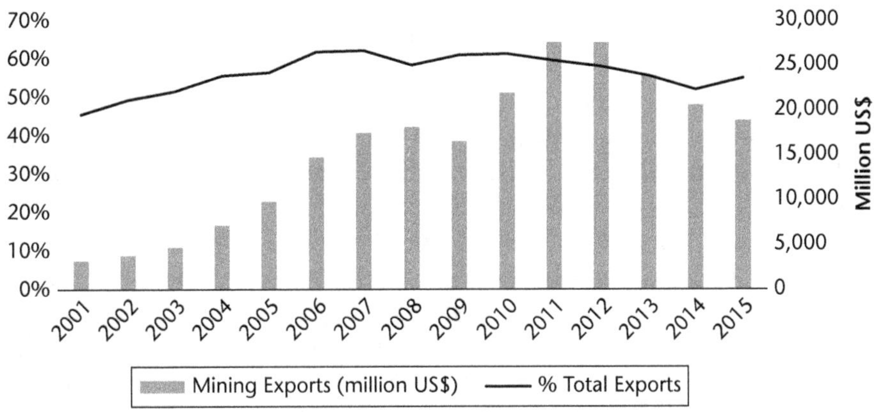

Figure 2.3. Mineral exports in value (US$ million) and share of total exports, Peru, 2001–15

Source: Authors' elaboration with data from BCRP (2017).

According to one Peruvian historian interviewed for this chapter, this was aimed at providing security to private investors, after years in which warring *caudillos* used state power to obtain resources through expropriation (see also Contreras y Cueto, 2009: 208).

As a result of these measures, the US-owned Cerro de Pasco Mining Company (CPMC) accumulated significant economic and political power through the purchase of existing small- and medium-scale mines from local investors and huge expanses of land from Peruvian owners, as well as buying shares in other mining companies and smelting plants, and participating in 1904 in the construction of a rail route from the mines. This enormous accumulation of

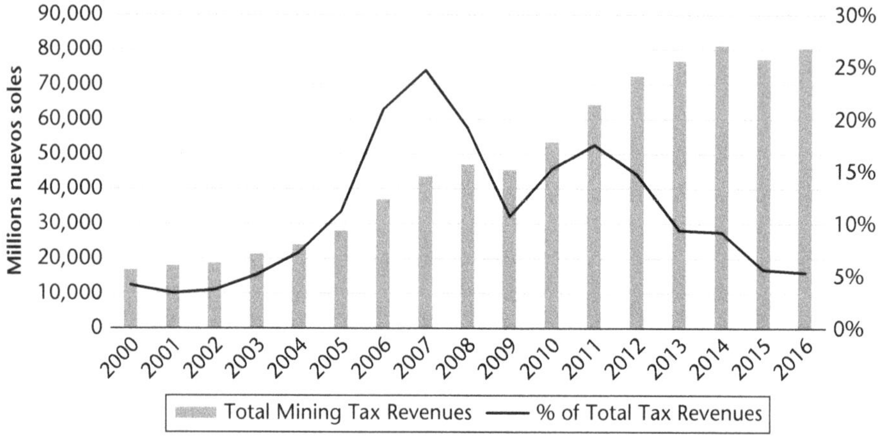

Figure 2.4. Total tax revenues and share from mining (millions of nuevos soles), Peru, 2000–16

Source: Authors' elaboration with data from SUNAT (2017).

power and capital by CPMC made it difficult for successive governments to regulate the firm's activities (Klarén, 2004; Thorp and Bertram, 2013).

After a period of rapid growth of mineral production between 1895 and 1929, the bonanza came to a halt with the Great Depression (Seminario, 2014). However, production by foreign mining firms remained important to the country, going from 97 per cent of total mineral exports in 1929 to 79 per cent in 1939 (Thorp and Bertram, 2013). During this period, domestic capitalists began to exploit other minerals that were gaining in importance over copper: first gold and then lead and zinc. Along with commercial fishing and cotton production, this primarily medium-scale mining helped to boost economic recovery. The resurgence of domestically-owned mining was supported by the state through a series of measures, including preferential access for Peruvians to non-concessional gold deposits (until 1936), the creation of a national Mining Bank in 1941 to provide credit to Peruvian miners, and the introduction of price and import controls (Dore, 1986; Orrego, 2012). During this period, Peru also saw an initial phase of expansion in artisanal gold mining along riverbanks in Cuzco, Puno, and Madre de Dios (Pachas, 2012).

During the brief democratic opening (1945–48), the government also introduced a new framework for labour rights, including recognition of trades unions and procedures for dismissal and retirement that were more favourable to workers, helping to strengthen the mine workers' confederation, among other labour groups (Kruijt and Vellinga, 1983: 72–75). However, by the 1950s the expansion of domestically owned mines was limited by the tendency of the large American firms to accumulate and retain the largest mineral deposits and vast expanses of land. While Peruvian firms' finances began to improve again in the 1940s, unfavourable price conditions for lead and zinc—the minerals most exploited by Peruvian investors—would also hold back national industry.

The 1950s marked another milestone in the dominance of large-scale, foreign-owned mining operations in Peru, linked to technological progress in the global mining industry, as well as more favourable government policies such as a decrease in tax rates. The military government of General Manuel Odría dismantled protectionist measures introduced during the 1930s and 1940s, under pressure from business and in the interests of replacing underground mines with investment in larger, open-pit mining that was then dominating the international copper industry. Without this technology, Peruvian copper production had become less competitive (Dore, 1986).

Under the new Mining Code of 1950, two major contracts for open-pit projects were signed with US-owned companies. The first, with Marcona Mining Company (MMC), was signed in 1952 to launch the development of an iron ore mine on the southern coast. The second, with Southern Peru Copper Corporation (SPCC), was signed in 1954 to enable exploitation of a copper deposit further south, in Tacna (Toquepala). Both deals led to a new mining boom, with increased exports and significant benefits to foreign capital. By 1960, the three largest US-owned companies accounted for 73 per cent of total mineral production (Thorp and Bertram, 2013). However, some medium-sized Peruvian mining companies also emerged in this period, notably Arias-Ballón, the Benavides Group, and Picasso (Becker, 1983).

As mentioned in Section 3, in the late 1950s social mobilization grew stronger around demands for agrarian reform and national sovereignty over natural resources. Land possession by mining companies in the central highlands was a primary focus for protest. The civilian government of Manuel Prado, who governed in a widely criticized alliance with the then-banned APRA party (the so-called '*Convivencia*'), responded timidly, creating an Institute for Land Reform and Colonization (*Instituto de Reforma Agraria y Colonización*, IRAC), which focused on studies aimed at laying the groundwork for future reform. This government also promoted the creation of a steel plant in the port of Chimbote on the northern coast, with the idea of industrializing production, and launched the beginning of the commercial fishmeal industry in the same area. The most lucrative mining projects, however, remained in foreign hands, and tax rates on mining remained around 20 per cent, which nationalist forces considered too low (Contreras and Cueto, 2009).

Under the more reformist government of Fernando Belaúnde, tax rates on mining were increased to 48 per cent, generating opposition from influential mining interests claiming that the existing mining code guaranteed them tax stability (Hunt, 2011). At the same time, official commissions were created in parliament to investigate alleged excess profit repatriation by MMC and

SPCC. These measures reflected government efforts to gain greater control over foreign capital.

During this period, there was another major expansion of mining production, led by the large-scale operations of SPCC (40 per cent of total mineral production), MMC (22 per cent) and the expansion of the CPMC operations (27 per cent) (Thorp and Bertram, 2013). Yet, despite increased world copper prices, during the 1960s there were no further major investments in the sector, apparently because of caution on the part of companies that held deposits in reserve in hopes that domestic political conditions would improve (ibid.). Map 2.1 shows the location of all mineral deposits that the Ministry of Energy and Mines in 1967 considered to be potential mining districts, the vast majority of which were not developed at that time. Meanwhile, small-scale gold extraction in the Amazon continued to grow in this period, with greater state support since 1950 in terms of concessions and of finance through the Mining Bank (Pachas, 2012; Torres, 2013).

3.2 *Nationalism and State Ownership (1968–90)*

While the GRFA also conceived mining to be important to growth as well as a source of financing for an ambitious industrialization programme, the generals initially hoped that private investors would continue to take part (Ballantyne, 1976; Sánchez, 1981). For the most part, however, the mixed investment schemes did not encounter private sector enthusiasm (Conaghan and Malloy, 1994).

In 1969, the junta negotiated with SPCC for a major new copper project (Cuajone), obtaining more favourable tax, trading, and foreign exchange arrangements than the state had previously enjoyed. The company also returned the exploitation rights over a deposit (Quellaveco) located between Cuajone and Toquepala that the government wanted to exploit to expand domestic production.[7] However, negotiations failed with the other two US mining companies, ending in nationalization of the huge CPMC in 1974 and of MMC in 1975.[8] During the 1970s, the participation of some national investors in the mining sector did increase, as foreigners transferred shares to Peruvians to avoid being expropriated (Torres, 2013), but this was primarily in small- and medium-sized mining operations, while the state remained the major large-scale operator (Becker, 1983; Glave and Kuramoto, 2007).

The military regime also brought important changes in mining governance, including the creation of the first Ministry of Energy and Mining (*Ministerio de Energía y Minas,* MINEM) in 1969 and a new Law of Mining in 1970, which re-established the leading role of the state in production (Becker, 1983; Guasti, 1985). Two large state-owned enterprises, CENTROMIN and HIERRO PERU, were created by the nationalization of CPMC and MMC, respectively.

Map 2.1. The national distribution of mineral deposits and potential mining districts identified by the Ministry of Energy and Mines, Peru (1967)

Source: Elaborated on the basis of original map identified in the archives of the Ministry of Energy and Mines, Institute of Geology and Mining (1967).

CENTROMIN would own and operate the seven mines that had belonged to CPMC, as well as its concentration plants, foundry, and refinery based in La Oroya. Both would later participate in a third project, *Minera Asociada Tintaya.*[9] MINERO PERU was also created to operate a zinc refinery, the Cerro Verde copper mine, and the still-to-be-exploited mines of Quellaveco and Antamina, while MINPECO was created as the state-owned minerals trader.

In a situation similar to that experienced by Zambia (see Chapter 4, this volume), the global economic recession after 1973 led to a significant slowdown in mineral production, while the state appropriations left the private sector very reluctant to make new investments. This led to a decline of average annual growth in production from 9.4 per cent in the 1960s to just 3.5 per cent between 1970 and 1979 (McClintock and Lowenthal, 1983; Aste, 1986). The pending debt crisis after 1976 and successive stabilization programmes further limited state capacity to invest in this sector. During this period, the state actively promoted small-scale gold mining through the national Mining Bank, both in the Amazon and in the Puno region near the border with Bolivia. These are areas where efforts to eradicate ASM would take place decades later (Torres, 2013; Cano, 2015a). Near the end of its term in 1978, the military government promulgated a new Law of Promotion of Gold Mining in the Peruvian Amazon, and also granted concessions to ASM organizations that had been left unemployed by the departure of foreign investors or by expropriations that were not considered profitable.

Although 1980 brought a change in political regime, governance of the mining sector did not change dramatically in the subsequent decade. A new General Mining Law (*Ley General de Minería*) was passed in 1981, with the goal of promoting more benefits for private companies and eradicating the government monopoly over the metals trade. This was not enough to revive private investment, however, and major operations remained largely under the control of state-owned enterprises. Ideologically, President Belaúnde and his finance minister, Manuel Ulloa, were favourable to privatization of this sector, but their party followers did not necessarily share that agenda. Interviewees with both public and private experience[10] noted that strong resistance from public employees' and mine workers' unions, as well as the Marxist Left parties, also made it politically risky to attempt such a move, and within a few years that government would be mired in crisis and replaced by leaders with no desire to privatize.

During the 1980s, mining production and exports decreased, because of a combination of low world prices and the anti-export bias of prevailing economic policies. Mining investment was also affected directly by internal armed conflict initiated by the Shining Path in the 1980s, with millions of dollars in losses due to sabotage and work stoppages, leading in some cases to the full militarization of mining camps and operations (Comisión de la

Verdad y Reconciliación 2003). The decade ended in economic and political disaster for the country as a whole, with increasing external debt, unprecedented inflation, and public finances nearly bankrupt. In the mining sector, new explorations for large-scale deposits were virtually halted, and state-run companies, which continued to account for 60 per cent of total mining production in the 1980s, operated under the burden of generating foreign exchange for other public expenditures, and were also subject to considerable internal corruption (Fitzgerald, 1979; Glave and Kuramoto, 2007).

3.3 *Neoliberalism and Mining in Two Stages (1990–2016)*

After 1990, both internal and external pressures made the political settlement based on state-centred development strategies unsustainable. What followed was a period in which neoliberal reforms were rapidly and radically implemented by central government technocrats, and the most productive sectors of the economy were all returned to private hands and opened to global competition. Large-scale mining in primarily foreign hands returned to a position of prominence. Major aspects of this neoliberal settlement remained in place, with the return to democracy after 2000, while new social demands and actors emerged with force, accelerated by a process of partial political decentralization. Greater political competition and more conflict around mining operations has been manifest after the turn of the century. Hence, we see the post-Fujimori period as one of realignment and modification of the mineral governance regime, while not yet constituting a distinctive new settlement.

3.3.1 FIRST STAGE: PRIVATIZATION AND EXPANSION IN THE 1990S

According to most direct accounts from the 1990s, promoting the mining sector was not initially a priority for Fujimori and his advisors. Yet the international context, together with the quality of Peru's mineral deposits and its new policy environment, led the sector to account for 64 per cent of the total investment received as a result of privatizations in this period, while just 13 per cent of these privatizing transactions were mining related (Pasco-Font and Saavedra, 2001).

Reform of the mining sector drew collaboration from experienced professionals within the state-owned mining enterprises, as well as from some private sector miners who assumed public functions.[11] At the outset, government officials also worked to resolve outstanding conflicts between private companies and the state.[12] Measures were also taken to guarantee tax and exchange rate stability and offer attractive tax incentives (Muñoz and Vega, 2000). Mineral commercialization was also liberalized and the concession system simplified.[13] These measures, encouraged by World Bank advisors and domestic experts, were considered necessary to attract new investors to what was still a high-risk country.

Policymakers in this period had reduced space for negotiation with investors around purchase prices, given the risk involved and the poor shape of some of the existing assets, which would require considerable new investment to modernize. From 1991 to 2000, the privatization of mining operations generated an estimated US$1.2 billion in direct income for the state (Ruiz Caro, 2002: 28; Bury, 2011). And while mineral exploration activities doubled worldwide in the 1990s, they multiplied twentyfold in Peru in this period (Poveda, 2007). This involved expansion not only in areas with existing mining operations, in the central and southern highlands, but also into parts of the country where people were not accustomed to large-scale mining, including areas with fragile ecosystems or thriving agricultural interests. According to the Geological, Mining, and Metallurgical Institute (*Instituto Geológico, Minero, y Metalúrgico*, INGEMMET), a government agency, and as shown in Figure 2.5, the total land area authorized for the granting of concession rights grew from 7.8 per cent of national territory in 1991 to 12 per cent in 1999. Transnational capital also renewed its predominance in the mining sector in the 1990s, alone or in partnership with national firms (Aste, 1986; Bebbington and Hinojosa, 2011). By 2000, eleven of the world's twenty major transnational mining companies were operating in Peru (Bury, 2011).

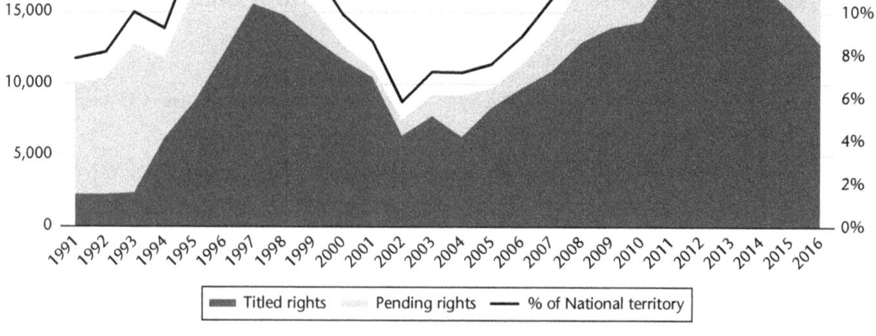

Figure 2.5. Evolution of mining rights and share of national territory, Peru, 1991–2016
Source: Authors' elaboration, based on data from INGEMMET (2017) and Glave and Kuramoto (2007).

Trades unions and professional associations saw their political and economic power recede significantly under neoliberalism, while business and associations of business interests—the National Confederation of Private Business Institutions (*Confederación Nacional de Instituciones Empresariales Privadas,* CONFIEP), the National Society of Mining, Oil, and Energy (*Sociedad Nacional de Minería, Petróleo y Energía,* SNMPE), and, to a lesser extent, the National Exporters' Association (*Asociación de Exportadores,* ADEX)—gained in prestige and access to power. In the mining sector, transnational firms held most of the large new mining projects, such as Antamina (one of the ten largest copper mines in the world), while some national industry leaders also had considerable political power.

In this period, World Bank and IMF staff also encouraged Peruvian policymakers to establish new environmental and social legislation that could more effectively prevent or reduce the negative impacts left behind by past extractive activity (Szablowski, 2002; Arellano-Yanguas, 2011). Instead of creating a separate authority for oversight of environmental standards in this and other industries, however, policymakers opted to incorporate enforcement of environmental norms into each line ministry. For example, an environmental office was established for the first time within MINEM in 1992: the General Direction of Environmental Issues in Mining (*Director General de Asuntos Ambientales Mineros,* DGAAM). This produced an apparent conflict of interest in regard to mining, as MINEM was charged with both promoting new investment, and implementing regulatory standards often resisted by the companies that invested (Charpentier and Hidalgo, 1999; World Bank, 2005).

Peru also introduced the requirement for investors to present an environmental impact assessment (EIA) for new projects during this period, as well as an environmental adjustment and management plan (*Programa de Adecuación y Manejo Ambiental,* PAMA) to manage legacies of past operations. However, testimonies from this period suggest that, in practice, the environmental norms established in the 1990s were driven by international pressures, but, as with other such policy innovations (including the 1989 Indigenous and Tribal Peoples Convention of the International Labour Organization—ILO 169; see Section IV-C-2-c), these were not priorities of the elites within Peru's existing political settlement, and were not implemented with the kind of institutional and political support necessary to give them teeth. Furthermore, in the 1990s, environmental conflicts around mining were not as salient as they would become in the next decade, as more mining investments moved into the operation stage.

In terms of ASM, the Fujimori administration did not adopt any new legislation or policy initiatives in the first half of the 1990s. From 1995 to 2000, however, the government took limited steps to formalize and regulate the expansion of ASM in the Amazon, including the first Registry of Artisanal

Miners. However, the overall liberalization of the mineral trade and liquidation of the state-run Mining Bank, in a context of favourable international gold prices, not only contributed to the largest expansion of this sector to that date, but also to a proliferation of informal producers and the atomization of gold traders operating parallel to the state (Cano, 2015a).

3.3.2 SECOND STAGE: CONTINUITY AND CHANGE IN MINING GOVERNANCE IN THE TWENTY-FIRST CENTURY

The return to democracy in 2001 was followed by a new bonanza period in global mineral prices, and the entry into the production stage of several new large-scale mining operations (Glave and Kuramoto, 2007; Portocarrero et al., 2007). From 2002 to 2012, total mineral exports increased in value from US$3.2 billion to US$27.4 billion, accounting for over half of total Peruvian exports. Mining concessions also continued to expand nationwide after 2000. By 2015, around 14.2 per cent of national territory had been titled for mining rights or mining rights in process, although a far smaller share—just 1.22 per cent—had been authorized for mining activity (MINEM, 2016; Map 2.2 shows the national geography of these different types of mining rights at the beginning of 2017).[14] From 2005 onwards, this boom in extractive activity began to generate considerable net profits for investors, and hence enormous tax revenues. At its peak in 2007, the mining industry accounted for a third of all profits generated, a quarter of all direct taxes, and half of all income taxes paid in the country (Zegarra, 2014).

In this period, ASM also gained in numbers of miners and political influence, becoming funders, powerbrokers, and even candidates in subnational elections, but—in contrast with the Bolivian case discussed in Chapter 3—without relatively stable pacts with the national level and political parties. They also provided funding to national level politicians and parties who promised to defend their interests. Initially, this sector was also allied with international aid organizations, including the World Bank, which saw the formalization of this activity as a route to inclusion (World Bank, 2005; Mosquera, 2006). With the support of regional and local politicians, the first legal framework to formalize small-scale miners was enacted in 2002. However, the intensity of 'gold fever' after 2005, induced by booming prices, undermined attempts by the state to establish order and encourage more sustainable practices. With political decentralization, the authorization and regulation of ASM was transferred to regional governments, some of which were run by prominent small- and medium-scale miners, and lacked either the technical capacity or political motivation to enforce high environmental and social standards (Cano, 2015a).

After 2006, central government policies surrounding ASM took a sharp turn towards an emphasis on contention and repression (Medina, 2014; Valencia,

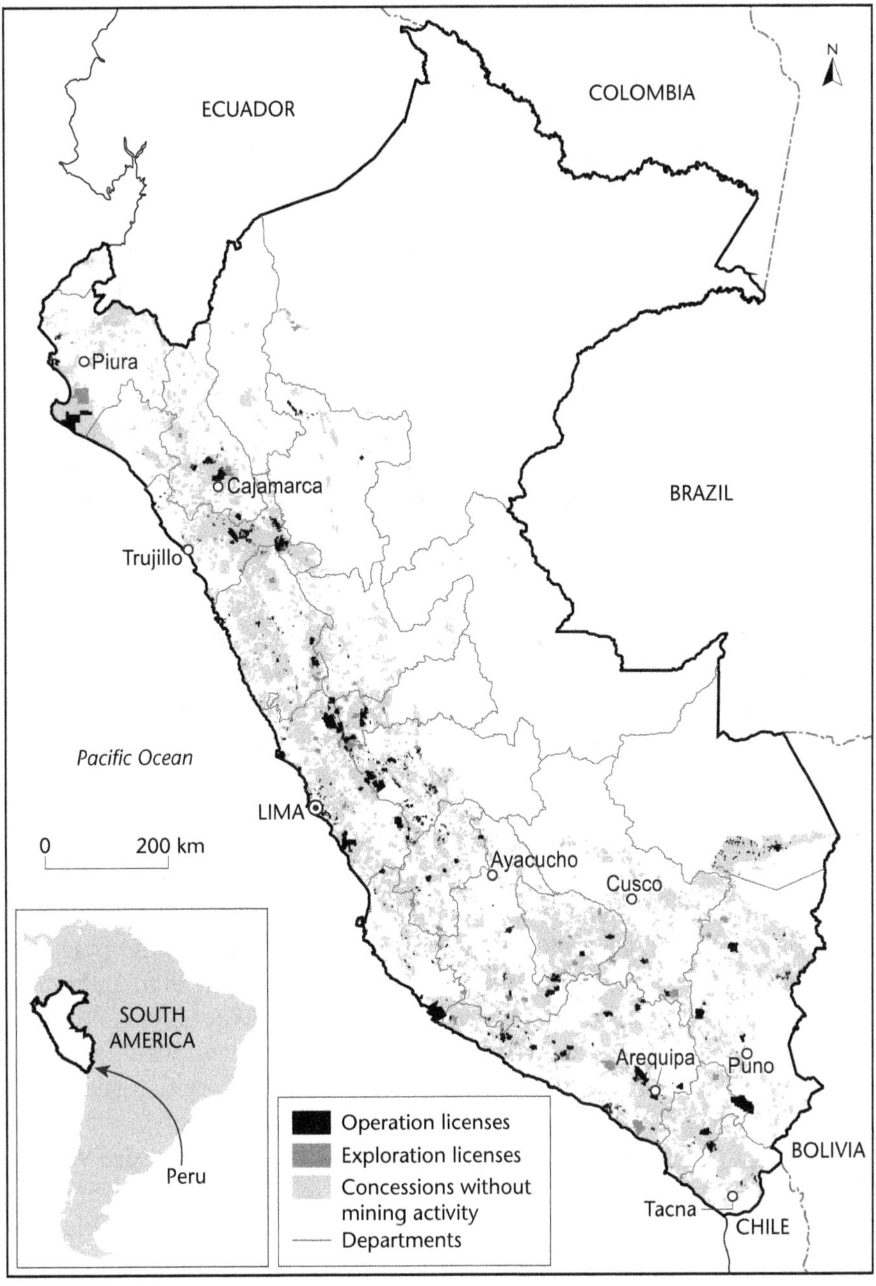

Map 2.2. The national distribution of different types of mining licence, Peru, January 2017

Source: Elaborated on the basis of maps produced by INGEMMET, 2017.

2014). This change coincided with the negotiation of a Free Trade Agreement (FTA) with the US, under which Peru committed to the creation of a new Ministry of the Environment (*Ministerio del Ambiente,* MINAM) that received significant support from the US, Germany, Japan, and other international donors. At the same time there was also strong pressure from international and local conservationists to do something about the 'ecological catastrophe' being created by artisanal miners, especially in parts of the Amazon. Increases in scale and intensification of extraction methods employed in ASM certainly contributed to this reaction, as well as an association of the sector with money laundering and other illegal activities (Cano, 2015a). Indeed, in some of its maps, the government associates ASM as much with illegality as informality (Map 2.3). For its part, MINAM was 'colonized' by professionals from environmental NGOs and movements who formed part of global networks in which eradication of this unregulated small-scale activity was a high priority. They thus gave this task new prominence, but with a focus on suppression rather than formalization (ibid.).

ASM also created tensions in some areas with larger, formal sector mining companies. In some regions, there were overlapping claims for land and minerals between larger firms and artisanal miners, who were also community leaders and authorities. The emphasis on containing ASM is thus framed as favouring the claims of the larger firms. Although Ollanta Humala's Nationalist Party received political support and alleged campaign donations from ASM, under that administration the militarization of this effort and intensification of interdiction actions increased, while efforts at formalization were largely abandoned (Cano, 2015a).

An additional key theme of this period is that the return to democracy came with a significant increase in social conflicts related to mining activity. These involved a variety of demands, including respect for indigenous rights, claims related to environmental and social impacts, disputes over land and water resources, and demands for greater distribution of the tax revenues and other economic benefits obtained. These conflicts led Peru's governments to introduce reforms aimed at reducing tension or responding to underlying demands associated with mining expansion (Bebbington, 2012). Although a detailed analysis of these policy changes and reforms is beyond the scope of this chapter, what follows is a summary of the major reforms.[15]

3.3.2.1 Taxation and revenue redistribution and transparency

The mean rate of income tax on mining operations has been around 30 per cent in Peru in the last decade and a half, which is average relative to other countries with major mineral exports in South America (EY, 2014). By 2006, however, there was growing public opinion critical of the alleged windfall profits that large firms were making as a combined result of price increases and tax stability

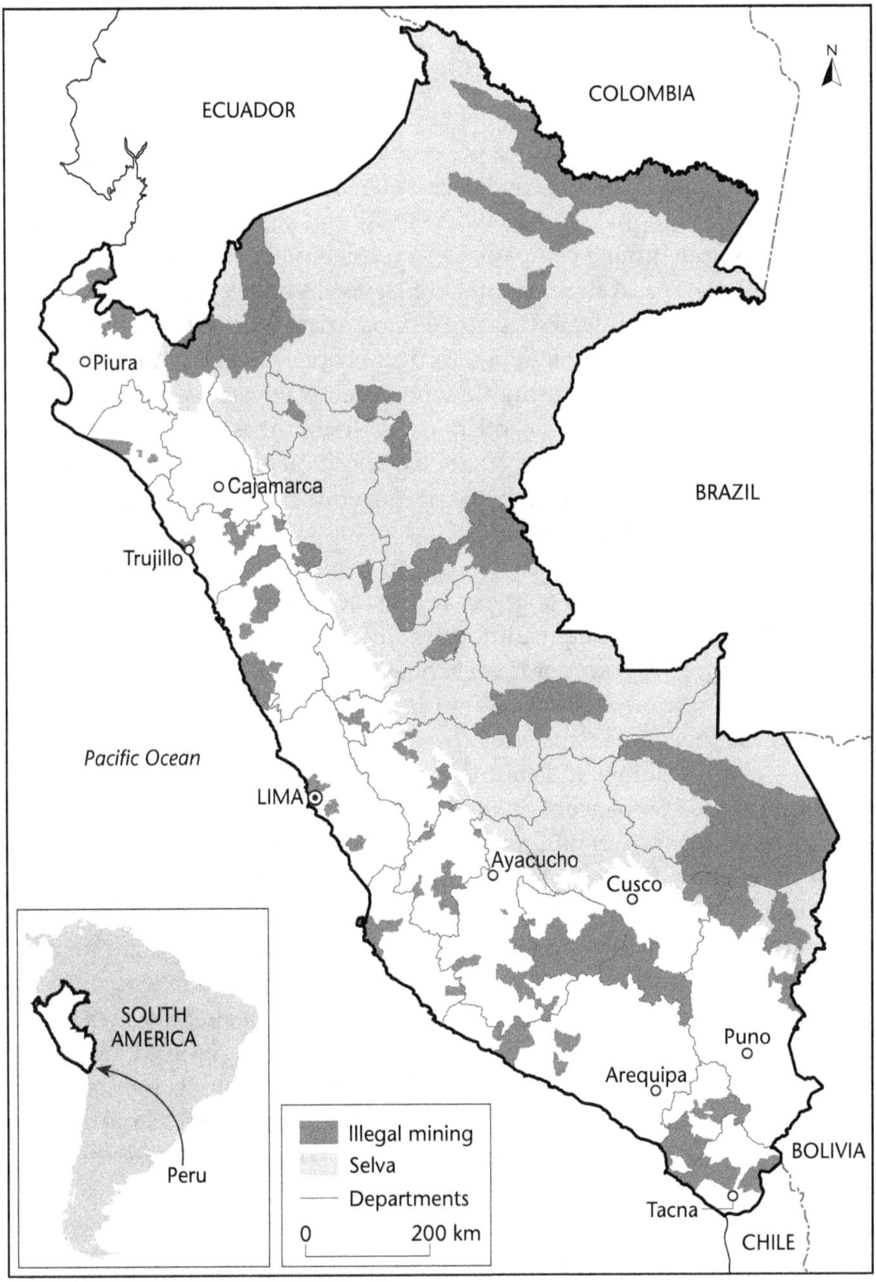

Map 2.3. Areas with presence of illegal and informal mining, as identified by the Ministry of Environment, Peru, 2015

Source: Elaborated on the basis of maps produced by the Ministry of Environment (2015).

agreements negotiated under the Fujimori administration. This resulted first in the 'Mining Programme in Solidarity with the People' (*Programa Minero de Solidaridad con el Pueblo,* PMSP), established by President Alan García, which required forty companies to implement direct social investment in their areas of operation, for the equivalent of a 2 per cent windfall profit tax (MINEM, 2011). Five years later, amid renewed conflict and public demands on the industry, the Humala administration discontinued the PMSP and implemented a mandatory contribution from mining companies.[16] A former military officer, Humala had run as a nationalist and strong admirer of General Velasco, placing him to the left of his closest contender, President Fujimori's daughter, Keiko. According to a former prime minister interviewed for this chapter, industry leaders, fearful that Humala would take more drastic action against private property, accepted this change after a series of negotiations. Although these fears would prove unfounded, and his administration adopted a position more favourable towards the mining industry, distrust between government and business leaders remained mutual during this period.

Meanwhile, beginning under the Toledo administration (2001–06), there was increased pressure for political and fiscal decentralization. Because of lobbying by local government authorities and some industry leaders, congress expanded the total amount of tax revenues from mining to be transferred to subnational government coffers. As in the case of Ghana, where 10 per cent[17] of mining tax revenue is transferred to subnational authorities (see Chapter 5, Section 4.2, this volume), in Peru the 'mining canon' was established in 2001 to distribute a full 50 per cent of all the income tax revenues captured by the central government from mining to subnational governments, to be used for public investment in the regions and districts where the mining operations take place.[18] This has meant that large sums of money have flowed to some regional and municipal governments, which were often unprepared to manage them effectively and transparently, while others with high levels of poverty and basic needs received very few. According to most analysts, in fact, this tax distribution scheme created more tension than it resolved (Arellano-Yanguas, 2011; Ponce and McClintock, 2014),[19] and attempts to establish a more equitable formula for distribution of revenues to non-producing districts were not successful (Arellano-Yanguas, 2016). Figure 2.6 shows the total amount of transfers distributed to regions from 2006 to 2015, and Figure 2.7 breaks this down by region for the same period.

Within Latin America, however, Peru has been a leader in the adoption of revenue transparency measures in the extractive industries. Considerable information about concessions, contracts, and EIAs are available on government websites, and a diversity of watchdog NGOs focus on large mining companies, trying to bridge the communications gap. Also beginning under the Toledo administration, Peru signed up to become a member of the

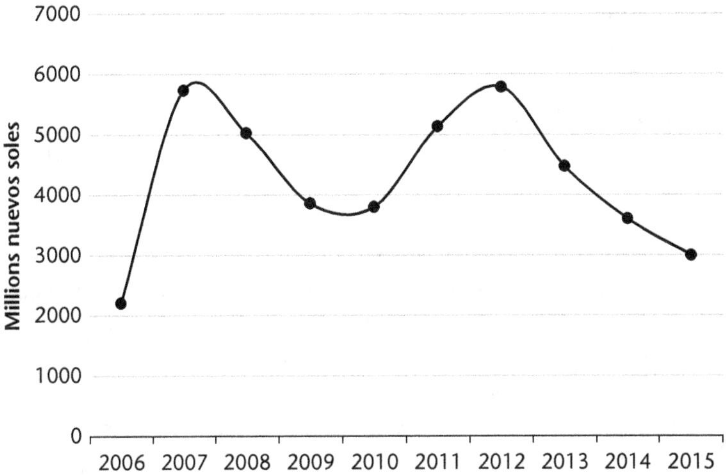

Figure 2.6. Total transfers to regions, Peru, 2006–15 (mining canon, royalties, and concessions payments, millions of nuevos soles)
Source: MINEM (2016).

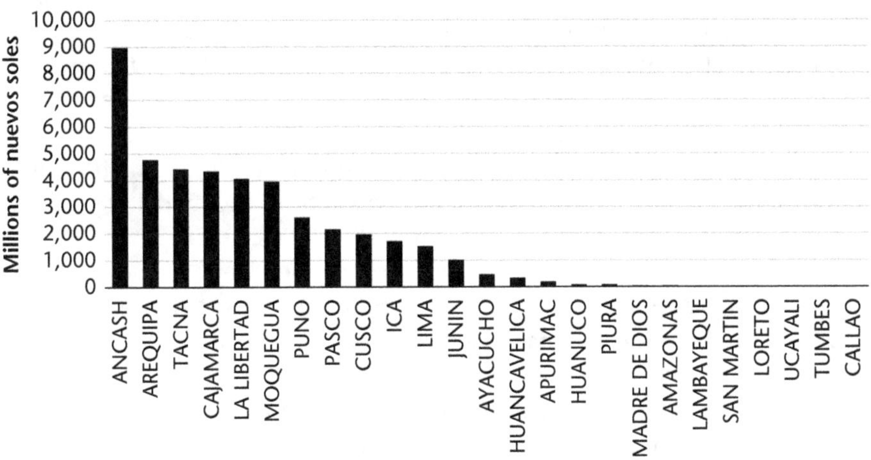

Figure 2.7. Total transfers to regions by region, Peru, 2006–15 (mining canon, royalties, and concessions payments, nuevos soles)
Source: MINEM (2016).

Extractive Industries Transparency Initiative (EITI), and in 2011 it became the first country in the Americas to be deemed compliant with the standards of this voluntary reporting programme. Among the four countries in this study, Peru was the third to join EITI (after Zambia and Ghana); Bolivia has not yet joined (Bebbington et al., 2017). Under the EITI, a majority of large mining and oil companies in Peru agreed to open their books to an independent evaluation and publish the amounts that they pay in taxes to the state.

3.3.2.2 Environmental regulation

Although Peru adopted modern environmental legislation for the mining sector in the 1990s, grassroots community organizers and pressure from mainstream international actors motivated the government to prioritize these issues more fully in the twenty-first century. The creation of MINAM in 2008 occurred in the context of increased demands from IFIs as a condition for approving energy projects, and of the negotiation of the FTA between Peru and the United States (Barandiarán Gomez, 2008).

Within MINAM, an important change for the industry was the establishment of the regulatory agencies with authority across all sectors, such as the Organism for Environmental Evaluation and Fiscalization (*Organismo de Evaluación y Fiscalización Ambiental,* OEFA) charged with monitoring environmental performance, and the National Service of Environmental Certification of Sustainable Investments (*Servicio Nacional de Certificación Ambiental para las Inversiones Sostenibles,* SENACE), charged with reviewing and approving EIAs. The latter was established in the wake of violent protests against the Conga mining project in Cajamarca in the north of the country, in which citizen mobilizations together with national and international NGOs and even other public officials, questioned the legitimacy of the EIA, which had been approved in order for the project to be implemented (Lanegra, 2015). This led to a proposed transfer in 2015 of all environmental functions from line ministries to the new agency, a notable change from the model of sectorial environmental authorities settled on during the 1990s.

In general, the operationalization of these independent agencies of environmental regulation was met by resistance from the Ministry of Economy and Finance (*Ministerio de Economia y Finanzas,* MEF), and the industry. Their main concern has been that environmental regulation will further slow investment in a period of economic downturn and will create more bureaucratic burden. Near the end of its term, in fact, the Humala administration passed a series of decrees curtailing the ability of environmental authorities to sanction violations, while a group of mining companies went to court to resist paying a mandatory corporate contribution to the agency.[20] Hence the enforcement of rules regarding regulation of the environmental impacts of large-scale mining, and hydrocarbon operations have remained a challenge for public authorities (Pulgar Vidal, 2008; De Echave and Diez, 2013).

3.3.2.3 Implementing ILO 169 and the right to prior consultation

Peru signed ILO 169 in 1994, under the Fujimori administration, along with numerous other international norms considered to be important on the road back to international acceptance. However, it took more than fifteen years, and particularly violent protest actions by indigenous peoples of the Amazon and their supporters, for congress to approve legislation designed to implement this right, which was signed into law by President Humala in 2011.[21] The Ministry of Culture and its Vice Ministry for Intercultural Affairs is tasked with supervising and guiding consultations under this framework (Sanborn, Ramírez, and Hurtado, 2017). The first consultation processes began in 2013 and by the end of 2016, thirty-three processes had been initiated, thirteen of which involved hydrocarbon concessions in the Amazon and ten of which involved permissions for mining exploration or exploitation activities. To date more than thirty processes have reached some level of agreement between the state and the indigenous peoples consulted (Ministry of Culture, 2018). As we have written elsewhere, this has represented an important step forward for indigenous rights in Peru, as for the first time in history the state has been required to identify who its indigenous peoples are, and to communicate with and consult indigenous peoples in transparent and culturally appropriate processes. At the same time, resistance to applying the Law of Prior Consultation to decisions related to mining activity, on the part of both central government and private investors, contributed to the stalling of implementation of this right in the Andean highlands—where most Quechua and Aymara peoples live—until late 2015 (Sanborn et al., 2016). When the first cases of consultation about mining began, the staff of the Ministry of Energy and Mines lacked the intercultural capabilities to conduct these processes in an appropriate way, while the Vice Ministry for Intercultural Affairs lacked the authority to guarantee compliance with the numerous agreements reached during the consultation processes (ibid.).

In summary, when comparing mining governance in the 1990s and after 2000, we see continuity in the promotion of private investment, the concentration of power and decision making in the executive, and the influence of technocrats with global ties (Arellano-Yanguas, 2016: 180). There has been change, however, in the emergence of a wider variety of actors with influence on policy debates, promoting norms and institutions related to decentralization, revenue transparency and redistribution, environmental oversight, and indigenous and rural community rights. In some cases, these changes have been the result of social mobilization and violent protest, while in others they have come from engagement with international agencies whose agendas combine an uneasy balance of commitments to growth, private investment, and socio-political inclusion, including the US government (in the context of negotiating the FTA) as well as the World Bank/International Finance Corporation (IFC). However, neither pressure from outside nor from within has produced a significant shift in the development paradigm, towards a more significant diversification of production with expansion of opportunities to larger numbers of citizens and a more effective commitment to environmental sustainability.

4 Politics, Extractive Governance, and Development in the Twenty-First Century

Figure 2.8 tracks social and socio-economic conflict reported by Peru's Ombudsman from 2005 to 2016. How can we account for the fact that neither domestic pressure nor international influence has been sufficient to significantly reduce such conflict and generate broader social consensus around the role of mining in development in the twenty-first century, or to sustain more significant mining governance reforms? In this section, we address this question by stressing three cross-cutting factors: state weakness and fractured politics; the power of private capital; and transnational forces. We then examine the outcomes of these dynamics for inclusive development in Peru.

4.1 *State Weakness and Fractured Politics*

There are three variables that evidence the weakness of the Peruvian state: its limited territorial reach, autonomy from non-state actors, and capacity to deliver essential public goods and services and protect fundamental rights

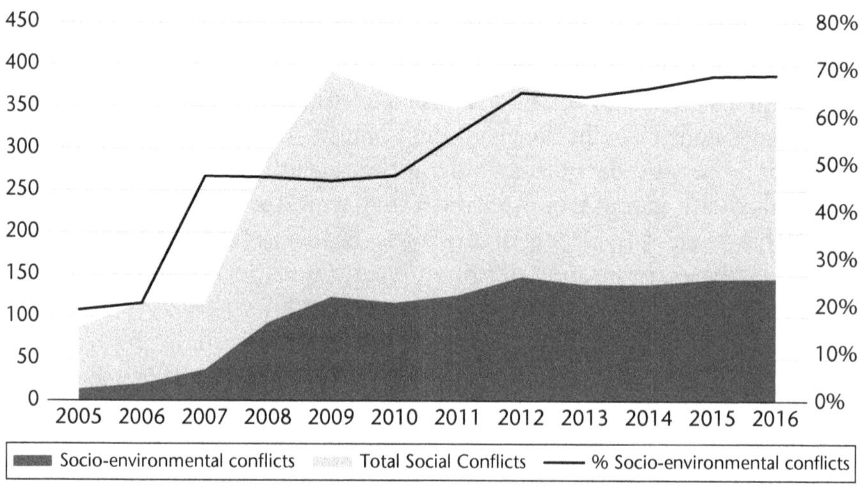

Figure 2.8. Total social and socio-environmental conflicts reported by the Ombudsman, Peru, 2005–16

Note: These numbers show the total conflicts registered by December.

Source: Defensoría del Pueblo (2017).

(Mann, 2006; Soifer, 2012). Our review of Peruvian history stresses the perpetuation of these long-standing weaknesses, as prior settlements as well as external constraints affect elite priorities and capacity for broader inclusion.

The military regime of 1968–80 tried to radically alter state capacity by achieving autonomy from oligarchic landowners and foreign interests, including US corporations. However, the junta failed to achieve its stated development goals, including building a more dynamic and national mining sector to channel the rents obtained into an industrialization programme.

A context of multiple crises throughout the 1980s created political and ideological space for the authoritarian restructuring of the 1990s, with support from conservative sectors of the armed forces and private business. The liberal reforms of this period reduced the debt burden, and increased state capacity in areas fundamental to promoting private investment and market-led growth, without returning to dependency on any one specific country or narrow set of corporations. They did not, however, promote state autonomy from private capital per se. While they set the basis for institutional modernization of those agencies involved with macroeconomic stability, they did not do the same for the improvement of state capacity for longer-term planning and human development.

Despite the political salience of mining in each electoral process since 2001, no political party has constructed and sustained a clear position on the role of this sector in the broader economy and society. Neither are there any national parties with significant power to defend indigenous peoples' rights to be consulted about development policies and plans in their territories, even though most mining and hydrocarbon investments are in the Andes and the Amazon, respectively, where indigenous communities are concentrated. And while some political candidates have toyed with the formalization and inclusion of small-scale miners in a national development agenda, as of 2016 this had not become a significant concern of the governing coalition or parties to the dominant settlement.

4.2 *The Power of Private Capital*

As we have shown throughout this study, the political weight of private capital and especially of foreign investors has been significant in government decision making for most of Peru's post-Independence history. The reforms of the 1990s undermined the influence of certain private interest groups that emerged in the 1970s and 1980s, particularly industrialists accustomed to rent-seeking and unable to withstand international competition. Yet these same reforms empowered private business as a whole, ideologically and economically, and gave renewed priority to large-scale mining interests in particular. They also empowered technocrats, who moved between the public and private sectors with ease, and who continue to favour mining as a driver of growth.

In twenty-first-century Peru, however, it is important to avoid treating the 'mining sector' as a unitary actor. Most of the leading transnationals in this industry are present in the country, including at least sixteen of the twenty-three firms participating in the International Council on Mining and Minerals (ICMM), an industry association oriented towards improving standards in the industry and promoting sustainable development.[22] Most of the home offices of ICMM firms have declared support for transparency and consultation measures. However, other long-standing foreign and domestic mining companies operating in Peru have strongly resisted key reforms, and their voices tend to prevail within the main industry guild, the SNMPE.

While the SNMPE may act as one force when negotiating with incoming governments, in recent years the power and effectiveness of this guild has come under question from its larger international members, who criticize the local leadership as being overly conservative, elitist, and clubby and, as such, proving largely ineffective in promoting legitimacy and public support for the mining industry per se.[23,24] While guild leaders may act in the collective interests of members in the pursuit of certain policy goals, such as in the initial negotiation with each new political administration, executives of the largest firms tend to focus more on their specific interests and build direct ties to policymakers and local authorities, rather than invest time and energy in the guild as a whole.[25]

4.3 *Transnational Actors and Forces*

Peru has historically experienced high levels of influence by external actors in its internal affairs. While powerful US corporations and their political allies saw their influence reduced in the 1970s, they were replaced by the IMF and other creditors. In the 1990s, the World Bank played an important role in diffusing policy ideas and frameworks promoting trade liberalization, overall reduction of the state, promotion of large-scale mining, and the alignment of extractive industry governance with broader World Bank and Organization for Economic Co-operation and Development (OECD) commitments.

The weight of external actors changed in the twenty-first century, as the debt burden was reduced significantly and as China and other non-Western actors moved into the region. Large-scale mining remains largely in the hands of transnational firms and depends on international demand. In the last two decades, however, transnational social movements and NGOs have also played a role in promoting institutional changes and challenging the power of both firms and government, in alliance with local actors.

As we have seen, since the early 2000s mining-related mobilization and conflict has been increasingly influential. The announcement of a new mining project or the construction of a mine can create incentives for local and regional political actors to compete for access to subnational government posts and, once in office, their survival may be associated with the delivery of public goods and services and distribution of canon revenues. At the same time, local protests over environmental concerns and human rights often become linked with transnational networks of activists and with national political debates, which has led to the resignation of cabinet ministers and the destabilization of governments. However, given the weaknesses of the political system, they have not had the kind of holding power necessary to significantly improve the capacity of the state to implement these reforms, nor to alter the overall focus on large-scale mining as an engine of growth and the lack of definition of the place of artisanal and small-scale miners.

4.4 *Outcomes for Inclusive Development*

The unofficial alliance between business and government in favour of export-led growth has been stable for most of this period and in particular in a context in which the national economy grew fairly steadily from 2000 onwards, reaching annual rates of around 6 per cent from 2005 to 2013. Indeed, Peru's GDP growth rate remained among the highest in the region, while levels of public debt and inflation have remained low (World Bank, 2016b). As one of the fastest growing sectors of the economy in the 2000s, large-scale mining has been a large part of this story, contributing around a quarter of total foreign direct investment (FDI) and between 11 and 17 per cent of GDP (World Bank, 2016b; EY, 2017). It is not the whole story, as the value of Peru's non-traditional exports grew fivefold between 2002 and 2014, led primarily by the expansion of commercial agriculture. Yet traditional mineral commodities continue to constitute around 60 per cent of total exports (BCRP, 2016; EY, 2017).

Although exports are vital to Peru's small open economy, continued reliance on non-renewable natural resource exports makes it vulnerable to international price changes, which affect the economy as a whole. This became more apparent after 2013, when declining export income translated into reduced transfer of canon revenues and an overall slowing of growth to 2.4 per cent in 2014. While increased mineral production and export volume helped to drive Peru's growth rates back up to 3.3 per cent in 2015 and nearly 4 per cent in 2016, the economy remains highly sensitive to fluctuations in external commodity prices (BCRP, 2016; World Bank, 2017a).[26]

Along with the risks of increased dependency on global demand for minerals, analysts critical of the weight of mining in Peru's economy tend to stress its weak links to growth in other sectors, and the low levels of direct employment it generates (Schuldt, 2013; Seminario, 2014; Ghezzi, 2015). This argument has been disputed by government technocrats and private industry leaders, who argue that mining has a stronger ripple effect and creates more indirect jobs than critics recognize (SNMPE, 2012; IPE, 2013).

In regard to taxation, total tax revenues quadrupled from 2001 to 2015, largely as a result of export-led growth. However, policymakers have had little ability or incentive to expand the country's overall tax base, relying instead on the revenues generated from a relatively small number of large firms, with mining contributing up to 25 per cent, and from a general consumption tax (*Impuesto General a las Ventas*, IGV), which represents around 26 per cent (SUNAT, 2017). Tax revenue as a percentage of GDP has remained around 16 per cent since 2006, below the average rate of 21 per cent for Latin America as a whole (World Bank, 2016b).[27]

As for the use of these revenues, public investment as a percentage of GDP increased from 2.8 per cent in 2002 to 5.8 per cent in 2015 (MEF, 2016b), and successive elected governments have invested in expanding access to education and health care, electricity, running water, and sewage.[28] Social programmes targeted specifically at the poor, including income transfers, were also expanded. Progress has been slower in improving the *quality* of these services and their equitable distribution, while social spending has remained low as a share of GDP in Peru when compared with similar economies (World Bank, 2016a).[29] Peruvian levels of spending on science and technology, critical to economic diversification, are also among the lowest in the region, reinforcing the priority on primary sector development (PRODUCE, 2014; Concytec, 2017).

One of the most important successes of the post-2000 focus on growth was a dramatic reduction in poverty. While 55.6 per cent of the population was officially poor in 2005, based on income measures, this dropped to 21.8 per cent by 2015, while the share of people living in extreme poverty declined from 15.8 per cent to 4.1 per cent in the same period (INEI, 2016; Work Bank, 2016b). Furthermore, in the last decade Peru has seen a modest decline in overall income *inequality*, as the Gini index declined from 0.49 in 2004 to 0.44 in 2014 (Castro et al., 2016; World Bank, 2016b).

For the most part, these important reductions in both poverty and inequality can be attributed to the 'rising tide' of overall economic growth, associated with expanding labour markets and shifts from unpaid family workers into wage employment (Inchauste et al., 2012; Cord et al., 2015; Castro et al., 2016). However, some evidence suggests that, since 2011, government social policies may have contributed more significantly to reducing inequality (Castro et al., 2016)—policies that also rely heavily on a still narrow tax base. It should be stressed, however, that Peru remains a very unequal society, with

Gini levels twice those of more developed countries and higher than Chile's, the most unequal country in the OECD. This is seen not only in income levels, but also in the persistent gaps between urban and rural areas and between diverse regions, and the vulnerability of millions of Peruvians who have climbed into the middle class, but precariously so. Although one in three Peruvians had joined the middle class by 2012, according to the World Bank, an estimated 40 per cent are considered to be vulnerable to falling back into poverty as overall growth levels subside—slightly above the average of 37.8 per cent for the region as a whole (Cord et al., 2015).

Neither have the benefits from growth to date overcome the country's long-standing geographical disparities. In 2015, 45 per cent of rural residents remained poor and nearly 14 per cent still lived in extreme poverty, compared to 14.5 per cent and just 1 per cent in urban areas, respectively (INEI, 2016). Furthermore, if we use a measure of multidimensional poverty, involving diverse indicators related to education, health, housing, and access to vital social services, some 60 per cent of the rural population in the Andean highlands remained poor in 2014 (Vasquez, 2016). This includes areas of intensive, large-scale mining activity.[30]

It is hard to assess the actual results of the huge revenue flows from the mining tax canon in producer districts and regions. Several studies conducted in producer areas argue that there has been limited positive impact on local welfare, especially among rural communities (see for example, Arellano-Yanguas, 2011; Paredes et al., 2013). Others stress that canon resources have increased the relative importance of public investment, but also note development gaps between regions (Fort and Paredes, 2015).

Peru also continues to stand out for having some of the highest levels of informality in the developing world, comprising 70.9 per cent of the total labour force and 61 per cent of the non-agricultural labour force, according to official government data (INEI, 2016). This is partly the historical result of a predominantly primary economy, a weak state, and a lack of elite commitment to investment in human capital, translating into low levels of educational achievement and hence labour productivity (Loayza, 2007).

As mentioned in Section 3, informality was also exacerbated as a result of the rollback of labour rights and deregulation in the 1990s (Chong et al., 2007). While informality appears to have declined modestly—around 5 per cent—since the early 2000s, and especially since 2005, it remains very high for what is now a middle-income country. The National Institute of Statistics and Informatics (*Instituto Nacional de Estadística e Informática,* INEI) concluded that the informal sector generated 61 per cent of total employment, but just 19 per cent of GDP in 2015 (INEI, 2016). This situation reinforces the relative narrowness of the country's tax base, as well as the weakness of its organized labour movement. While up to 40 per cent of the economically active population belonged to a trades union in the 1980s, this declined to 2 per cent in the late 1990s and has remained between 4 and 6 per cent since 2012 (Villavicencio, 2015: 344; ILO, 2017).

The persistence of this situation well into the twenty-first century also reflects the continuity of neoliberal ideas among the technocrats in the central government, and their strong identification with private sector elites. Although candidates may appeal to workers during electoral periods, promising increases in the legal minimum wage or improved public sector salaries, no government since 2001 has focused on labour rights once in power. Successive ministers of economy and finance have been more sympathetic to the demands of employers' associations, which regularly call for a further rollback of labour rights and wage guidelines, claiming that the costs of formalization are too high, especially for small businesses.[31] The Ministry of Labour remains one of the least modernized public institutions, and authorities have limited capacity or incentive for supervising Peru's diverse labour markets and enforcing the rules on the books. In addition, no political parties with presence in congress have an explicit working-class identity or agenda.

Since 2001, Peruvian democracy has had a weak capacity for interest representation overall. On one hand, it is positive that elected governments have remained in place since 2001, the military have largely remained out of politics, and dominant elite agreements must be legitimated, at least in part, through the democratic process. Furthermore, the electorate is now very broad based—nearly 70 per cent of the total population is of voting age—and there have been advances in political and fiscal decentralization, especially under the Toledo administration. On the other hand, the rule changes and 'anti-party' rhetoric of the 1990s left a party system that is weak, fragmented, and volatile. Fewer than 5 per cent of Peruvians belong to any party, and short-lived electoral 'movements' tend to win subnational elections. The majority of members elected to Peru's small congress are newcomers, and are not re-elected to a second term. While some analysts argue that the decline of parties and traditional interest organizations is a global phenomenon, others claim that in the Peruvian case economic informality also feeds political informality (Cameron, 1997). The weakness of mass-based representative institutions makes it harder for voters to hold politicians accountable after elections, and facilitates the persistent influence of wealthy and powerful elites and high levels of political corruption.

In addition, the participation of indigenous peoples and organizations in the democratic process remains weak in twenty-first-century Peru. Although there are now laws establishing quotas for indigenous candidates on regional and municipal party lists in areas with high shares of indigenous voters, to date, the indigenous presence in elected offices remains limited, and indigenous voices are rarely present in national political arenas, where the quotas do not apply.[32] Leaders of some national indigenous organizations charge that in practice, few parties have indigenous members with decision-making power, and they have few incentives to recruit and train indigenous members (ONAMIAP, 2014; Sanborn et al., 2016). Efforts by indigenous firms to organize their own parties and field candidates have also failed to gain much voter support. Instead, protests often remain the main mechanism through which indigenous demands have been heard by, and had impact on, national public opinion and dominant elites.

A major advance in recent years has been the national Law of Prior Consultation, which, despite the problems involved in its implementation, has obliged the state to embark on an unprecedented effort to identify and communicate with its indigenous citizens. Mining investors today also need to obtain explicit permission from indigenous and peasant communities for mining activities on their lands, and a qualified majority of communal assembly members if their land is to be used or sold (Ley N° 26505). These policies represent a language and practice of inclusion that is relatively new in Peru (De Echave and Diez, 2013). Yet they have not changed the main legal and property regime that has governed mining activity since the 1990s. Decisions concerning the granting of concessions remain a Lima-based central government attribute, and legal frameworks for the protection of peasant communities' lands have been frequently threatened by efforts to encourage more investment.

As for the environmental dimension, as mentioned above, there have been several advances in the promotion of environmental regulation during the last five years. These include the creation of institutions aimed at evaluating the EIAs presented by investors, monitoring compliance with existing norms, sanctioning violators, and simplifying administrative oversight. However, maintaining the authority and autonomy of environmental regulators is an ongoing political struggle that requires the support of other cabinet members, the media, and civil society organizations, in the face of pressures by the more powerful members of the executive branch—aligned with private interests—to reduce the social and environmental protections demanded of investors.

In summary, these various dimensions of inclusive development in Peru in the twenty-first century should be understood in relation to the weight of past political settlements, and the potential unravelling or modification of the most recent neoliberal one. In a context of rising global prices, policymakers in the post-Fujimori era did not have incentives to significantly alter a primary export-oriented economy, promote greater diversification, reform labour markets, or improve the underlying social conditions that distort them. Investment in social programmes for the poor has been substantial but insufficient to compensate for more structural challenges, and, as a result, a significant section of the Peruvian population remains vulnerable to the impact of external shocks, and at risk of falling back into poverty.

5 Conclusions and Final Reflections

This chapter began with three general questions about the Peruvian case. When have there been periods of political realignment and settlement, as reflected in the institutions and policies of the state? How have such settlements shaped the governance and exploitation of Peru's mineral resources? And how have the relationships between dominant elites, mineral extraction, and the state affected patterns of inclusive development over time?

The first question is addressed primarily in Section 2, where we identify three broad periods as having *relatively* stable institutional arrangements that have been crucial for the development of economic models and the distribution of holding power among key actors. These are the very long period of oligarchic predominance (1895–1968), a second period we call statist (1968–90), and the neoliberal period, which dates from the early 1990s to the present. Although marked by diverse social and economic pressures, we argue that each period is reflected in particular patterns of state building and dominant economic models. However, in the face of global market forces, and with pressure from new ideological trends and mobilization from excluded actors, the chapter has discussed how each settlement lost strength and eventually became radically altered, and which groups benefited and lost out in the process.

How did these arrangements shape patterns of governance and exploitation of Peru's mineral resources? As discussed in Section 3, the oligarchical period was most strongly associated with the exploitation of land and labour for agriculture, while Peruvian elites ceded power over mineral resources to foreign (largely US-based) corporations with the necessary capital to exploit large deposits and, eventually, to build and manage large open-pit operations. For decades, the large landed estate, or *hacienda*, and the mining *enclave* coexisted, and the state benefited from tax collection, while labour rights were only gradually introduced. Over time, however, the demands of urban and rural workers, peasant communities, and emerging middle classes grew enough to challenge this dominant model.

Mining governance during the second settlement period (1968–90) cannot be understood without looking at this precedent. One of the main features of the Revolutionary Government of the Armed Forces was its stated commitment to reducing dependency on foreign capital, empowering a national bourgeoisie, and expanding the domestic market, goals shared simultaneously by broad sectors of the Peruvian population, as in much of Latin America at the time. This meant a radical transformation of the ownership and management of the mining sector, as well as broad land and labour reforms. However, the goal of an alliance between the military and private Peruvian investors was not achieved, and instead most large-scale mining operations were concentrated in state-run enterprises. This radically altered the composition of ownership in the sector for two decades, but proved unsustainable, for reasons of profound economic and political crisis in the 1980s. This ownership model was dismantled in an equally radical neoliberal shift starting in the early 1990s.

In the third period (1990 onwards), large-scale mining shifted back into private and primarily transnational hands, and became a major driver of economic growth. A new alliance of military and civilian elites set Peru on a radically liberalizing pattern of state reforms, and the resulting empowerment of the liberal technocracy maintained continuity after the return to democracy (2000 onwards). However, the balance of power remained less stable because of the growing conflicts around expanding mining operations, and because of some of the very reforms introduced to stem such conflict, such as the mining canon. In recent years, there have also been institutional innovations within the state associated with environmental regulation and politics of recognition of indigenous rights, which introduce counterweights without significantly altering the pattern of mining ownership and governance.

Section 4 addressed our third question, about the relationships between dominant elites, mining, and inclusive development. Here we argue that three cross-cutting factors—state weakness and fractured politics, the power of private capital, and transnational forces—help account for the difficulties in overcoming social conflict around the role of mining in development, and in sustaining more significant mining governance reforms. The section ends with a discussion of how these dynamics ultimately restrict the prospects for inclusive development in contemporary Peru.

5.1 *Final Reflections*

Although the fate of mining-dependent countries such as Peru is often considered to be largely determined by international markets and capital flows, this project has focused on issues of political relationships and the interaction of domestic and transnational actors. The results of these interactions have important consequences for the governance of the extractive industries, and for the capacity of the state to achieve more inclusive and sustainable development.

In the Peruvian case, at the helm of the state we have seen both economically liberalizing coalitions which give priority to primary exports, and more statist coalitions, which tried (and failed) to promote greater industrialization. These different coalitions have significantly altered the patterns of mineral production and regulation as part of broader agendas. We have also seen private actors resist the political directives of the state, halting investments or waiting for changing political tides when policies were not in their favour. The balance of power around mining governance in Peru has been asymmetrical, but also unstable.

Through the twentieth century, the most radical changes in mineral governance were undertaken under authoritarian rule, in which the dominant elites had little incentive or commitment to negotiate with other groups in society, especially if they were weak and dispersed. The democratic opening in 2001 appeared as a favourable scenario to change this pattern and to modify the ways in which mining itself is governed. As we have seen, on various levels, Peru has made strides in this century towards overcoming its historical 'resource curse', taking advantage of the rising global demand for minerals and other commodities, achieving sustained economic growth for nearly two decades, and implementing an unprecedented degree of decentralization of the revenues generated.

Yet as we have also discussed, the implementation of extractive governance reforms has been largely in response to conflict, and difficult to sustain in practice. Some of these reforms created or empowered local interests prone to corrupt or authoritarian forms of behaviour, and some have generated new conflicts. The mining canon, for example, has become not only a source of revenue for local governments, but also something that is considered an acquired right by local and regional actors. Yet the weakness of subnational governments and local political organizations inhibits their ability to invest these resources effectively, build alliances, and serve as a counterweight to central executive power. This is also reflected in the fact that policymaking towards large- and medium-scale mining is concentrated in the national government, while the only mining governance functions transferred to subnational government involve regulating artisanal mining. In recent years, decentralization has also coexisted with diverse schemes of public–private partnership, which aim to reduce the infrastructure gap in Peru, but have been criticized for potentially undermining efforts to strengthen subnational government institutions, curb corruption, and reinforce still incipient efforts at citizen deliberation over public spending.

In this context of 'fractured politics' (Crabtree, 2011), technocrats have remained fundamental to operating the central state in Peru, and this has contributed to a higher degree of stability and responsibility in macroeconomic policymaking than in past eras (Dargent, 2015). However, they do not have the kind of party affiliations and holding power that their counterparts in Chile and elsewhere have. Furthermore, the power of technocrats has not been consistent across the state, and their lack of political experience and skills leaves them ill-equipped to prevent or manage social conflict, especially around mining. Yet it is often the frustration on the part of those who live outside of Lima and feel left out of this most recent 'Peruvian miracle' that fuels such conflict, which tends to be channelled through more violent means, and to be met with considerable violence from the state as well.

The lack of stronger and more representative parties and civil society organizations in Peru, exacerbated by the political violence of the 1980s and the attack on representative institutions in the 1990s, has limited the quality of democracy, as well as the ability of elites to agree on models of longer-term, inclusive development. The economy remains unable to create more effective counter-cyclical policies, promote greater productive diversity, and build more decent employment. As a result, it remains highly vulnerable to external markets, and the newly emergent and in large part informal middle classes remain vulnerable to falling back into poverty. The need to promote new mineral production to sustain these revenues—to offset the effect of declining world prices—has also led policymakers to backslide on environmental and social safeguards, and to resist implementing new rights, especially those of indigenous peoples.

The fact that the general liberal economic direction of the 1990s has continued through this century does not mean there is broad social consensus around it, nor the drive by ruling elites to expand extractive activity nationwide. The combination of sustained growth and targeted social policy partially contributed to the important reduction in poverty levels. However, this did not serve to effectively 'include' more citizens in alliances, pacts, or coalitions able to overcome the country's historical political instability and fragmentation. In class, ethnic, and regional terms, there has been limited change in the main parties to Peru's dominant political settlements.

In current Peruvian academic and policymaking circles, there is growing recognition of the limits of development centred on macroeconomic growth alone, and of the need to focus more on the development and quality of institutions (Ghezzi and Gallardo, 2013). There is less awareness, however, of the power dynamics that lie behind institutions or the challenges to building political alliances and coalitions to change them. The challenges faced by Peru, like many other mineral exporters, include the diversification of the economy and the reduction of informality, as well as more equitable distribution of public investment and services. This demands not only technocratic policy decisions, but also broader state reform that can be promoted and sustained by political and economic elites. In this chapter, we have identified the origins of what Arellano-Yanguas (2008) calls a 'dual bureaucracy' within the Peruvian state, in which certain sectors and agencies linked to market opening and macroeconomic stability have benefited from reforms oriented towards professionalization and modernization, while other long-standing social ministries (labour, health, education), and new ones created because of international pressure or social conflict, such as the ministries of the environment and of culture, still lack the power to defend policies not popular with primary export interests.

In this sense, we find that even after nearly two decades of uninterrupted democracy, high levels of political instability and fragmentation have inhibited the development of effective institutions and longer-term policies in Peru. To date, there are still few powers within the state that can serve as checks and balances on the executive and particularly the ministries that promote mining-led growth. The absence of organizations that represent interests beyond the local sphere limits the effectiveness and legitimacy of institutions created to improve mineral governance, regulate environmental impacts, and protect human rights. Instead, the response of recent governments to increased social conflict around mining has been characterized by short-term measures and the arbitrary use of force.

The persistent legacies of the 1970s' military regime, and of the neoliberal reforms of the 1990s, have also left an important sector of Peruvian elites averse to any serious effort at longer-term national planning on the part of the state. This ideological inheritance, combined with political instability, also helps to explain the lack of elite commitment that underlies limited capacity to promote a professional civil service, or implement more ambitious strategies for promoting economic diversification. To enact measures that more broadly modernize the state and put it more at the service of inclusive development requires politicians and technocrats who are committed to this goal over the long term, and are able to resist the short-term interests of those who benefit from the model at hand.

Acknowledgements

Tania Ramírez and Verónica Hurtado made considerable and important contributions to the development of the Peruvian case study. This chapter is based largely on an earlier and more extensive document published as Sanborn et al. (2017) 'Mining, political settlements and inclusive development in Peru', ESID Working Paper Number 79.

Endnotes

1. See, for example, Gonzáles de Olarte and Samamé (1991), Tuesta (1996), Cameron (1997), Tanaka (1998), Parodi (2002), and Schmidt (2008), cited in Moron and Sanborn (2007).
2. This includes specialized survey data produced by the National Institute for Statistics and Informatics (*Instituto Nacional de Estadística e Informática*, INEI), the Central Reserve Bank (*Banco Central de Reserva*), National Superintendency of Tax Administration (*Superintendencia Nacional de Administración Tributaria* SUNAT), the

Geological, Mining, and Metallurgical Institute (*Instituto Geológico, Minero, y Metalúrgico,* INGEMMET), the ministries of Energy and Mines (*Ministerio de Energía y Minas,* MINEM), Production (*Ministerio de Producción,* PRODUCE), and Culture (*Ministerio de Cultura,* MC), and the National Society of Mining, Oil, and Energy (*Sociedad Nacional de Minería, Petróleo y Energía,* SNMPE).

3. Peru has one of the largest indigenous populations in South America, yet their total numbers are difficult to measure. As of 2016, national census data did not include questions of racial or ethnic identity, only the maternal language of heads of household. Using this indicator, the most recent census of 2007 estimated the total number of indigenous people at four million, or roughly 15.7 per cent of the population (INEI, 2007). Alternative measures range from as low as 5 per cent when only self-identification is used, to as high as 75 per cent when taking into account ancestors, traditions, and customs (Sulmont 2012). The Ministry of Culture has identified fifty-five main indigenous peoples, the largest being Quechua and Aymara, and over fifty-one smaller groups of Amazonian peoples (INEI, 2007; Ministry of Culture 2017b).
4. The Law of Highway Conscription, in 1920, mandated that all men aged eighteen to sixty do unpaid roadwork for a certain number of days per year. Only a few could buy their way out of this obligation (Contreras and Cueto, 2009).
5. The UNO was a party created by former dictator Manuel Odría (President 1948–56) and linked to sugar and cotton barons. Its alliance with APRA allowed for an opposition majority against Belaunde from 1963 to 1968 (Manrique, 2009).
6. The Fujimori regime after 1992 has been called 'competitive authoritarianism', because elections were held without major fraud and there were spaces for political opposition in the new congress, local governments, and a sector of the media (Levitsky and Way, 2010). The 1993 constitution remained in place by democratically elected governments after 2000.
7. According to an interview with a former executive of a leading foreign mining company in Peru. See also Becker (1983).
8. Apparently, the military leaders initially wanted a joint venture with CPMC and a part of the stock that company held in SPCC, which was refused. The nationalization was then presented as a political victory in a famous speech by General Jorge Fernández Maldonado (Sánchez Albavera, 1981; Becker, 1983).
9. According to an interview with a former general director of mining of the Ministry of Energy and Mines and board member of Hierro Peru and Centromin. See also Pasco-Font (2000).
10. A former minister of energy and mines; a former minister of transport and communications, minister of energy and mines, and minister of the presidency; and a former executive of a leading foreign mining company in Peru.
11. According to interviews with a former general director of mining in the Ministry of Energy and Mines and board member of Hierro Peru and Centromin, and a former minister of energy and mines.
12. According to interviews with a former minister of transport and communications, minister of energy and mines, and minister of the presidency; and a former executive of a leading foreign mining company in Peru.

13. According to interviews with a former general director of mining of the Ministry of Energy and Mines and board member of Hierro Peru and Centromin; the regional coordinator of an international NGO; and a former minister of transport and communications, minister of energy and mines, and minister of the presidency.
14. The share of national territory that remained off-limits for mining activity in 2015, because of various factors, including creation of national parks and protected nature areas as well as urban zoning, was estimated at 65 per cent. The granting of mining rights alone does not authorize holders to engage in active mineral exploration, mine construction, or extraction, all of which require numerous steps, from negotiating purchase or lease of surface lands, to obtaining approval of EIAs—procedures that can take years to complete (MINEM, 2016).
15. For more details on these measures, see Sanborn and Chonn (2015); Sanborn and Paredes (2015).
16. According to an interview with a former prime minister. See also EY (2014).
17. Note that the Office of Administration of Stool Lands (OASL), which oversees this distribution, is allowed to retain 10 per cent of it for its own costs, so 9 per cent is actually transferred to subnational authorities.
18. Since 2003, the formula for canon distribution provides 25 per cent to the regional government where the operation is based, 25 per cent to the provincial municipality and related districts, 20 per cent to the producer district, and 40 per cent to all other municipalities in the region (Sanborn and Dammert, 2013).
19. The main regions dependent on mining are Moquegua (40 per cent of regional GDP), Tacna (34 per cent), Pasco (27 per cent), Ancash (26 per cent), and Arequipa (24 per cent) (McKinsey, 2013).
20. See for example: 'Exigen a Tribunal Constitucional responder demanda contra Ley 30230' (22 July 2015). *SERVINDI.* http://www.servindi.org/actualidad/135812; 'Aporte por regulación: OEFA gana nuevo proceso a minera' (21 July 2015). *La República.* http://larepublica.pe/impresa/economia/16893-aporte-por-regulacion-oefa-gana-nuevo-proceso-minera; and 'Medida judicial no permite que OEFA cobre 56 multas ambientales a mineras' (10 July 2015). *SPDA Actualidad Ambiental,* http://www.actualidadambiental.pe/?p=31113.
21. In 2009, after months of strikes and protests by native Amazonian peoples over not being consulted on new legislation related to forestry and extractive investments, a confrontation broke out in the city of Bagua, in the Amazonas region, when police tried to forcibly disperse a fifty-nine-day roadblock. In what is known as the 'Baguazo', twenty-three police officers and ten civilians were killed and hundreds wounded (Barrera-Hernández, 2009; Amnesty International, 2014). This violence spurred Humala to approve the implementation of ILO 169 as one of his first actions in office.
22. See: http://www.icmm.com/en-gb/members/member-companies.
23. According to interviews with a former general director of mining of the Ministry of Energy and Mines and a board member of Hierro Peru and Centromin; a former minister of energy and mines; and a former executive of a leading foreign mining company in Peru.

24. 'The National Mining Society is one of the most ineffective, inefficient and unequal organizational messes in the hemisphere', said one foreign mining executive based in Peru. 'If a mining company really wants to get something done, they sit down with the corresponding authority directly. If it is a company with more than a billion dollars' worth of investment, they can have a direct talk with the minister.' Furthermore, 'there is no clear strategy in their actions, and the studies they once promoted for the sector have been left behind'.
25. According to interviews with a former general director of mining of the Ministry of Energy and Mines and a board member of Hierro Peru and Centromin; and a former executive of a leading foreign mining company in Peru.
26. Copper production in particular jumped from 1.6 million tonnes in 2015 to 2.3 million tonnes in 2016, thanks largely to two mega-projects coming on line, the Cerro Verde mine in Arequipa and Las Bambas in Apurimac (EY 2017: 37).
27. See also: 'Latin America and the Caribbean: Tax Revenues remain stable' (10 March 2015). *Inter-American Development Bank*. Retrieved from http://www.iadb.org/en/news/news-releases/2015-03-10/revenue-statistics-in-latin-america-and-the-caribbean,11082.html.
28. To review the historical evolution of public spending in these services, see: MEF (Ministry of Economy and Finance) (2016a).
29. For example, investment in education in 2012 represented 2.9 per cent of GDP—well below levels of neighbouring countries with similar dependence on natural resource exports, such as Chile (4.6 per cent of GDP), Argentina (5.1 per cent), and Bolivia (6.4 per cent) (World Bank, 2016a).
30. According to Vasquez (2016), using a measure of multidimensional poverty, the five poorest regions of Peru in 2014 were Huancavelica (52.63 per cent), Cajamarca (49.89 per cent), Amazonas (46.79 per cent), Puno (45.27 per cent), and Huánuco (43.99 per cent). These regions include areas of intensive mining activity.
31. See: 'Excesiva regulación y altos impuestos gravan ingreso al sector formal en Perú' (19 October 2014). *Gestión*. http://gestion.pe/economia/excesiva-regulacion-y-altos-impuestos-gravan-ingreso-al-sector-formal-peru-2111487.
32. Various electoral laws in Peru promote participation of historically excluded indigenous peoples, as well as women and youth. Law 26859, for example, states that at least 30 per cent of candidates on the parliamentary lists of all parties must be women, while Law 27734, passed in 2002, states that a minimum of 15 per cent of candidates for regional and municipal councillors should be of indigenous or native origins in those regions and provinces determined by authorities to have a high percentage of indigenous residents. As mentioned at the outset, while the national census does not measure ethnic or racial identities, some 15.6 per cent claim an indigenous mother tongue, and an estimated 40 per cent of the population claims to descend from native Andean or Amazonian peoples (Sulmont, 2012).

3

Political Settlements, Natural Resource Extraction, and Inclusion in Bolivia

The concept of 'political settlement' draws attention to the need to understand institutional arrangements as the products of bargains among elites (Di John and Putzel, 2009). That is, contention and relationships of power among elites produce institutions that will tend to distribute benefits more or less in line with differences in power (Khan, 2010; see also Acemoglu and Robinson, 2012). The nature of the state will reflect this distribution of power and these bargains, as well as institutions inherited from historical distributions of power.

As noted in Chapter 1, Khan (2010) suggests that the overall mode in which state authority is exercised depends on what he refers to as 'horizontal' and 'vertical' distributions of power. The vertical distribution refers to the way in which power is distributed within the coalition of ruling elites (the parties to the 'bargain'), while the horizontal distribution refers to the relationships of power between the ruling coalition and so-called 'excluded factions', who were not party to the bargain and are not therefore directly involved in rule and benefit capture. These two distributions of power draw attention to the ever-present possibility of instability in the settlement. The greater the relative power of excluded factions, as well as of weaker ('lower-level') groups within the ruling coalition, the greater the likelihood of instability. Another factor in determining relative instability is the extent to which the form of development delivered by the ruling coalition produces benefits for factions that are excluded from, or are little more than sleeper members of, the ruling coalition. For Khan, the nature of this development depends on the extent to which ruling elite interests are aligned with economic growth. Booth (2015) adds that the quality of this development will also depend on the capacity of elite parties to the bargain to act collectively around a shared vision of society and economy. In some sense, the issue here is whether the bargain arrived at hinges around a shared vision of change or a simple divvying up of the spoils of government.[1]

These different observations are important because although the term 'settlement' implies some type of equilibrium, the pacts underlying the settlement can be unstable and even ephemeral. This has been the norm for Bolivia. Understanding the sources of such instability, and also the conditions in which settlements become more stable, is therefore important for understanding how development processes are governed. In a case such as Bolivia, where governance and development were traditionally characterized by chronic instability, only to enter a period of remarkable stability since 2005, it becomes particularly important to find a framework whose concepts help explain both the drivers of instability and the conditions that have now helped favour stability.

The Bolivian case also suggests the value of making natural resources central to political settlement thinking. This is for several reasons: access to and control over resources and resource rents are central to elite bargains; the transnational valorization of resources serves to bring political actors into being and into demise; and the economic and cultural values apportioned to natural resources become critical elements of both state- and nation-building (Bebbington, 2013b). The *'longue durée'* perspective of political settlements taken in this book reveals 'unresolved tensions' (Crabtree and Whitehead, 2008) in Bolivia over who should control natural resources, how those resources should be used and by whom, how their benefits should be distributed socially and spatially, and the type of state that should be built for a particular mode of natural resource governance (state-led vs market-led, centralized vs decentralized, linked to indigenous governance vs Weberian state forms, etc.).

In this context, this chapter considers the following:

- How far have prior political settlements and coalitions in Bolivia structured the forms taken by an expanding extractive economy, and how far have these settlements subsequently been shaped by this expansion?
- To what extent have conflict, coalitional change, and learning processes driven institutional innovation in the governance of extractive industries in Bolivia?
- How have interactions among actors operating at different scales affected these processes of institutional change and the overall governance of mining and hydrocarbons in Bolivia?

We address these themes by first offering a short introduction to minerals and hydrocarbons in Bolivia, followed by a brief periodization of Bolivian political dynamics and settlements from 1899 through to the present. This serves to introduce a more detailed discussion of the interactions between mining, hydrocarbons, and political settlements over time—the theme of Section 3 (mining) and Section 4 (hydrocarbons). The final section, Section 5, concludes with a discussion of the relationships between resource extraction and political settlements over the long term, emphasizing the recurring importance of subnational politics and ideas of resource nationalism in these settlements.

The argument draws on historical analysis from secondary sources, complemented by a series of key informant interviews. Specifically, field research and interviews were conducted in the departments of Tarija, the primary centre of natural gas production in Bolivia, and Potosí, the historical centre of the hard-rock mining economy since pre-Hispanic times. Both structured and informal interviews were conducted with a range of actors representing businesses, popular organizations, elected representatives, and local authorities in Potosí, Tarija, and the capital city of La Paz. The analysis is further informed and complemented by documentary analysis drawn from newspaper articles, government publications and presentations, and published and unpublished reports from Bolivian research centres and non-governmental organizations (NGOs).

1 Resource Extraction and Political Settlements in Bolivia: an Overview

1.1 *The Simple Geographies of Mining and Hydrocarbons in Bolivia*

Mining has been part of Bolivia's identity and economy since well before it existed as a modern nation, and even before Spanish colonization of the central Andes. Until recently, this mining has been concentrated in the western highlands of the country. This region is one of high altitude plains (the *altiplano*), mountain peaks and valleys, and historically was the home to advanced pre-Incaic forms of government and rule. These highlands continue to be populated primarily by indigenous Aymara and Quechua groups. Mining labour has been almost entirely indigenous throughout the history of the sector (Nash, 1993; Oporto, 2012).

The highland concentration of mining is largely an artefact of geology, with Andean mineralizations yielding deposits of silver, tin, zinc, nickel, gold, copper, and wolfram, among others (see Map 3.1). These resources have traditionally been extracted through underground operations, but these began to give way to open-cast operations headed by transnational companies during the 1990s. In terms of size, mining in Bolivia has long consisted of a mix of large-scale and small-scale operations. Beginning with the period following structural adjustment in 1985, however, substantial

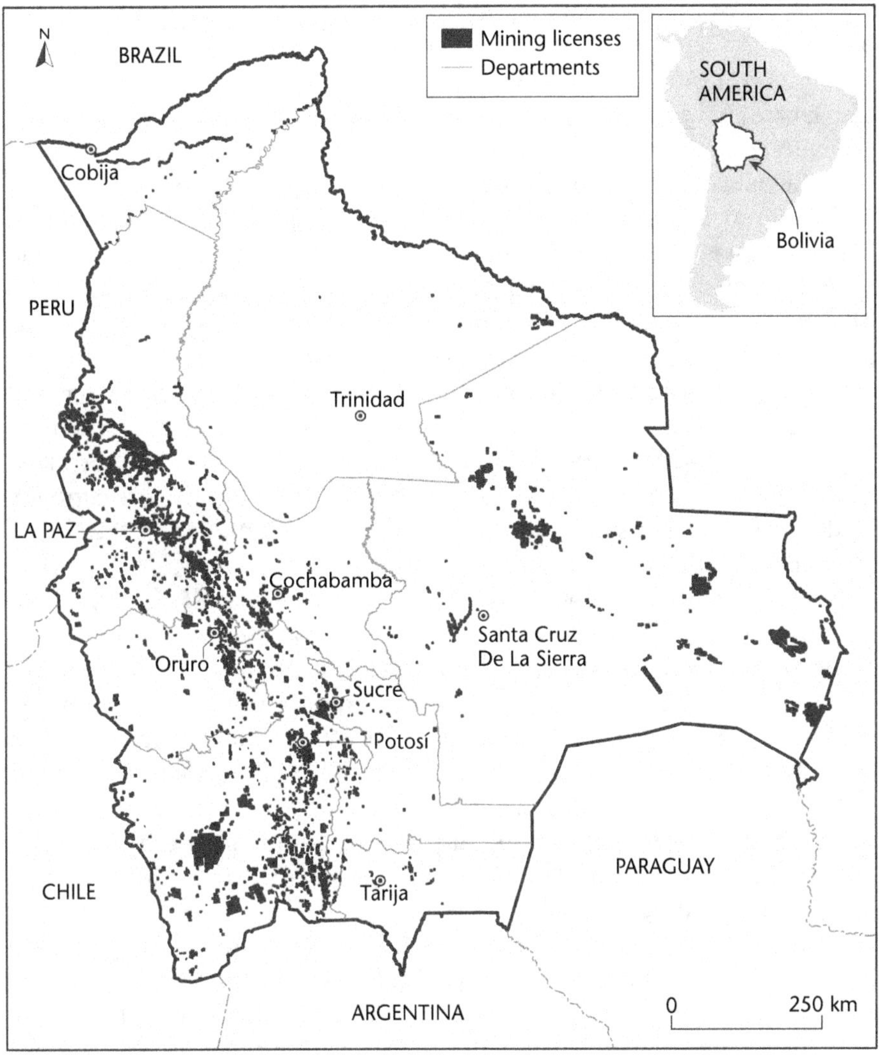

Map 3.1. Mining areas, Bolivia

Source: Map prepared by Chandra Jayasuriya on the basis of maps made available by CEDIB, Cochabamba, Bolivia, 2017.

growth emerged in small- and medium-scale production. This is characterized by cooperative mining, in which groups of miners organized through hierarchically structured networks of control and informal labour gain preferential access to mine sites provided by the state mining company, the Bolivian Mining Corporation (*Corporación Minera de Bolivia*, COMIBOL). These networks have come to dominate the mining sector and have been politically important actors since 2000.

Mineral extraction in the humid tropical lowlands to the north and east of Bolivia is a far more recent phenomenon taking two forms (see Map 3.1). To the north, informal gold mining has become increasingly important in alluvial areas, where gold has been carried downstream from the Andes over geological time and deposited in areas bordering what are now Peru and Brazil. This alluvial gold extraction should be viewed as part of a larger complex, of which the socio-politically and economically significant alluvial mining in Madre de Dios, Peru, is a prominent manifestation (see Cano, 2015b and Chapter 2, this volume). In Bolivia, this alluvial gold mining has produced murderous violence, as in Peru, but is yet to generate socio-politically strong actors in the way that has occurred in the Peruvian lowlands or Bolivia's highlands. The second form taken by lowland mining involves actual and planned large-scale operations in the eastern parts of the Santa Cruz department. Most significant among these are the Don Mario gold mine (Hindery, 2013, 2013b) and the very large iron ore deposits of Mutún that are currently held by the Bolivian state following the withdrawal in 2012 of the Indian company Jindal.[2]

The geography of hydrocarbons is the obverse of that of minerals, with primary reserves being concentrated in the Chaco, a narrow band of lowlands of the eastern/southeastern departments of Santa Cruz, Tarija, and Chuquisaca (see Map 3.2). These deposits are part of a larger belt of hydrocarbons and gas stretching along the eastern flank of the Andes through to Argentina. In Bolivia, these reserves are also concentrated in historically indigenous territories, primarily of Guaraní peoples. However, unlike mining, these populations have played scarcely any role as labour in the hydrocarbon economy and have more typically (until recent years) been displaced and ignored by operating companies.

The first hydrocarbon operations in Bolivia were along the Aguaragüe mountain range of the Chaco of Tarija in the 1920s. By the 1940s, operations extended into the Chaco of Santa Cruz and Chuquisaca, as well as more humid areas of Santa Cruz. Santa Cruz steadily became the heart of operations for Bolivia's hydrocarbons sector at the same time as it was becoming the overall economic centre of Bolivia. It also emerged as an important hub for more conservative political parties and movements with a strong regional identity and more or less overt expressions of racism centred on differentiating themselves from highland indigenous populations (Perreault, 2013). Over the last two decades, large gas fields were discovered and brought into production in the Chaco of Tarija, making the department of Tarija by far the largest producer of hydrocarbons and recipient of hydrocarbon revenue in the country (Humphreys Bebbington, 2010). However, the city of Santa Cruz continues to be the administrative centre of the hydrocarbon economy, with companies maintaining their primary offices there.

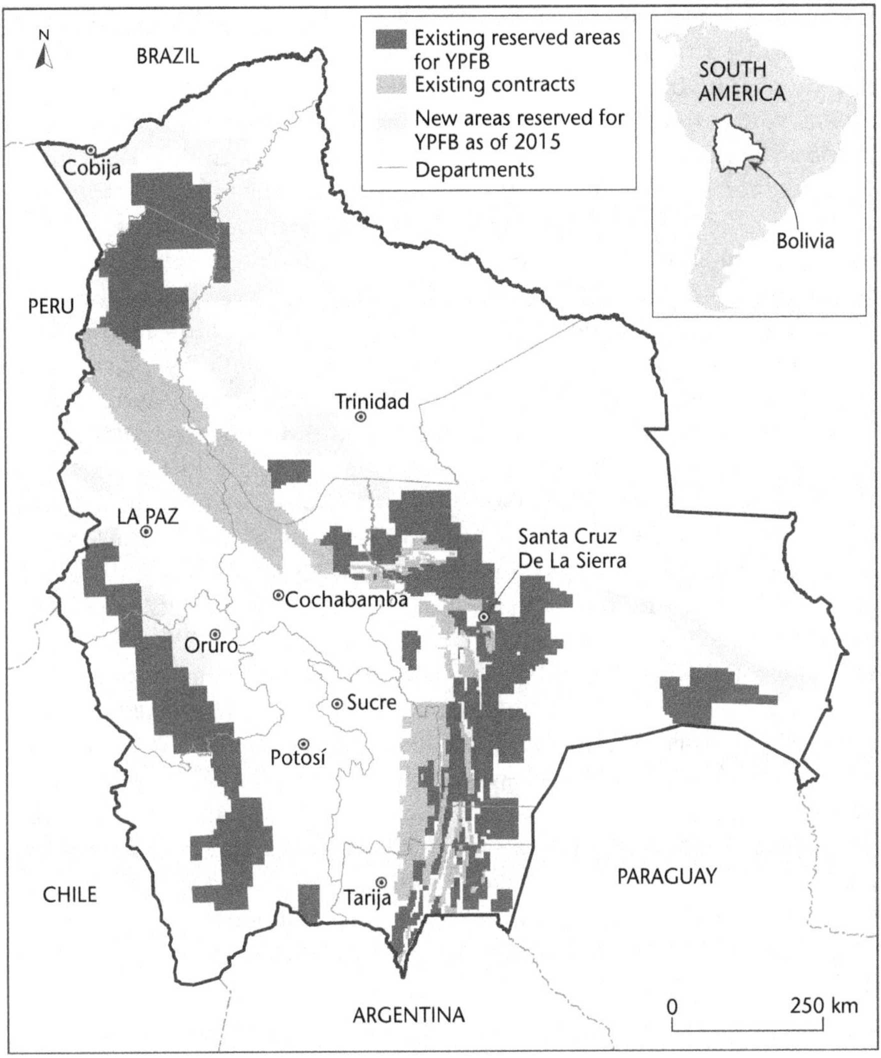

Map 3.2. Hydrocarbon areas, Bolivia

Source: Map prepared by Chandra Jayasuriya on the basis of maps made available by CEDIB, Cochabamba, Bolivia, 2017.

The geography of revenue distribution from hydrocarbons (discussed in Subsection 4.2) has meant that these three departments have gained significantly from gas and oil extraction. This has given rise to tensions with other departments and the national government, one result of which has been an effort by the Movement to Socialism (*Movimiento al Socialismo,* MAS) central government to encourage hydrocarbon exploration in non-traditional areas such as the Amazonian lowlands of the department of La Paz.[3] While there appear to be strong indications of reserves there, the cost of establishing operations is high, and government efforts to drill wells lag behind the traditional hydrocarbon-producing areas (*Página Siete*, 2016).

The geographies of mining and hydrocarbons have been the mirror image of each other, but over time each has extended into the primary 'territory' of the other. These geographies are important because, through their interaction with geographies of race and ethnicity, they have helped produce politically important actors and some of the discourses of justice, sovereignty, and autonomy that these actors mobilize in arguments over natural resources.

Not only have mining and hydrocarbons been politically salient, they have also dominated Bolivia's economy throughout history, and certainly since 1899, the starting point for this chapter. Mining production dominated early, with a peak in the 1950s as a result of a decline in the quality of ore grades beginning in the 1930s. In contrast, oil accounted for less than 1 per cent of total GDP in 1953 (Klein and Peres Cajías, 2014). However, by 1972, the opening of markets for natural gas quickly led that sector to surpass oil exports. Following the collapse of international tin markets, natural gas became Bolivia's most important commodity. Indeed, in the 1980s, taxes from the hydrocarbons sector constituted nearly 50 per cent of national income.

Aggregating across minerals, mining, and hydrocarbons now make comparable contributions to GDP: 6.6 per cent for hydrocarbons and 6.8 per cent for mining. Each subsector likewise contributes similarly to total exports: 42.3 per cent for hydrocarbons and 34.3 per cent for mining. However, there is a significant difference in terms of taxes paid, with hydrocarbons accounting for 29.2 per cent of government revenue and mining a paltry 1.9 per cent (Arellano-Yanguas, 2014). Conversely, mining continues to provide employment to significant numbers of Bolivian families, which is not the case for the hydrocarbons sector.

2 A Brief Periodization of Bolivia's Political Settlement and Instability

2.1 *Continuities and Instabilities among Elites and Extractivist Institutions*

Interpreting Bolivian history and contemporary events through the lens of political settlements is no small challenge in light of the often unruly and rupture-prone nature of national politics (Dunkerley, 2007). The main difficulty lies in balancing attention to detail, which can shed light on the forces that lead to new settlements, with the need to tease out larger patterns. We argue that political settlements beginning in the late nineteenth century and extending into the twenty-first century have been characterized by competition, instability, shifting alliances of power, and deeply entrenched forms of clientelism.

As we build this interpretation, we draw upon the work of both institutional economists and historiographers of Bolivia. In their work on the colonial origins of economic development, Acemoglu et al., (2001) explore the 'riches to rags' trajectories of a group of once wealthy but now poor countries first colonized by European powers in the sixteenth century—a category into which Bolivia would fall. Seeking to explain this 'reversal of fortune', the authors turn to an analysis of the kinds of institutions that European colonial powers introduced to these settings. They hypothesize that the different economic trajectories can be explained by taking a closer look at the organization of society at the time of colonization. More specifically, in those territories of great wealth, Europeans introduced 'extractivist institutions',[4] which favoured control by a small elite; conversely, in more marginal environments with less obvious resource wealth, the tendency was to ensure property rights ('institutions of property') to a broader swathe of society (Acemoglu et al., 2002: 1235; Acemoglu and Robinson, 2012). Extractivist institutions are seen as a brake on investment and long-term economic development, because such institutions allow groups that hold power to capture rents and maintain power, while institutions of property are seen as contributing favourably to the conditions necessary for investment in capitalist development.[5]

Acemoglu et al.'s emphasis on the 'stickiness' of institutions, and the *longue durée* of history, is important. However, there is more than a suggestion of path dependence in their argument, as 'extractivist institutions' remain firmly in the hands of a small but cohesive elite that retains its power and privilege through the control of rents over an extended period of time. In the case of Bolivia, however, recent historiography suggests that the nature of elite cohesiveness and power is more nuanced, complex, and potentially fragile (Barragán, 2008). Economic historian José Peres Cajías (2011) argues that the 'oligarchy hypothesis', which suggests the presence of a coherent and powerful elite exercising hegemonic power over national territory from 1880 to 1930, is not supported by evidence. He argues that it is more useful to analyse power relations through the prism of negotiation and accommodation, rather than domination. Through this prism, Peres Cajías details a chronic struggle of the weak (*lucha de débiles*) among sectors whose relative strength and capacity to influence politics is uneven and generally insufficient to consolidate a true national-level hegemony sustained over time (2011: 99). He points to the tensions between 'national elites' and regional elites over the construction of railway lines, which resulted in clear winners and losers (Rodriguez, 1994, cited in Peres Cajías, 2011: 111). Importantly, one upshot of this chronic struggle is the production of prolonged uncertainty that in turn dampens the expectations of economic actors, dissuades investment, and generates negative consequences for economic growth.

Bringing these insights together, we argue that the roots of political settlements and coalitions that underlie Bolivia's extractivist economy can be traced to historical institutional arrangements first introduced by Spanish colonizers and later modified during the Republican period (1825–80).[6] These early institutions were focused on extracting silver for export to Europe and resulted in the suppression of other economic activities not linked to extraction. This helped perpetuate arrangements in which a few elites linked to the control of natural resources were able to dominate national politics, even if they were not the only groups to draw some benefit from these institutional arrangements.[7] The emergence of oil and gas production in the eastern lowlands in the second half of the twentieth century then brought into being new elites, as well as a new set of institutional arrangements, reflecting significant divergences from mining sector practices with regard to how financial resource flows were collected, redistributed, and spent.

2.2 *Periodizing Political Settlements: 1899–2016*

With these observations in mind, we suggest that the broad dynamics of political settlements in Bolivia can be discussed across five periods between 1899 and 2016. The transitions between these periods are marked by some combination of change of government, period of crisis and revolution, and/or dramatic economic change (see Table 3.1).

2.2.1 1899–1935

The first period is bookended by the termination of the Federal War (1898–99) and the Chaco War (1932–35). The former pitted liberals supported by tin mining elites, mostly in the La Paz area, against conservatives, who were more linked to silver interests, and large landowners based in and around Sucre. This tension between Sucre and La Paz was indicative of this period, which was one of regional oligarchies competing among themselves and with national elites.

The end of this period of settlement, in which the so-called tin barons were dominant, was ushered in by economic crisis and war. The beginning of the Great Depression in 1929 and associated collapse of export markets revealed the chronic dependency of Bolivia on commodity market volatility, and marked the beginning of the end for the tin barons. Then the Chaco War, waged between 1932 and 1935, saw Bolivia and Paraguay in a dispute over inhospitable eastern lowland territory that was becoming known to host oil reserves. The Chaco War became a disaster for Bolivia, while also marking the delegitimation of the old political order and setting the stage for the emergence of modern political parties, the ascension of younger military officers with more progressive ideas, and new forms of popular political consciousness.[8]

2.2.2 1936–52

The Chaco War changed Bolivia and Bolivians in profound ways. All Bolivian men had been conscripted to fight: miners stood alongside students, urban workers, highland peasants from 'free' communities, and peasants labouring on semi-feudal estates. In the wake of the conflict, the political system collapsed, and a period of social protest and disorder followed. In 1936, two war heroes, David Toro and Germán Busch, launched a coup installing Toro as president, and shortly afterwards Toro announced his intent to pursue a project of 'military socialism'. Political life expanded in many directions as students and intellectuals explored radical politics through the creation of new political parties, at times influenced by international currents.

Meanwhile, the continuing stagnation of the global tin economy marked a period in which the traditional political parties (liberal, conservative, republican) unravelled, and the power of mining and landed elites began to break down. This period was also marked by 'increasing polarization between labour and capital in the industry' (Contreras, 1993: 20), as well as the undoing of old elites replaced by coalitions of new elites. This was reflected in a series of regime changes and coups leading to periods of liberal military rule and reform. The combination of liberal-minded militaries and increasingly organized and radicalized labour also gave rise to a growing prominence of nationalist ideas and discourses around natural resources. This period of extended political disequilibrium marked the absence of any clear settlement and a profound churning of elites, with industrial elites increasingly challenged by new elites emerging from labour, new political parties, and factions in the military.

2.2.3 1953–84

The churning of elites culminated in the revolution of 1952, led by the National Revolutionary Movement (*Movimiento Nacionalista Revolucionario*, MNR). While the period from 1952 to 1964 was hardly one of political quiescence, the MNR's sustained hold on government power allowed for the roll-out of thoroughgoing institutional and social reforms. These included broad-based expropriation of rural estates and land reform, the nationalization of mines (and thus the end of the tin barons), mass education, universal suffrage,[9] and social programmes. A period of dominant party politics, with increased attention to the promotion of class alliances, these twelve years changed the structures of access to and control of resources in the country, of political participation, and of class alliances. Indeed, in this period, the peasantry and workers became central to the ways in which settlements were negotiated, largely because they became increasingly organized from local to national level with the creation in 1952 of the Confederation of Bolivian Workers (*Central Obrera Boliviana*, COB) and the National Confederation of Peasant Workers of Bolivia (*Confederación Nacional de Trabajadores Campesinos de Bolivia*, CNTCB) in 1953.[10] The MNR extended its hegemony using a mix of clientelism and authoritarian methods, in particular with the increasingly restless miners' unions.

In 1964, a military coup brought MNR rule to an end, and the following six years combined both coup-based and elected military rule. Conflict within the military regarding both style and content of rule, and a mixture of pacted, contentious, and at times violent relations with organized labour and the peasantry characterized a period of little direction. The absence of any settlement about how politics should be done, who should lead, and how power and property should be distributed, characterized this period.

The period of 1971–85 is characterized by a high degree of political instability and the absence of any clear view of models of development. Military rule (albeit by quite distinct factions of the military at different times) resulted in varying combinations of military-society pacts, clientelism, kleptocracy, and outright repression. Governing ideas of development and societal organization changed often in this period, though importantly, there was a sustained commitment to the eastern lowlands whose economies and elites benefited considerably. The lowland city of Santa Cruz emerged as the increasingly obvious economic capital of the country, benefiting especially from the policies of the government of Hugo Banzer (1971–78). Military rule came to an end in 1982 with the election of an unstable political coalition of centrist and left-of-centre groupings that culminated in economic chaos and hyperinflation in 1984 and 1985.

2.2.4 1985–2002

This period begins with a textbook case of economic shock therapy and structural adjustment in August 1985, but is also characterized by elected rule and a party-based democracy associated with a progressive withdrawal of the military and labour unions from political life. Governments of this period were all characterized by coalitions among parties, because no party ever won much more than 20 per cent of the popular vote at election time. Thus, while the conduct of elections was all about party-based competitive clientelism, at the moment when governments were formed, the competition also manifested itself as one between coalitions of parties. The other stable feature of this period is the agreement among elites on the need to institutionalize neoliberal rules of economic and social management in the wake of the economic chaos of the mid-1980s.

Politics in these two decades are dominated by 'pacted democracy' (Assies, 2004: 31), in which rule was mostly characterized by carefully negotiated elections and outcomes among political elites (including the military). While these coalitions were highly fluid, with parties choosing governing allies for pragmatic rather than ideological reasons, the constant was the necessity of government through pacts. Another constant is the gradual undoing of the developmental state (a process that began in the 1970s and accelerated from the mid-1980s onwards), because of a combination of unmanageable debt, government incompetence, ideological desire to weaken organized labour, neoliberal commitment to the progressive marketization of society, and rejection of any pretence that the state might have the capacity to foster development itself. One consequence of this process was the closure of state-owned COMIBOL mines across the highlands in the mid-1980s.

2.2.5 2003–18

The last period runs from the collapse of the final government of pacted democracy in 2003 to the present. This has been a period characterized by profound disillusion with elite pacts, the resurgence of state-led development, and a centrality of social movement discourse and mobilization in national politics. The period begins with the fall of the government of Gonzalo Sánchez de Lozada in the wake of broad and violent social protests. While these protests had different origins, the primary drivers were related to natural resource politics (Perreault, 2006; this topic is discussed more fully in Subsection 4.2). An important actor in each of these protests was the political movement led by Evo Morales, who had narrowly lost the 2002 presidential elections to Sánchez de Lozada. Morales's movement was itself a product of resource governance, in that its initial bases had been coca growers, many of whom were themselves former miners who had been displaced by the closure of state-owned mines in the highlands. Morales and MAS prevailed in the 2005 elections, and have ruled via a self-described government of social movements ever since. Though MAS has been sustained by consistent electoral victories, in part this has been made possible by constitutional changes and interpretations that allowed for the successive re-elections of Morales. In some regard, the period has, therefore, been characterized by the increasing consolidation of a dominant party/dominant leader mode of rule.[11]

Ideologically, the Morales government rejects neoliberal modes of economic and social organization, and is committed to a form of state-led development that combines both nationalist and socialist sentiments. The government marks the most settled period of rule in the country since the first two decades of the twentieth century. This stability is grounded primarily in a settlement among most national social movements, but also with certain private capitalist interests (lowland agricultural elites) that have been able to

Table 3.1. Periodization of political settlements in Bolivia: 1899–2016

Period	Characterization of ruling coalition	Type of political regime	Configuration of political organizations	Broader development ideology	Modes of inclusion in extractive industry
1899–1935	Single party/tin barons	Multiparty	Limited access order, elite control characterized by *caudillismo*	Modernization	Employment in mines
1936–52	Fluid elite pacts with strong military presence	Military and multiparty	Limited access; new military and class elites emerge; old elites unravel	Resource nationalist	Employment in mines
1953–84	Single party/corporatist followed by military dictatorships (in pacts with different sectors)	Military and multiparty	Competitive clientelist with military presence	Nationalist–populist/ modernization	Employment in mines
1985–2002	Elected 'democratic pacts' among regional and sectoral elites	Multiparty	Competitive clientelist	Neoliberal	Access to mining areas (cooperatives)
2003–16	MAS and the Government of Social Movements	Multiparty	Electoral politics with de facto dominant party/ dominant leader	State-led transformation and redistribution	State ownership; taxation and redistribution through social transfers; ownership of mining cooperatives

continue operating in ways that allow for significant profit. Completely excluded from this settlement, however, have been historical political elites from the east as, in another similarity to the liberal period, the settlement is politically centred in the highlands.

In each of these five periods (summarized in Table 3.1), therefore, it is clear that overall political settlements cannot be discussed separately from mining and (later) hydrocarbons, given the overwhelming economic and political significance of these sectors. The interactions between political settlements and natural resources across these periods are discussed in more detail in the following two sections: mining in Section 3, and hydrocarbons in Section 4.

3 Mining and Politics: The Long Journey from Oligarchs to Cooperatives

3.1 *From Oligarchic Private Mining to the Unravelling of Resource Nationalist Mining*

From the late nineteenth century until post-World War II (WWII), mining in Bolivia was dominated by a small group of elite Bolivian families, first linked to silver mining (known as the Patriarchs of Silver) and later supplanted in the early twentieth century by families linked to tin mining (the tin barons).[12] These families increasingly dominated the national economy and politics, though in slightly different ways: while the former exercised direct control of the presidency at times, the latter exercised power indirectly and behind the scenes through the so-called '*rosca*'[13] and lawyers and politicians under their control (Mesa et al., 1998). At the same time, the emergence of tin as a valuable commodity led to the rise of new mining elites, who were both more entrepreneurial and more liberal than silver elites. More importantly, tin also sparked a shift in Bolivian politics as the (tin-based) Liberal Party and La Paz-based regional interests demanded the creation of a federalist system, greater revenue sharing, and more autonomy from the Conservative Party government in Sucre.[14]

Tin production was dominated by three Bolivian producers: Simon Patiño, the Aramayos, and the Hochschilds. The most famous and important of these was Patiño, a self-made man rising from humble origins to become the richest man in Bolivia and the Americas. At its peak, Patiño's tin empire controlled 10 per cent of world production and 80 per cent of tin smelters (Capriles Villazón, 1977; Granados, 2015). Patiño also played an important, though controversial, role in the Chaco War by lending the Bolivian government money and donating planes for the war effort.[15] The Aramayos were descendants of an old silver family and active in the mining sector until the 1952 reforms, while the Hochschilds, a family of Jewish immigrants from Europe, eventually left Bolivia to develop mining interests elsewhere in Latin America.[16] Tin cemented the importance of La Paz and the centrality of the altiplano in Bolivian politics, and the new tin elite exerted enormous influence over infrastructure investment and fiscal policy. The barons were also favoured by the commodities boom from 1922 to 1929, in which tin prices rose significantly, as did international demand and production.

The tin boom drove increasing government debt, which grew fivefold from 1900 to 1922 as the state took on loans to invest in railway networks to support the sector, but failed to impose any significant taxes on the mines until the 1920s. Disputes between national and regional elites emerged over public investment in railway lines, roads, and other public infrastructure. The inability of economic and political elites to agree on how to diversify the economy, combined with an increasing reliance upon tin revenues to finance government, not only reinforced the narrow base of the Bolivian economy, but also fed national–subnational disputes over budgets, stunted institutional development, and derailed the pursuit of broader development initiatives (Orihuela and Thorp, 2012: 32–3).

At the same time as the tin elite exercised significant control over capital and politics,[17] the period was characterized by growing mine labour and indigenous organization, a series of strikes (one of which ended in the appalling Uncía massacre in 1923), and a growing instability in pacts among mining interests following the Depression.[18] The government needed more tax revenue to pay off burdensome loans, including those for infrastructure to support the mining sector, and by the 1920s had managed to install something of a tax system and a fiscal commission (*Comisión Fiscal Permanente*) which 'exhaustively reviewed the books of mining companies and succeeded in collecting significant amounts from many of them in back taxes' (Contreras, 1993: 11). Meanwhile, a boom in tin prices from 1922 to 1929 ended with the collapse of world markets after the 1929 Depression, leading the government to introduce a system for distributing export quotas among mining companies that pitted companies against each other and weakened their national representative association. Finally, despite enjoying a relatively stable political settlement, the period was characterized by development disappointment. Given the explosive growth of the tin economy, Contreras (1993: 8) argues that:

> [T]he mining industry was not the great 'engine of growth' of Bolivian development that it could have been, [primarily because of] (i) governmental incapability to extract higher taxes from the mining industry, particularly during the first

> decades, together with the inefficient use of that income which was generated; and (ii) the factor that the major mining companies, after obtaining large profits, did not invest in the country.

These were, without doubt, important factors though it is also true that mining failed as an engine of growth in later decades when taxes were higher, and that the relative paucity of business opportunities in Bolivia may have been a factor in miners' decisions not to invest in the country. Whatever the case, in many respects it is the ghost of this development disappointment that hangs over the MAS government today as it negotiates how to manage large but unstable resource rents, this time from natural gas, and seeks to convert them into lasting and significant social change and development.

These dynamics played out in the context of a more serious structural challenge: the country's increasing isolation and limited prospects for economic growth in the wake of its loss of coastal territory in the War of the Pacific (1879–83) and the imposed constraints from the peace settlements that followed.[19] In many ways, Bolivia never fully recovered from the loss of these Pacific ports, and this certainly constrained the expansion of mining and other investments in the altiplano, while also contributing to the country's eventual turn eastward for economic growth and development.[20]

Following the Great Depression and crises in the tin sector of the 1930s and post-WWII era, the mining sector entered a profound slump (Whitehead, 1972). The viability of agro-pastoral production and mining in the altiplano came into question. The government, which had already begun to support colonization of the eastern lowlands and the promotion of commercial agriculture, redoubled its efforts. Support came from the Bohan Commission, a US government mission sent to Bolivia in 1941–42 to help draft a strategic plan for economic development and cooperation. In addition to supporting the expansion of a modern, commercial agricultural sector, the 'Bohan Plan' called for increased development of hydrocarbon resources in the eastern departments, which had been discovered and developed by Standard Oil of New Jersey in the 1920s and later nationalized in the 1930s. Hydrocarbon production would be revitalized through private investment to generate the revenues needed to fund government and replace lost income from a declining mineral sector. The plan was embraced by political elites from the east and uncontested by elites elsewhere. It served to orient US development assistance to Bolivia for decades, though it would take sixty years and another round of privatization before the hydrocarbons component of this vision would come to full fruition.[21]

While development planners and some elites were looking east, mining labour was becoming increasingly organized and militant, with closer links to political parties—both of the far left, and the emerging (centrist) MNR. This strength won labour a series of favourable legislative provisions, which also had the effect of increasing mines' costs of production. Struggles between mine owners and labour became increasingly acute, including through the massacre of striking miners at Patiño's Catavi mine in 1943. This was immediately followed by the creation of the Union Federation of Bolivian Mine Workers (*Federación Sindical de Trabajadores Mineros de Bolivia,* FSTMB) in 1944, which subsequently called for greater militancy and the seizure of mines through the Trotskyist-inflected 'Tesis de Pulacayo' in 1946.

The FSTMB, and especially more radicalized elements such as the tin miner militias from the altiplano, played an important role in the MNR revolution of April 1952, which became the first 'national-popular' revolution of post-WWII Latin America (Hylton and Thomson, 2005: 42). A coalition of these mining groups, urban-based middle-class reformists, radicalized students, and workers from La Paz ushered in the government of President Paz Estenssoro, which pursued an ambitious and wide-ranging reform agenda. These reforms sought the definitive end to oligarchic privilege and power, which, inter alia, required separating the oligarchy from natural resource ownership through agrarian reform and nationalization of the mines. The ideas and discourses mobilized in this period reinforced the centrality of extractive industry in the country's economic development process and imaginary, with effects felt through to the present.[22]

The state only nationalized the mines of the tin oligarchs (Patiño, Hochschild, and Aramayo) as they were seen as anti-patriotic and responsible for Bolivia's economic weakness. The tin barons sought to establish joint operations with the state, but this proposal was rejected. Eventually, the state took control of 80 per cent of mineral production (see Contreras, 1993). The MNR government created COMIBOL to administer these newly nationalized mines, and introduced the concept of co-government of mines with mine workers. Meanwhile, in the absence of any countervailing power, and under pressure from the US government, the hydrocarbons sector was reopened to foreign investment.

If the 1952 revolution effectively disrupted the old regime, it also profoundly reshaped peasant–indigenous–worker interactions with the Bolivian state. The government pronounced all rural workers to be *campesinos* (peasants), and quickly moved to create a dense network of rural unions (first linked to the expropriated landed estates, but then to more traditional communities—especially in the altiplano). The rural unions became vehicles for rural populations to gain access to government services and programmes, among them the newly introduced food programmes supported by international aid.[23] Corporatist ties were cemented between the state and the peasantry that would last far beyond the MNR government, re-emerging in important ways in the MAS/Morales period. From this point forward, the *campesinado* (peasantry) became a central actor in Bolivian politics. The military dictatorships that immediately followed the MNR government were quick to institutionalize the alliance in the form of the *Pacto Militar Campesino* (Military Campesino Pact).

Following the overthrow of the MNR government in 1964 by René Barrientos, formal politics entered a period of hyper-political instability described by James Dunkerley as a 'continuity of ruptures' (2007: 114). Over an eighteen-year period, fourteen governments came to power, almost all of them military, and many via the ubiquitous 'coup d'état'. Violations of human rights were frequent, and a culture of violence and impunity took root.[24] Significantly, under authoritarianism, the conservative right tended to forge alliances with military regimes, while the progressive left sought alliances with more progressive officers within the armed forces. With no single political party strong enough to challenge military rule, party loyalties tended to be fluid and pragmatic (Dunkerley, 2007: 118). Economic management was poor and the mining sector suffered because of repression of unions, but also from a lack of any strategy to invest in or strengthen COMIBOL.

Profound divisions within the military ultimately led to a return of a (weak) civilian political coalition first elected in 1980, but prevented from taking office until 1982. The return to civilian rule coincided with the emerging debt crisis in Latin America, an empty treasury, and a restless citizenry. Sliding into social crisis, Paz Estenssoro, the president who had led the revolution of 1952, and now in the role of elder statesman, was elected to power in 1985. He promptly announced a programme of stabilization, including a package of emergency economic measures, to stem hyperinflation. The country's plight was compounded by the dramatic collapse of tin markets in 1984 and the resulting crisis of tin mining, a key source of rural employment and export revenues. Among the measures taken to reduce public expenditure and open the economy to external competition, the national mining company, COMIBOL, was 'decentralized' into a series of regional units, and a policy of *relocalización* (relocation) was introduced.[25] Nearly 80 per cent of COMIBOL's workforce, comprised largely of indigenous highland miners, was dismissed. The FSTMB fought the closures and negotiated with the state to maintain production at some sites. But this time, strikes and road blocks—the tactic of choice in so many previous conflicts with the state—held no sway. With little left to negotiate, rural families headed to urban settlements in El Alto and Cochabamba, the Chapare to cultivate coca leaf, and further afield to Argentina and Brazil. The ensuing exodus from the mining sector has had profound implications for Bolivia's social and political landscape, as seen in the capacity of ex-miners to organize the Juntas Vecinales at the forefront of the 2003 Guerra del Gas conflict, and more recently the role of colonist families (many of them ex-miners from the highlands) in the Isiboro Sécure Indigenous Territory and National Park (*Territorio Indígena y Parque Nacional Isiboro-Sécure,* TIPNIS) conflict of 2012.[26]

However, not all families abandoned mining, and an important number of them negotiated with the state in order to obtain concessions and equipment to continue mining activity on a small-scale basis as organized cooperatives. This was not a new institutional arrangement; mining cooperatives had long existed in the highlands, in particular in the department of Potosí. From colonial times, miners practised *Kachi,* arrangements in which miners were allowed to enter certain areas of the mine and work independently, sharing the value of the minerals they produced.[27] In the twentieth century, this practice persisted and was consolidated in times of economic crisis. Analysts today continue to maintain that the rise of the cooperative sector is linked to the long practice of *Kachi* and the state's legalization of independent mining via the measures introduced by Gonzalo Sánchez de Lozada, the planning minister and implementer of the stabilization programme (Poveda, 2012; Francescone and Díaz, 2014). In hindsight, the government's recognition and support of the cooperative sector might be seen as a so-called *salida de paso*—a pragmatic exit from an immediate problem. It certainly was neither part of a longer-term view of developing the mining sector, nor an attempt to increase popular access to mineral resources. The organization of cooperatives and the transference of concessions and equipment for the purposes of exploitation at least partially resolved the immediate question of what to do with mining families. It also complemented the government's larger plan of reopening the mining sector to foreign capital in the hopes of revitalizing a long moribund industry, inter alia to satisfy the personal interests of the president (Hindery, 2013a; Kaup, 2013).[28]

3.2 *Emergence of Cooperativism and the Return of Large-Scale Private Mining*

While many subaltern actors in Bolivian politics have gained visibility and power over the last thirty years, the trajectory of the mining cooperatives from assertive excluded faction to prominent actor in the current political settlement is most noteworthy. One interviewee, a former Assembly representative from the department of Potosí, noted:

> The cooperatives have always made pacts: with neoliberal governments of the past, with the MIR, with ADN, with the MNR and NFR, in order to have access to mining concessions and benefits. Before MAS, the cooperatives had these pacts. The mining cooperatives were against the Constituent Assembly [to reform the constitution] and they marched against it with dynamite in hand. Today, after opposing the new constitution, the cooperatives are now *the* transcendent political

> allies of this government, not the Federation of Mine Workers, not the Confederation of Workers [COB]. It is the Federation of Cooperative Miners [FENCOMIN] and its departmental and regional affiliates that are part of this political alliance. (Authors' translation).

The emergence of mining cooperatives has produced wide-ranging impacts on the development of Bolivia's mining sector (Francescone, 2015). This is evident in the significant influence they exerted to shape the policies, practices, and governance of the sector in the new *Ley Minera* (Mining Law) of May 2014. The sector is also one of the closest allies of the MAS/Morales government, as they can be relied upon to mobilize their massive numbers (estimated at over 100,000 families), eclipsing the importance of the state's historical ally, the FSTMB.[29] In acknowledgement of their political power, one former minister of mining explained that the MAS/Morales administration created three vice-ministry positions, assigning each key sector either a vice-minister's or minister's seat: the cooperative sector; the FSTMB; and private, medium-scale miners. Moreover, a representative of the cooperative sector was appointed minister in 2013, though was later replaced in the midst of negotiations around the new Mining Law in favour of a more conciliatory figure not linked to a particular mining constituency.[30]

To secure their unconditional support, the mining cooperatives receive highly favourable treatment that is at times better than that received by the FSTMB miners who labour for COMIBOL. This is not lost on the latter, who have seen their power diminished, both politically and at times physically, as in the case of the Huanuni mine conflict of 2005.[31] According to one ex-minister of mines interviewed, the cooperative miners pay only the mining royalty, which is 5–7 per cent of the total value of their production. They do not pay IVA (value-added tax) and are exempt from additional (social) costs that private mining firms and COMIBOL are obliged by law to cover. The smaller, less organized cooperatives do not contribute to pension schemes (though the larger, better organized cooperatives do). Cooperatives are not required to present an environmental licence for their activities nor fulfil other environmental requirements.[32] The new Mining Law of 2014 also provides for low-cost loans, technical assistance, and social benefits to the cooperative sector.

The cooperative sector also enjoys preferential treatment in terms of receiving concessions for areas to work, a practice which appears to be in contradiction to a stated government agenda to consolidate a state-led mining economy. In a highly fluid context, cooperatives attempt to gain access to mines through two routes. The first involves petitioning COMIBOL for concessions, which may be pursued through the violent occupation of a (private or state-owned) mining operation in order to force the government to give them more areas to work. The second tactic involves a more collaborative approach, in which private mining interests sub-contract cooperatives to work specific areas and/or carry out tasks, as in the case of the San Bartolomé mine in the vicinity of Cerro Rico.[33,34] What is markedly different from previous eras of extraction is the high level of social conflict and violence associated with the expansion of mining (CEDLA, 2014; Fundación UNIR, 2014). While the government has moved to discourage violent occupations of mines, police presence in rural areas is weak, and the government is hesitant to send in the military to remove the occupiers. Analysts criticize the government for doing too little, too late, pointing to the now entrenched modus operandi of cooperativists (and other opportunists masquerading as cooperativists) that has constrained the prospects for developing a vibrant, modern, state-led mining sector (Espinoza Morales, 2010; Oporto, 2012).

The emergence of the cooperative sector is critical to understanding the changing structure of capital investment and economic development, as well as to interpreting shifts in the political base of the MAS/Morales government of social movements. However, it would be incorrect to suggest that this marks the beginning of the end of transnational mining and private investment in Bolivia. Indeed, cooperatives contribute little to the national budget by way of taxes or royalties. Instead, mining revenue comes largely from a single operation, the San Cristobal mine in southern Potosí, which accounts for 30 per cent of all export mining revenues (CEDIB, 2013). Operated by Sumitomo, a Japanese firm, the mine produces silver, zinc, and lead. In 2011, the mine paid US$150 million in royalties and taxes. The rest of Bolivia's private mines, while not as large, also contribute important sums in terms of royalties and taxes. These are medium-scale mines with investors from Canadian, US, Australian, and Korean firms, who often partner with Bolivian firms represented by the National Association of Medium-Scale Mining (*Asociación Nacional de Mineros Medianos*, ANMM). In recent years, private investment in the mining sector has stagnated, as only the most risk-tolerant firms move forward with projects. One national mining authority interviewed noted that privately, the government promotes foreign investment in mining, though its public message is more antagonistic.[35]

Under the 2014 Mining Law, the Bolivian government will convert all existing mining concessions to joint contracts with COMIBOL, with the objective of reasserting sovereignty (if only symbolically) over the country's natural resources and deterring speculation.[36] Of the various actors in the sector, COMIBOL, the FSTMB, and ANMM stand to lose the most. In the case of COMIBOL, the government is forced to cede its plan to forge a modern, dynamic, state-owned mining sector, and instead focus on attracting foreign capital (when possible) and pursue initiatives to exploit and industrialize iron ore (via the Proyecto Mutún in the department of Santa Cruz) and lithium (via a joint investment in Potosí). These are both long-term projects that have the potential to radically reshape Bolivia's mining industry. However, they require enormous investment over a long period of time, and the MAS/Morales government has not shown the capacity to negotiate contracts that can support the development of iron ore and lithium reserves. Meanwhile, the FSTMB has been displaced by a more vocal and militant cooperative leadership that has extracted major concessions from the government. While they continue to be important allies as a social movement, their relatively unimportant role in the negotiation of the new Mining Law suggests a very different trajectory for COMIBOL, and a less visible political role for unionized mine workers. Finally, medium-scale mining companies will have to negotiate complicated arrangements with the Bolivian state (via COMIBOL), as well as with communities, cooperatives, and in some cases with formally recognized indigenous communities.

3.3 *Summary*

In this section, we have demonstrated that the control of mining in Bolivia shifted broadly over time from international–national capitalist control, to national capitalist control, to state control, to a return to international and national capitalist control, followed finally by increasing—and increasingly prominent—cooperative influence. These changes reflect shifts in the larger development ideas and discourses across the settlement periods outlined earlier: from liberal capitalist, to developmental statist, to neoliberal, to statist/resource nationalist and social movement-based. These changes reflect the shifting influence and politics of different actors within national settlements, at the same time as they have helped to constitute certain actors as particularly powerful. The changes also point to the complex relationships between economic and political power: as much for nineteenth-century mining elites as for cooperatives today, while their economic power has been a basis for their political power, they have also used their political power to secure and enhance their economic power. The current context is one characterized by the increasing power of the cooperatives and a pragmatic institutional pluralism that accommodates their demands, but also permits private capital to coexist and participate profitably in the sector.

Changes in the sector also reflect shifts in the relative importance of different modes of inclusion through mining. In earlier periods, mining policy was not very inclusive, except through labour. With the creation of COMIBOL in the 1950s, inclusion took place through labour that sought both economic and political inclusion for miners, through co-government, with miners taking up positions in the bureaucracy, and also through government-administered clientelist programmes funded by rents generated by COMIBOL. In the neoliberal period, at least initially, there was limited inclusion of either type (few jobs, and low tax revenues). However, the economic crisis at the moment of adjustment (1985) sowed the seeds for a new model of inclusion. First, the government's transfer of mining rights to displaced miners organized as cooperatives created the basis for what has now become a large sector. In this case, what was initially an effort to foster limited economic inclusion (through allocating mining rights) triggered processes that have culminated in far greater political inclusion demanded by an organized sector with substantial capacity (or 'holding power', in Khan's terms[37]) to exercise influence over other actors, national elites, and the nature of the national political settlement. Second, adjustment in 1985 was accompanied by the creation of the Social Emergency Fund, an effort to foster very basic inclusion under conditions of crisis. In retrospect, this initiated the model of fund-based social protection financing that has since become central to the MAS government's efforts to foster inclusion.[38]

4 Hydrocarbons, Regionalism, and Economic Development

4.1 *The Rise and Demise of Hydrocarbon Nationalism*

The emergence of oil as an additional source of rents began in the early years of the twentieth century, far from the disputes and struggles of the La Paz-based mining and landed elites. Some minor investment, speculation, and exploratory activity took place prior to this period, but it was not until 1921, when Standard Oil of New Jersey began exploring for oil in the Chaco, that the sector attracted any real interest. The first fields brought into production were in the area of Bermejo (1924), just north of the frontier with Argentina, in the department of Tarija, followed by a series of discoveries along the *Serranía de Aguaragüe* in the Chaco of Tarija (which has become an area of renewed gas exploration in recent years). These were remote sites in a marginal region occupied by a mix of lowland indigenous groups, cattle ranchers, missionaries, and indigenous peasants tied to landed estates.

The purported role of oil companies in fostering the Chaco War (1932–35), in which over 50,000 Bolivian soldiers died, changed how Bolivians viewed the role of the state in administering and protecting the country's natural resources. Political analyst Carlos Toranzo Roca (2009) argues that historical interpretations of the Chaco War as having been fought over oil produced an *idea fuerza* (dominant idea) that oil is part of Bolivia's strategic wealth and that the state must retain control over the hydrocarbons sector. This idea persists among the general public through to the present, and underlies the MAS/Morales discourse.[39]

The post-war, coup-installed military government moved to regain control over the country's hydrocarbon resources by confiscating the oilfields owned by Standard Oil, and in so doing established yet another *idea fuerza*: that of the military as defender of Bolivia's natural resources. In 1937, the government created a national hydrocarbons agency, Bolivian National Oilfields (*Yacimientos Petrolíferos Fiscales de Bolivia*, YPFB). In addition, a Ministry of Mines and Petroleum was established to oversee the development of the extractive sectors and to promote a modern, technical management of the country's resources. For the next fifteen years, YPFB was the sole operator in the sector, drilling at different sites in the Chaco and gaining expertise in the emerging oil and gas sectors.

As a relatively small actor providing modest amounts to the national budget, and with physical operations in a distant territory, YPFB was able to grow, develop technical capacity, and consolidate its operations relatively undisturbed. The hydrocarbons industry in Bolivia never produced a national hydrocarbon elite of oilmen and speculators (as it did in the United States, or as mining had already done in Bolivia; Kaup, 2013). Instead, as YPFB grew, it produced an important, if small, number of engineers and managers. Some of these were trained in Mexico, and therefore knew the experience of state-led Mexican Petroleums (*Petróleos Mexicanos*, PEMEX), while others were trained in the United States, particularly in Texas, and forged ties with international oil companies. Those who worked in the industry in Bolivia in the decades from the 1950s to the 1970s often came to occupy important positions in central bureaucracy and in the governments of oil-producing departments, established technical services firms serving the industry, or took up consultancy work as analysts in the country and abroad.

In contrast to the royalties produced from the mining sector, which were sent to the national treasury (mining rents never formed an important part of departmental budgets), the system of royalties for oil (and later gas) followed a different trajectory. This system was first laid out in legislation dating to 1921 and later reaffirmed in the Organic Petroleum Law of 1938, which established that a royalty payment of 11 per cent of the value of oil production would be paid to the region where it was produced. The Busch Law of 1957 ratified the arrangement again, though there were efforts by central government to modify these payments. While the amount paid was initially modest (in 1954 the department of Santa Cruz received only US$76,000 in oil royalties), payments rose quickly as production increased (Barragán, 2008). When, in the mid-1950s, the MNR government sought to rein in these payments, the response was a regional citizen revolt in Santa Cruz, in which the *Comité Cívico* (Citizen's Committee), a group of prominent citizens lobbying for departmental interests, launched a two-year protest to receive their 11 per cent royalty in support of their economic development (Roca, 2008).

Eventually, the government ceded to the demands of the Santa Cruz rebels. The department of Tarija, a more modest producer of oil, allied with the Santa Cruz *Comité Cívico* to demand to be included in the same arrangement, and thus Tarija also began receiving royalties paid directly by YPFB to departmental coffers.[40]

Importantly, these social mobilizations organized by regional political and economic elites to institutionalize the payment of hydrocarbon rents to departments reinforced another set of *ideas fuerza*. The first of these was that producing regions were *entitled* to a direct flow of the financial resources linked to the amount of hydrocarbons produced in their territory. The second idea was that these resources were needed in order to promote the economic development aspirations of regions that had been neglected and harmed by the excessive centralism of La Paz and the highlands. A third *idea fuerza* was that regional governments must be vigilant against efforts by the central government to reclaim departmental revenues.[41] These dominant ideas linked to hydrocarbon rents have persisted over the last six decades, fuelled significant social conflict in recent years, and continue to shape the current (post-2003) political settlement, despite the efforts of MAS and Morales to reform how hydrocarbon rents are distributed and spent across national territory.

Under pressure from the US embassy, the MNR government agreed to sign the Davenport Code in 1956, which transferred potential areas of production held by YPFB to the US-owned Gulf Oil. In 1969, another military government, led by General Alfredo Ovando, reclaimed sovereignty over Bolivia's oil and gas fields with a second nationalization. Advising Ovando were two influential public intellectuals: Marcelo Quiroga Santa Cruz, later named Minister of Mining and Petroleum, and Sergio Almaraz, a strategist of the left. Both effectively mobilized nationalist–populist sentiments that resonated with the working and urban middle classes and with YPFB workers and technocrats. Through nationalization, the country recovered about 90 per cent of its gas reserves—considered to be illegally controlled by Gulf Oil. Bolivia was then able to negotiate a long-term agreement to deliver natural gas to Argentina's expanding market. Shortly thereafter, during the Banzer dictatorship, the natural gas sector further expanded with the possibilities of serving new markets in Brazil (1972).[42]

By the early 1990s, however, the sector was again confronting a shortage of capital to invest in exploration and the development of new fields. With the decline of tin revenues, the Latin American debt crisis, and constraints imposed on public expenditure through neoliberal measures, the coffers of YPFB were empty (Morales, 1992). To further aggravate YPFB's woes, an erratic payment arrangement between Bolivia and Argentina for the delivery of natural gas meant that YPFB did not always receive what it was owed. As the contractual arrangement allowed Bolivia to be paid 'in kind', repayment would take the form of equipment, processed fuel, or other inputs, among other things. As both countries suffered from significant currency devaluations and general economic mismanagement, keeping track of deliveries and payments became exceedingly complex. This led to the infamous *borrón y cuenta nueva*, when both countries threw up their hands and agreed to settle accounts with a 'clean slate'.[43]

The period from the 1930s to the 1980s was therefore one of oscillation between private and state control of the industry. While the state was never able to adequately strengthen a national hydrocarbons company, social and political leaders were recurrently inclined to deploy ideas of resource nationalism because of historically inherited distrust of transnational companies. In parallel with this, regional actors in hydrocarbon-rich areas became increasingly strong and able to make claims for the earmarking of tax and royalty revenue for regional needs. The seeds of hydrocarbon nationalism planted in the 1960s would re-emerge in the twenty-first century, again in a context of regional claims for revenue sharing. This time, however, these claims also emerged in the context of a government based on a stable settlement with negotiated relations, both with parties to the settlement (mostly social movements) as well as with strategic excluded factions. This has led to greater stability in hydrocarbons governance, as discussed in the following section.

4.2 *Resource Regionalism, Social Movement Nationalism, and the Governance of Natural Gas*

By the 1990s, the combination of a pacted democracy (Assies, 2004) and inter-elite agreement on neoliberal economic management became progressively less stable in the face of new, more radical political currents in the Andean highlands, the coca growers' movement (*cocaleros*) in the Chapare, and the increasing mobilizations of lowland indigenous groups in the east. The combined effect of these distinct forms of 'holding power' forced political leaders to address issues of political, economic, and social inclusion. In response, the first Sánchez de Lozada government (1993–97) launched a broad-ranging reform programme that created new vehicles for grassroots political participation and decentralization. These programmes sought to appease excluded factions (especially subnational ones), while at the same time actually deepening market reforms and opening up new opportunities for capital investment in natural resources (Kohl, 2002; Farthing and Kohl, 2005). Through a series of new laws, the government announced the creation of 311 new municipalities with elected town councils. These would be supported by municipal citizen oversight committees and have control of modest budgets.[44] These new municipalities would now receive a direct flow of resources from the central state—an arrangement that has been reaffirmed and expanded under the MAS/Morales government. Sánchez de Lozada did nothing, however, to recognize regional demands for greater political autonomy,[45] fearing this would 'Balkanize Bolivia' (Roca, 2008: 66). This was therefore an attempt to build a mega-pact with municipal governments which would allow the central government to work around entrenched and hostile political elites in the departmental capitals.[46] In the end, though, the effort to incorporate subnational factions through resource transfers rather than the delegation of political powers was insufficient to sustain the settlement.

Political and economic elites generally supported these neoliberal reforms, even though the power of La Paz elites and the dominant position of the western departments and the mining economy were significantly impacted (those in La Paz, for example, saw their access to government posts and public funds diminish: Molina, 2008: 7). Bolivia pursued its own version of the privatization of state assets through a programme of 'capitalization', in which the government retained only a minority share in former state enterprises. YPFB was broken down into various operations and sold off to foreign investors, retaining only minimal functions of promotion, information, and regulation. Attracted by extremely favourable terms, some of the world's largest oil companies became involved in the sector as the 'fire sale' of YPFB's assets coincided with a worldwide boom to search for and bring into production new oil and gas reserves. Numerous scholars have argued that this sell-off of state assets was an act of betrayal by the political elite, and ultimately gave rise to an environment of hyper-social mobilization and conflict that would eventually end decades of pacted democracy in 2003 (e.g. Kaup, 2013; Farthing and Kohl, 2014).

The break-up of YPFB thus effectively put control of the hydrocarbons sector in the hands of international firms, who moved to develop their projects in a highly fluid and competitive environment influenced by international hydrocarbons and capital markets. By the turn of the century, the natural gas market was booming, and 'new discoveries' led by Petrobras (Brazil) and REPSOL-YPF (Spain) led to projections that Bolivia would be a major producer and distributor of natural gas for the Southern Cone region (Brazil, Argentina, Paraguay, and Chile). It is important to note, however, that several authors, as well as former YPFB officials and Bolivian geologists interviewed for this project, argue that YPFB already knew about the existence of these 'newly discovered' wells, and that they were on the maps that YPFB had to turn over to foreign firms under privatization. The sting in the tail is that the tax regime was much lower for new discoveries: 18 per cent versus 50 per cent for existing wells. This fed the public perception of an all-out pillage by transnational firms and nurtured a grievance that culminated in MAS/Morales' nationalization of oil and gas fields in 2006.

A series of mergers and acquisitions—exercised far beyond the borders of Bolivia—produced a landscape of investors, speculators, and operators that were beyond the control of the state. The public perception, especially in the highlands, was that transnational firms and institutions were now in control of Bolivia's gas resources (Perreault, 2006). In contrast, regional leaders and elites in the departments of Santa Cruz, and especially Tarija, where the gas boom was centred, were less critical of the presence of transnational firms and actively participated in the promotion of major investments. In interviews with a range of social actors in Tarija, most noted that there was generally a positive reaction to gas projects, as this would mean that departmental revenues would increase along with employment and other economic activities. As *petroleros* (a term used to describe all workers/officials linked to the oil and gas industries) had a long-established history in the region, and hydrocarbons had contributed to the development of the Chaco and the city of Tarija, there was less animosity towards their presence. While there was some opposition by indigenous groups on whose territories much of the resources were located, their mobilizations were dismissed as little more than an attempt at rent-seeking (Humphreys Bebbington, 2010).

In the rest of the country, and in particular the highlands, the expansion of hydrocarbon investments in the 1990s and early 2000s was generating anxiety over the sense of lost wealth, as well as increasing animosity towards political leaders. Ethnic tensions flared between east and west. The rise of MAS, which was linked to the *cocaleros* in the Chapare (Cochabamba) and their standard-bearer, Evo Morales, emerged as the most coherent and organized force among Bolivia's political movements. MAS would lead the demand for greater political participation and an end to neoliberal policies. A series of violent confrontations between social movements and the government over the privatization of water services in the city of Cochabamba, known as the Water War, led to social mobilizations elsewhere in the country (Assies, 2004; Perreault, 2006). From Cochabamba, street mobilizations spread to the altiplano. Initially, social mobilizing centred on opposition to the *Ley de Aguas* (Water Law) and an end to concessioning water, but then encompassed public rejection of coca eradication policies and the proposal to export Bolivian natural gas via Chile.

Facing the spread of unrest, Sánchez de Lozada called in the military to restore order. Dozens of protestors were killed and hundreds were injured in the resulting conflict. Images of bloodied protestors projected in televised news reports provoked immediate outrage at the outsized use of force by the government, prompting Sánchez de Lozada to resign and depart the country. After some thirty years of pacted power sharing, the political settlement collapsed. Though the original grievances behind the 'Gas War' had been diffuse, the multiple sites of protest coalesced into a unified public demand that the state retake control of the nation's natural resources. As we will show further, this reflects once more the centrality of natural resources to the formulation (and demise) of Bolivian political settlements.[47]

The incoming president, Carlos Mesa, was seen as a more moderate and conciliatory figure, and he moved to introduce a series of reforms to calm tensions. To appease both protesters' concerns as well as calls for greater regional autonomy from the bloc of eastern departments (Santa Cruz, Tarija, Beni, and Pando) he offered to allow regions to elect their prefects directly (previously they had been appointed by the president).[48] Under the Mesa government, the Hydrocarbons Law 3058 (2005) was passed, which has since become the basis for the current political settlement. The law helped resolve a crippling political crisis by creating a framework for sharing the financial resources generated by extraction. It increased the taxes levied against foreign companies' revenues, while also expanding distribution to a broader range of sectors and interest groups, with important implications for how different social and political projects are pursued and sustained. Once again, then, a mechanism was created to allow the fashioning of political settlements on the basis of natural resource revenues.

Despite these efforts, tensions continued to flare across the country, resulting in Mesa's resignation and a special election in 2005. Morales and MAS were easily elected to power in the first round, through the support of a coalition of highland and lowland social, indigenous and peasant movements (his closest allies), urban intellectuals, NGOs, urban middle-class workers, and trade union members. Much of Morales's base came from the altiplano, but he also received significant support from the ever-expanding migrant communities (largely from the altiplano) in urban centres and from poorer sectors throughout the country (even in the four eastern departments). The Morales/MAS government represented a return to state-led capitalist development under the control of a movement-based party. The basis of its economic project is a continuation of the extraction and export of natural resources (especially hydrocarbons), with a programme of redistribution via cash transfer programmes. Industrialization of Bolivia's natural resources is also part of the larger vision, with a view to altering how Bolivia participates in the global economy.

One of Morales's first moves was to renationalize Bolivia's hydrocarbons. Through a decree referring to the fallen Heroes of the Chaco, and mobilizing the 'political mythology'[49] of a war purportedly fought to defend Bolivia's natural resources, Morales travelled to the most important gas field (operated by Petrobras) to declare: 'the gas is ours'. The enormously popular move produced reverberations in international financial markets and put Bolivia in the category of poor investment environments (in ratings such as those produced by Verisk Maplecroft Risk Index, 2013). More practically, it provoked tension with Bolivia's biggest neighbour and consumer of gas, Brazil.

Petrobras, the hybrid state firm, effectively produces about 60 per cent of all Bolivian natural gas, and consumes upwards of 70 per cent of all gas produced by the country. In addition, it operates several major pipelines and provides important technical assistance and support to YPFB.

In the end, the renationalization was more symbolic than real, insofar as it did not confiscate the camps, equipment, and related infrastructure. Petrobras continued to produce and transport natural gas and ensure that financial resources flowed to government coffers. What the nationalization did accomplish, however, was the unravelling of some of capitalization's most egregious errors. It re-established sovereignty over natural resources, abolished concessions, and forced all companies to enter into joint contracts with the state via YPFB. It addressed the imbalance caused by the 18 per cent tax on new discoveries, increasing Bolivia's take to 50 per cent on all wells, new or old. It re-established YPFB as the state authority responsible for hydrocarbons production, returned areas reserved for development to the agency, and set about restoring its ability to produce and distribute hydrocarbons. In addition, Bolivia renegotiated the contract price of natural gas with Brazil and Argentina closer to market rates.

As a result, government revenues nearly tripled overnight, injecting a sense of national euphoria that Bolivia had recovered what rightfully belonged to the nation. Ironically, this change benefited the regional governments in opposition to MAS/Morales more than any other group. The financial windfall, however, did little to calm tensions between these eastern regions and the central government. Instead, it led to increasingly acrimonious conflict. Hamstrung by an agreement that left few resources for the central government and his projects, Morales announced his intention to alter the percentages contained in the Hydrocarbons Law 3058 and to claw back resources for the national treasury. Almost immediately, regional governments responded with threats of revolt, and a 'catastrophic stand-off' ensued (García Linera, 2008). The four regional governments receiving the highest royalty and tax transfers (Santa Cruz, Tarija, Beni, and Pando) mobilized their bases, set about writing charters for autonomy, and organized departmental referenda to adopt them. Once again, distributional fights seemed to threaten the country's internal cohesion.

In the end, confrontation was averted when the central government left tax transfers to regional governments mostly intact and instead focused on redirecting revenue linked to the increased production of gas to municipal governments.[50] The combination of increased production and higher prices swelled departmental and municipal government coffers, and there was no shortage of central government largesse to be used to garner support for its positions. The MAS/Morales government has been able to consolidate political power through a mix of bold political tactics and hydrocarbon revenues. Since the passage of a new constitution in 2009 and the re-election of Evo Morales in 2010, regional political elites have largely been subdued, and redistributive fights have been resolved.

4.3 *Summary*

Hydrocarbons have been pivotal to the nature and constitution of national political settlements over the last century in Bolivia, as well as to the political negotiations between central and subnational elites. Indeed, the period discussed here is bookended by two phenomena reflecting the great significance of oil and gas. Whether or not the Chaco War was actually catalysed by Standard Oil's machinations to secure access to oil, the war is imagined to a very great extent through *ideas fuerza* about oil. The war is viewed as symptomatic of the need for Bolivia to secure its hydrocarbon resources and protect them from foreign capture. Moreover, the loss of thousands of highland lives in the war is the critical point of reference for arguing that oil wealth is national property, not subnational. In the contemporary moment, hydrocarbons are at the centre of the MAS/Morales political project, providing the fiscal resources for national programmes of redistributive social investment. At the same time, struggles over hydrocarbon revenues have been at the core of tensions between a highlands-dominated central government, and the subnational elites of Santa Cruz, Tarija, and Chuquisaca.

The governance of hydrocarbons has changed repeatedly over this period, from private to state control on three separate occasions. This has reflected the shifting national political settlement, and the rise and demise of resource nationalist ideas about oil and gas. This general instability has meant that hydrocarbons and development have been only poorly coupled at a national level—indeed, the only success in strategically converting hydrocarbon revenue into development had, until the latter 2000s, been at a subnational scale, primarily in the department of Santa Cruz. This pattern shifted, however, with the consolidation of the MAS/Morales political settlement, under which hydrocarbon revenues have been increasingly secured by the centre, and then deliberately used to finance social inclusion through a range of social protection measures. The success of these transfer programmes has in turn helped to further stabilize the settlement through the vertical incorporation of lower-level factions into the settlement.

Given that hydrocarbons have been a constant since the 1920s, it is clearly *not* the case that oil can be said to have any necessary relation to the nature of the political settlement. The nature of the political settlement *does*, however, affect how oil is governed and used. As the settlement has increasingly become one of a dominant party/dominant leader, coupled with some significant checks and balances on power, hydrocarbons have become more obviously developmental.

5 Conclusions: Resource Governance, Region, and Political Settlements in the *Longue Durée*

By establishing and discussing five key periods of Bolivia's modern history, this chapter has attempted to understand how political settlements among elites have affected and been affected by natural resource governance in the country. In this concluding section, we focus on the following: (1) the patterns that recur across these periods, in particular those that relate to the centrality of national–subnational relations within Bolivia's political settlements; (2) the centrality of ideas about, and the materiality of, natural resources for the nature of these settlements; and (3) the implications of this analysis for political settlements theory.

5.1 *Historical Continuities and Subnational Dynamics*

While the constitution of political settlements in Bolivia has shifted over the last 120 years, with corresponding shifts in their implications for inclusivity and exclusivity, certain themes have been recurrent. The first is the importance of subnational elites and politics to the ways in which a national settlement is fashioned, and the consequent instability of any such settlement. Second is the increasing importance of the east of Bolivia to the constitution of settlements, given the concentration there of powerful agrarian, agro-industrial, and hydrocarbon elites who have been included factions or excluded actors with significant ability to exercise power over or within the dominant settlement. Third is the use of natural resources, and above all the rents deriving from these, in any strategy to build national settlements around the exchange of loyalties and patronage. Fourth is the ebb and flow between employment, redistribution, and direct control of natural resources as the primary mechanisms of socio-economic inclusion, and the tendency for inclusion-through-employment and resource control to produce subaltern actors with significant 'holding power', who have been able to exercise influence over national settlements. These four themes intersect substantially with each other, and will be present throughout our discussion in the remainder of the chapter.

The role of subnational elites in Bolivia's settlements, their ability to undermine national settlements, and the relationship between this ability and the presence of natural resource endowments within their territories, is striking. There has been a constant tension between projects to create a unitary state and demands for more decentralized forms of government. This goes back to the very beginning of our period of interest, when inter-elite debates over the levying of taxes and public expenditure reflected the preference for a unitary state over a federalist arrangement, with poorer departments constantly clamouring for more resources from central government. Historian Rossana Barragán notes that the strengthening of the central government and the departments happened simultaneously, based on the raising and sharing of revenues beginning in the late nineteenth century: 'we see the fragility of the central state and how it had to fight to impose itself over economic sectors and groups through endless disputes' (Barragán, 2008: 84).[51] From the late nineteenth century onwards, mining revenues from the departments of Potosí, Oruro, and La Paz subsidized poorer departments that lacked the capacity to raise revenue through taxes. Mining revenue was also the source of funding for financing transportation infrastructure investments (mostly railways, but also roads) to support the growth of the regions and their articulation to markets (Orihuela and Thorp, 2012).

Once hydrocarbons came on the scene, a different tax and redistribution model slowly came into being, strengthening the hand of eastern subnational elites. Beginning in the 1920s, with the production of oil in the eastern departments of Santa Cruz and Tarija, oil revenues (from royalties) were assigned to poorer regions (Pando, Beni) to support their growth and consolidation. However, unlike with hard-rock minerals, royalties from oil (and later natural gas) also went to departmental government coffers, allowing producing departments to grow and develop.[52]

These arguments between subnational elites and national elites have long histories. Some of this history is related to the traditional strength of departmental prefects, who in the past were in charge of education, agriculture, industry, and commerce; who supervised the treasury and customs offices; and who recruited, clothed, and fed troops. Barragán notes that the historical power of this institution:

> explains how every revolution or change in government arose from agreements and pacts between departmental leaders, whether prefects or those who aspired to the position, and why every government established itself on the basis of the same strategic geography – in essence a network between capital cities and the main urban centres of each department. (2008: 91)

The importance of these subnational elites in the state-building project has also given them power, and indeed relations between departmental treasuries and the central state were always problematic. There were constant disputes over which income streams were national and which were departmental, as well as over what and whom would be taxed. Thus, central state and departmental relations were characterized by both mutual need and constant feuding, in which departmental authorities were seen as more powerful, cohesive actors negotiating with a weaker central state. This pattern clearly persists into the contemporary period and has been one of the critical factors affecting natural resource governance. That said, beginning in 2009 with the passage of the new constitution and the referendum reaffirming the MAS/Morales government, we see a significant consolidation of political power. Regional elites that were once avowed enemies of MAS/Morales joined the ranks of MAS, either by running as candidates in local, regional, and national elections, or through appointments to the public bureaucracy.

5.2 *Natural Resources and the Constitution of Political Settlements*

> The question we should be asking ourselves is not 'why is it that our greatest wealth was lost?' but rather 'how do we save ourselves from our natural wealth?'
>
> (Fernando Molina, 2011)

An enduring set of ideas around the reasons for Bolivia's underdevelopment centres on the oligarchies hypothesis, in which Bolivia's economic and political elites are seen as a tightly hegemonic group. Acemoglu and Robinson (2012), among others, challenge this view of elites as a homogenous group, offering a more nuanced approach that views inter-elite disputes and bargaining as critical to explaining development trajectories. Through a close examination of the evolution of the mining and hydrocarbons sectors, the shifting composition of political settlements, and the persistent tensions between national and regional elites over the distribution of revenues, we find a story that does not support the oligarchies' hypothesis.

Different regimes, under different settlements, would forge alliances with urban-based regional elites, hoping to reduce the chronic instability that characterized Bolivian political life. Indeed, even in the present day, the MAS/Morales regime has constructed a careful coalition of Andean-based regional support to counteract the political and economic power of the eastern departments. Subnational agreements appear to be an important part of the story—with the department of Santa Cruz perhaps the best example of a long-standing subnational political settlement. In the most recent settlement period, subaltern actors have significantly increased their holding power or become part of a dominant coalition at both the subnational and national levels. More generally, subnational actors—both departmental and municipal—have played important roles in constituting and contesting settlements over the course of the last century.[53]

By the second half of the last century, the emergence of a dynamic oil and gas sector in the east of the country eclipsed the mining sector and ultimately the long-standing power of elites linked to mining in the west. This transition picked up speed with the dramatic collapse of tin markets in the 1980s, coupled with a debt crisis and years of mismanagement from military rule, followed by the introduction of neoliberal reforms. But the blueprint for this transition was set in motion decades earlier, through the little-known US-sponsored Bohan Plan, which concluded that Bolivia's future lay to its east. Indeed, the receipts from oil and gas development have surpassed the collective imagination. Vice-President García Linera has described natural gas as 'the goose that lays the golden egg'—*the* source of funds that will seed Bolivia's development in the twenty-first century (García Linera, n.d.: 11). The centrality of gas came quickly, though it will produce long-lasting impacts on the organization of economic, political, and social life. In departments like Tarija, where some 80 per cent of all natural gas is produced, and a nearly equal percentage of the country's gas reserves are located, gas revenues contribute over 95 per cent of the budget. Even in the department of Santa Cruz, whose economy is more diversified by the presence of a strong agro-industrial sector, oil and gas revenues still dominate the budget.

At the national level, oil and gas revenues are vital to the MAS/Morales 'Process of Change', the wide-reaching project to refound Bolivia. Gas and oil rents are the currency by which social inclusion is delivered and efforts at nascent industrial transformation are initiated, as well as the means by which patronage is extended and loyalties are consolidated. The ambiguity and flexibility of the MAS/Morales process of change allows for new alliances to be created according to fluctuating needs and distinct political contexts. In this way, political enemies of MAS can be incorporated into the bureaucracy through *peguismo* (the creation of posts), or added to political rosters with relative ease. Such flexibility allowed Morales to cement an agreement with and gain the loyalty of conservative subregional elites in the Chaco, in exchange for their being granted direct receipt of royalty payments. This in turn allowed him to suppress the political power of urban-based regional elites in the city of Tarija by placing a gas-funded wedge between them and these subregional elites. *Peguismo* inside YPFB and the central government has continued to flourish, despite Morales's insistence that MAS adherents should not expect to benefit from employment arrangements in exchange for party loyalty. The first director of YPFB, Santos Ramírez, a former close confidant of Morales, who is now in prison for corruption charges, was known for hiring party-based technicians who knew nothing about hydrocarbons.[54] In a different sort of redistributive fight, as YPFB was being reconstituted, the government was forced to divide the state-owned company into a series of vice-presidencies so that each producing department (Tarija, Santa Cruz, Chuquisaca, and Cochabamba) would host an office in addition to La Paz.

Generally, hydrocarbon rents have been used to foster inclusion through redistributive spending. Up to the mid-1950s, rents were fairly modest, and so did not draw much attention or give rise to major social mobilization. However, the political significance of rents changed as the scale of production grew and royalty and tax payments increased. The Hydrocarbons Law 3058 established the parameters for the central government to distribute hydrocarbon taxes to regional and municipal governments (as well as to universities, the police, and a special development fund for indigenous groups). Within regions, the distribution of rent-funded expenditure has also become central to political dynamics.

MAS and Morales have also used the distribution of oil and gas rents to shape the settlement in new ways. Until recently, rent distribution usually took place in one of two ways: by territory or by sector. With the introduction of social programmes[55] targeted at individuals, a new dynamic has been introduced. Through such transfers, new entitlements (and relationships) between the central government and citizens are formed that in turn have long-term implications for Bolivia's future economic development path. In the near-to-medium term, the government must produce more hydrocarbons in order to pay for these programmes, and indeed, the government uses this argument as a way to validate its preferential treatment of the hydrocarbons industry. This stands in some tension with the government's other need to invest in the industrialization of minerals, oil, and gas, as well as in other sectors of the economy, in order to move beyond the extraction–export model.

In the case of the mining sector, which historically provided opportunities for participation either through labour (as a mine worker), or, to a lesser extent, through direct control of the means of production (a mine owner), the government increasingly appears to privilege the mining cooperatives. Mining cooperatives resolve employment issues for many more rural families in the highlands (an important segment of MAS' political base) than do large-scale mines—even if such a resolution is only partial and such mining is usually combined with other livelihood activities. More importantly, the new mining law allows rural families the possibility of controlling the means of production (or to do so at least jointly with the state) as a means of receiving greater benefits. However, larger-scale investment in exploration cannot be pursued under conditions characterized by uncertainty and social conflict—two significant problems affecting mining areas today, partly as a consequence of the increased strength of cooperatives. Furthermore, the imposition of cooperative mining in some agro-pastoral communities constrains the possibilities for pursuing other productive (and less environmentally damaging) economic activities. In the most recent political settlement, we see increasing social conflict over the negative impacts of uncontrolled mining activity and the inability of the government to address long-standing sites of environmental contamination, raising the question as to the role that environment and contamination will play in a new settlement.

Natural resources have long been at the centre of Bolivian political economy and political bargaining. Not since colonial times, however, have they been a sufficient basis of power for any one settlement to become consolidated to the point that it could begin to view these resources as part of a medium- to long-term developmental project, and manage those resources accordingly. The combined effect of changes in global markets (both in terms of prices and shifting patterns of demand), the distinct regional geographies of different resources within Bolivia, and the country's substantial and often powerful subaltern populations, have meant that efforts to build alliances between the centre and regions, across regions, and across classes have never succeeded for long. As a consequence, the incentive for elites has consistently been to control revenue streams from resources in order to spend on managing political alliances, rather than to invest in economic and social development.

5.3 *Implications for Theory*

The case of Bolivia also suggests that relative 'settlement' in political relationships may be more the exception than the norm. Certainly, the last 120 years in the country have been characterized by great instability, deriving largely from the inability of elites to act collectively across spatial and social differences and agree on models of development that offer broad inclusion in benefits and opportunities. The relative exceptions to this instability have been the periods of liberal rule in the 1900s and 1920s, the decade or so of MNR rule from 1952 to 1964, and the period of MAS hegemony since 2005. One might argue that the period from 1985 to 2003 was also characterized by sustained elite agreement that Bolivian political economy should be governed through electoral democracy and neoliberal modes of management.

Interestingly, these more settled periods of relative party dominance have also been characterized by significant policy roll-out: policies that supported the rapid growth of the tin economy in the liberal period, and socio-economic reform policies that dramatically changed forms of natural resource governance and benefit distribution in both the MNR and MAS periods. While this pattern is consistent with the claim that periods of dominant party rule can be associated with more transformational and developmental policies, the very significant exception is the institutionalization of neoliberal government between 1985 and 2003, which occurred under conditions of competitive clientelism. This suggests that analytical distinctions regarding the developmental implications of competitive clientelism and dominant party rule need to be made with care. One implication, perhaps, is that regardless of the domestic mode of rule, transnational pressures from financial and commodity markets, rolled out through networks of technocrats and traders, can discipline settlements regardless of their form, and can determine the models of development that flow from these settlements. This disciplining effect can be just as strong as any disciplining coming from excluded factions, and certainly helps explain why neoliberal commitments became taken for granted among political and economic elites after 1985. Furthermore, in Bolivia, this external disciplining has come not only from historical imperial powers (the US) but also countries such as Brazil and Argentina as they seek to consolidate their regional authority.

This does not imply that the emphasis of political settlements literature on bargains among elites, the influence of excluded and lower-level factions, and domestic political drivers is not relevant. These factors are clearly important in understanding how natural resources have been governed over the *longue durée* in Bolivia. Pressure from excluded labour in the 1930s and 1940s, excluded social movement constituencies during the 1980s and 1990s, and excluded eastern lowland elites under MAS rule have all ultimately shifted prevailing bargains and driven important, and in some cases profound, changes in mining and hydrocarbon governance. In some instances, the holding power of excluded groups has ultimately driven reversals in the overall political settlement—as reflected in the emergence and coming-to-power of both the MNR and MAS.

The Bolivian experience suggests elements of a framework for explaining the emergence of actors with the political power necessary to shift settlements. In broad terms, actors who have challenged settlements have emerged either on the basis of geographically dependent subnational power or changes in economic organization. Examples of the first include eastern lowland elites (powered by economic resources and a sense of regional identities) and highland elites linked to the particular geographies of mining (this is the case as much for tin miners in the 1900s as for the mining cooperatives today). Social movements defined by territorial identifiers also fall into this category, and have become more powerful either because they have been threatened by particular economic activities or because other actors (perhaps especially transnational activists) have given greater cultural and political value to their geographical origins (e.g. by recognizing the value of indigenous territory). In the second instance, examples include the miners' unions of the 1940s onwards or the mining cooperative movement today. Thus, the emergence of actors with holding power can be endogenous to the prevailing political economy (e.g. miners' unions, authorities receiving benefit transfers, etc.) also aided by transnational support.

Finally, both in the processes underlying the emergence of new actors, and in those through which ruling elites consolidate their authority, the mobilization of ideas (especially those related to natural resources) has been of critical importance. These ideas serve to catalyse collective action of both elites and excluded groups, and also to persuade others, domestically and internationally, of the legitimacy of their claims. Many of these ideas have been derived from Bolivia's own historical experience, such as the failure of tin to catalyse development or the fortunes taken out of the country by international mining companies in the past. In addition, they have been derived from the country's geographies, such as through the coupling of nature and nation (cf. Perreault, 2013) and the territorial bases of racial, regional, and ethnic identity. Other ideas have been more international in origin, such as international labour organizing and socialist principles.

Making sense of the relationships between political power and natural resource governance in Bolivia therefore requires attention to the nature of political settlements (including their relative stability or lack thereof), the particular history and geography of natural resource governance, and the relationships among actors operating at different geographical scales.

Acknowledgements

Celina Grisi Huber provided tremendous support to this chapter, in collecting data, commenting on the text, and correcting errors. José Alejandro Peres Cajías also offered extensive commentary and guidance.

The maps in this chapter are courtesy of the Bolivian Centre for Documentation and Information (*Centro de Documentación e Información Bolivia,* CEDIB) in Cochabamba, and we are extremely grateful to Marco Gandarillas for allowing us to work with the maps, as well as for the great work that CEDIB does in Bolivia.

Endnotes

1. Such an agreement to 'divvy up' can be an agreement to distribute control of resources and benefits simultaneously, or to allow parties to the bargain to take turns in controlling these benefits (e.g. with different parts of the elite coming to power at different times through some form of electoral process).
2. As of January 2016, the government signed a contract with SINOSTEEL Equipment to proceed with the extractive project.
3. Considered part of the Sub-Andean belt of hydrocarbons linking the Camisea gas fields in Peru to the lowlands of La Paz, Cochabamba, and Beni.
4. Extractivist institutions were already in place at the time of colonization, as the Incans employed the 'mita', a tribute in the form of labour that conquered populations had to deliver. The Spanish were adept at maintaining and expanding those prior institutions which were useful for their purposes (Stern, 1993). In Bolivia, forced labour practices such as *pongeaje* and *mitaje* were not eliminated until the

reforms of the 1952 National Revolution. Before the revolution, only property-owning males with a certain income were eligible to vote.

5. Acemoglu et al. further argue that population density and prosperity at the time of colonization were important influences on the policies introduced by Europeans (2002: 1236).
6. On the long-term effect of colonial institutions on the contemporary Andean economy, see Dell (2010).
7. The nature of such elites was not, however, constant across time and space, and they were only able to secure dominance by negotiating power and resources with other groups which had some degree of political capacity.
8. This has of course been a frequent effect of war (Tilly, 2004).
9. Previously, only about 10 per cent of the male population was eligible to vote in any given election.
10. The Unified Confederation of Unionized Peasant Workers of Bolivia (*Confederación Sindical Única de Trabajadores Campesinos de Bolivia*, CSUTCB), was created in 1979.
11. In February 2016, Bolivians returned to vote on a proposal to allow Morales to run a third time, potentially extending his presidency until 2025. The 'No' vote won 51.3 per cent to 48.7 per cent, indicating a potential return to a competitive clientelist form of settlement.
12. The focus of this chapter spans the late nineteenth century to the present for the mining sector and the early twentieth century to the present for the hydrocarbons sector. In the period immediately following independence (1825–41), Bolivia continued to participate in global trade circuits dominated by Peruvian foreign mining interests. Later in the century, the sector became dominated by Chilean and British companies, which were very influential in the liberal government, in particular in terms of pressing for railroad construction. From the late 1840s to 1880, Bolivia was governed by a series of military *caudillos* (military strongmen) resulting in political violence and lawlessness, though Klein (2011) remarks that colonial social and political institutions persisted into the 1880s.
13. *Rosca* referring to an inner circle.
14. Following the Federal War of 1899 between liberals based in the city of La Paz and conservatives based in the city of Sucre, liberal politics prevailed in Bolivia until the coup of 1921. The post-war settlement transferred most government functions to La Paz, but retained the unitary system and elite control over politics. Reflecting long-standing, unresolved tensions between regions, the issue of where to locate Bolivia's capital returned to national political debate during the Constituent Assembly process of 2006–07.
15. Undoubtedly, Patiño's influence was huge, buttressed by his enormous personal wealth and the success of his international businesses. For an interesting take on Patiño's role during the Chaco War, see *Página Siete* (2013).
16. Patiño had consolidated his global economic power by World War I—well before the Hochschilds (who did so after the Great Depression)—while the Aramayos never controlled such a large share of the tin economy, though their economic power dated back much further, to the mid-nineteenth century.

17. Other authors suggest that the agricultural sector also exercised significant control over politics because it had a majority presence in parliament (Gallo, 1991).
18. On long histories of indigenous and peasant resistance and struggle, see Gotkowitz (2008).
19. Since independence in 1825, Bolivia lost over half of its territory through war and poorly negotiated treaties with problematic neighbours—yet another reflection of a fragmented elite and the chronic weakness of the central state.
20. Fernando Molina argues that historical patterns of economic activity, combined with geographic constraints, forced Bolivia's regions to seek integration into global circuits and economic development through different axes. The altiplano looked towards the Pacific Coast—though this was complicated with the loss of access to ports, first to Peru and later to Chile—while the southeast looked towards Asunción and Buenos Aires, and the northeast looked towards the Amazon and Brazil's Atlantic Coast (2008: 5).
21. In addition to expanding hydrocarbons production, the Bohan Plan called for investing in pipelines to link oil fields (and later gas) with markets in Argentina and northern Chile. The idea of Bolivia serving as an energy hub for its larger neighbours was at the centre of the natural gas boom (and ensuing conflict) between 1995 and 2005.
22. For example, many of these nationalist sentiments around Bolivia's natural resources continue to be echoed in the publications of the Committee for the Defense of National Patrimony *Comité de Defensa del Patrimonio Nacional,* (CODEPANAL), among others.
23. International aid was almost entirely from the United States, and it is precisely during this period that US opinion began to influence internal politics in Bolivia.
24. During much of this period, Bolivia's neighbours were also governed by military dictatorships in which civilian repression, torture, and violence were commonplace. However, unlike its neighbours, there was no organized leftist guerrilla movement in Bolivia, and the level of political violence was significantly less than elsewhere.
25. In contrast to COMIBOL and the mining sector, the draconian economic measures strengthened the operations of the national hydrocarbons agency, Bolivian National Oilfields (*Yacimientos Petrolíferos Fiscales de Bolivia,* YPFB), by liberalizing the prices charged to customers. As a result, the agency's contribution to the national treasury increased from 12.7 per cent of total public revenue in 1983 to 56.7 per cent in 1986 (Dunkerley, 2007: 152). It is at this point that the hydrocarbons sector definitively replaces tin at the head of the national economy in terms of share of total public revenue and total exports.
26. This conflict was triggered by government plans to build a highway that would run through TIPNIS, a region that is designated both as indigenous territory and a protected area. It was supposed by some parties that the road would benefit colonist (including coca) farmers in the lowlands and would also support the expansion of hydrocarbons within TIPNIS. While positions and identities assumed around the conflict are complex, in a very broad sense lowland indigenous groups tended to protest against the road, while colonists and coca producers favoured it. The

conflict was ultimately violent, and indeed became viewed as the first time that the Morales government had used police and military violence indiscriminately against the population.

27. The first mining cooperative can be traced back to Potosí in 1929, when the *Palliris K'ajcha Libre* was organized, later to be transformed into the *Sociedad Cooperativa K'ajcha Libre*.
28. Gonzalo Sánchez de Lozada served as planning minister and architect of Bolivia's structural adjustment programme (with support from Jeffrey Sachs) of the Paz Estenssoro government of 1985–89. He was later elected president (1993–97) and introduced a series of sweeping reforms, among them the privatization initiatives known as capitalization. He was elected again in 2002, but did not finish his term, as rising social protest over economic policy, the 'transnationalization' of Bolivia's natural resources, and an unpopular drug eradication policy descended into increasingly violent confrontations between the state and social movements. A highly contentious figure in Bolivian politics, Sánchez de Lozada was part of the mining elite. He was founder and owner of the Mining Company of the South (Compañía Minera del Sur, COMSUR), which operated several important mines, including the Porco Mine in Potosí and the Don Mario mine in the Chiquitania of Santa Cruz. See Kaup (2013) and Hindery (2013) for critical views of the economic reforms he pursued. Both argue that such reforms benefited his personal financial interests. Kaup also notes that his governments strengthened the hand of private mining interests (and the power of La Paz elites) while effectively neutralizing regional and agro-industrial elite challenges to central state authority.
29. Rolando Jordan (2012) refers to the mining cooperatives as an 'untouchable political and social power', and links their emergence to *relocalización* and the politics of accommodation pursued under Sánchez de Lozada.
30. Interview with a former Minister of Mining, August 2014.
31. On 5–6 October 2006, a bloody conflict between two rival groups of miners exploded any perception of stability in the mining sector under the Morales government. Some 4,000 mine workers linked to mining cooperatives came to blows with some 800 state mine workers (FSTMB) over control of the richer veins of Pokasoni Hill. COMIBOL began operating the mine after a private firm was forced to return the concession to the Bolivian state. A former cooperative Huanuni mine worker himself, Wálter Villaruel, Morales's first minister of mining, supported the position of the cooperatives. Failing to negotiate an agreement with COMIBOL, the minister called on the cooperatives to take over the mine. Sixteen miners were killed and dozens more injured. The government intervened in favour of COMIBOL by nationalizing the mine, incorporating cooperative miners into COMIBOL, and abolishing cooperative mining. However, the move did little to strengthen COMIBOL or the unionized mine workers. Since then cooperative miners have continued to either threaten—or have indeed carried out—invasions of mines, forcing COMIBOL to grant them areas to work (see Espinoza Morales, 2010; Stein, 2010).
32. In July 2014, a spill involving a cooperative-owned mine in Potosí sent thousands of gallons of toxic chemicals into a nearby stream and eventually into the

Pilcomayo River. An interview with the then mining minister indicated that he noted that government supervision of cooperative mining operations was nil.

33. *Cerro Rico*, or 'Rich Hill', is a large, cone-shaped mountain in Potosí that towers over the surrounding landscape. Discovered by the Spanish in 1545, the mine led to the founding of the city of Potosí, also known as the *Villa Imperial* (Imperial City) at its foot. It was the first colonial city of the Americas, and quickly grew to surpass by the early 1600s the populations of London and Paris (Brown, 2012: 46). Nearly 500 years later, Cerro Rico remains an important source of employment for the largely indigenous, cooperative miners and workers who labour alongside private investment and the state mining agency.
34. In some cases, such as the Colquiri mine, the government moved to nationalize the mine and then proposed joint exploration between COMIBOL and cooperatives.
35. Interview with Vice-Minister of Mining, 2013.
36. In August 2016, cooperative miners protested the government's efforts to regain control over concessions obtained by cooperatives to work in partnership with third parties, mostly ANMM mines, leading to the death of Vice-Minister Rodolfo Illanes and the delegitimation of cooperative mining leaders.
37. The concept of 'holding power' for Khan refers to 'how long a particular organization can hold out in actual or potential conflicts with other organizations or the state', and is 'a function of a number of characteristics of an organization, including its economic capability to sustain itself during conflicts, its capability to mobilize supporters to be able to absorb costs and its ability to mobilize prevalent ideologies and symbols of legitimacy to consolidate its mobilization and keep its members committed' (Khan, 2010: 20, cited in Hickey et al., 2015: 47–8).
38. The government has three very popular cash transfer programmes providing a minimum pension for the elderly (*Renta Dignidad*), a stipend for pregnant and lactating mothers (*Bono Juana Azurduy*), and a stipend for school-aged children (*Bono Jacinto Pinto*).
39. Historians generally agree that the Chaco War was not over oil (Klein, 2011), and that tensions within the Bolivian elite were key factors in the decision to go to war with Paraguay.
40. According to an interview with a former supervisor of hydrocarbons in Tarija.
41. These ideas were very much invoked during conflicts between Santa Cruz, Tarija, and the central government in 2008.
42. Though large-scale exports to Brazil begin only around 2000.
43. Interview with a former supervisor of hydrocarbons, department of Tarija. The term, loosely translated, would be 'clean the slate and begin again from scratch'.
44. The government allocated 20 per cent of state revenues to the municipalities, based on population.
45. Indeed, he blocked them. A draft decentralization law, crafted by representatives from a range of social and political groups in 1993, was ignored by Sánchez de Lozada. Previous efforts during the Paz Estenssoro government of 1985–89 were blocked for the same reason.
46. Subsequent governments of Carlos Mesa and Evo Morales pursued a similar strategy.

47. See García Linera (2008) on the institutional crisis brought on by the resignation of President Sánchez de Lozada and the breakdown of the neoliberal project.
48. Reflecting the complicated nature of expanding political participation and to avoid any issue of constitutionality, President Mesa said that he would then 'ratify' the winner of the election by appointing them to the position (Roca, 2008).
49. See Molina (2011).
50. Despite this, it is important to note that Vice-President García Linera has indicated that the government will try again in the future to reform the Hydrocarbons Law 3058 of 2005.
51. It is important to note that from post-independence (1825–80) up to the tin mining boom in the late nineteenth century, some 35 per cent of the revenues managed by the Bolivian government came from taxes paid by indigenous peoples, with La Paz, Oruro, and Potosí being the largest contributors. After the 1880s, taxes from the mining sector increased significantly, and the state began to live from mining revenues (Barragán, 2008: 90).
52. The creation of the departmental royalty (11 per cent of production from the department) comes from the initial negotiation between the Bolivian government and Standard Oil of New Jersey in the early 1920s.
53. In some cases, such municipal actors have themselves been produced, in part, by decentralization policies (Faguet, 2012).
54. Interview with former YPFB official, 2013.
55. *Juancito Pinto, Juana Azurduy,* and *Renta Dignidad* are the primary examples of such programmes. See n. 38 for further explanation of these programmes.

4

The Politics of Natural Resource Extraction in Zambia

Copper extraction has dominated Zambia's economic and political development since the first European exploration of the region in the late 1880s under the British South Africa Company (BSAC). A classic example of a mineral-rich country, Zambia has always counted on its vast copper reserves to carry it to the status of a fully industrialized and 'modern' state. Yet though copper accounts for over 75 per cent of its current (2015) exports, the country has high poverty rates and is also one of the most unequal.[1] Despite recurrent rallying cries for economic diversification in support of the latent agricultural sector, Zambia's rural areas have remained marginal to its development.

Three key historical themes help to explain why Zambia's copper endowment has not resulted in better economic development outcomes. First, as Fraser and Larmer (2011) note, Zambia has been particularly unfortunate when it comes to the timing of mining policies. For example, just two years after the country nationalized mining operations, copper prices dropped precipitously, due to the 1976 global economic crisis. Yet shortly after the country reprivatized operations in the late 1990s—when copper prices were at their lowest and generated little revenue—a boom in prices ensued that yielded windfall profits to private firms. Second, though the national government in Lusaka, located more than 300 kilometres from the Copperbelt, is formally charged with the redistribution of national wealth, the Copperbelt historically produces and dominates the political sphere that determines how this is done.

Third, Zambia lacks indigenous entrepreneurship, and the state is central to class formation. With no feasible alternative income sources, such as secondary industries or a robust agricultural sector (Sutton and Langmead, 2013), state-led enterprise has remained the most important source for potential income mobility from independence in 1964 to the present (Szeftel, 1982). Yet because government revenue depends on fluctuating copper prices, campaign promises and public expectations for wealth accumulation were never fully met, leading to disenchantment with political parties. As a result, except for trade unions, which now represent only a small group of formal workers, constituents remain distant from the political parties that drive national policies, thus ensuring a continued marginalization and under-representation of the most vulnerable sectors of society.

In this chapter, we will analyse how and why these dynamics have emerged in Zambia through the lens of the political settlements framework. This framework operates on the premise that underlying conditions for development are established first and foremost by the character of inter-elite relations, and especially the ways in which elites use the power at their disposal to shape policy reforms and institutional changes (North et al., 2009; Khan, 2010; Hickey, 2013). This breaks with a more singular and apolitical focus on the role of institutions, which was a dominant theme in development theory in the 1990s.

In particular, we use a political settlements approach to explore the dynamics of the governance of natural resources and their ability or inability to bring sustainable and substantial development to a country. We do so by comparing and contrasting historical periods of high and low social and economic investments in Zambia. In addition, we investigate the consequence of political settlements on mineral income by examining Zambia's mining taxation policies, a process that is highly influenced by international actors. We operate under the assumption that an inclusive/exclusive distribution model of Zambia's mineral wealth requires a closer understanding of its political leaders' interaction with its constituents and social base.

Using the vocabulary of political settlements theory, we argue that Zambia mostly resembles a meta-settlement, which is founded on a long lineage of the power of foreign influence in shaping economic and social policies. What we propose is the equivalent of what historians refer to as the '*longue durée*', a long-term historical assemblage that can show signs of slowly evolving structures and incremental changes. This analysis is tied to what Bayart has called 'extraversion': a way of understanding long-term historical patterns by which 'the [African] continent has been inserted into the rest of the world', and how this became 'a resource for . . . internal politics of power and authority' (Englund, 2002: 19).

We proceed as follows. In Section 1, we describe our conceptual framework for understanding natural resource governance in Zambia. In Section 2, we give a history of natural resource extraction in the country. In Section 3, we analyse the history of political settlements in Zambia, including by identifying specific periods of political settlements, beginning with occupation by BSAC in 1896. Finally, we offer a summary of our conclusions in Section 4. Our argument is based on a combination of literature review, analysis of press and other grey material, discussion workshops and, above all, a series of interviews in Zambia. These interviews were conducted with people from the following categories: former ministers of mines and lands, former political advisors to presidents, the Office of the Vice-President, business people (local and international), corporate lawyers, directors of mining companies, civil society leaders, diplomats, politicians, and academics. Given the sensitive nature and the political context during which the work was conducted, we have kept all interviewees anonymous.

1 Conceptual Framework

The existing literature on the political economy of copper in Zambia has given us insufficient insight into the historical relationship between mining governance, resource allocation, and development outcomes. In this chapter, we apply the political settlements framework in an attempt to address the gap in our understanding of the history of the political incentives and systems that inform this relationship. Political settlements have been defined as 'an interdependent combination of a structure of power and institutions at the level of a society that is mutually "compatible" and "sustainable" in terms of economic and political viability' (Khan, 2010: 20), or more simply, as 'the balance or distribution of power between contending social groups and classes, on which any state is based' (di John and Putzel, 2009: 4). As discussed in Chapter 1, at the core of this concept is the claim that development outcomes are shaped largely by the character of inter-elite power relations, especially the ways in which elites use the power at their disposal to shape policy reforms and institutional changes, and how these in turn shape the varied socio-economic entitlements of different actors. Specifically, with regard to countries that are rich in natural resources, Khan (2010) argues that the ability to create an open economy and prevent it from being strangled by the special interests of rent-seekers is bound up with the transformation of the economy from a natural resource-based enclave into diversified, export-based activity and especially export-based industrialization. This emphasis on the role of exporters in moving the economy forward demonstrates a shift in the role of capital and elites away from the powerbrokers of the natural resource enclave to a more competitive system, both economically and politically (Eifert et al., 2003, quoted in Mosley, 2014).

The transition from low- and middle-income status towards high-income status is primarily propelled by the interplay between the polity and the economy (North et al., 2007). Governance institutions and, in particular, competitive political parties, create the environment for economic development. As North et al. (2007: 21) state: 'Political competition in the presence of open access to organizations provides opposition political parties with incentives to monitor the government and oppose proposals that threaten open access and competition.' Increased political competition could then arguably make a difference in response to the overall dilemma of mineral wealth and development, since ruling elites must gain legitimacy to maintain power. However, North cautions that this is a long-term process and development is not automatic.

This emphasis on political competition as a prerequisite for economic growth is in some ways paradoxical. Throughout the developing world, the 'wave of democratization has also served to highlight the blight of poverty' (Mkandawire, 2006: 9), and we can now add inequality to this. Strong economic policies are not immediately born out of democracy. Indeed, in certain contexts, democracy can take a fruitless form. In the case of Zambia, the shift from a one-party state to a multiparty democracy was in fact coupled with massive economic reform that only further enhanced unemployment and inequality, as well as a decline of important countervailing powers like the trades unions. This points to the fact that in order to avoid making easy assumptions about developmental dynamics, we need to improve our understanding of the underlying forces that determine inclusive development *within* a specific context and tradition. We therefore subscribe to the idea that 'any effort to understand the governance of extraction and of its relationships to development *must* be spatially and historically explicit' (Bebbington, 2013b: 2). By taking this approach, we move away from a crude resource curse analysis and give space to a detailed description of the forces and interests that have shaped Zambia's trajectory.

2 A History of Natural Resource Extraction in Zambia

Beginning with mineral exploration by BSAC in the late nineteenth century and continuing to the present day, copper extraction has dictated not only the economic history of Zambia, but its political and social histories as well. Founded by Cecil Rhodes, the BSAC sought to develop the mining industry throughout Southern Africa. In return for effectively occupying North-Western Rhodesia and North-Eastern Rhodesia and developing infrastructure to support the mining industry, the BSAC was granted the first mining concession at Broken Hill (now Kabwe, the capital of Zambia's Central Province). The two protectorates were combined in 1911, continuing to be administered by the BSAC as a crown colony until 1924, when administrative control was taken over fully by the British government.

Zambia's copper deposits could not be exploited commercially until the Southern Rhodesian railway had extended across the Zambezi and continued northward, to reach the Belgian–Congo border, which it did in 1909. By that time, mining had started in Katanga, in southern Congo. In Northern Rhodesia, the surface ores were of poorer quality, and copper was only worked intermittently at Bwana Mkubwa, until in 1924 rich copper sulphide ores were discovered. As a result of Northern Rhodesia's preference for large-scale deals with major commercial mining companies, throughout the colonial era and into the early 1970s, all mines in Zambia were owned by two mining companies: the Anglo-American Corporation (AAC), owned by the Oppenheimer family in South Africa, and the American Roan Selection Trust (RST), chaired by Sir Ronald Prain, a British businessman.

While copper was dominant in Zambia from early in its colonial history, Roberts (2011) notes the mining industry only began to prosper in 1949 as a consequence of the devaluation of the pound sterling against the US dollar. Because the British government based the price it paid for Northern Rhodesian copper on the dollar, revenues from sales increased due to the shift. Another important element was the outbreak of the Korean War in 1950, which led to a fresh demand for copper. Rising demand and prices meant that by 1951 all four copper mines were paying dividends for the first time. It is thus clear that global economic trends have had a crucial impact on the Zambian industry (see also Figure 4.1).

Administration in Zambia underwent a massive shift in 1953, with the creation of the Central African Federation (CAF). The CAF brought together the colonies of Northern and Southern Rhodesia (present Zimbabwe) and Nyasaland (present Malawi) into a centralized administrative structure run from Salisbury, which became a mini-metropole, serving as the seat of government and industry. The CAF privileged white settlers and those in Southern Rhodesia in particular. Northern Rhodesia was seen solely as an extractive state, particularly in terms of minerals, as well as agriculture.

For the first several years after the creation of the CAF, mineral prices rose, and Southern Rhodesians prospered from the north's extraction. However, prices fell in the late 1950s, coinciding with agitations for political independence from Northern Rhodesia. The CAF was dissolved in 1962, and shortly thereafter, on 24 October 1964, Zambia was granted its independence.

Expectations of a higher standard of living for all Zambians were high in this new period of independence, known as the First Republic. In the context of a stable and expanding economy, enormous investments were made in education, health, and infrastructure as the governing United National Independence Party (UNIP), under the leadership of President Kenneth Kaunda, had envisioned and promised to deliver a development state. Copper at independence represented half of Zambian GDP and almost the entirety (96 per cent) of exports for the country. Yet despite high global prices, the copper wealth did not translate into countrywide development. Infrastructure, urban growth, education, health care, and other indices of development were mostly apparent along the so-called 'Line of Rail', which included the Copperbelt (Ndola, Kitwe, etc.), Lusaka, and, at a smaller level, development in the southern part (Livingstone), where there were a large number of white settler and indigenous agricultural enterprises. Map 4.1 shows the location of these sites, as well as others referred to throughout this chapter.

The emphasis in the early post-colonial years was on the 'Zambianization' of the workforce or the steady replacement of British and other expatriates in the public and private labour force with indigenous Zambians. The emergence of the 'Second Republic' in Zambia in the early 1970s brought many changes that affected the structure of the extractive state. In December 1972, Kaunda signed the declaration of the one-party state, the climax of a process of the consolidation of power that began with the nationalization of major industries beginning in 1968. It was partially driven by an external force, namely the Unilateral Declaration of Independence (UDI) in Rhodesia in 1965, which turned Zambia into a frontline state and put pressure on it to forego the influence of white settler capital. Zambia's colonial history as a member of the CAF left a legacy of economic dependence on its southern neighbour. At the time of UDI, Zambia was still almost entirely reliant on shared infrastructure, particularly the 'Line of Rail', controlled by Rhodesia Railways. Zambian copper exports were exported via this line, and almost all imports were brought in on it as well. Yet despite this economic dependency, a direct lineage of the CAF, the UK placed great pressure on Zambia to participate in sanctions against Rhodesia. The pressure, carried out through the United Nations, was so great that Zambia threatened to leave the Commonwealth, and began to turn to alternative development partners to achieve economic independence.

Internally, nationalization was driven by pressure from certain sectors of society (labour unions, party cadres, nationalist leaders, civil servants) that demanded greater material rewards from political independence than those they perceived were being handed to them by private capital. Leading up to this shift, the existing political settlement with the state and erstwhile mining companies—in existence from early colonial days—gradually broke down. The Matero Economic Reforms of 1969 resulted in the government purchasing 51 per cent shares from the AAC and RST, leading to partial nationalization of the copper industry. The AAC and RST retained 49 per cent of the shares and were renamed Nchanga Consolidated Copper Mines (NCCM) and Roan Consolidated Copper Mines (RCM), respectively. They remained under foreign management. Subsequently, with the full-scale nationalization of the mines in the 1970s, they were integrated into the Zambia Consolidated Copper Mines (ZCCM), now entirely under Zambian management.

The Zambia Industrial and Mining Corporation's (ZIMCO), the state holding company that was charged with the supervision of the state-owned

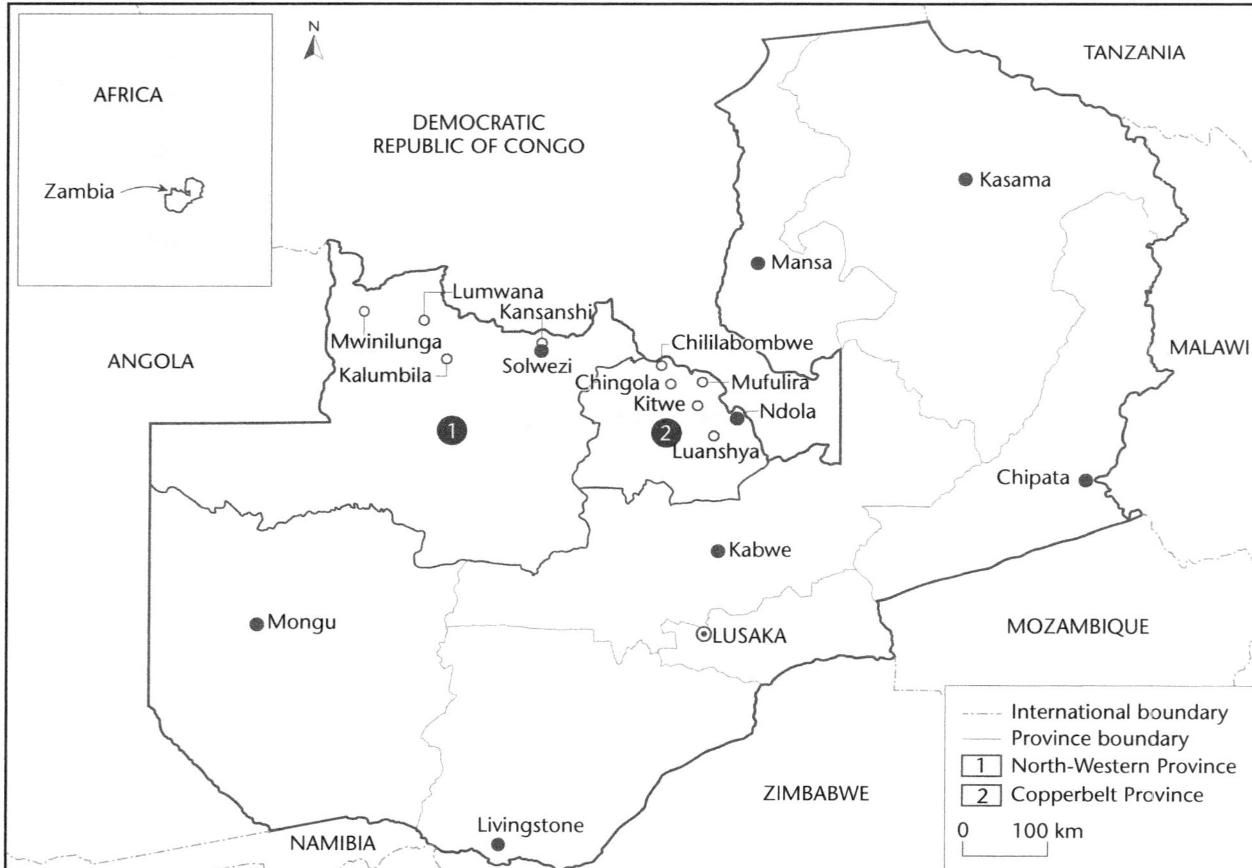

Map 4.1. Mining provinces and key mine sites, Zambia

Source: Elaborated on the basis of maps produced by flexicadstre.com, accessed September 2017.

mining enterprises under its wing, was originally structured to minimize political interference in the running of state-owned businesses by serving as a buffer between the government and its investments. In practice, however, government officials exercised increasing control over ZIMCO. Managers of sub-holding companies reported directly to the relevant government ministries, which in turn reported to Kaunda, who retained the title of company chairman. ZIMCO's process of purchasing bonds in order to buy out the remainder of the foreign shares and management demonstrates how these dynamics led to (costly) mismanagement: when the bonds were redeemed in 1974, they effectively wiped out Zambia's foreign reserve base (Craig, 1999: 40).[2] Thus, while the government now fully controlled the mining industry, some of the fundamental problems that had prompted nationalization remained or worsened. The global economic crisis of the 1970s placed an enormous strain on the country as it faced rapidly falling revenues.

By the late 1980s, Zambia's economy was in free fall, leading to lost mining jobs and an acute shortage of basic goods. On the heels of violent protest and an attempted coup, Kaunda yielded to pressure and Zambia held multiparty elections in 1991. Frederick Chiluba, the former president of the Zambia Congress of Trade Unions (ZCTU) and leader of the Movement for Multi-Party Democracy (MMD) was installed as the President of the Republic. Though Kaunda had started the process of structural adjustment under the auspices of the International Monetary Fund/World Bank (IMF/WB) in the late 1980s, it was under Chiluba that large-scale privatization actually took place. The Mines and Minerals Act of 1995 paved the way for the dismantling of ZCCM and the sale of individual mining companies. In place of a uniform tax regime and code of conditions within which private mining companies were to operate, the act provided for the negotiation of unique Development Agreements (DAs) with each company. Several state officials who were involved in these closed-door negotiations have since been the subjects of corruption charges, and some have been convicted. In addition, social pacts linking the state-led industries to their workers and communities were disbanded and replaced with corporate social responsibility (CSR) programmes (Negi, 2011: 30).

The process of privatizing the mines proved to be a challenging exercise for the MMD. Considering depressed world copper prices, the increasingly deplorable state of the mines, and the pressure on the Zambian government to sell the mines as part of the conditionalities attached to the debt relief by the International Financial Institutions (IFI), buyers could strengthen their negotiation position. Thus, the state essentially lost its ability to extract revenues from the mining sector. The copper boom that followed shortly afterwards added to a deepening sense of the lack of legitimacy of the entire privatization process, both for the Zambian state and the new mine owners

(Fraser and Lungu, 2007). This is an important theme to which we will return below.

3 A History of Political Settlements in Zambia

As shown in Table 4.1, Zambia's history of economic growth and decline does not necessarily follow political transitions, but rather mirrors the fluctuations of international commodity prices as reflected by the country's economic performance during different commodity prices conditions presented in the table. However, political settlements come into play when examining the governance and distribution of natural resources affected by these commodity prices. In this section, we thus draw on the history of natural resource extraction summarized above to identify and describe five key periods of political settlements in modern Zambian history. These periods are summarized in Table 4.1.

3.1 *1896–1924*

The early period of colonial occupation under the BSAC was characterized by corporate colonialism. The colonial administration was thin on the ground, with most of Northern Rhodesia's colonial boundaries only enforced as late as the 1930s. While it was not destined to become a white settler colony like Southern Rhodesia, a small agricultural white settler community had settled in the north that began to call for representation. Colonial authorities introduced a household-based 'hut tax' to support administrative structures, leading to a migration of labourers to gold mines in Tanganyika (Tanzania), copper mines in Elizabethville (Lubumbashi), and as far afield as South Africa.

3.2 *1924–64*

British Colonial Rule, introduced in 1924, saw the opening of the first session of the Northern Rhodesian parliament, with limited white settler representation. The British also introduced Indirect Rule, a system in which the local chiefs became administrative agents employed by the colonial regime. These traditional leaders participated in the hut tax collection and labour recruitment. Labour migration within Northern Rhodesia now also included the rapidly expanding Copperbelt, a series of mining towns in the western part of the country that borders copper-rich Katanga (Congo). By 1930, the African labour force on the Copperbelt had risen to 32,000, where, with the gathering of various ethnic groups, a national identity was forged and the basis for a nationalist movement was laid. Traditional authority associations

Table 4.1. Zambian political settlements, 1896–present

Period	Name of ruling coalition	Type of political regime	Configuration of political organizations	Broader development ideology	Modes of inclusion in extractive industry	International commodity price performance	Zambia's economic growth performance
1896–1924	BSAC	Colonial rule	Advisory council, little settler representation	Industrial capital	Hut tax/labour migration	Favourable	Positive
1924–64	BSAC and CAF	Colonial rule	Political representation of white settlers	Industrial capital	Hut tax/labour migration	Favourable	Positive
1964–73	UNIP	Multiparty	Dominant	Industrial capital	Tax/labour	Favourable	Positive
1973–91	UNIP	One-party state	Vulnerable authoritarian	State-led	Nationalized industry	Unfavourable	Negative
1991–to date	MMD, PF	Multiparty	Competitive authoritarianism*	Neoliberal capitalist, with some spells of resource nationalism	Tax/labour	Unfavourable Favourable from 2001	Negative positive from 2001

* Here we depart from Levy (2012) and use the following definition: 'civilian regimes in which formal democratic institutions exist and are widely viewed as the primary means of gaining power, but in which the incumbents' abuse of the state places them at a significant disadvantage vis-à-vis their opponents. Such regimes are competitive in that opposition parties use democratic institutions to contest seriously for power, but they are not democratic because the playing field is heavily skewed in favour of incumbents. Competition is thus real but unfair'.

Source: Levitsky and Way, 2010: 6.

were present in the Copperbelt but were less influential than the rising labour and nationalist movements. The main commercial economic interest, represented by the white settler community, was the agricultural sector—specifically sugar, tobacco, and maize. The first demonstration of the political weight of the Copperbelt took place in the 1930s, when both African and European trade unions went on massive strikes after the international financial crisis led to widespread job losses. The strike was partially blamed on the Watchtower Church, which had entered the urban areas with returning labour migrants from South Africa.

The formation of the CAF in 1953, described in detail in Section 2, represented an important move towards independence. It was premised on the notion that white settlers in the region, dominated by Southern Rhodesian settlers, would work towards self-rule. Generally, Northern Rhodesia's white settlers (a paltry 3 per cent of the total population) opposed the federation, as it worked against their economic and political interests. With the ever-expanding production of copper and stabilization of the Copperbelt workforce, the influence of trade unions increased. The early nationalist movement began to form around the mission-educated elite, often of royal establishments. Their positions were soon taken over by a generation of younger men, equally mission-educated but with no traditional power base. Missionaries generally favoured the nationalist movement and, as a result, the churches remained influential players in post-colonial Zambia.

3.3 *1964–73*

On 31 December 1963, the Federation of Rhodesia and Nyasaland was formally dissolved. Less than a year later, on 24 October 1964, Northern Rhodesia became an independent republic, now known as Zambia. UNIP's charismatic Kenneth Kaunda, a teacher born in Zambia, but from a Malawian missionary background, became its first president. His main contender, Harry Nkumbula of the African National Congress (ANC), remained an influential political player, but the settler parties almost immediately lost their erstwhile influence. Despite enormous investments in social and physical infrastructure, discontent with UNIP quickly emerged, due to uneven distribution and so-called 'thwarted expectations' (Macola, 2006: 56). Opposition coalitions took shape among groups with (temporary) common cause: unionized workers (clashes with mine workers already occurred in 1965–66), business people, marginalized rural communities, students, and intellectuals. UNIP felt especially threatened by the rise of former Vice-President Simon Kapwepwe's United Progressive Party (UPP), which gained a stronghold in the Copperbelt and the Northern Province. It also faced resistance from Barotseland, which felt aggrieved by the abrogation, shortly after independence, of an agreement granting them a high degree of autonomy. This period also saw the rise of the importance of the civil service as a bargaining force. After independence, it was 'Zambianized' and increased nearly threefold by 1974. During this period, political office became a crucial means to acquire resources from both public and private sectors.

3.4 *1973–91*

The Second Republic, associated with nationalization of the mines and the declaration of the one-party state, represented an important shift in political settlements that specifically promoted social welfare. However, to call Zambia a staunchly socialist state in this period would be a misnomer. Begun in a period of economic prosperity, nationalization was a reaction to the global shift towards government ownership for more equal economic growth seen throughout the developing world in this period. Yet for Zambia, growth was hampered by global economic contraction, and equality was not realized.

The global economic crisis of the 1970s placed tremendous strain on the government as it worked to deal with rapidly falling copper prices. Despite a contraction in revenue, it tried to maintain a high level of support for the mining industry and the mine workers, continuing welfare programmes and development that were begun by privately owned companies during the colonial period. Yet by placating urban workers, it further exacerbated the uneven development of the country, with most of the rural areas left behind.

Though opposition movements were banned, both underground political movements and the trade unions threatened UNIP throughout this period. Yet unlike in Ghana, Peru, and Bolivia, the military was unable to take control of the government during this era of economic decline, with UNIP successfully resisting two coup attempts in the 1980s. Unlike other countries, the military had not been part of the liberation movement in Zambia and did not become an influential factor.

3.5 *1991–Present*

In the late 1980s, a coalition comprised of trade unions, politicians, lawyers, students, academics, and the business community came together under the banner of the MMD to call for the dissolution of the one-party state. This, combined with pressure from bilateral and multilateral donors, forced UNIP to open the country to multiparty elections in 1991. International actors deepened their neoliberal economic engagement with the new MMD government, tying debt relief to privatization of national companies—most notably the mines. Moreover, the government was rewarded for privatization with massive amounts of foreign aid, which came to make up more than 40 per cent of the national budget in the early 1990s.

Civil society also expanded rapidly during the 1990s and became especially influential when aligned with more established non-state actors like the Law Association of Zambia (LAZ) or the powerful mainstream churches. This period also saw the rise in influence of the independent media, especially *The Post* newspaper.

Elections became gradually more competitive from 2001 onward, rendering the MMD highly vulnerable. This dynamic created an incentive for short-term, politically motivated public spending, which arguably explains the lack of a long-term development vision for the Zambian mining sector. As Poteete (2009) argues, elite commitment to such a vision is possible only when ruling elites feel that they will stay in power long enough to reap the benefits of accumulated investments.

At the same time, debt relief and a copper boom granted the MMD increased fiscal space, with export revenue increasing from US$670 million to US$4 billion. The government responded by defying the existing DAs to increase mining taxation. They expanded pro-poor expenditure in the social sectors and released huge funding for political projects, such as road construction and a Fertilizer Import Support programme. These investments had a limited developmental impact, especially in rural areas and the urban informal sectors.

In September 2011, the Patriotic Front (PF), which had broken from the MMD in 2001, came to power on a left-leaning manifesto and with the support of the young, informal urban populace. The party ran on a platform opposed to the laissez-faire attitude and neoliberal policies of the previous regime, especially vis-à-vis the mining sector. In practice, Zambia witnessed a 45 per cent increase in public sector wages, as well as expanded mineral royalties and private sector wages under the PF. Yet these are not solely attributable to the party, as they were conceived in the context of a number of African Union (AU) declarations that encouraged governments to adopt fixed budgetary allocations for education and health.

An interesting development is the newly introduced concept of a sovereign wealth fund in the 2015 budget, signalling that the government is thinking about a long-term national development trajectory. It also demonstrates the influence of the Norwegian cooperation partners in the field of mineral taxation. The Norwegian embassy's project aims at improving Zambia's revenue out of the copper industry, by building capacity within the Zambia Revenue Authority in obtaining accurate information on production, processing, and export volumes in the mining sector.

The contemporary period has been marked by an emerging geographical shift in power. While the Copperbelt region has historically been the home of opposition political parties (UPP, MMD, PF), recent elections show that it now shares that role with Lusaka, which has grown tremendously in recent decades. This is partially attributable to interurban migration as a result of the economic crisis in the Copperbelt in the 1990s. Decades of job losses, reliance on casual rather than contract labour, and an increase of the number of participants in the informal sector have hollowed out the powers of the trade unions. Civil society and media organizations have weakened as well and have become hyper-partisan due to their co-optation by political parties for short-term electoral gains. The liberal United Party for National Development (UPND), which was founded in 1998 and has since become the largest opposition party, has an especially strong base in the non-labour migrant areas in what used to be called North-Western Rhodesia, though it has also made inroads in Lusaka and Copperbelt.

Finally, political parties have witnessed a shuffling of allegiances in the wake of the death of PF President Michael Sata while in office in October 2014. Factionalism has led to a three-way split in the MMD, leaving it severely weakened. One group merged with the PF to support its candidate, Edgar Lungu, in the by-election to replace Sata, and another partially merged with the UPND. Lungu and the PF won the presidential by-election in 2015, as well as the controversial general election of 2016, which was marred by violence and intimidation, as well as accusations of widespread rigging.

3.6 *Commonalities Across the Settlements*

To adequately historicize the political settlements described above, we highlight here some of the more enduring characteristics that have shaped Zambia's political culture and civic norms. These ultimately determine leaders' conduct and interests, regardless of apparent (ideological) shifts in the numerous political transitions the country has experienced. Importantly, as we will spell out in the next section, these characteristics influence the natural resource governance of the country.

Two key lasting features of post-colonial Zambia's political culture are authoritarianism and a narrow elitism. Macola (2008) traces this trend to the roots of Zambia's nationalism in which party and nation were seen as the same. Alternative views and political projects were viewed with suspicion and regarded as unpatriotic. This authoritarianism emerged through a simultaneous concentration of power in the hands of the executive branch and a weakening of institutions of accountability, including parliament and the judiciary. Despite the re-introduction of multiparty democracy, Zambia's ruling parties remain authoritarian and dominant. During elections, the opposition parties are given no space in the public media and the ruling party uses the (colonial) Public Order Act to limit the opportunities to campaign.

Larmer (2006) argues that these dynamics are related to the uneven nature of Zambia's nationalist struggle, which led to political and economic divisions in the post-colonial state that were never entirely ironed out by the process of state formation. A small, closely networked political elite emerged from the nationalist movement to lead the new state. Yet it is important to note that the majority of this group had received little formal training: on the eve of independence, out of a population of 3.5 million people, Zambia counted fewer than 100 university graduates.

As a result, a limited choice was offered to the electorate by Zambia's post-democratization political parties, contributing to a 'recycling' of leaders. This in turn contributed to the pattern of splits and mergers in the history of Zambia's political parties. Consequently, there is a consensus among our informants that, in many respects, Zambia's political system has not undergone any fundamental changes from the time of transition from a one-party state to multiparty democracy in 1991. Instead, Zambia is de facto still characterized by imperial or executive presidentialism. This is reified through the system's structure, in which all incentives centre around the president. The weakening of trade unions and decline of civil society since the1990s meant a reduction in countervailing powers.

Another salient feature of Zambia's political landscape is 'elite insecurity' (Migdal, 1988), in which ruling politicians are in constant fear of being ousted. These circumstances existed long before the era of competitive politics, with challenges to ruling authority including: the emergence of ethno-regional political movements that defied the legitimacy of the first post-colonial governments (Fraser, 2010: 191, 214) and led to the introduction of the one-party state in 1972; pressure by domestic commercial interests, trade unions, and the Church (1973–91); and growing electoral competition between the country's two or three dominant parties since the return to multiparty democracy (1992 to present). As Fraser (2010: 221) notes, 'just as UNIP ruled in fear of urban disorder, the MMD governed Zambia under the shadow of a constant crisis of physical security, ideological self-confidence, and political legitimacy'.

In some forms, elite insecurity could be viewed as an important democratic accountability measure. Yet it has taken on such intensity in Zambia that politicians operate myopically, to the long-term detriment of the country. The turnover of members of parliament at each election is one of the highest in Africa with the number of those remaining seated averaging only 30 per cent. The absence of a registered party membership, combined with historical fluid voter behaviour, makes the PF insecure of the size and loyalty of its base.

Simuntanyi (2015) notes that the short-term policy focus that this kind of insecurity generates is particularly acute under competitive clientelist settlements, where the *raison d'être* of political alliances is to win and hold onto state power. In such a system, an electoral strategy based on targeting benefits or applying sanctions is apparent from the new government's first day in office and dominates the government's policy decisions thereafter. This makes coherent policy structured around a long-term vision—including and, especially, development—extremely difficult.

4 Political Settlements, the State, and Extractive Industry Governance

In this section, we present a historical overview of Zambia's copper industry in light of the salient features of the political settlements set out above. In particular, we consider the changing nature of capital and ownership in the industry, government policies regarding income (taxation) and expenditure (distribution), and the impact of political competition on policies of inclusive development. For a general overview, see Table 4.2.

4.1 *1924–64*

A key theme across both the colonial and post-colonial regimes in Zambia has been a struggle to obtain what the government considered to be a fair share of the wealth generated by Zambia's copper deposits. The determination of the level of royalties and taxation in both periods has always been a process of lengthy negotiations. For the Northern Rhodesian government, its share in the country's copper wealth was boosted by changes in company taxation by an agreement in 1949 with BSAC, whereby the government took one-fifth of the gross value of royalties paid by the mining companies.

This agreement boosted government revenue nearly fivefold, but because of the existing political settlement, it did not translate into an increase in overall living standards. The British Colonial's office attempted to pursue a progressive development ideology through a ten-year plan in 1947 committed to supporting the 'uplift of the African population'. However, white settlers, through their control of the local economy, hijacked his attempt at inclusive development, and revenues were directed towards their own needs instead (Roberts, 2011: 21–22).

The establishment of CAF in 1953 solidified the trend of state revenue flowing to the capital in Salisbury and to the white settler population (mostly in Southern Rhodesia)—who were, until the late 1950s, generally envisaged as the drivers of agricultural development (Larmer, 2011). Sir Ronald Prain, the chairman of RST, recognized the consequences of the prevailing income inequalities between the European and African workers. He argued that 'it would always be difficult to keep the Copperbelt's African miners contented in the face of the violent contrast between African wages and the exceptionally

Table 4.2. Political settlements in relation to the extractive industry, Zambia

Periods	Global market prices in $ (period minimum–maximum price) (US$)	EI production (period minimum–maximum annual output in tonnes per annum)	Presence of transnational actors	Measures of overall state capacity in EI sector	Key dimensions of EI governance/policy	Patterns of resistance
1896–1924	293*		BSAC		Corporation is the state	
1924–64	293–683	66–886	BSAC; AAC and RST	Royalty tax of 13.5% since 1949	Colonial mining policy, revenue mostly to the centre (London)	Trades unions, nationalist movement
1964–73	683–1,130	632–750	AAC and RST; British; Non-Alignment Movement	13.5% up to 1969, replaced by mineral tax (income tax of 45% and profit tax of 35%, flat fee of 73.5%)	Zambianization of mining workforce. CIPEC	Trades unions
1973–90	1,130–2,410	228–700	IMF/WB	Mineral tax (as above)	Nationalization, ZIMCO, ZCCM	Trades unions
1990–2001	2,401–1,690	257–500	IMF/WB	Royalty tax. Based on DAgs (between 0.6 and 2%), corporate tax between 25 and 35%	Liberalization and casualization	Trades unions, civil society
2001–Present	1,690–8,950	251–710	China; IMF/WB	Royalty tax raised to 3%, corporate tax 25 to 35% Royalty tax 6%, increased in late 2014 to 8% (underground) and 20% (open-pit). Dropped in Jan 2015 to 6% and 9%. Six tax policy changes and reversals since then	Liberalization and casualization Growing resource nationalism Joined EITI in 2009	Trades unions, resistance against casualization, civil society and community-based activity, PF opposition politics

* In the first period (1896–1924) we adopted 293 as the minimum figure for the period 1924–1964 because then the country had not formally started exploiting minerals.

Source: EITI: Extractive Industries Transparency Initiative.

lush conditions which our European labour enjoys' (quoted in Phimister, 2011: 132). These dynamics led to high wage expectations on the part of African workers on the eve of independence. There was an additional anticipation that mining companies would provide welfare services for their workers, including housing, education, and healthcare, just as they had done for the European workers. Because of the dominance of the mining sector, the Copperbelt trade unions became influential non-state actors and, over time, obtained significant political leverage to achieve these demands. This was the setting that in large part determined Kaunda's dealings with the mining industry after independence and created a new setting of unequal distribution and uneven development.

The consequences of these structures, which can be termed a colonial labour-reserve type of economy, were long lasting. A labour-reserve economy is characterized by a dualistic formal labour market and a migrant labour system that in Zambia tied vast amounts of peasants to the white-owned mining industry and settler agriculture. Self-employment and entrepreneurship by Africans in the cities was limited, and there was little stimulus for peasant production either, since both could have undermined the supply of labour to commercial farms and industry. Combined with limited public investment in African education, the formation of an African middle class was very limited.

4.2 *1964–73*

The post-colonial government recognized the risk of being overly dependent on copper wealth to sustain large social and physical investments after independence, especially given the erratic nature of international copper prices, and committed to addressing it. In 1967, Kaunda brought together leaders of four of the world's main copper exporting countries (Zambia, Chile, Peru, and the Congo/Zaire) in Lusaka, with the aim of establishing a price- and quota-fixing copper cartel similar to the Organization of the Petroleum Exporting Countries (OPEC), which was formed in 1960. The group, which became known as the Intergovernmental Council of Copper Exporting Countries (CIPEC), was later joined by Australia, Indonesia, Papua New Guinea, and Yugoslavia. Their effort to control prices failed, however, and in practice, CIPEC served merely as an information exchange. The fundamental barrier to controlling prices was that the member states lacked access to capital to stockpile copper reserves, which was crucial to effectively managing supply. In addition, CIPEC member states controlled less than 60 per cent of world copper trade, and fewer than half of identified reserves, and major copper producers like Canada did not join CIPEC (Larmer, 2011). The failure of CIPEC to control copper prices led to the realization that the global system was beyond the reach of the member states, and that only local policies and ownership patterns could be subject to conscious management by Africans (Fraser and Larmer, 2011).

As shown in the other chapters, Ghana and Peru have both earmarked varying degrees of mining revenue for specific regions, local governments, or sectors. Specifically, in Ghana, 10 per cent of revenue is reserved for subnational authorities (see Chapter 5), while through Peru's 'mining canon', half is distributed to support development in the regions in which the mining takes place (see Chapter 3). Zambia is more similar to Bolivia in this regard, however. In both cases, mining revenues traditionally accrue directly to the national government, with little input from regions. In Zambia, the national government focuses mining revenues on overall national development through five-year development plans. The initial plan, launched in the transition phase of 1962, emphasized the expansion of physical and social infrastructure, especially to benefit the marginalized African population. This was followed by the First National Development Plan (1966–71), which aimed to diversify the economy away from its overdependence on copper mining, including by promoting rural development. Both development plans led to a period of sustained economic growth, accompanied by the improvement of social indicators. On paper, the high levels of revenue benefited the whole population equally; in practice, the expenditure was highly uneven.

This turned out to be a short-lived period of progressive development. A perfect storm developed in the early 1970s, which threw Zambia from a middle-income country to a low-income country status with high levels of unsustainable debts in the mid-1980s. To illustrate this: between 1974 and 1994, per capita income declined by 50 per cent, leaving Zambia as the twenty-fifth poorest country in the world (Fraser and Lungu, 2007: 8). Regional and international factors played an important role in the difficulties faced by the fledgling state, including the UDI in Southern Rhodesia, as described above. The legacy of the CAF was that of deep economic and infrastructural linkages between Zambia and Rhodesia, which made Zambian participation in UN-sponsored sanctions on Rhodesia impossible until such time that infrastructural independence, particularly in terms of transport and electricity, could be realized. Several nations played an important role in assisting Zambia with its goal of economic independence, including western states like Great Britain (mostly as a direct reaction to UDI), China (specifically, through construction of the TAZARA railway as an alternative export route for copper through Tanzania), and Yugoslavia, through non-aligned economic development cooperation. The Cold War dictated the international geopolitical order in this period, complicating negotiations between Zambia and its potential development partners.

4.3 *1973–91*

Among Zambia's neighbours, violent independence struggles and subsequent civil strife erupted not just in Rhodesia, but also in Congo, Angola, Namibia, and Mozambique. At the same time, as the global economy collapsed, copper prices nosedived, with heavy consequences for Zambia's economy, as shown in Figure 4.1.

The economic crisis made government expenditure on social and physical infrastructure and high wages for mine workers unsustainable. The nationalization of the economy and the introduction of the one-party state was a way of dealing with these major economic and political crises of the late 1960s, as well as a reaction to changing global ideas of the state. Throughout the developing ('Third') World, leaders sought ways to unify ethnically diverse states (a hangover of colonialism) and ensure equal development for all citizens, as imagined by the Non-Alignment Movement and leaders such as Yugoslavia's 'benevolent dictator', Josip Broz Tito. One-party states and nationalization were regarded as viable alternatives to what were considered to be the disruptive outcomes of multiparty democracy. They would ensure development at all levels and reduce incidences of violence and civil war.

Szeftel (1982: 15) asserts that the centrality of the state in newly independent Zambia was one of the primary underlying factors that led to the

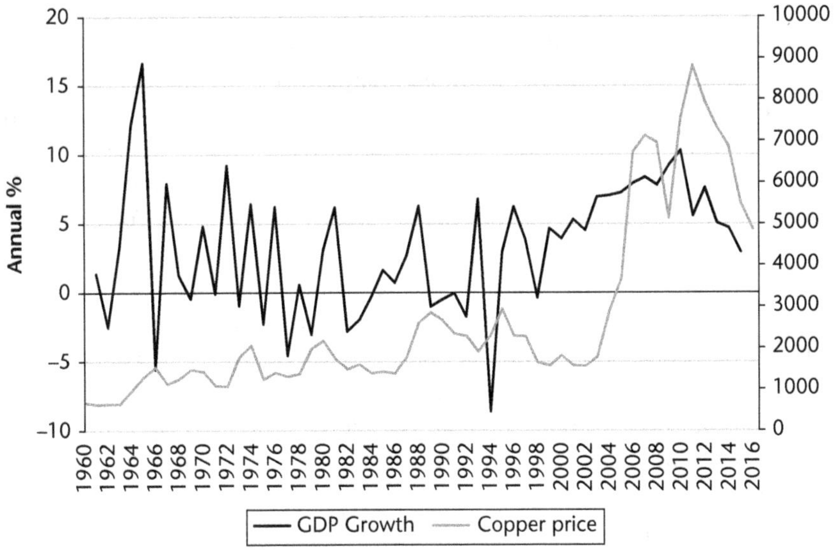

Figure 4.1. Annual GDP growth and copper price trend, Zambia, 1960–2016

Note: Copper prices represent the price for Grade A copper, electrolytic wire bars/cathodes, London Metal Exchange, cash.

Source: World Bank (2017a), UNCTADSTAT (2017). Graph format based on ICMM (2014: 6).

emergence of the one-party state at this specific moment in time. He argues that the so-called 'accumulation of spoils' from the mining sector had led to factionalism and reproduced regional lines of cleavage. The allocation of senior party and government positions reflected the need to balance the claims of these contending factions. The cabinet, for instance, had been characterized by a (shifting) balance of posts between provinces. These dynamics threatened to boil over into dangerous conflict, as they did when a powerful faction from the Bemba-speaking Northern and Copperbelt provinces threatened to alter the balance drastically, first by claiming dominance within UNIP and thereafter by splitting off and setting up a powerful opposition party.

These political tensions were exacerbated by the continuing unequal distribution of (mining) revenues driven by the uneven nature of Zambia's political settlement. Economic activity was distributed inequitably and concentrated in the three provinces along the axis of the railway line that included the Copperbelt. Inhabited by 43 per cent of the population, these provinces contributed 89 per cent of the country's gross domestic product (Craig, 1999: 17). Ethnic balancing, therefore, was seen by the marginalized regions as cosmetic, as the resistance and political formations around the Barotseland issue and other tensions like in the North-Western Province (Larmer and Macola, 2007). In describing a detailed history of the Mwinilunga district in North-Western Zambia, Pesa (2014: 52) points out that during early post-colonial elections, 'allegiances in Mwinilunga were more easily stirred by playing on connections with Angola and Congo, than by reference to a national Zambian state with the remote Copperbelt and "line of rail" areas as its centre...' Another prominent manifestation of this theme is opposition from the Southern Province, which primarily represents a peasantry and cattle-keeping economy that persists through to the present, and was never appeased by the appointment of politicians from the prominent Tonga ethnic group to cabinet positions (Macola, 2010).

With the process of nationalization of the copper mines starting in the late 1960s, the Copperbelt began to look like a mini-welfare state, with the state and the mining companies famously providing social services from 'cradle to grave' (Fraser and Lungu, 2007: 8). ZCCM provided facilities beyond the mining compounds and made the Copperbelt an attractive place to live—a veritable hub of 'modernity' (Ferguson, 1999). The mini-welfare state was, in a way, a continuance of the social welfare policies of the colonial mining industry, but now benefiting a larger population. ZCCM as a state entity, however, was increasingly treated as a 'cash cow', and was milked without matching investment in machinery and further prospecting. As ore bodies within the existing mines were found deeper underground, the cost of production also rose. To illustrate the drastic decline: ZCCM production collapsed from a high of 750,000 tonnes in 1973 to 257,000 tonnes in 2000. Craig (1999: 87) notes that the drop in copper prices was not the only reason for the decline in production and income:

> In common with the rest of the Zambian economy, the mines suffered from a number of difficulties. As a bulk exporter, the transportation difficulties which afflicted Zambia were particularly severe. The situation had deteriorated to such a degree that by the second half of the 1970s the transport system was not able to carry all of the copper produced, leaving the mines accumulating stocks of finished metal. The mines also suffered from the declining capacity of the economy to fund imports. Although the companies themselves were net foreign exchange earners, their supply of currency was rationed by the Government along with other sectors and fell short of their requirements.

ZCCM was under constant pressure from the government, who needed to appease the mine workers, to keep the reductions in the workforce to a minimum. The goals of diversification into the agricultural sector had not been achieved either (Hern and Achberger, 2014).

Methods to prevent the rise of alternative centres of power affected overall productivity in the public sector. A variety of methods were utilized: powers of appointment to shuffle senior management to prevent them from developing their own power base, and non-merit appointments to maintain leaders' own support base. To prevent people from becoming entrenched, reshuffling of positions became the order of the day, with some provincial ministers staying less than half a year in one position before being 're-appointed'. Political appointments in the nationalized industry, including the copper mines, proved disastrous for its functioning, as they undermined technocrats and professionalism more generally. Zambia's first secretary to the cabinet, Valentine Musakanya, expressed disenchantment with government as early as the late 1960s, pointing out that the politically driven restructuring of the civil service was intended to effectively put UNIP in control at all levels (Larmer, 2010).

The causes of the crisis were already known at the time, as can be seen from the 1977 *Report of a Special Parliamentary Select Committee* that was appointed to examine the country's economic problems. It noted:

> With the exception of the mining sector, few parastatal bodies have exported anything of substance... Government annually makes a large allocation of capital funds to support projects undertaken by parastatal organisations. This has arisen largely because these bodies are notable to generate their own capital for plant renewal and new investment... Poor management, absence of inventory control, overstaffing, inadequate pricing of products and political interference have been named as some of the reasons for the poor performance of the parastatal sector (quoted in Craig, 1999: 79).

The private sector was similarly affected. Whereas the 'Zambianization' of the economy was aimed at producing an indigenous entrepreneurial and managerial class, UNIP was ideologically opposed to capitalism and detested profit-making. An independent entrepreneurial class was also regarded as a potential political threat, which came to fruition in 1980, when a group of marginalized entrepreneurs and professionals actively opposed the UNIP regime by engaging in a coup attempt.

The consequences of Zambia's political and economic plunge in the 1970s were dire. Desperate about the economic crisis and the related political insecurity, government policies became increasingly ad hoc and unpredictable. Within a space of a few years, UNIP first flirted with scientific socialism, and then turned to the business community and eventually, in 1984, secured external support in the form of a grant from the European Community and the African Development Bank for a rehabilitation programme of the mines. As a result of its substantial debt levels, Zambia had also come under the influence of the IFI, which forced a structural adjustment programme (SAP) in the 1980s. These measures consisted of the removal of subsidies (especially those benefiting urban consumers), a reduction of the workforce, and liberalized foreign exchange rules. The uncontrollable urban maize riots of 1986 threatened UNIP's survival and Zambia decided to break with the IMF and reintroduce the subsidies. This measure was short-lived, and the government was soon forced to re-enter the IMF fold. Within the context of further economic weakening of the 1980s, an alignment of non-state actors came together under the banner of the MMD and called for the dissolution of the one-party state. Faced with an international democratization wave caused by the end of the Cold War and pressure from bilateral and multilateral donors, UNIP had to accede to the demands. It dissolved the one-party state and called for multiparty elections in 1991.

4.4 *1991–Present*

Simuntanyi (2015) characterizes the period of Zambia's multiparty democracy as a competitive clientelist political system, defined as an informal or tacit agreement by the political elite that they will compete for control of the country's political and economic resources through periodic elections in which the strongest political group takes power, rather than through repression of opponents or violent conflict. Within this system, political competition takes place largely on the basis of distribution of patronage/targeted resources to allies and supporters; it is also characterized by the existence of several fragmented political factions. The authoritarian streak never left Zambian politics. While elections took place and the dominant party was ousted in 2011, elections generally remained an uneven playing field in which the ruling party allowed limited space for opposition. Whereas there is some continuation from the UNIP era, there are also some distinct features that mark the Third Republic. As Gould (2010: 11) rightly observed:

> [T]he ambitions of various players – for power, influence, and the control of resources – had been held in check, to a large extent, by the patrimonial structures of the UNIP machinery. As the regulatory mechanisms of the Party-State crumbled, new self-interested players with a wide range of interests and ambitions emerged. Some of these are associated with the rapidly changing gallery of political parties, some with business and commercial interests. Others are linked to the mushrooming array of organizations that compete for government and donor contracts.

The 1990s could also be defined as a 'choiceless democracy', in which governments had little space to determine their own budgets, given the conditionalities imposed by external financing agreements (quoted in 'Strengthening', 1998). Rakner (2003, cited in Hickey, 2013: 15) suggests that economic and political reforms in Zambia, taking place during the exact same period, led to the breakdown of the organizational power of important economic interest groups, such as businesses, unions, and agricultural cooperatives. The privatization of state companies like the mines and the traditional mode of patronage made State House (the office of the Zambian president), political parties, and political actors more susceptible to the special interests of politico-economic entrepreneurs, in the process undermining the formal structures that normally guide accountability and oversight of business lobbying and deals. Mosley (2014) also highlights the risk of the rise of a new class of Zambian rentiers. Because rentiers invest their wealth in the import-export business and depend on mining companies and/or government ties for procurement, their interests go against the need for policies that would advance value-added manufacturing and an overall reduction of costs.

In addition, the privatization process of the Zambian copper mines during this period was seriously flawed. For example, the Chiluba government has not accounted for the sum of US$35 million that it was supposed to have received from the sale of the Roan Antelope Mining Corporation of Zambia in Luanshya. Similarly, the foreign accounts of the government have been utilized for personal benefit by the leadership, as well as for political patronage purposes (Osei-Hwedi, 2003). So, after decades of job cuts and declining living standards, communities on the Copperbelt, the political hotbed of Zambia, rather than simply welcoming the new boom, resented the companies' unexpected opportunity to generate profits from exceptional world copper prices (Fraser and Larmer, 2011). There were good material reasons for disgruntlement. In the five years from 1995 to 2000, as the Zambian government prepared ZCCM for sale and then sold it, employment in the mines had halved. Although new investments did create some new jobs, companies took advantage of weak unions and non-enforcement of employment laws. Casual and contract labour became the new norm. Moreover, the tax incentives 'locked in' under these terms were so generous that the Zambian state was applying an effective tax rate of 0 per cent. Any money made from mining was expatriated before Zambians could see the benefits of the 'boom'.

In short, many of the presumed benefits for the Zambian economy from privatization did not materialize, and this in turn became a rallying point for opposition parties in the 2000s. As happened to UNIP shortly after independence, MMD lost its hegemonic position after the introduction of multiparty democracy. Like UNIP, it was exposed to rivalling regional forces and opposition forces in the urban areas. While MMD won by a large margin in 1996 (also since UNIP boycotted the election), it lost most of its popularity in its second term (1996–2001). Its fall was a result of a combination of factors: privatization (and its dire consequences), rampant corruption, and Chiluba's attempt to run for an unconstitutional third term in office. Defeated by opposition forces (a similar coalition of civil society, churches, trade unions, and intellectuals), Chiluba stepped down and appointed Levy Mwanawasa, a lawyer, as his successor. Mwanawasa controversially won the 2001 election from UPND's Andy Mazoka, with 29 per cent of the vote, thereby lacking a clear mandate.[3]

Mwanawasa's quest for political legitimacy and increased leverage within the context of a rapidly growing economy and high copper prices shifted Zambia's economic policies of mining taxation and distribution. The much-derided Mining DAs were abrogated and renegotiated with a heavy hand. Higher mining tax rates and debt relief from the World Bank's Heavily Indebted Poor Countries Initiative (HIPC), which tied debt relief to expenditure in the social sectors, led to a tentative reduction in poverty between 2005 and 2012, though mainly in urban areas. This slight reduction in poverty is associated with a movement towards 'pro-poor expenditures', which support labour-intensive activities or in other ways support poor people's needs. We have also shown, however, that the focusing of government expenditures in this arena has been partial and imperfect, especially for two reasons: first, leakages away from the target group towards the non-poor, as with the Farmer Input Support Programme (FISP), consisting of seed and fertilizer subsidies to poorer farmers; and second, political barriers which obstruct the flow of public resources into the poorest regions.

The ruling class's resistance to increasing the tax base away from the over-reliance on copper income was closely linked to the way post-liberalization resources were distributed. As Rakner (2003) and di John (2010) point out, prior to liberalization, the state was able to create rents through a series of interventions that included posts in public enterprises and parastatals, infant industry protection via trade barriers, and subsidized credit through control of the banking system, among others. With economic liberalization, the levers of state patronage were reduced. Thus, while privileged positions in government remained important, the tax system became an ever-growing source of dispensing patronage and privilege. While the Zambian tax system is relatively effective, the demands of accommodating elites (and their allied interest with mining companies) have constrained the ability of the state to develop a more robust tax system.

Despite rhetoric surrounding the need to grow indigenous entrepreneurship under MMD's liberal regime in the 1990s, the government did little to facilitate the growth of (independent) entrepreneurs. The SAP did not help either, as shown by the prescribed investment incentives like tax concessions and tax rebates that favoured large, foreign companies, creating an uneven playing field. Moreover, subsequent governments have continued to feel threatened by Zambian businessmen as potential sources of opposition party funding. A successful entrepreneur commented that, during the privatization process, Zambian businessmen were side lined because of their alleged political affiliation to one of the major opposition parties (interview). A former managing director of Zambia's Privatization Agency remembers a specific case in which a local entrepreneur was shelved in the early 1990s, despite having obtained finance to buy one of the public companies that was in the process of being privatized. In most cases of privatization, the government showed preference to either a foreign or a non-indigenous entrepreneur (Mkandawire, 2006). In Zambia's case, the white, Indian, and Lebanese communities still dominate the private sector (Sutton and Langmead, 2013).

The recent unstable settlements show the resilience of the bureaucracy. While the president continues to control decision making regarding the allocation of substantive rents (e.g. state ownership of resources, major contracts, trade agreements, etc.), Levy (2012) suggests that patronage-relationships and rent-seeking behaviour in general have become much more decentralized throughout the hierarchy of the political and bureaucratic elite. Members of the business community testify to this. They observe that there is a class of professional middlemen who, on behalf of their businesses, traverse the political and bureaucratic elite. Businesses can choose the 'high politics' route—to directly influence the ministers, the vice-president, or the president himself—but this is seemingly only undertaken by large companies. Foreign multinational corporations also choose diplomatic channels, via their embassies, mostly to great effect.

In terms of leverage in wage negotiations, the civil service has overtaken the erstwhile power of the miners' trades unions. Their role has also strengthened because of the structural adjustments programmes of the 1990s. One has witnessed a professionalization in specific departments, especially within the Ministry of Finance, the Zambia Revenue Authority, the Ministry of Commerce, and the Bank of Zambia. Ideas around fiscal responsibility, debt levels and macroeconomic stability are quite firmly settled within these departments. Bureaucrats are immovable and a constant factor in society. With their emoluments taking over 60 per cent of the national public sector budget, this all comes at the expense of much-needed social investments to bridge the inequality gap.

In the period since 2001, while continuing to reflect the features of competitive clientelism, Zambia has begun to show signs of becoming a vulnerable/unstable settlement. This is caused by an expanding informal economy, demographic shifts (a large unemployed youth electorate), and low educational standards, aggravated by the death of two presidents in office, which has caused disruptive presidential by-elections. Without a clear line of succession within the political parties, the presidents' deaths have caused deep factionalism within the parties. We have seen a high level of fluidity in Zambian governance, which, especially when compared to its neighbouring countries, makes the political scene even more unpredictable. The link between politicians and constituents becomes increasingly indistinct. Thus, political parties are short-lived and disintegrate once out of office or past the need for coalitions. The main opposition party, UPND, has a stronger link with its (rural) constituents and has been consistently liberal in its outlook, but in recent years has watered down its identity by forging coalitions. It is important to keep in mind that the youth, the largest demographic group in the country (66 per cent of the population are less than twenty-four years old), largely grew up in a post-liberalization economy that is entirely de-industrialized and increasingly informal. They have no recollection of the welfare state and are unlikely to belong to any social movement or have membership in any political party. As the social base of the electorate changes, so does its expectation vis-à-vis the state (see Raftopolous' parallel observations on Zimbabwe, 2014).

Despite this fluidity and many electoral cycles, especially between 2006 and 2016, we can discern shifts in the political settlement that have caused some changes to Zambia's political and economic landscape. As we noted before, change is most evident from 2001 onwards—the moment from which MMD faced opposition and eventually lost a fiercely competitive election in 2011. Civil society, fragmented and disunited in the 1990s, proved that when aligned it could still constitute a formidable force, as it did in 2001 when it united to prevent Chiluba's attempt to run for an unconstitutional third term in office. The year 2001 is significant in other respects as well, namely that it coincides with the return of Chinese capital and the turnaround of the economy stemming from the rapid rise of copper prices. Political competition and the growth of the mining sectors, as two former MMD ministers testify, put pressure on the government to increase fiscal space to allow for social expenditure. Civil society aligned itself with the then opposition party, PF, to influence the mining tax debate. The online leaks of secret DAs by civil society campaigns also added to the pressure for urgent tax reforms. With key documents in the public realm for the first time, media and parliamentary debate focused on the injustice of the long-term tax breaks enjoyed by the companies. The Zambian government was offered technical assistance from several bilateral donor agencies who now realized that the DAs unfairly disadvantaged Zambia. All donors, however, insisted that any changes to the tax regime be endorsed by the companies, respecting the principle that a contract has legal value. In this case, both sides publicly stated a willingness to negotiate. In January 2008, President Mwanawasa surprised everyone by announcing the unilateral imposition of windfall taxes on mining companies. He appeared to have consulted more broadly on this issue with his ministers than other presidents had, when he reached this conclusion. This momentum was short-lived, however, as his successor, Rupiah Banda, revoked the windfall tax as soon as he came into office after the death of Mwanawasa in August 2008. Former ministers feel Banda could have easily amended the tax regime to appease the mining industry, without revoking the windfall tax altogether. While Banda introduced other measures to increase taxes from the mining sector, like a variable profit tax, these were less visible and did little to substantively increase state revenue from the mining sector.

Tax revenue and evasion was tackled head-on by the incoming PF government in 2011, with a substantial increase in the royalty tax and the closing of loopholes regarding the export of the ore. News reports following President Sata's death in October 2014 indicated that mining companies were trying to renegotiate the tax rates. Possibly with an eye on the presidential by-election of January 2015, which was tightly contested and needed a popular appeal, the new Mining Act was passed in December 2014. In response, Barrick Gold, the Canadian company that owns the Lumwana open-pit mine in North-Western Province, issued a statement that it would suspend its operations. Shortly after the elections, as expected, the mining tax rates were immediately renegotiated and reversed and Lumwana continued its operations. It follows the pattern that once a new government is in place, one can almost be guaranteed that mining interests will come to the fore, in line with the prevailing political settlement, and, as always, in keeping with fluctuating copper prices that hold Zambia hostage. It also points to the continued individualized negotiations and business influence over State House, as it was the president who announced the revocation of the mining act, not the minister of mines or finance. The most valuable observation from a tax political economy analysis is that, independent of the various tax regimes with their merits and demerits, there has been one constant, namely:

> The system is plagued with incentives both for mining and across sectors. These individual deals are tantamount to an individualized tax system, which makes administration impossible, particularly when tax administrators may not have access to specific provisions of the individualized DAs or other contractual provisions. Definitions and rules are not clear, there appears to be significant discretion about how tax provisions are applied, and public information about how the rules should be applied is scarce. This situation raises the potential for honest taxpayers to exploit the legal ambiguity for their benefit, for dishonest taxpayers to evade taxation, for corruption within the tax administration (Conrad, 2014: 15).

Following a period of sustained economic growth, the major donors had a diminished influence on government policies, including those related to mining taxation. Grants from cooperating partners to Zambia have decreased from 40 per cent of the government's national budget in 2007 to 6 per cent in 2013 (OECD), and to a mere 2.6 per cent in 2015. In 2011, the World Bank reclassified Zambia as a lower middle-income country, though it still ranks 163 out of 186 countries on the 2012 Human Development Index. With this changing tide, political parties like PF were now able to enter the political arena on an anti-neoliberal platform and offer a return to a 'UNIP-style' developmental state, albeit without the suggestion of a full-blown renationalization. Donors, on the other hand, are increasingly caught between the contradictory policies underlying the shift from 'aid to trade'. This has led to an ambiguous situation, where donor governments are funding their own activist organizations to fight the consequences of the dominance of mining capital, while at the same time protecting the investment interests of their own mining companies.

As can be seen in Figure 4.2, over time the composition and origin of capital itself has also significantly changed character. We challenge the notion of a monolithic nature of international capital. The recently privatized mines were purchased by firms from a diverse array of countries, including Canada, Switzerland, and China. Indeed, the Zambian mining industry remains dominated by global capital, with a small percentage of shares being owned by ZCCM Investment Holdings (IH), a state-owned enterprise. In Lee's book on Chinese capital and labour in Zambia (Lee, 2017), she makes a distinction between shareholder capitalism, which is based on shareholder value maximization, and Chinese state capitalism, which also aims at profit, but not profit maximization. Thus, the profit horizon of the latter is conceived to be in the long term, and its capital is therefore less footloose. Lee argues that it is thus unsurprising that when the global financial crisis of 2008 hit Zambia, the shareholder companies

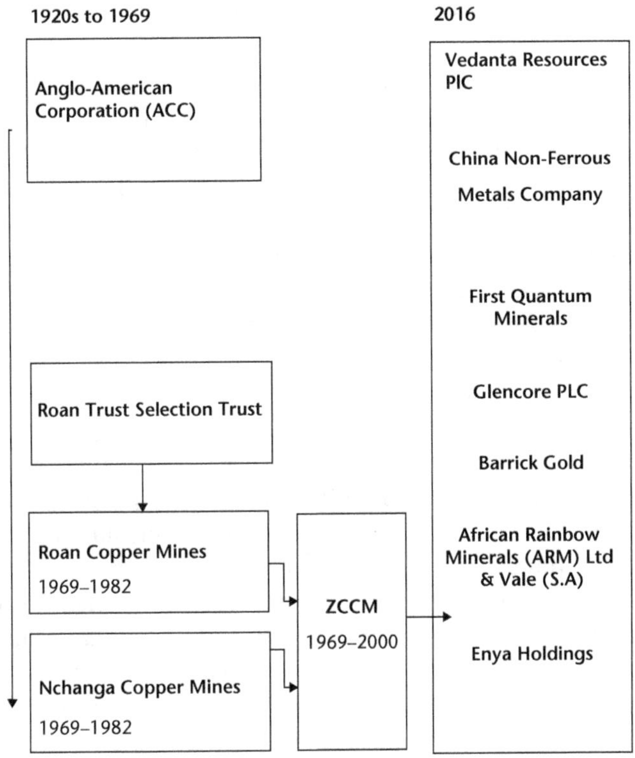

Figure 4.2. Private ownership patterns in Zambian copper mines, 1920s to the present
Source: Author's work.

immediately retrenched thousands of workers, in contrast with Chinese state-owned companies that kept all workers in place. Whether this trend will continue in the current downturn will be an important test case for this proposition.

In earlier articles, Lee (2014) also argued that another motivating factor for long-term commitment is that China actually has a need for the copper ore for its own development. This contrasts with other holding companies, which use the copper merely as a trading commodity and have no direct use for the commodity itself. The consequence of the long-term nature of these investments is that the companies are forced to be compliant with regulations/taxation and to maintain a high level of political influence. In the Zambian context, the adaptation of the Chinese to the changing regimes and populist responses has been remarkable. Lee (2014) concluded that for Zambia, 'Chinese state capital's logic of encompassing accumulation makes it more accommodating and negotiable than global private capital to the Zambian state strategy of development, if there is a vision and political will.' Chinese state capital, however, is more vulnerable to political moods, as the Chinese were particularly targeted by opposition politicians who exploit and channel popular sentiment of resource nationalism against Chinese investment. The Zambian state has space to negotiate their relationship with China, but rarely does, lacking a coherent China policy. China's long-term planning includes bringing manufacturing to Zambia. Investment in the establishment of several multi-facility export zones (MFEZs) is indicative of this development.

Another significant shift in the mining sector in this period is the establishment of new mining enclaves in and near Solwezi District in North-Western Province (see Maps 4.1 and 4.2).[4] Three relatively large open-pit copper mines—Kansanshi, Kalumbila, and Lumwana—(re)started operations there in the last ten years, employing more than 7,000 workers. Both holding companies, First Quantum and Barrick Gold, have headquarters in Canada. Solwezi is at the centre of these developments. By 2007, Solwezi's population had grown to somewhere between 120,000 and 150,000—triple what it was in the year 2000. This transformation is visible in the influx of allied activities—like engineering and transportation—and supporting services, both formal (such as banks, mobile phone and internet companies, and retail) and informal (such as taxicabs, street vendors, and sex workers), making the place a frontier of what has been labelled extractive capitalism (Negi, 2014). But unlike the old Copperbelt, Solwezi has shown no signs of emerging urban politics that link to the national level. Given its status as an opposition stronghold throughout Zambia's political history but more especially in recent years against the PF, the central government has halted much needed infrastructure developments in this area, most notably the Chingola–Solwezi highway.

Historically this region has been largely excluded from elite bargaining at the national level. While there has been a significant rise of political consciousness, clamouring for a percentage of the royalties from mining operations, the area lacks the political powers, the unity, the numbers (it represents only 5 per cent of the national vote), and local activism to force this issue. The potential political brokers in this area are not the trade unions, as was the case in the old Copperbelt, but rather the local chiefs. Their income, however, is derived from government and mining companies and influences their decision making. Overall, the communities feel marginalized in these areas. The lack of communication between government, chiefs, and the local population in relation to the establishment of mining companies in this area reflects the top-down, centralized approach of the government and comes to the fore in the following exchange quoted by Cheelo (2008):

> Us, as a community, had had no role to play in the negotiations of mining investments at Kansanshi – we did not participate at all. We just saw the chief come and introduce the investors to us telling us that we should keep them well.

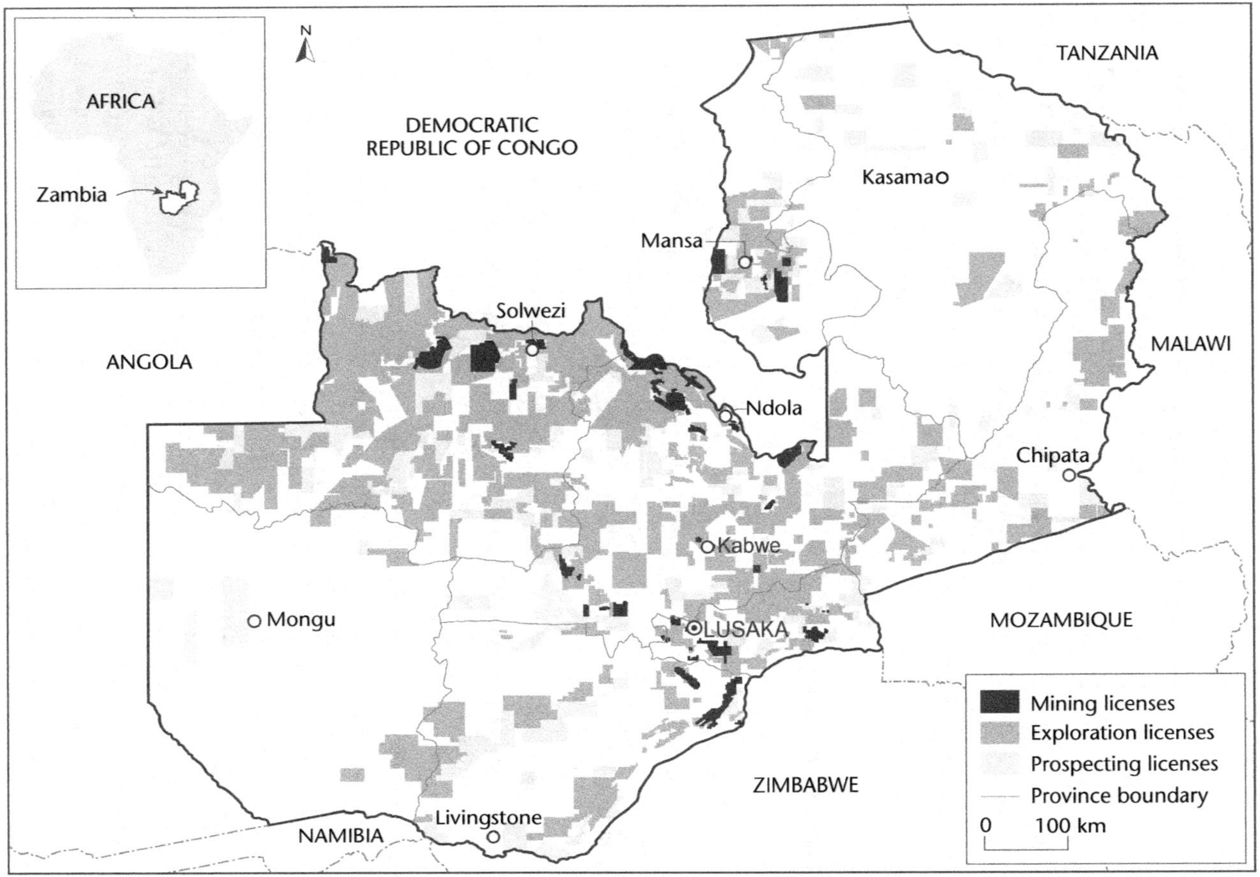

Map 4.2. National distribution of mining licenses in Zambia in 2017, showing particular concentrations in North-Western and Copperbelt Provinces

Source: Elaborated on the basis of maps produced by flexicadstre.com, accessed September 2017.

> He told us that 'you shouldn't steal from them; you shouldn't do bad things to them. If you keep them well, they will develop this region' (Cheelo, 2008: 169).

It is not clear how elite relations will develop in the context of the post-2016 general elections. It is interesting to note that an unprecedented level of campaigning by the ruling party took place in North-Western Province, which was an important indicator of the region's growing political importance. Despite these efforts, the province overwhelmingly voted for the opposition. For now, the mining industry in North-Western Province continues to be a classical enclave economy, where mines and mining compounds are literally fenced off from the local communities. The interface between international companies and the Zambian government takes place in Lusaka, where the corporate affairs offices are based.

5 Conclusion

Zambia's economic growth strongly depends on cyclical changes in international commodity prices. Over time, these changes have prompted reform, be it in the shape of nationalization, privatization, or, more recently, the abrogation of DAs. But overall, there has been a certain continuity in state–natural resources relations. This existing order was formed during the early colonial era, in which the extractive industry came to dominate the economic, social, and political landscape. Designated as a labour-reserve economy, the focus of development has always been on the mining industry at the expense of the rural hinterlands. The political culture in Zambia has largely been shaped by urban labour migrants, the current-day urban dwellers.

Zambia's developmental outcomes then, in part, have been determined by the type of international capital that dictates the mining industry. The industry was initially dominated by what Ferguson (2006: 35) called a 'socially thick' type of capitalism, in which miners and their extended families enjoyed extensive welfare programmes. The Copperbelt, in many ways, resembled a mini-developmental state during this period. As we have seen above, this form of capitalism was replaced in the late 1990s by a more footloose neoliberal form involving significant Chinese capital and in which the industry wound down all erstwhile social contracts with the mining communities. The resentment about the privatization process, the accompanying corruption among local and international brokers, and the limited revenue derived from a booming industry led the opposition party to mobilize around the issue of resource nationalism, without the suggestion of a full-scale nationalization of the industry. A state-led development model thus made a return but was accompanied by increasing misgivings about the potential politicization of this process.

To what extent, then, does a political settlements approach help to characterize and explain the way in which politics, natural resource governance, and development interact in Zambia? On the one hand, the political settlement approach to power and institutions offers a clear sense of how elite-level politics play out in Zambia, most notably by helping to identify the significance of building broad ruling coalitions that stretch across the main urban areas and ethno-linguistic groupings. But whereas these coalitions proved useful for establishing stability in Zambia, they have not stimulated development and pushed non-dominant groupings to the margins. Patron–client politics deepened in response to competitive pressures during the 1990s, most notably through the distribution of agricultural subsidies and the (brief) introduction of the windfall tax on mining profits. Along with the executive type of presidentialism that was institutionalized under Kaunda's period of dominance, these dimensions also help to explain why political mobilization has lacked any socially coherent basis that was sustained over the long term. It helps us to understand why these organizations, even with a clear manifesto and ideology, have in practice largely turned out to be clientelist rather than programmatic. It also clarifies the failure of political leaders to form sustained followers among lower-level factions, as reflected in the personalized nature of political parties, which lack a persistent social basis over time. With the rise of the informal sector and the coming of age of younger generations ('the post-IMF babies'), the social base is becoming even less defined and more fluid.

What the political settlement framework is perhaps less adept at explaining is why the social bases of political mobilization matter, as these can shape the developmental tendencies of ruling coalitions. Overall, in Zambia's history we can see short periods in which inclusive development was briefly actualized, from the 1960s until the early to mid-1970s, and again from the early 2000s to 2014. This was always in the context of high copper prices, increased fiscal space, and nationalist/populist pressure to distribute the copper wealth. The recovery was never sustained for a long period and its potential was never fully realized. Besides the challenge of maximizing tax revenue, proceeds were often spent in an unproductive manner. The consequence of this was that during an economic downturn, the consumptive nature of the state immediately gave rise to external and domestic debts. Neoliberal capitalism took an especially unproductive form in Zambia: it not only diffused social organizations (such as trades unions and farmers' cooperatives), but it also undermined the processes of class formation that could, in turn, have led to class-based mobilization. Ideas and memories matter more than the political settlements approach seems to imply. These elements are especially clear for countries that have a long mining history with a formative influence such as that of Zambia.

Table 4.3. Indicators of inequality, poverty, and extractive industries in Zambia

Indicator	Period				
	1964–72	1973–90	1991–2001	2002–10	2011–14
Inequality					
Gini	–	–	51.95	51.24	57.5
Poverty					
Poverty headcount ratio at national poverty lines (% of population)	–	–	–	60.5	54
Poverty headcount ratio at $1.25 a day (PPP) (% of population)	–	–	61	68	60.5
Poverty headcount ratio at $2 a day (PPP) (% of population)	–	–	78	84	–
Life expectancy at birth, total (years)	48	49	41	49	56
Literacy rate, adult total (% of people ages 15 and above)	–	65	68	65	70.6
Access to electricity (% of population)	–	13	17	18.5	22.1
Primary completion rate, total (% of relevant age group)	70	83	66	86	91
Lower secondary completion rate, total (% of relevant age group)	–	18.5	27	54	60
Mortality rate, infant (per 1,000 live births)	111	103	108	75	57.4
Extractive Industries					
Mineral rents (% of GDP)	26.08	11.51	9.25	14.03	22.06
Total natural resources rents (% of GDP)	27.25	14.84	0	17.92	25.14
Ores and metals exports (% of merchandise exports)	98.04	97.49	76.25	76.93	74.55

Source: Compiled by the authors from World Bank Reports, UN reports, and the Central Statistical Office of Zambia.

Acknowledgements

Jessica Achberger helped enormously in the preparation of this chapter. Justine Sichone also assisted with preparation of the figures.

Notes

1. For more indicators on inequality, poverty, and extractive industries in Zambia, see Table 4.3.
2. Details were as follows: the government had agreed to compensate for the abrupt cancellation of the service contracts by paying K55 million and had to pay an additional K146.6 million to redeem the bonds. Additional costs were incurred in the redemption of the bonds which carried a coupon of 6 per cent, with funds borrowed at 12–13 per cent (Burdette quoted in Craig, 1999: 40, n. 108). There are different versions of the causes and beneficiaries of this expensive saga.
3. According to a former intelligence agent and other sources, the 2001 election was rigged in favour of MMD.
4. In 2015, Solwezi District was subdivided into three districts (Solwezi, Kalumbila, and Mushidano) each containing one of the big mines.

5

Competitive Clientelism and the Political Economy of Mining in Ghana

Ghana has a long history of mineral resource extraction, with mechanized large-scale mining often traced as far back as the nineteenth century. The country is endowed with substantial mineral resources in commercial quantities, including oil, gold, diamonds, manganese, bauxite, limestone, and salt. Gold has been the predominant mineral produced, reflecting the country's colonial name, the Gold Coast. Once the leading producer of gold in the world and accounting for about 35.5 per cent of total world gold output between 1493 and 1600 (Republic of Ghana, 2014: 4), Ghana currently ranks around tenth in the global league of major gold producers, but is still Africa's second largest producer after South Africa (Kapstein and Kim, 2011).

However, the actual contribution of mining to the country's development prospects has long been called into question. For some (e.g. Aryee, 2001), mining has played a crucial role in Ghana's development efforts, especially when viewed in terms of its contribution to government revenues. Between 1999 and 2014, the mining industry was consistently the highest gross foreign exchange earner (Republic of Ghana, 2014: 12).[1] Presently, mining contributes about 27 per cent of government revenue in terms of domestic tax collections (ibid.), and accounted for 43 per cent of total merchandise exports in 2012 (Ghana Chamber of Mines, 2013). Export revenues from the mineral sector amounted to US$5.1 billion in 2013 (Aryee, 2014). Yet there is a strong sense in both the academic literature and national policy debates that Ghana is far from obtaining sufficient developmental benefits from its mining sector. One close industry observer concludes that 'mining has... not fulfilled its poverty reduction role' (Akabzaa, 2009: 49). A World Bank-commissioned study concurs, describing the sector's contribution to overall national development efforts as 'disappointing' (Ayee et al., 2011: 6), and the Natural Resource Governance Institute's Resource Governance Index for 2017 assessed Ghana's performance in mining revenue management as 'poor' (NRGI, 2017).

Why has Ghana been unable to effectively translate its massive mineral wealth into more inclusive forms of development?

This is an important question in view of Ghana's recognition as one of the best governed countries in Africa, with multiparty democracy increasingly entrenched. In 2013, Ghana was the highest ranked African country (and fifteenth out of fifty-eight countries globally) in the Resource Governance Index, which measures the quality of countries' natural resource governance performance in terms of transparency and accountability; in 2017, the index for Ghana's oil management was still the highest of rankings for African countries, though its mining management was ranked twenty-fourth, lower than that of Botswana, Burkina Faso, and South Africa (NRGI, 2017). Ghana is also held up as 'a model of best practice' (Standing, 2014), based on its policy of distributing a proportion of mining rents to subnational authorities in mining communities. Judged from the perspective of the resource curse literature, which emphasizes the quality of governance and institutions as the best route to translating natural resource wealth into broad-based development, Ghana's experience with natural resource governance is therefore puzzling.

In this chapter, we use insights of the political settlements literature to explore the politics of mining sector governance in Ghana and deepen our understanding of why the utilization of natural resource wealth for broad-based development has historically proven 'to be difficult' (Boakye et al., 2012: 1). In particular, we work with the claim that institutions are the products of elite bargains, and that their role in shaping development outcomes can therefore best be understood within the context of embedded power relations. This approach not only helps us understand why very similar sets of formal institutions often produce divergent development outcomes, but also allows an analysis of the contending interests that exist within any state, which constrain and facilitate institutional and developmental change. Poteete (2009) uses similar ideas to argue that, in Botswana, variation in the governance of extractives is a product of elite commitment and capacity to overcome clientelist pressures and channel mineral rents into long-term development goals. She argues that:

> Politicians with narrow and unstable coalitions see rentier politics as an attractive coalition building strategy; their responses to this political problem hinder state building . [. . Conversely,] [p]oliticians with broader and more stable coalitions are less likely to turn to rentier politics to bolster political support, in part because they are more apt to believe that they will reap the benefits from investments in state building (Poteete, 2009: 545).

Poteete also insists that a fuller account of the Botswanan experience requires taking external factors into account.[2] Building on these ideas, we ask: what roles do power relations, ideas, and transnational actors/factors play in shaping mining sector governance in Ghana (including issues around the distribution of rents), and how have these, in turn, shaped prospects for mining-led development? The chapter proceeds as follows: in Sections 1 and 2, we discuss the overall interaction of mining governance and political settlements over the long sweep of Ghana's history, from the pre-colonial period to the present. Section 3 then focuses on the period since the early 1990s, drawing particular attention to the ways in which a competitive clientelist settlement has affected mining governance and helps explain the generally disappointing impacts of mining on poverty reduction. Sections 4 and 5 then address two particular features of the Ghanaian mining context: the roles of the chieftaincy institution and of central–local relationships; and the significant small-scale, extra-legal mining sector. In each instance, we argue that the nature of national–subnational relationships within the political settlement affects patterns and means of inclusion in the mining economy and the quality of its effects on local development.

1 Political Settlements in Ghana: A Periodization

Until the return to multiparty democracy in 1992, the political history of Ghana was essentially a story of political instability. With the notable exception of the First Republic under Nkrumah (1960–66), the interludes of civilian governments under the Second (1969–72) and Third (1979–81) Republics were short-lived, unable to survive for longer than three years without being overthrown in a coup d'état. With each military takeover, state power shifted from one ethnic group to the other (Chazan, 1982). This section attempts to periodize Ghana's political settlements dynamics, starting with how processes of decolonization laid a foundation for the emergence of competitive clientelism. During the first three decades after independence, Ghana's political settlements oscillated between competitive clientelism, vulnerable authoritarianism, and a dominant leader type of settlement, before reverting to competitive clientelism from 1993 to the present. See Table 5.1 for a summary of these settlements.

1.1 *Decolonization and the Emergence of Competitive Clientelism in Post-Colonial Ghana, 1874–1965*

Prior to the formal declaration of the Gold Coast as a British Colony in 1874, pre-colonial Ghanaian societies were organized largely into centralized and hierarchical kingdoms, the most powerful of which was the Asante Kingdom. In 1844, the British signed a political agreement with several Fanti chiefs.[3] Dubbed the Bond of 1844, this agreement extended British protection to the

Table 5.1. Periodization of Ghana's national political settlements dynamics, colonial period to date

Time period	Characterization of ruling coalition based on Khan's (2010) typology	Name of ruling coalition	Name of ruling coalition	Type of political regime	Broader development ideology
1874–1956	Dominant settlement	1874–1950: British Crown 1951–Feb. 1957: power sharing government between Nkrumah's CPP and colonial officials	British Crown	British colonial rule	–
1957–66	Competitive clientelism	1957–64: CPP led by Nkrumah	CPP, led by Nkrumah	Multiparty democratic (First Republic)	Nationalist/socialist
		1964–66: CPP, led by Nkrumah	CPP, led by Nkrumah	Legal One-Party	
1966–81	Vulnerable authoritarianism	1966–69: National Liberation Council	National Liberation Council	Military–bureaucratic	–
		1969–72: Progress Party, led by Busia	Progress Party, led by Busia	Multiparty democratic (Second Republic)	Liberal
		1972–74: National Redemption Council	National Redemption Council	Military-bureaucratic-chiefly	–
		1975–78: Supreme Military Council (SMC I)	Supreme Military Council (SMC I)	Military (only)	
		1978–79: SMC II	SMC II	Internal military coup	
		4 June 1979: Armed Forces Revolutionary Council	Armed Forces Revolutionary Council	Military	–
		Sept. 1979: People's National Party, Limann	People's National Party, Limann	Multiparty democratic (Third Republic)	–
1982–92	Dominant leader settlement	31 Dec. 1981 to Jan. 1993: PNDC, led by Rawlings	PNDC, led by Rawlings	Military-bureaucratic	Militant-populist and neoliberal
1993–2017	Competitive clientelism	1993–2000: NDC, Rawlings	NDC, Rawlings	Multiparty democratic (Fourth Republic)	Social democratic/resource nationalist
		2001–08: NPP, Kufuor	NPP, Kufuor		Property-owning democracy and private sector-led growth
		2009–12: NDC, Mills*	NDC, Mills[a]		Social democratic/resource nationalist
		2012–16: NDC, Mahama	NDC, Mahama		Social democratic/resource nationalist
		Jan. 2017–date: NPP, Akuffo-Addo	NPP, Akuffo-Addo		Property-owning democracy and private sector-led growth

Note: [a] President Mills died while in office in July 2012, and Vice-President Mahama became president. The next national elections were held in December 2012, at which Mahama stood for president as the NDC party candidate and won, and the NDC took a majority in Parliament, giving the NDC a second term in government.

Source: Authors' work.

signatory Fanti states and gave Britain a degree of authority over the coastal part of Ghana. From here, the British extended their jurisdiction inwards over the rest of the southern part of contemporary Ghana. British expansion provoked a war with the Asante Kingdom in the middle of the country, with several battles leading ultimately to Asante defeat in 1901. British rule was subsequently extended over the Asante Kingdom and its hinterland to the north, which became the Northern Territories. Thus, the Gold Coast was an amalgamation of: the Colony (the coastal part), where societies had a long history of interaction with European traders; the Ashanti territory in the middle belt; Togoland, which had been part of the German empire but came under British mandate after World War I; and the Northern Territories (NTs) (i.e. the present-day Northern, Upper East, and Upper West regions). These territories had different experiences of social and economic change, as a result of their varying interaction with the colonial government (see Whitfield et al., 2015; Abdulai, 2012).

Because mining and agricultural production were concentrated in the Ashanti territory and Gold Coast Colony, these regions received the bulk of colonial capital investments. In contrast, the NTs were integrated into the colonial capitalist economy as a pool of reserve labour (Plange, 1979). These differential terms of incorporation led to a fragmented elite front during the decolonization process (Abdulai, 2012). Moreover, the concentration of educational and economic opportunities in the Colony and Ashanti during the colonial period resulted in multiple distinct but overlapping social groups with varying economic interests, which often conflicted with each other. These conflicts of interest led to a high degree of political mobilization and dispersion of power in society, leading to a fractured nationalist movement towards decolonization (Whitfield et al., 2015).

As a result, the decolonization struggle in Ghana was not so much a conflict between Africans and the British colonial authorities as one among societal groups in the colonial territories (Whitfield, 2018). When the decolonization process started with elections in the major towns in 1950 for African members to form a power sharing government with the British, it played out in a context of extremely dispersed power among groups of elites, as well as significant political mobilization and organization across sections of society. Several political parties emerged, and their alliances and composition changed over time, as three elections were held before independence. The educated elites, led by J. B. Danquah, formed the United Gold Convention Party (UGCC) in 1947, which was essentially an African business lobby seeking to capture the trade of European merchant-importers. Kwame Nkrumah, who was the General Secretary of the UGCC, split off to form the Convention People's Party (CPP) in 1949, under pressure from a group of educated 'commoners' to be their leader (Whitfield et al., 2015; Whitfield, 2018).

The Nkrumah-led CPP won national elections organized by the colonial administration in 1951 and 1954, and Nkrumah became Leader of Government Business in a power sharing arrangement between the CPP and the colonial administration. At this point, opposition to the CPP came mainly from the UGCC and the state council of chiefs, who either stood as candidates themselves or used their machinery of sub-chiefs to support other local elites. The majority of representatives of the chiefs were not sympathetic to the CPP government. After joining the power sharing government with the British, Nkrumah and CPP politicians took steps to reduce the political authority and economic base of chiefs with the objective of curtailing political opposition to the CPP ruling coalition.

Shortly after the 1954 elections, a new political coalition—the National Liberation Movement (NLM)—was formed in the Ashanti territory.[4] Composed mainly of Ashanti chiefs, cocoa farmers, commoners' associations, and UGCC elites, the NLM rejected the CPP's call for a unitary constitution in favour of a federal one. Their purpose was to enable 'Ashantis to use their region's wealth to benefit themselves rather than to subsidize development in the less affluent parts of the country' (Smock and Smock, 1975: 68). Though the 1954 election was supposed to determine to whom the British would transfer political authority at independence, the NLM's agitations prompted the colonial administration to insist on national elections in 1956 to determine the population's wishes regarding the character of the independence constitution. Although the CPP again managed an overall victory in this election and formed the first fully independent government, the various ethnic and regional-based parties demonstrated their strength in their respective ethno-regional strongholds, with the largely Asante-based NLM winning 'nearly two-thirds of the vote in the "true Ashanti" states' (Austin, 1964: 353).

Having successfully survived the 1954–56 political struggle, and now at the helm of a fully independent state, the CPP ruling elites adopted several measures to manage their growing vulnerability in power. One such measure was the co-optation of opposition politicians into the ruling coalition, a strategy facilitated by the distribution of public resources along patronage lines (Ladouceur, 1979: 174–5; Songsore et al., 2001; Whitfield et al., 2015). The second measure was the suppression of opposition elements through the passage of various laws. Moreover, by 1960, Nkrumah had pushed through a new Republican Constitution, which concentrated extraordinary powers in the hands of the president, and in 1964, Ghana became a *de jure* one-party state under Nkrumah's CPP.

1.2 *Vulnerable Authoritarianism, 1966–81*

In February 1966, the CPP government was violently overthrown through a military coup, marking the beginning of vulnerable authoritarianism in

Ghana. Following this coup, the Ghanaian economy floundered under a succession of short-lived military and civilian regimes, 'each apparently too caught up in internal rivalries and personal ambition to give serious attention to the economy' (Berry, 2008: 39). Between 1966 and 1981 there were seven regime changes, signifying a period of constant power struggles and high levels of conflict between factions of political elites, both military and civilian, for control over the state (Whitfield, 2018). Coups d'état prompted by macro-economic crises deposed two democratic regimes (the Second and Third Republics), but the subsequent ruling coalitions of both military and civilian regimes could not maintain power for long in the face of mounting pressures from excluded political elites (Whitfield et al., 2015). Consequently, no political coalition was able to hold power for more than seven years, and the country oscillated between periods of democratic rule and military governments until the return to multiparty democracy in 1992 (ibid.).

1.3 *Dominant Settlement under the PNDC, 1982–92*

By 1981, Ghana was in the midst of a severe economic contraction that led to a crisis of legitimacy for the political, military, and bureaucratic elites that had been ruling Ghana since independence. The crisis reached so far unheard of proportions, to the extent that 'the average Ghanaian family consumed at least 30% less food in 1982 than the same family did in 1970' (Donkor, 1997, quoted in Armstrong, 2008: 14). Jerry (J. J.) Rawlings, who had led a coup in 1979 before yielding to democratic authority in the Third Republic, now reversed course. He mobilized junior ranks in the military to overthrow the elected government and called for a 'people's revolution', resulting in a temporary mobilization of the lower sections of society. The severity of the twin economic and political crises thus created a window of opportunity for changing the political settlement, and the emergence of a new group of ruling elites led by Rawlings under the Provisional National Defense Council (PNDC) (Whitfield, 2018). The PNDC government got the country out of the economic impasse and restarted economic growth by implementing an Economic Recovery Programme (ERP) in 1983, followed by a structural adjustment programme (SAP) from 1986 to 1991 with support from the International Monetary Fund (IMF) and World Bank (WB) (Aryeetey and McKay, 2007: 147). The impacts of these reforms have been hailed as 'salutary' (Oelbaum, 2007: 15), especially with regards to restoring economic growth and macroeconomic stability.

Unlike previous military regimes, the PNDC was characterized by a large degree of cohesion among the higher-level factions of the ruling coalition, which enabled it to implement difficult economic reforms that previous regimes were too vulnerable to undertake (Whitfield et al., 2015). These high-level factions included: technocrats who were in charge of economic policy, and who came from the universities or had served in previous governments; a conservative wing, composed of traditional authorities and established elites, who were largely in charge of the political strategy after 1984; leaders of the 'revolutionary organs', who after 1984 had little political or policy influence; and so-called 'securocrats', who were responsible for security of the ruling coalition. Power became centralized around Rawlings, as the small group of PNDC elites owed their positions to him and had no independent power bases of their own (Whitfield, 2018). Meanwhile, the established political elites were seen as the major cause of the country's economic decline, and thus had little legitimacy with which to challenge the PNDC.

The PNDC government also had unprecedented financial support from the Bretton Woods institutions for undertaking its economic measures. Large aid inflows from the WB and IMF helped to buffer the impact of the reforms and softened the blow to the population of massive cuts in government expenditure and public sector employment, price increases, and currency devaluation. Foreign aid also allowed the PNDC government to increase 'development' spending that helped shore up its legitimacy among the population (Whitfield et al., 2015; Whitfield, 2018).

However, towards the end of the 1980s and in the early 1990s, the excluded political factions formed an alliance and increased pressure on the PNDC government to return to multiparty rule. Following the introduction of democratic local elections in 1988, in which newly created district assemblies were to be the highest authorities responsible for developmental decision making at the local level, Rawlings returned the country to multiparty democracy in 1992.[5] This marked a return to competitive clientelism in Ghana.

1.4 *Return to Competitive Clientelism: 1992–Present*

Following the return to multiparty democracy in 1992, a *de facto* two-party system emerged, in which the National Democratic Congress (NDC) and the New Patriotic Party (NPP) have dominated all elections. The NDC is the civilian metamorphosis of the PNDC, while the NPP has its roots in the Danquah-Busia political tradition, which evolved from the UGCC, the NLM, the United Party, and the Progress Party led by K. A. Busia during the Second Republic. In ideological terms, the NDC professes to be a social democratic and statist party that seeks to 'ensure optimum production and distributive justice' (NDC, 2004: 12), while the NPP regards itself as a pro-market party, and touts the private sector as the main engine of growth (NPP, 2012). The period from 1992 marked a return to competitive clientelism, in which these two dominant parties compete for electoral power. With each electoral cycle, the NDC and NPP have become increasingly competitive, and the margin of votes by which candidates win the presidency has been declining.

During the last decade and a half, power has alternated thrice between these two parties (in 2000, 2008, and 2016) with presidential elections sometimes won by a margin of less than 0.5 per cent of the total votes. Despite this equal strength, the party that wins elections monopolizes power and state resources, irrespective of the margin of its electoral victory. Consequently, each ruling coalition is characterized by a high degree of vulnerability, providing strong incentives for ruling elites across both parties to focus on short-term objectives of political survival. In this context, ruling elites often prioritize initiatives that can deliver immediate visible benefits in order to win the next election, while avoiding initiatives that have political costs, as with reforms concerning land ownership and the role of chiefs in land transactions.

The implications of competitive clientelism have been well discussed in the literature (e.g. see Oduro et al., 2014; Whitfield et al., 2015). Here, we focus on two issues that have had specific implications for natural resource governance. First, the increasingly competitive character of elections effectively undermines prospects for building a broad and enduring political consensus on a national development agenda. As a result, 'the national interest has become fragmented along party lines, with the result that each new administration has followed its own short-to-medium-term development agenda and spending priorities based on its party's election platform' (Gyimah-Boadi and Prempeh, 2012: 102). Second, securing and remaining in power has become an increasingly expensive endeavour. The increasingly competitive nature of elections has created large political financing needs, and the money 'invested' by party financiers and individual politicians needs to be 'recouped'. Recouping investments and refilling party coffers is typically done through kickbacks on state contracts awarded to party members, who in turn expect to be rewarded with political appointments or business contracts (Bob-Milliar, 2012). In the following section, we explore the ways in which these two dynamics have shaped the relationships between political leaders and mining companies, and the implications of this for the governance of the mining sector.

2 Political Settlements and Mining Governance over the *Longue Durée*

In this section, we discuss how mining governance has shifted in relation to the changing political settlements outlined in Section 1. We will show that while there are clearly causal relations to be drawn here, they are not direct. Thus, while mining governance has changed as a consequence of shifts from pre-colonial, to colonial, to early independence and neoliberally-oriented

Table 5.2. Periodization of political settlements in mining, Ghana

Time period	Dominant actors in shaping the settlement	Modes of inclusion in extractive industry
Pre-colonial period	Chiefs, clans, and families	Retention of one-third of mining proceeds by local populations
1874–1956: Colonial capitalism	British mining companies, chiefs	Employment in mines
1957–85: State dominance and the nationalization of mines	State-owned enterprises	Employment in mines
1986–2008: Liberalization of mines	Multinational corporations, Bretton Woods institutions, chiefs	Employment in mines
2009–16: Return to resource nationalism	Multinational corporations, Bretton Woods institutions, chiefs	Employment in mines; increased taxation and redistribution through social transfers; artisanal and small-scale mining (both legally and illegally); allocation to communities through Minerals Development Fund

Source: Authors' work.

settlements, the changes are not perfectly aligned in time. Furthermore, while competitive and clientelist-oriented logics have dominated much of the post-colonial period, they have been associated with quite distinct forms of mining governance. While changes in governance may represent responses to the pressures and incentives created by clientelism, their diversity shows also that ideas and international influences are as important as the nature of the settlement. Table 5.2 offers a summary of the periodization of political settlements in mining.

2.1 *Pre-Colonial Period: Chiefly Dominance over Mineralized Lands*

While it remains uncertain when gold mining commenced in Ghana, there is consensus that the local inhabitants were accustomed to gold mining long before the Portuguese arrived in 1471 (Arhin, 1967; Anin, 1994; Dumett, 1998; Hilson, 2002). At the centre of resource extraction and control during this period were chiefs and kings, who acted as trustees for the care of the land owned by all the people (Dumett, 1998: 16). During this period, any individual or group could mine gold almost everywhere they chose, so long as this was within the limits of their own lineage or stool lands (ibid.: 68). Stool land is collectively owned land held in trust by a collective authority, usually a chief, on behalf of an extended family, a clan, or a community of ancestrally related people.[6] Over the centuries, revenues from gold mining provided one of the most important building blocks for state formation and consolidation in all the important kingdoms in pre-colonial Ghana (ibid.: 41). Among the

Ashantis, in particular, gold became 'the mirror of kingship and imperial splendour and the nexus that undergirded the state, the social order, and the entire culture' (ibid.).

Dumett (1998) identified three main ways by which chiefs used their powers to extract surplus from gold mining. The first, and most prevalent, approach was the *abusa* share system, by which miners retained one-third of their proceeds and turned over one-third to the local chief, or stool, leaving the remaining third for the king or paramount ruler. The second was the direct power of political authorities to tax, which derived from both the traditional territorial controls of the ruler as well as from the kinship obligations of the people to him. At the peak of Asante power in the nineteenth century, major revenue sources included a poll tax, levied at the rate of one-tenth of an ounce of gold per man. The third was through a system of compulsory community labour,[7] when 'special days were set aside for all the citizens to mine solely on behalf of the paramount ruler' (Dumett, 1998: 71).

The overall evidence suggests that, whereas the political settlement on mining could be characterized as inclusive at the level of the elites, it remained generally exclusionary for the greater majority of the population in terms of the distribution of material benefits. Much of the available literature suggests that artisanal gold extraction in pre-colonial Ghana was not worth the effort expended. Analysing the returns from gold extraction vis-à-vis the efforts required, G. A. Robertson concluded that 'Working for gold was not a profitable form of employment' (Robertson, 1819, quoted in Dumett, 1998: 77). Although Dumett (1998) emphasizes the need to understand traditional mining as an income supplement for farmers outside of the farming season, he also draws attention to the generally exclusionary character of gold revenues in terms of its socio-economic relevance for the masses. In particular, he draws attention to instances when 'chiefs . . . might enter a mining district any time they chose and, in total defiance of the *abusa* share and legitimate taxation systems, forcibly confiscate all gold dust and gold jewellery possessed by miners and their families' (Dumett, 1998: 75–6).

Writing specifically on the Asante Kingdom, Arhin (1978: 97) similarly concludes that 'gold mining and trading did not have as much developmental effect on Ashanti society and economy as could have been expected from the amount of wealth' accumulated via gold extraction, in part because much of gold revenues were 'used in the building of state power, a means of further wealth-acquisition by the Ashanti state'. Moreover, a large portion of the gold acquired from taxation was used for the refinement of chiefs' regalia which, in the cultural milieu of the historic period, was a means of social and political control. As will be see in Subsection 4.2.2, this problem has persisted right through to the present, with some chiefs continuing to use their share of mineral royalties on themselves and their palaces.

2.2 *Colonial Capitalism and the Subtle Decline in Chiefly Powers, 1874–1956*

The advent of colonialism and expatriate-led capitalism catalysed significant changes in the relationship between the political settlements and mining governance, in part because it marked the beginning of the commercialization of mineralized lands and the subtle decline in chiefly control over such lands. Following an extensive period of stagnant gold production—a direct result of the 200-year slave trade—European interest in Gold Coast gold was suddenly renewed in the 1870s. Following the mass gold rushes in the early 1880s, significant European capital was invested in the Gold Coast Colony and Ashanti, as hundreds of buyers applied for land concessions.[8] The period from 1892 to 1901 has been characterized as Ghana's first 'Jungle Boom', when some 400 newly established companies invested £40 million to develop gold mining properties. Between 1901 and 1902, gold production in the Gold Coast increased 400 per cent, as investors began withdrawing interests from South Africa during the Boer War of 1899–1902 (Hilson, 2002: 22).

One serious consequence of the gold rush associated with colonial capitalism was 'the commercialization of stool lands, which resulted in inter-village boundary disputes that threatened the stability of the state' (Ofosu-Mensah, 2016: 32). For Dumett (1998: 272), this movement towards the commercialization of land was 'the most disruptive dimension to the encroachment of Western capitalism on the traditional economy and society of southwestern Ghana', not least as paramount rulers, sub-chiefs, and village headmen soon learned to attach money values to lands believed to contain gold-bearing soil.[9] Partly because of the absence of landmarks to clearly distinguish land boundaries, access to mining leases triggered waves of litigation between competing traditional landlords.

A related issue was the slow deterioration in the authority of chiefs. Dumett (1998: 175) identifies three converging forces that contributed to the erosion of traditional authority structures during the colonial period: (1) slowly diminishing respect for coastal chiefs as a long-term aspect of colonial rule and westernization; (2) further fragmentation of chiefly power in the interior amid the lure of payoffs by European prospectors and African middlemen as a consequence of concession leasing; and, finally (3) arbitrary actions by the colonial government, such as the occasional destoolment of 'recalcitrant' chiefs. The commercialization of mineralized lands complicated these patterns. While some chiefs gained in wealth and power through the very considerable leverage placed at their disposal by the lease of mineral properties to Europeans (Dumett, 1998: 75), others suffered from a loss of authority and control. Under Akan law, the leasing of mineral lands fell mainly under the powers of chiefs (the *ahenfo)*, enabling them to increase their powers and wealth from expatriate mining leaseholders. In contrast, the paramount rulers (or *omanhene*) saw far too few of the returns from concessions leasing, and they increasingly complained that their traditional political powers and roles in decision making had been 'eroded or bypassed' (Dumett, 1998: 273).

Overall, however, it was the capitalist expatriate companies 'who had become the real dispensers of wealth and fonts of authority' from the gold trade, along with some African coastal concessions middlemen—like Joseph Dawson—who sometimes doubled as advisers to the kings and chiefs (Dumett, 1998: 275). That European mining companies were the main beneficiaries of gold mining during this period is supported by the significant pressure they exerted on the colonial government to create an environment conducive to their operations, through both the provision of infrastructure and a regulatory framework.[10] As Tsikata (1997: 9) notes, the interests of British mining companies had a significant influence on the formulation and implementation of mineral policy in colonial Ghana. For example, the passage of the Mercury Ordinance Law of 1933—which banned the use of mercury in mining activities—was facilitated by British mining companies at home, who pressured both the colonial office in London and the Gold Coast governor to create opportunities for their entry into the Colony. With the use of mercury banned, mining activities by local populations were impaired. This in turn weakened the control of chiefs because they lost leverage in terms of labour demands (Tsuma, 2010: 12). That this new law effectively criminalized small-scale mining also meant that it contributed to the exclusion of significant segments of rural populations in terms of the distribution of mineral wealth.

Yet until the mid-1890s, the colonial administration stoutly resisted programmes for revenue-supported education and public health measures on behalf of the local populations, on the grounds that such expenditures would saddle the colonial treasury with huge debts (Dumett, 1998: 278). Where public investments were undertaken, as in the areas of infrastructure provision, these were often done to help facilitate further resource extraction, with the result that areas without substantial mineral and other resources of interest to the colonial state were excluded. This is the origin of the contemporary north–south inequalities in Ghana in which the north has remained much poorer (Abdulai, 2012, 2017).

2.3 *Post-independence Reforms and the Nationalization of Mines: 1957–85*

After colonial rule, most independent African governments engaged in a process of assuming total sovereignty and control over their natural resources and economies more broadly. In addition, all four countries discussed in this book experienced a nationalization of mining operations in this general time period. In Ghana, the period 1957–86 was characterized by active state involvement in the mining industry and other sectors of the economy. Following a series of laws in the early 1960s, nearly all mining companies were fully nationalized, and the State Gold Mining Corporation (SGMC) was established in 1961 to take over existing mines. Various post-independent ruling coalitions justified this 'nationalization project' on the grounds of generating mass employment and providing maximum access to the foreign exchange obtained through the sale of minerals (Tsikata, 1997).

One challenge faced, however, was the question of how to deal with the enduring control of chiefs over mineral-rich lands. As already noted, despite a series of direct and indirect factors that contributed to the erosion of chiefs' authority during the colonial period, rural areas remained largely under their dominion at the end of colonial rule. Yet within the overall framework of centralizing decision making and gaining total sovereignty over valuable natural resources, the first post-independent government under Nkrumah embraced the colonial mining legislation that vested all mineral-rich lands in the hands of the colonial governor.

In 1962, the CPP-led Nkrumah government passed the Minerals Act (Act 126), which vested the ownership of minerals in '... the President on behalf of the Republic and in trust for the People of Ghana' (Tsikata, 1997: 10). This provision has found itself in various Ghanaian constitutions since 1969 and has also been repeated in statutes such as the Minerals and Mining Law of 1986 and subsequent amendments in 1993 and 2006. The Minerals Act and Administration of Lands Act (Act 123), both passed in 1962, also gave the executive substantial powers to decide upon the use and management of all lands, including those owned by a community presided over by a chief, known as 'stool lands'. These laws further provided that payments in respect of stool lands be made, not directly to the representatives of the owning community, but to the sector minister, who would allocate portions for 'the maintenance of the traditional authority, projects for the benefit of the people of the area, and the local government bodies of the area' (Tsikata, 1997). This arrangement has remained essentially the same today, with only very marginal changes.

This era of state-owned mining witnessed a significant deterioration in Ghana's economic situation, as the protectionist policies of various governments strangled investments in the country's export sector more generally. Lack of public and private investments left the state-run mines uncompetitive. As a result, the SGMC was operating at a loss and had to close down most of its operations. By 1982, gold output had declined to 232,000 oz—approximately one quarter of the 1960 output (900,000 oz). The importance of the mineral sector to the wider economy declined accordingly and, in

1982, the sector's share of GDP was 0.3 per cent, down from 2.5 per cent in 1968 (Addy, 1998: 234).

2.4 *Structural Adjustment and the Rise of Multinational Corporations, 1986–2008*

While the 1982 PNDC government clearly marked a new political settlement, it was only the pressures of deteriorating economic conditions and 'the political imperatives of regime survival'[11] that led the quasi-military ruling elites to shift clearly to a neoliberal agenda and adopt structural adjustment in 1986. As part of the SAP reforms, the country took IMF and WB loans with conditionalities that included the privatization of the extractive industry. Of the several policy initiatives adopted to revive the mining sector during this period, the most significant was the promulgation of the Minerals and Mining Law (PNDC Law 153 of 1986), which, among other things, established a Minerals Commission to regulate the sector, liberalized the mining regime, and extended significant new benefits to private investors. The content of this law was driven significantly by the WB's continent-wide strategy on mining (Akabzaa and Darimani, 2001; Akabzaa, 2009), which described the facilitation of private investment as 'the main objective of donor intervention in African mining' (World Bank, 1992: xii).

The new mining law provided a number of extensive tax incentives to foreign mining investors, including generous capital and investment allowances that permitted 80 per cent of total investment to be written off in the first year. Mining companies could also maintain negotiated levels of their gross minerals sales in offshore accounts. These measures, coupled with a rise in gold prices, sparked substantial new interest in the Ghanaian mining sector: more than fifty-five gold prospecting licences were issued between 1986 and 1989 (Campbell, 1998, cited in Hutchful, 2002: 83). These reforms resulted in significant increases in mineral outputs (see Figure 5.1), enabling gold exports to regain prominence in the overall national economy. Between 1984 and 1995, gold exports as a percentage of total exports increased from 22 per cent to 45 per cent (Tsuma, 2010: 23). However, this period did not witness greater inclusivity in Ghanaian society, with regional, gender, and rural–urban inequalities actually increasing throughout the 1990s (Ghana Statistical Service, 2007). Nor did mining seem to have made any significant impact on poverty reduction in mining-affected communities. One WB internal evaluation report reads:

> A field visit to Wassa District, which contains the largest share of Ghana's mines, confirmed the competition between mining and agriculture for arable land, the poor state of local infrastructure, inadequate public services, and high

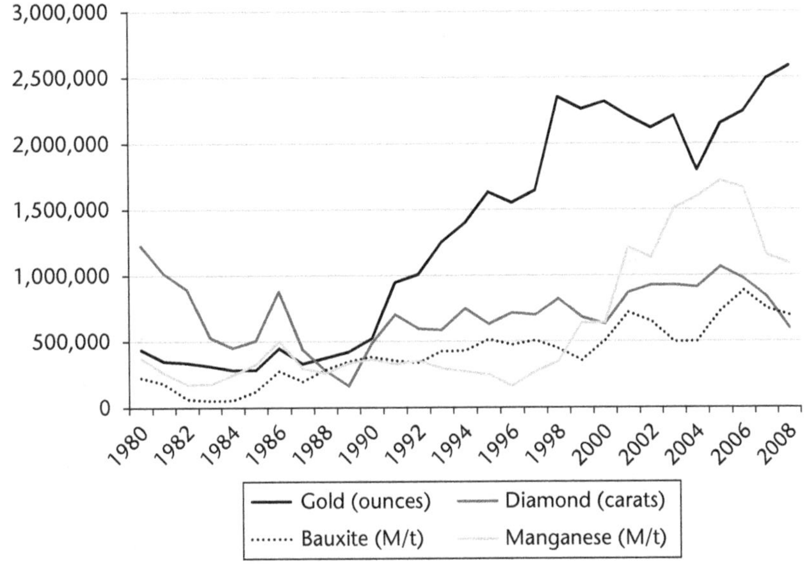

Figure 5.1. Key mineral production trends, 1980–2008
Source: Based on raw data from the Minerals Commission, Accra.

> unemployment. The local economy in Wassa does not appear to have benefited from large-scale mining through sustained economic growth and improved public services. . . Local people feel no perceptible benefit from the resources extracted from 'their' land. (World Bank, 2003: 20)

The surge in multinational investment in the mining sector was accompanied by a significant shift from underground to surface mining (see Map 5.1 for the distribution of different types mining licence by 2014). Because surface mining requires the acquisition of large tracts of land, this led to heightened competition over land between companies and local residents. The late 1980s and early 1990s therefore marked the beginning of increased agitation from dissatisfied residents in mining communities.[12] At the same time, the capital-intensive nature of large-scale mining meant that very few local people could gain employment in the new mining economy.

By the late 1980s, the problem of land-use conflicts arising from local community resistance had resulted in the promulgation of three laws aimed at bringing artisanal and small-scale (ASM) gold mining into the official economy. In 1989, and as part of the SAP reforms, the Small-Scale Gold Mining Law (PNDC Law 218), the Mercury Law (PNDC Law 217), and the Precious Minerals Marketing Corporation Law (PNDC Law 219) were passed, all in an attempt to legalize and regularize the previously illegal ASM sector.[13] Under PNDC Law 218, artisanal miners could apply for a concession of a maximum of 25 acres in designated areas, and then obtain a licence to mine

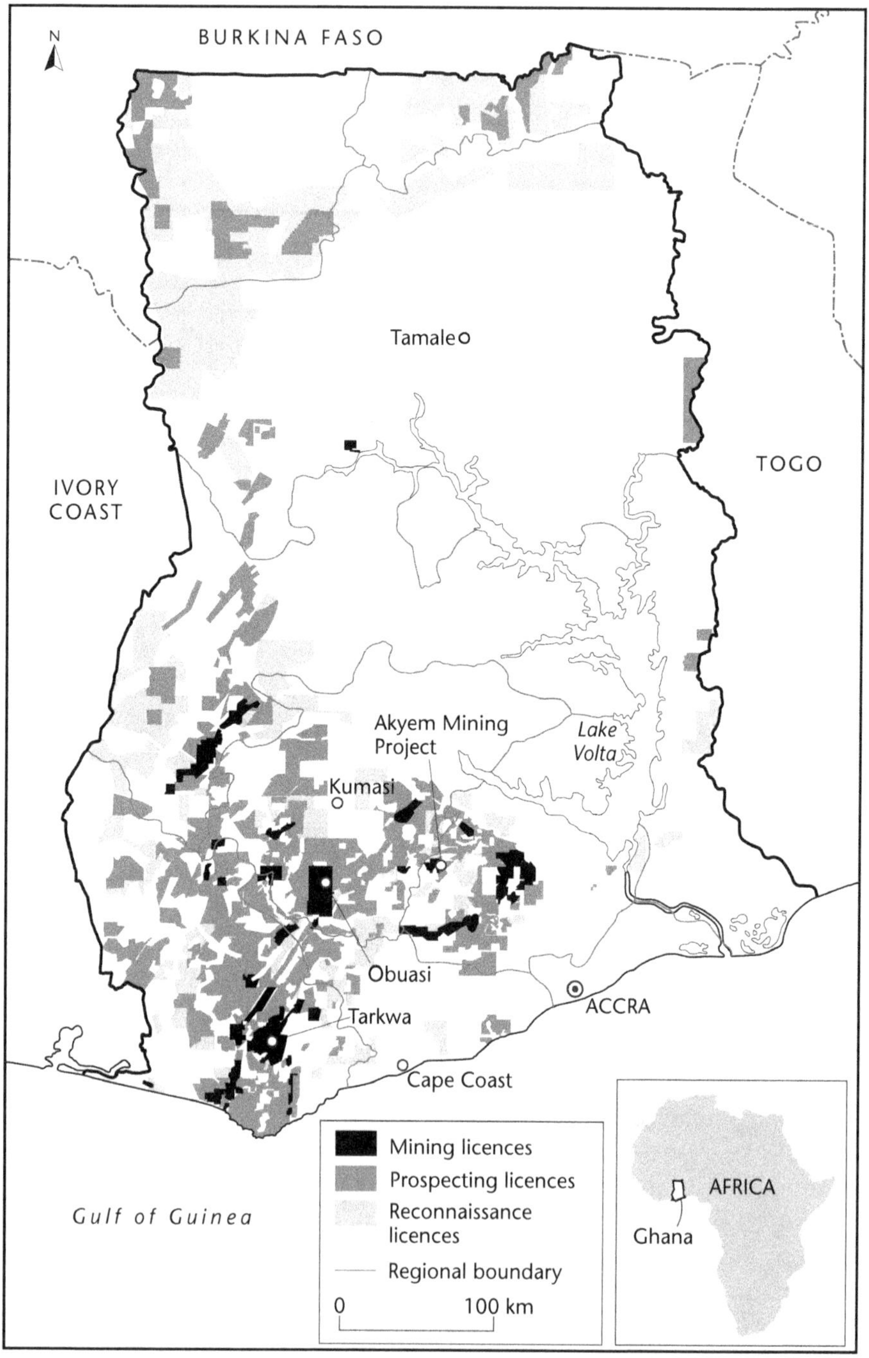

Map 5.1. Geographical distribution of mining licences in Ghana, 2014
Source: Oxfam America (2014).

through the Minerals Commission. The Mercury Law legalized the purchase of mercury from authorized sellers for purposes of gold production, while PNDC Law 219 established the Precious Minerals Marketing Company (PMMC) to provide a market for small-scale mined gold (Tsikata, 1997). Prior to this, most gold produced by ASM operators was smuggled to neighbouring countries (Addy, 1998; Teschner, 2012).

The 1986 law remained the substantive legislation for the mining sector until its replacement in 2006. Here again, the influence of transnational ideas and actors was very significant. After more than a decade of its implementation, multinational mining companies and international financial institutions (particularly the WB) began to express dissatisfaction with the 1986 mining code, arguing that it could not compete with those of other mineral-endowed African countries, and that Ghana was losing investment to countries such as Tanzania, Guinea, and Mali, which had far more liberal codes. Thus, in 2001, Ghana contracted consultants to review its mining code with the objective of staying internationally competitive (Akabzaa, 2009). The World Bank (2008: 32) described the resulting 2006 Mining Act as 'more investment friendly... in line with international best practices in the industry'. For example, the corporate income tax rate was reduced from 35 per cent to 25 per cent, while an additional profit tax[14] of 35 per cent was scrapped altogether. One consequence was that when mining companies began to make supernormal profits following rising commodity prices from the mid-2000s onwards, there was no legal basis for imposing additional taxes on them, and the government's attempt to introduce a new windfall tax backfired.

The passage of this more liberal 2006 mining code was relatively straightforward during the administrations of the NPP government under President Kufuor (2001–08), given the closeness of its 'property-owning democracy' ideology to the World Bank's pro-business ideological perspective, coupled with the relative absence of a sustained and systematic challenge from Ghanaian civil society. Akabzaa (2009) notes that although the consultative processes leading up to the new act involved several actors within the mining industry—including the Chamber of Mines, traditional rulers, a representative of small-scale miners, and the Third World Network, which represented the National Coalition of NGOs in Mining (NCOM)—the uneven power relations among these actors resulted in domination by the mining companies. Thus, whereas the draft act included several proposals that were submitted to parliament by various civic actors, subsequent 'behind the scenes consultations changed the fortunes of the concerned community and civil society groups' (Akabzaa, 2009: 39).

While the privatizations of this period involved direct negotiation between multinationals as investors, and the state as the owner of the subsoil, parallel developments involved direct negotiations between chiefs and ASM operators. Indeed, the continuing influence of chiefs over land has given rise to parallel systems of mineral licensing in Ghana—one formal (granted by the state to large-scale mining companies) and the other informal (granted mainly by chiefs to illegal small-scale operators [Nyame and Blocher, 2010; see also Section 5]). Under the present arrangements, though all minerals are vested in the president, much of the gold-bearing lands remain firmly under the control of traditional councils. This dichotomy between land rights and mineral rights has posed significant challenges for controlling illegal mining activities in Ghana, as illegal operators continue to obtain lands from chiefs and other customary owners for their operations, a point to which we return later.[15]

2.5 *A Return to Resource Nationalism? 2009–16*

The period from 2009 to 2016 may be characterized as a return to the resource nationalism of the early post-independence reforms. This time, however, the government resorted to various fiscal reforms that encouraged private mine ownership to earn more revenue from natural resource extraction. In 2009, the NDC government introduced a National Fiscal Stabilization Levy, which imposed an additional 5 per cent levy on the profits (before tax) of companies in certain industries, including mining. This was soon followed by an amendment to the Mining Act in 2010, The Minerals and Mining (Amendment) Act (Act 794), which provided for a fixed 5 per cent royalty rate across the board and abolished the sliding 3–6 per cent scale provided in the 2006 Mining Code. However, the most radical reforms were announced in the 2012 national budget statement, which proposed to increase the corporate tax rate by 10 per cent (i.e. to 35 per cent) and install a new windfall tax of 10 per cent. A seven-member Mining Review Committee was also established to review all mining agreements that were deemed detrimental to the national interest.

The boom in commodity prices was the most significant driver of these fiscal reforms.[16] With rising commodity prices (see Figure 5.2), concerns over the national interest were widely held up as a key political justification for many of the newly proposed policy reforms. In presenting the 2010 budget statement, the finance minister expressed concern that foreign multinational companies had responded to the price hikes in gold by increasing production, but without a corresponding contribution to government revenue (Republic of Ghana, 2009: 19).

> The issue with mining is about fair and transparent sharing of the benefits and windfall gains from the exploitation of the country's precious and irreplaceable natural resources... [D]uring the recent global financial crisis, prices of gold, cocoa

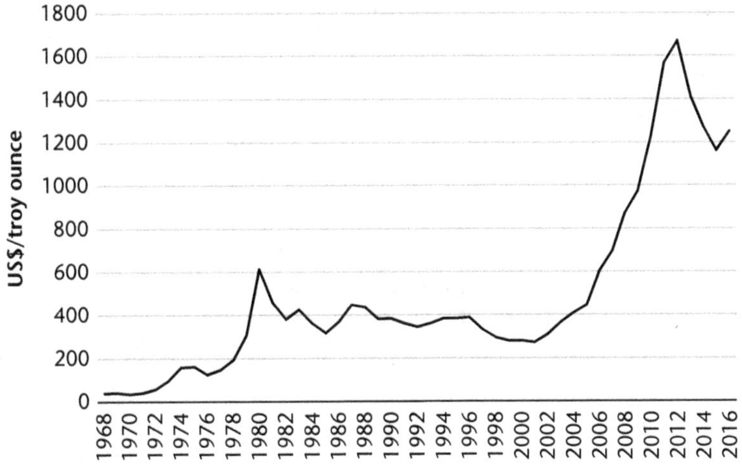

Figure 5.2. World gold price (US$/troy ounce), 1968–2016. Price based on 99.5% fine, afternoon fixing, London
Source: UNCTADSTAT (2017).

> and oil reached their peak levels ever. Yet, the country did not benefit at all from the price hikes . . . The Government has, therefore, taken a bold step to critically review the fiscal regimes and mining agreements, with the view to ensuring that the country benefits adequately and fairly from the gains in the mining sector. (Republic of Ghana, 2011: 54).

A second important explanation relates to changes in transnational support and ideas, with both the World Bank and the IMF openly supportive of the government's initiatives. As the Chief Director of the Ministry of Energy and Petroleum told us in an interview, 'this time, the IMF and the World Bank were rather actually on the side of government'. The soaring gold prices triggered calls on the government from even the traditional architects of the liberalized mining regimes (i.e. the World Bank and the IMF) to raise certain taxes in order to maximize the benefits of resource extraction (National Coalition on Mining, 2011). In 2011, the head of the IMF mission in Ghana, Christina Daseking, specifically recommended that Ghanaian authorities explore ways of improving tax revenues from the mining sector, stating that the fund 'supported adoption of additional tax policy measures, particularly in the area of natural resources' (Quandzie, 2011).[17]

There is also evidence to suggest that the new tax reforms were reflective of, and partly driven by, the social democratic philosophy of the NDC ruling coalition and the party's recognition of 'distributive justice' as an important guiding principle for its approach to governance (NDC, 2004). As far back as 2008, when the party was in opposition, it emphasized the need to redefine the role of mining in the national development agenda.

Specifically, it highlighted the need to 'optimise national benefits or retained earnings from mining investment in the country' by'[s]trengthen [ing] the mining fiscal regime to capture more rent for the state and mining communities through greater State carried interest, higher royalties and more realistic resource rent-based taxation' (NDC, 2008: 58).[18] That these pledges were made by a party in opposition makes it difficult to interpret such pronouncements as purely instrumental attempts to secure greater mining revenues to address fiscal constraints and gain re-election. Importantly, these pledges differed substantially from those of the more pro-business NPP ruling coalition at the time, whose 2008 election manifesto pledged to further cut corporate taxes in order 'to encourage and support businesses' (NPP, 2008: 6). This analysis suggests that responses to resource booms are driven not only by the degree of stability/vulnerability of ruling coalitions (Poteete, 2009), but also by the ideological orientation of dominant elites within such coalitions.

That said, most interviewees suggested that material interests played a more significant role in motivating the new tax reforms than the ideological orientation of the NDC ruling coalition. According to one interviewee in the Ministry of Lands and Natural Resources, at the peak of the mining boom, 'the government was in a tight corner and needed money; they needed to come up with a way of dealing with the fiscal gaps'. With mining increasingly replacing cocoa as the 'cash cow' of successive ruling elites, the interviewee asserted that 'the government didn't have any other option than to look at the natural resources sector'. The respondent further noted that it was this overriding need for cash that explained why the reforms were initiated and championed by the Finance Ministry rather than the Ministry of Lands and Natural Resources, which has a direct mandate over mining activities.

Implementation of the government's proposed reforms was patchy, however, with the windfall tax not implemented at all, due partly to intense pressure from mining companies.[19] At the 2014 World Economic Forum in Davos, the Ghanaian president at the time, John Dramani Mahama, noted that his government's suspension of the windfall tax was based on companies' threats to cut off jobs and shift their production investments to other countries: 'They threatened to lay off workers if we implemented the windfall tax and because we needed the jobs and you don't want workers laid off you are coerced to go along' (*Ghanaian Chronicle*, 2014). Some key industry actors also attribute the suspension of the windfall tax mainly to 'bad timing' (Aryee, 2014), in that just when the government began to introduce it, gold prices began to dip, undermining the government's argument for the tax (ibid.). The fact that other African countries (e.g. Mali) were reducing tax rates at the same time 'put additional restraining pressures on the government's reform directions' (ibid.).

This said, as shown in Table 5.3, it is important to note that the 10 per cent increase in the corporate tax rate and the 5 per cent royalty rate have been effectively implemented since 2012, contributing to improved government revenues from mining. However, the table also shows that as gold prices started to decline from 2013 onwards, government revenues from corporate income taxes, as well as the mining sector's overall contributions to revenues collected by the Ghana Revenue Authority (GRA), also began to dwindle, even as gold output remained fairly high and continued to increase until 2015. This underscores how global commodity price fluctuations can place major strains on the public finances of resource-dependent countries like Ghana, with potential implications for the development imaginaries of ruling elites. As one of our respondents aptly put it: 'Ghana depends so much on the mining sector that as soon as prices of minerals fluctuate, our budget has to.'[20]

The period of the boom coincided with increased government revenue from mining and significant declines in the incidence of poverty and extreme poverty in Ghana. Indeed, by the early 2010s, the mining sector contributed 37 per cent of export revenues and 19 per cent of all direct tax payments, making it the largest tax paying sector in the Ghanaian economy (Ghana Chamber of Mines and ICMM, 2015). Meanwhile, between 2006 and 2013, the estimated national poverty rate fell from 31.9 per cent to 24.2 per cent, while extreme poverty declined from 16.5 per cent to 8.4 per cent during the same period. These reductions enabled Ghana to emerge as the first country in sub-Saharan Africa to meet the first target of the Millennium Development Goals, of halving extreme poverty by 2015. The three poorer northern regions in particular made substantial progress in poverty reduction, which translated into a reduction of regional income inequalities during this period (see Table 5.4). However, there remain significant disparities in poverty levels

Table 5.3. Gold production and government revenue from mining (GH₵, 2005–15)

Year	Gold production (ounces)	Royalty	Corporate tax	PAYE	Total mining contribution to GRA	% Mining to total GRA
2005	2,149,372	23,595	26,988.96	19,405,894	72,285,749	11.21
2006	2,244,680	31,625	40,436.18	21,652,578	74,822,760	10.20
2007	2,486,821	40,882	47,415,690	34,587,597	123,021,866	14.42
2008	2,585,993	59,005	73,554,697	47,139,242	179,978,383	15.32
2009	2,930,328	90,416	124,600,880	103,061,985	319,022,676	18.21
2010	2,970,080	144,697	241,578,780	132,469,710	519,682,174	21.29
2011	2,924,385	222,024	649,902,536	161,822,107	1,034,221,712	27.61
2012	3,166,483	359,392,853	893,773,828	207,495,934	1,461,202,977	27.04
2013	3,192,648	364,673,038	518,545,259	220,131,571	1,104,047,315	18.71
2014	3,167,755	470,356,949	441,235,059	259,459,815	1,172,117,330	15.38
2015	2,848,574	485,632,657	463,128,598	404,743,477	1,354,379,971	14.90

Source: Data from the Minerals Commission, Accra; see also Ghana Chamber of Mines (2016).

Table 5.4. Poverty trends in Ghana's poorer northern regions and the country as a whole, 2005–13

	Poverty incidence (% of population)		Extreme poverty incidence (% of population)	
	2005/06	2012/13	2005/06	2012/13
Northern	55.7	50.4	36.1	22.8
Upper East	72.9	44.4	56.9	21.3
Upper West	89.1	70.7	76.0	45.1
Ghana	**31.9**	**24.2**	**16.5**	**8.4**

Source: Ghana Statistical Service (2014).

between different socio-economic groups, rural and urban areas, and the three historically poorer northern regions and the rest of the country.

Whether the growth in mining revenues contributed to this trend is, however, an entirely different question. Direct causality between mining and inclusive development is difficult to establish, because mining revenues in Ghana are not set aside for specific development investments but are instead channelled directly into the consolidated fund for general budgetary support. However, the available evidence suggests that the increased revenues from mining, along with the commencement of commercial oil production in 2010, did influence the developmental imaginaries of the ruling elites. This is evidenced in the introduction of several special social intervention programmes aimed at increasing public expenditure on initiatives targeted at the poorest and the most vulnerable. Much of the recent poverty reduction in Ghana has been attributed largely to high GDP growth rates supported by increased government development expenditure. In particular, specific interventions, such as the launch of the Savannah Accelerated Development Authority (SADA) in 2010 and the Livelihood Empowerment against Poverty (LEAP), have helped to reduce poverty in the poorer northern regions.[21] With a goal of doubling incomes of northern Ghanaians and reducing the incidence of poverty to 20 per cent within twenty years (Government of Ghana, 2010), SADA has been widely recognized as the most comprehensive effort towards the reduction of the north–south developmental disparities in Ghana's history. The LEAP is Ghana's flagship cash transfer programme that provides bimonthly cash benefits for extremely poor families which also have at least one member that is elderly (those above sixty-five years), disabled and unable to work, or an orphan or vulnerable child (OVC). Figure 5.3 shows the budgetary allocations to LEAP between 2010 and 2016.

We are not suggesting here that mining revenues have always been expended in ways that help reduce poverty and inequality in Ghana. On the contrary, the distribution of power in Ghanaian society and the competitive clientelism that it produces have significantly undermined the effective utilization of mining

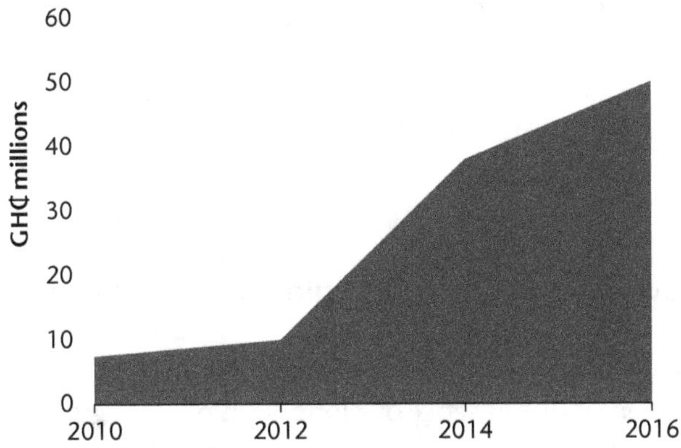

Figure 5.3. Budgetary allocations (GH₵ millions) to LEAP, 2010–16
Source: MOFEP (2017), NDPC (2017).

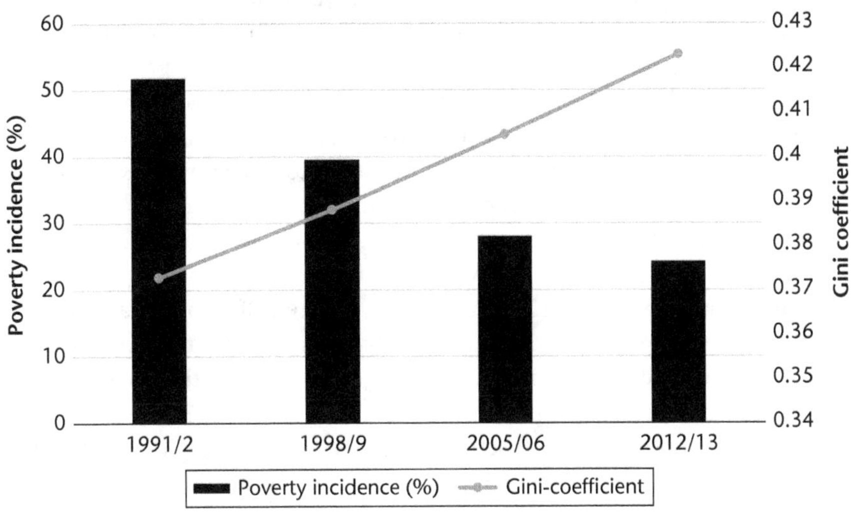

Figure 5.4. Poverty and inequality trends, Ghana, 1991–2013
Source: Government of Ghana (2014: 18).

revenues for fostering greater inclusion and for the pursuit of the national interest more broadly (see also the next section). For example, while greater access to mineral revenues might have enabled the government to launch a number of social intervention programmes, most of these, including the LEAP, suffer from politically motivated poor targeting, benefiting the better-off far more than the poorest (Jones et al., 2009; Wodon, 2012; Debrah, 2013; Abdulai and Hulme, 2015; Abdulai and Hickey, 2016). As shown in Figure 5.4, whereas overall poverty levels fell by 27.5 percentage points between 1991/92 and

2012/13, Ghana's Gini coefficient has consistently been increasing since the early 1990s. The government of Ghana acknowledges these rising levels of inequality as a major problem, describing it as 'a dangerous sign that the poverty reduction effort is not being properly targeted at those who need it most' (Government of Ghana, 2012: 22).

3 Competitive Clientelism and Mining Sector Governance

Most Ghanaian scholars attribute the limited impact of mining on broad-based development to the absence of a long-term plan for guiding the efficient utilization of mineral rents. It is argued that policy reforms have focused almost exclusively on revenue generation from mining, but 'without a policy for long-term investment' (Ayee et al., 2011: 36). Mineral rents have often been expended in a way that 'does not recognize the need to convert mineral revenues into long-term physical and human capital' (Ghana Chamber of Mines and ICMM, 2015: 51). In addition, as one interviewee noted, the government often '[collects] mineral royalty in cash and... [spends] it in the next budget'.[22] This leaves the mining sector as an 'economic enclave' (Akabzaa, 2009: 51; Bloch and Owusu, 2012). These dynamics are indicative of a competitive clientelist settlement, a designation which helps to explain Ghana's natural resource governance over time.

Elite commitment to investing mineral wealth in long-term development is shaped by the degree of stability/vulnerability of ruling coalitions (Poteete, 2009). In competitive clientelist settlements, where ruling political elites feel that they are unlikely to stay in power long enough to reap the benefits of accumulated investments, incentives are geared towards the use of mineral rents in securing short-term political gains. As Levy (2014: 35) reminds us, a competitive clientelist political settlement is based on a credible prospect of power alternation such that 'whichever faction is in power is likely to have a short time horizon'. Ghanaian politics has developed into a highly competitive and antagonistic game, in which each round of elections has seen one of the two dominant parties 'horizontally excluded' from power. Ruling coalitions, therefore, tend to be confronted by high levels of horizontal opposition of the powerful elite bloc left out of power. This political context incentivizes political elites to focus on initiatives that enhance prospects for their short-term political survival.

Whitfield (see Whitfield et al., 2015; Whitfield, 2011a, 2011b, 2018) has shown how this form of politics has rendered Ghana's quest for structural transformation elusive during the past several decades. She shows that political survival strategies have included distributive, consumption-driven expenditures designed to deliver resources and economic opportunities to higher and lower level factions of the ruling coalition, as well as visible goods and services to as much of the population as possible, in an effort to 'swing' voters their way. Whitfield notes that these expenditures depleted the wealth of the country without reproducing it, much less expanding it. She further argues that one consequence of these actions has been the absence of sustained political commitment to developing the productive sectors of the economy, which are critical for structural transformation and broad-based development.

These dynamics are particularly evident in the absence of a long-term development plan, in both the mining sector and the economy as a whole. One key industry observer interviewed for this project noted:

> Do we even have a long-term vision for the whole country? We don't... The winner-takes-all factor in our politics makes it necessary for everybody to think about the short-term political interest—that is, his political survival, party, and his interest—and as a result, does not look beyond an electioneering period.

Another interviewee, in the Ministry of Lands and Natural Resources, explained the challenge of a mining-led development in Ghana in terms of discrepancies relating to 'governments' short-term views versus the long-term view of mining'. He elaborated the point as follows:

> You have a mine which will probably operate for 20–50 years... You have the potential to ensure that it interfaces with the rest of the economy and creates an economic activity which is much bigger than the mine itself... Yet you elect a government which is going to be in place for four to eight years, maximum. If you are in charge of that government, what will you do? You are looking for benefits now to help you run your government; you are not looking for creating a base for your opponents to come and take the benefits.

Thus, while a national mining policy was fully drafted in 1994, it was not actually launched until 2016. The interviewee noted that this apparent lack of elite commitment towards a long-term development vision for mining has meant that regulatory frameworks within the industry have rarely been accompanied by a policy to guide day-to-day implementation:

> When you have natural resources, your long-term vision is important. Once you have your long-term vision, you now look at the policy that will take you to your long-term vision. Your policy will have specific objectives. These objectives will be pursued by the laws you put in place. And then you have regulations which will detail out how the various provisions in the law are to be interpreted and applied. But here is the case: in the mining sector, we have [had] a Minerals and Mining Act passed in 2006. We are in 2014, and what we have is a draft mining policy. So, we put the act in place before thinking about policy. So, all this while, what policy objectives has the law been pursuing?

Circumstances are similar in the hydrocarbons sector. Indeed, the Petroleum Revenue Management Act (PRMA) requires that spending of oil revenues be guided by a medium-term framework aligned with a long-term national development plan. Yet after seven years of commercial oil production, such a plan remains absent, allowing the continuous discretionary utilization of petroleum revenues by ruling political elites. Recent and ongoing attempts by the National Development Planning Commission (NDPC) to launch a legally-binding forty year development plan were initially met with stiff opposition from the two main political parties, on the grounds that such a plan would constrain their ability to implement their party manifestos. Kwesi Botchwey, then Chairman of the NDPC, recalled how a government white paper 'had attempted to sideline the call for long-term development planning', and President Mahama subsequently insisted that any such 'long-term development plan . . . must have a flexibility to accommodate political and ideological orientations' (Joy Online, 2015).

The preference for a high level of discretion for politicians in Ghana is also evident in the negotiation of mining agreements and in the allocation of mining licences. Under Ghana's mining laws, the minister has the power to 'negotiate, grant, revoke, suspend or renew mineral rights' (Minerals and Mining Act, 2006, Section 5[1]). Mineral licences are to be issued to companies 'in the form and conditions determined by the minister' (ibid., Section 6[3]), who also has the powers to enter into stability agreements with mining companies. Holders of such stability agreements are to be insulated from subsequent changes relating to the payment of customs or other duties, royalty rates, taxes, fees, and other fiscal imports, as well as laws relating to exchange control, transfer of capital, and dividend remittance for a period of up to fifteen years (ibid., Section 48).

Such powers have enabled the minister to enter into what some deem highly questionable agreements with mining companies, as with fiscal stability agreements with Newmont Ghana and AngloGold Ashanti during the 2000s, which give the two companies (which together account for two-fifths of total gold output: Boakye et al., 2012: 12) protected tax benefits. Thus, although the mining law pegs royalty payments on a sliding scale of 3–6 per cent, Newmont's stability agreement fixes its gross royalties on gold production at the lowest allowable rate of 3.0 per cent.[23] Companies without stability agreements now have a corporate tax rate of 35 per cent, compared to a ceiling of 32.5 per cent set in Newmont's agreement with the government. The company is also exempted from the payment of value-added tax (VAT) on all items it imports, and for all foreign and locally purchased services and supplies, to the extent that they are used in connection with operations. Moreover, contrary to the provisions of the Mining Code, which mandates a minimum 10 per cent equity stake for the state, the Ghanaian government has no stake in Newmont's operations.

Available evidence also suggests that the signing of such confidential stability agreements tends to occur during or just prior to election years. A further example from the oil sector is the 'scandalously generous' (Phillips et al., 2016: 30) deal with Kosmos Energy in 2004, which many believe was meant to generate kickbacks for allies in the Kufuor-led NPP ruling coalition. Industry analysts estimated that the Kosmos contract would mean the government would lose US$3.8 billion in tax revenues over the lifespan of the West Cape Three Points oil block, in comparison to Tullow Oil's terms for the adjacent Deepwater Tano block (Wood Mackenzie 2012, cited in Phillips et al., 2016). Ayee et al. (2011) also argue that overgenerous concessions granted to some mining companies may have been granted 'as a reward for political support and financial kickbacks' (2011: 21). These observations need to be understood within the context of the highly competitive form of patron–client electoral politics in Ghana, where 'big business interests seem to be particularly strong, with their influence deriving from personal relationships and the funding of political campaigns' (World Bank, 2009: 28).

A final indication of the clientelist nature of relations between state institutions and mining companies stems from a Mining Review Committee chaired by Professor Akilapka Sawyer. The government established the seven-member committee following resistance by some mining companies (specifically those with stability agreements) to the government's decision to raise taxes in the mining sector. The tasks of the committee were to review and renegotiate any part of the stability agreements between the country and mining companies and redesign existing or draft agreements to ensure that they yielded better social and economic returns for the state.

In 2013, Sawyer hinted that the committee was facing significant difficulties because of the nature of the relationships between the state and mining companies involved. He noted that 'the Committee has realised that the government at times raises resources from some mining companies and that such relationships have affected their negotiation' (*Daily Express*, 2013). These observations give some credence to suspicions that competitive clientelism has meant that the tendency of political leaders to bypass bureaucrats in mineral resource contractual processes in order to reach politically desirable decisions, and of ruling party members of parliament (MPs) to rush through major mineral resource agreements, has 'become the norm' in both the mining and oil sectors (TWN-Africa, 2016: 2; see also Hickey et al., 2015; Mohan and Asante, 2015). Thus, whereas the generally 'disappointing' impact of Ghana's mining sector has sometimes been blamed on the weak capacity of regulatory institutions such as parliament (Ayee et al., 2011: 6; see also Atta-Quayson, 2012), we argue that such weaknesses are the direct result of the mutual interests between ruling party MPs and the executive. The weak supervisory role of the Ghanaian parliament is much more political than technical, suggesting that such weaknesses are unlikely to be effectively addressed through *technical* capacity building alone.

4 The Politics of Central–Local Relations in Ghana's Mining Governance

One of the great challenges in Ghana's mining governance has consistently been that of aligning national aspirations with what is politically feasible at the local scale. This dilemma manifests itself in several ways, one of which is the phenomenon of ASM, discussed in the next section. This section addresses the particularly complex central–local politics that surround (1) the relationships between national authorities and chieftaincies in determining control of access to the subsoil, and (2) the distribution and use of revenues generated by mining. As we will see, the first of these issues affects the second.

4.1 *Chiefs, Politicians, and the Land Question from the Late Nineteenth Century to the Present*

The extreme dispersion of power in Ghanaian society and the competition that it generates has involved traditional authorities throughout Ghana's post-colonial history. To this extent, an historicized understanding of the relationship between chiefs and politicians is central to comprehending the politics of natural resource governance in Ghana from a *longue durée* perspective, and in particular to assessing central–local relations in governing the mining economy. Indeed, Amanor (2008, 2009) traces the political influence of chiefs in present-day Ghana to the failed attempts of the British colonial administration to control land and vest it in the colonial state, and to the ultimate creation of a system of indirect rule based on Native Authorities and chiefly rule.

One of the early concerns of British colonial rule was how best to vest all unoccupied land in the British Crown. This concern arose mainly from the colonial government's fear that foreign companies would acquire the land through speculation and by purchasing concessions from local chiefs during the mining boom. In 1894, the colonial government attempted to enact a Crown Lands Ordinance, which would place 'waste land, forest land and minerals' under the British Crown and enabled the colonial government to gain control over the granting of concessions (Omosini, 1972; Wardell, 2006). However, this was met with considerable resistance and opposition, manifested in the formation of the Aborigines Rights Protection Society (ARPS) in 1897.

The ARPS was an alliance of chiefs and business and intellectual elites on the Gold Coast that was formed to defend African rights over the land.

After decades of similarly unsuccessful attempts to take control over the administration and allocation of land rights, colonial administration was ultimately established through an alliance with traditional rulers organized into Native Authorities.[24] This system of indirect rule brought chiefly families into the ruling coalition, effectively as lower-level factions that could maintain political support for British ruling elites. The establishment of the Native Administration system resulted in the creation of 'a neo-traditional elite' in the Gold Coast (Whitfield, 2018) whereby 'Chiefs became responsible for appropriating land for public works, forest reserves, mining and timber concessions, and allocating land to farmers for export crop production' (Amanor, 2009: 102; see also Amanor, 2008: 60).

However, the indirect rule policy through which the colonial powers governed in collaboration with chiefs was to become a major source of rivalry between some traditional leaders and the educated elite during the decolonization processes. The CPP, the dominant nationalist party that led Ghana to independence, led a campaign against the chiefs—with some even pushing to abolish chieftaincy altogether—by drawing support from local youth groups and opportunistically exploiting local conflicts (Crook, 2005). After independence in 1957, however, Nkrumah followed a more complicated strategy, courting chiefs who supported him, while punishing his opponents (Berry, 2008). As Berry states, this punishment included 'stripping them of administrative and judicial authority, confiscating their stool lands, and putting some of their most outspoken opponents in prison' (ibid.: 41).

The military regime that overthrew Nkrumah in 1966 released his jailed opponents and restored their confiscated lands, and their successors varied in their reactions—from tacit acceptance to open support of chieftaincy as a time-honoured institution (Berry, 2008). With chiefs becoming an important source of political support and legitimacy for each new set of ruling elites, the NRC, which came to power in 1972, 'constructed a centre of political gravity based on a military–bureaucratic–chief alliance' (Chazan, 1982: 464). In effect, post-independence governments retained the customary land ownership and tenure system constructed during the colonial period, which gave chiefs and their traditional councils control over access to land and enhanced their authority. It is important to make clear, therefore, that the institution of chieftaincy not only survived in this period but gained strength after the 1966 coup. Chiefly authority over land was reaffirmed in the 1969 constitution, which restored chiefs' authority to allocate land rights and receive land tribute. The 1979 constitution went further to emphasize that the central government had no right to recognize or refuse to recognize chiefs, as this was the sole right of the community (Whitfield et al., 2015).

With the general vulnerability that characterized all subsequent political regimes after Nkrumah's overthrow, elections provided important moments for politicians to strike new deals with chiefs, in order to expand their electoral coalitions. One good example was a deal struck by the I. K. Acheampong military government (1972–78) with chiefs from the country's Northern and Upper regions in the run-up to a national referendum in the late 1970s (Chazan, 1982). Another example is Jerry Rawlings' deal with chiefs as the country was preparing to a return to multiparty democracy in 1992. During the 1980s, the Rawlings-led PNDC government initially challenged the authority of chiefs over land, especially in the important cocoa-growing areas. But by the early 1990s, when the return to multiparty rule was imminent, chiefs in the affected cocoa areas and the PNDC struck a bargain: chiefs helped mobilize support for the party, and the government allowed chiefs unfettered control over the land (Whitfield et al., 2015: 130). The continuing political influence of chiefs is also clear in the dynamics surrounding the distribution of mining royalties from which they benefit directly for their personal accumulation as part of an elite bargain.

4.2 *The Subnational Politics of Revenue Distribution*

The success of any mineral-led development strategy depends mainly on the share of revenues captured by national governments and the modalities that governments adopt in managing and distributing those revenues (Akabzaa, 2009). Mining sector revenues in Ghana are obtained mainly from royalties, corporate and personal income taxes, and the withholding tax on dividends and foreign outsourcing. Mining taxes (both corporate and personal) and dividends accrue directly and solely to the central government, while mineral royalties are distributed between the centre and subnational authorities.

Figure 5.5 summarizes how mining revenues are distributed in Ghana. Revenues from mining royalties are collected by the large tax unit of the Internal Revenue Service, which then dispenses the money into the consolidated fund. Of this sum, 80 per cent is retained by the government and used for general budget support, while the remaining 20 per cent is paid into a mineral development fund (MDF), which was established in late 1992 through an 'executive fiat' (Republic of Ghana, 2013: 21).[25] The 20 per cent allocated to the MDF is divided further in two: half (representing 10 per cent of total royalties) goes to the Minerals Commission and the Department of Mines, while the Office of Administration of Stool Lands (OASL) receives the remaining half. The OASL is charged with overseeing stool land. The OASL dispenses its allocated sum directly to beneficiary institutions at the subnational level, according to a formula outlined in the 1992 constitution and reinforced by the Minerals and Mining Act of 2006. This stipulates that the office retains

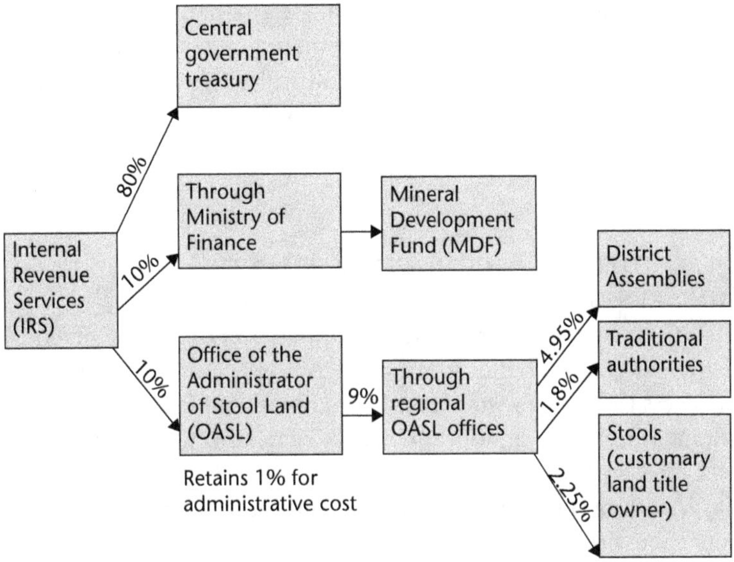

Figure 5.5. Distribution of mining revenues in Ghana
Source: Adapted from Boampong (2012).

10 per cent of the monies (or 1 per cent of total royalties) to cover administrative expenses, while the remaining 90 per cent (9 per cent of total royalties) is distributed as follows:

- 25 per cent to the stools through the traditional authority structure for 'the maintenance of the stool in keeping with its status';
- 20 per cent to the chiefs or other traditional authorities; and
- 55 per cent to the district assemblies located within the area of authority of the stool lands (Republic of Ghana, 1992).

Thus, with all taxes and 90 per cent of mineral royalties being retained at the national level, current procedures are inherently biased towards the central government and away from mining communities. This is particularly evident in comparison to Peru (see Chapter 2, Subsection 3.3.2.1, this volume), where the central government distributes half of its mining income tax revenues to the subnational areas that host mining operations.

The disparity between the state's share of royalties and that of mining communities has long been the basis of public grievances in the mining sector. Chiefs and mining companies have repeatedly demanded an increase in the share of mineral royalties going to local communities. In August 2016, one chief went so far as to advocate that all stools' share nationwide be paid to them directly by companies (as was the case in pre-colonial Ghana) rather than being channelled through the central state (Ghana News Agency, 2015; Swanzy, 2016). Yet such demands have remained unsuccessful in the face of an overall settlement among national political elites agreeing that mining revenues be centralized, as well as evidence of the misapplication of mineral royalties by subnational authorities. We will discuss this further in Subsections 4.2.1 and 4.2.2.

4.2.1 IDEAS, INTERESTS AND THE CENTRALIZATION OF MINING RENTS

Political elite consensus regarding the centralization of mining revenues has a long history in Ghana,[26] motivated by a combination of central elite incentives for access to a greater share of mineral rents, and ideas about sovereignty and national unity. Throughout the history of post-independence Ghana, the dominant idea articulated by both political elites and citizens is the notion of Ghana as a unitary state. In terms of natural resources, this idea is manifested in a belief that the state is best placed to exploit minerals and hydrocarbons and to share the benefits with its citizens and regions. One mining governance expert interviewed in Ghana traced this idea to the nationalist movements of the late 1940s and early 1950s, a period during which 'the control of natural resources was seen as a great gain of the anti-colonial movement'. He continued:

> In many of our countries, colonial companies controlled the resources. So [after independence], being able to now say that the nation owned the resources was an important political statement, and also that these resources would be applied to national development. Now if there is national ownership and the idea is that the resources are held in trust for the people by the state, how do you establish a basis for special treatment of a particular region?

Within this overall discourse of 'national ownership', allocating disproportionate shares of mineral rents to regions of extraction is generally seen as having the potential to foster divisive tendencies, and, as a consequence, undermine national political stability. Thus, although mining activities in Ghana have long been spatially concentrated in the Ashanti and Western regions, revenues generated from mining have historically been channelled for direct budgetary support and utilized without any recourse to the areas of their derivation. At the local level, such ideas also help explain why revenues from the MDF—which are meant to help mitigate the environmental costs of mining in affected communities—are sometimes extended to benefit non-mining communities (Quarshie, 2015). More broadly, it was also partly on the basis of such ideas about national unity that recent demands from chiefs from the oil-rich Western region, that 10 per cent of oil revenues be earmarked for developmental projects in their region, were generally rejected by elites across the political divide. As the Minister of Lands and Natural Resources explained in an interview:

> Could you imagine what would have happened if government had even entertained the idea? Obuasi will rise up, the Akyem people (referring to Newmont Mines in New Aberim) will rise up and ask what about us? Government will be fighting fires everywhere. I believe strongly that we need to collect the revenues to the centre and distribute. This is the only way we can ensure we stay together as a state. We can hold the country together.

Such ideas have endured throughout post-colonial Ghana in large part because it is also in the material *interests* of ruling elites to keep revenues centralized, so that they can control their distribution and uses. Within the context of competitive clientelism, the suppression of subnational challenges to how mining rents are distributed also enhances the prospects for the maintenance of ruling coalitions through patronage spending.

4.2.2 MISAPPLICATION OF ROYALTIES BY SUBNATIONAL AUTHORITIES

There is ample evidence that mineral royalties tend to be 'misused' by both chiefs and district assemblies (DAs), providing opportunities for the centre to justify its continuous centralization of revenues. Official government sources suggest that a large portion of the royalties received by the District Assemblies is often applied to expenses not intended by the distribution scheme (Republic of Ghana, 2013: 42).[27] Indeed, of some GHC 6.74 million of mineral royalties received by the three highest beneficiary District Assemblies during 2004–09, only GHC 0.69 million (14.2 per cent) was spent on health, water and sanitation and waste management, land degradation, and alternative sources of livelihoods—all areas directly affected by mining activities. Most beneficiary assemblies were found to have 'utilised MDF either in whole or partly for varied projects which do not mitigate the harmful effects of mining' (Republic of Ghana, 2013: iv).

Moreover, '[t]here is strong evidence that the payments to traditional councils and stools tend to finance expenditures other than those that benefit the local communities involved' (ICMM, 2007: 77). In some cases, chiefs 'have spent some of their mining royalties on erecting new palaces' (Boampong, 2012: 2) and on ceremonial clothing for the chief (CHRAJ, 2008). Part of the problem here relates to provisions of the 1992 constitution, which states that revenues accruing from stool lands 'be used to maintain the stool in keeping with its status'. In one stakeholder workshop on mining, traditional authorities took advantage of this constitutional provision to argue that their share of mineral revenues is 'not meant for development projects' (Aterkyi, 2007: 4). Moreover, as part of the Ghana Extractive Industries Transparency Initiative (GHEITI), the Minerals Commission drafted a template that sought to help chiefs report on their mineral royalty expenses, but the chiefs responded so harshly that the Commission 'had to backtrack'.[28]

The important question, therefore, is: why have political elites in Ghana continued to allocate mining revenues to local chiefs, despite clear evidence that such resources do not contribute significantly to the well-being of local populations? One explanation is that there is a 'genuine uncertainty as to the "appropriate purpose" of distributing mining revenues to chiefs in Ghana' (ICMM, 2007: 77). We contend, however, that two related factors lie behind this, both underpinned by Ghana's competitive clientelist political settlements: the logic of maintaining social order due to the significant leverage of traditional authorities over mineral-rich lands, and the desire of ruling elites to win and maintain political power through the support of chiefs.

As a result of the historical power struggles between politicians and chiefs over mineralized land since the colonial period, land ownership remains complex in Ghana. There are two main categories of land ownership today—namely, state lands, compulsorily acquired by the government through the invocation of appropriate legislation, and vested lands, belonging to customary authorities (stools, skins, clans, and families). Vested ownership entails allodial and user rights that are vested in paramount chiefs, who control access over the land on behalf of a community. In all, more than 80 per cent of land in Ghana is under the control of chiefs (Ministry of Lands and Natural Resources, 2011: 1; World Bank, 2013: 1), implying that most mineral operations, both by large-scale companies and ASM operators, occur on stool land (Tsikata, 1997; Nyame and Blocher, 2010).

Consequently, although mineral resources in Ghana are entrusted in the hands of the president on behalf of the people, the state depends substantially on chiefs for access to land, and governments often plead with chiefs to release lands for development projects. Chiefs have turned their control over land into widespread *de facto* power at the local and national levels, effectively utilizing it to exact tribute both from mining companies and the government. Thus, the allocation of mining revenues to traditional leaders by the central government needs to be understood as a *co-optation* strategy aimed at enhancing the cooperation of traditional authorities with ruling political elites so as to maintain the stability of ruling coalitions. In other words, it is primarily the capacity of chiefs 'to cause trouble' that has historically entitled them to a share of mining revenues. As one mining sector activist stated in an interview:

> If you look at the history of how what has been given to local communities through the chiefs has been spent, it has nothing to do with community interest; the chiefs take it as their entitlement, and the state allows that as part of a compromise. So, in a way, this is a continuation of the intra-elite struggles over the distribution of public resources.

One respondent described the allocation of mining royalties to traditional authorities as 'a pay-out to chiefs to keep them quiet', elaborating further that 'the idea is to silence them because chiefs can be very significant trouble makers... In the gold-producing areas, the chiefs continue to wield some power, and if they are not sorted out, they can be a problem'.[29] These observations echo suggestions that in countries characterized by 'limited access orders', the stability of ruling coalitions requires the distribution of rents to members of a 'dominant coalition' in ways that create incentives for elites to cooperate among themselves rather than fight (North et al., 2009).

In the Ghanaian context, such distributional strategies are also influenced by historical memories of the pre-colonial era, when mining royalties served as a key source of power and local control for chiefs. As Dumett (1998: 45) reminds us of the pre-colonial Ghanaian context, the power of chiefs over mineralized land was such that 'whenever a local chief granted the right to a stranger to mine for gold on stool lands, the *omanhene*, as paramount ruler, was entitled to a one-third, or *abusa*, share of the proceeds'. One respondent echoed this point:

> Historically, the chiefs gave the concessions to gold companies and collected royalties... So, in the memory of the traditional elites, there is this thing about how once upon a time, they were the ones collecting the royalties.[30]

In this context, the Ghanaian experience also illustrates the importance of historical memories around natural resource governance, whereby 'the ways in which history is recounted and remembered can, constitute an important variant of how ideas matter in struggles over the governance of extraction' (Bebbington, 2015: 107).

The second reason the central government maintains payments to subnational leaders is the importance of chiefs for winning elections and politicians' desire to court the political support of traditional authorities. While chiefs are constitutionally barred from taking partisan positions, many have continued to flout this with impunity, mainly because of their capacity to mobilize voters in support of ruling political elites (Fox et al., 2011). Indeed, Crook (2005) states that: 'Their power and authority are such that they are often more likely to be listened to than any politician' (2005: 4). As one government employee in the OASL stated:

> If you are a government and you don't give that recognition to chiefs, you are on your way out of office very quickly... You know the politicians go and solicit support from chiefs because, whether you like it or not, the chiefs still have influence over the people. And if you are a politician and you don't recognize and respect chiefs, that will be a big, big trouble for you.

Together, this means that politicians across the political divide 'are ready to "purchase" the allegiance or interest of local traditional leaders through the patronage available to them... in return for the influence over local voting that they can deliver' (Coffey International Development, 2011: 30).[31] The distribution of mining revenues is one typical example of such clientelist alliances between political leaders and traditional authorities. Moreover, competitive clientelism has meant that neither of the two dominant parties is prepared to undertake a politically costly reform that would deny chiefs from benefiting directly from mining royalties. For example, asked why GHEITI is not pushing for transparency and accountability from chiefs with regards to their utilization of mining rents, one bureaucrat from the finance ministry responded: 'You know the nature of our politics; they [politicians] will say the previous government has not done this, so why will this government... push it? They will look at it from the political angle.'[32,33]

In the specific Ghanaian context, clientelist exchanges exist not only between traditional leaders and political leaders, but also between the former and mining companies. Apart from their shares in mining royalties, traditional authorities have been the direct recipients of various forms of transfers from mining companies, in return for which they are expected to play a role in moderating community dissent against companies. In a study of three mining communities in Ghana's Western region, Bush (2010) notes how 'Chiefs were often used in the development of patron–client relations by companies as corporate largesse was distributed to them to encourage traditional authorities to control their youth, and to fulfil some tasks of labour hire for routine but mostly occasional mine maintenance' (Bush, 2010: 108). Such forms of collusion between chiefs and mining companies have often led to feelings of exclusion among unemployed youth, who have occasionally attacked local chiefs and looted or destroyed their palaces in revenge (World Bank, 2003; Standing, 2014).

In sum, all post-independence political elites have allocated a share of mineral royalties to chiefs, partly in exchange for political support, or non-opposition to their rule, enabling them to maintain social and political order. In the context of the high degree of vulnerability that has characterized all ruling political elites, political accommodation with traditional authorities has been important in ensuring that chiefs, who continue to wield substantial control over rural populations, do not support excluded political factions against those in power. In this context, policy fixes that ignore the political economy dynamics of natural resource governance are unlikely to be able to address the misuse of natural resource rents by national and local elite actors. Here, as Maconachie et al. (2015: 16) have noted, captured rents by local chiefs tend to 'serve an important function in securing political contracts, where revenues are used to strengthen relations with clients under systems of patronage'.

5 The Political Settlement and Illegal Mining in Ghana

This section explores the impact of Ghana's political settlement dynamics on the governance of the country's ASM sector. Although various governments have placed heavy emphasis on large-scale gold mining by transnational corporations (Hilson et al., 2014: 294), the small-scale sector has expanded dramatically in recent years (see Figure 5.6), and has the greatest potential for rural poverty reduction. ASM accounts for well over 60 per cent of Ghana's total mining labour force (Hilson and Potter, 2003; Carson et al., 2005), providing direct and indirect employment to over one million people (Afryie et al., 2016). In 2013, gold exports from ASM operators accounted for 34 per cent of Ghana's total gold export, which equalled the total contribution of the three largest multinational companies in the country (Acheampong, 2015).[34]

Although Ghana has had a formalized process for mining gold on a small scale, legal basis since the passage of the small-scale mining law in 1989, there remain two distinct types of small-scale mines in Ghana. The first group consists of registered ASM operators who have been awarded licences by the state to mine in designated areas. The second group comprises unregistered (and therefore illegal) small-scale operators commonly referred to as *galamsey*.[35] An estimated 85 per cent of Ghana's ASM operators are *galamsey* (Hilson and Potter, 2003; Ofosu-Mensah, 2016), and there is official government acknowledgement that 'illegal mining activities are on the increase' (Ministry of Lands and Natural Resources, 2013: 3).

Most *galamsey* operators have opted to remain unregistered, often with significant adverse implications. Some commentators have raised concerns

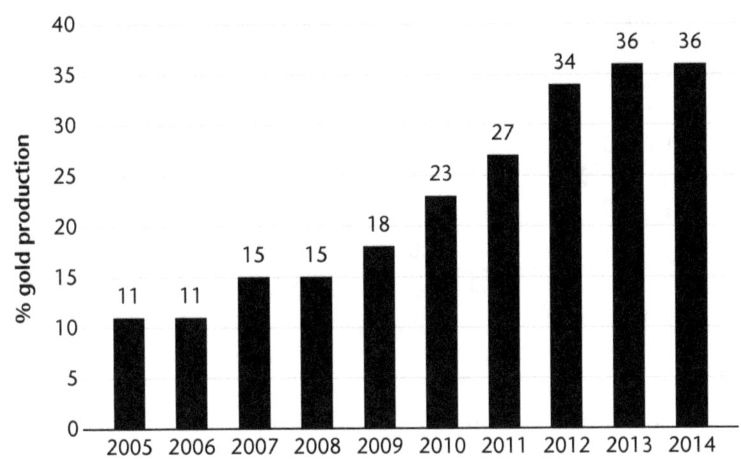

Figure 5.6. ASM contribution to total gold production (%), Ghana, 2005–14
Source: Based on raw data from the Minerals Commission, Accra.

over this dynamic, arguing that *galamsey* operators do not pay any tax to the state, while their activities continue to 'pose serious threats to other land users and the environment' (Bansah et al., 2016). In March 2017, the Ghana Water Company warned that the spate of water pollution by illegal ASM operators is approaching alarming levels, and that the country risks having to import water for consumption unless illegal mining activities are curbed (Joy Online, 2017). Moreover, reports of deaths resulting from the collapse of *galamsey* pits, as well as of violent confrontations between illegal ASM operators and formalized large-scale mining companies are common. Why has illegal mining continued to grow, despite the state's efforts to regularize the sector through various policies and programmes? Why have most ASM operators chosen to remain illegal, despite some opportunities for state support associated with the regularization of their activities? In addition to ambiguities around land and mineral ownership, we suggest two explanations, each related to the ideas and incentives generated by competitive clientelism in Ghana: law enforcement corruption, and elections and partisan polarization.

5.1 *Law Enforcement Corruption*

Scholars who study Ghana's small-scale mining sector often blame a lack of effective law enforcement capacity on the part of the state for the increase in *galamsey* operators (Hilson and Potter, 2003; Kuma and Yendaw, 2010), arguing that the Ghanaian state is unable to effectively broadcast its power in rural areas where illegal mining activities take place. Others attribute the blame to 'lack of political will' (Aubynn, 2009) or the 'intentional ambivalence' (Teschner, 2012) of politicians and law enforcement institutions.

Drawing evidence from Tawkwa, a major mining town in the Western region, Teschner (2012) contrasts the pervasive and open nature of illegal mining activities to the 'active' role of police officers in frequently enforcing laws in other aspects of public life. In this context, attributing the increase in *galamsey* to the state's insufficient law enforcement capacity is not convincing. Instead, illegal mining activities have persisted because of 'political leniency and law enforcement corruption' (ibid.). One interviewee from the Ministry of Lands and Natural Resources attributes the *galamsey* phenomenon to 'a complete lack of political will', arguing that the people who have the responsibility to curb illegal mining activities tend to benefit from them: 'the chiefs are culpable, the assemblies are culpable, some MPs are culpable, some ministers are culpable. That is how bad it is'. In this respect, illegal mining has continued to flourish because it serves the interests of a wide range of actors, including chiefs who gain through the royalties they receive in exchange for land; the government middlemen whose incomes depend on the unfinished products of *galamsey* work; and the political, business, and local elite who own the concessions that operate outside the legal mining framework (see also Tsuma, 2010). This suggests that calls for empowering security agencies as a way of addressing the problem of illegal mining (e.g. Kuma and Yendaw, 2010: 120) are misplaced. Nor does the answer lie solely in technocratic approaches, such as the demarcation of land plots suitable for ASM activities (e.g. Hilson and Potter, 2003). In a recent study of the influx of foreigners into the ASM sector, Crawford and Botchwey (2017) make a similar observation, stating that although various state institutions have often failed in performing their regulatory responsibilities; 'this was not due to weakness or lack of capacity. Rather public officials "turned a blind eye" to illicit gold mining' (2017: 2).

They conclude that 'collaboration and collusion in illegality occurred from local to national levels, within both official circles and society at large' (2017: 7). They note that this dynamic became especially prevalent at the time of the 2012 general elections, as politicians at various levels offered protection for illegal migrants 'in return for financial support to sponsor their campaigns' (2017: 14).

5.2 *Competitive Elections and Partisan Polarization*

Khan (2010: 68) reminds us that because of the vulnerability of ruling elites, countries characterized by competitive clientelism generally suffer from 'weak implementation and enforcement capabilities', especially around reforms that require the cooperation of several 'principals' within the ruling coalition. Our evidence suggests that the increasingly vulnerable nature of ruling elites resulting from the strength of excluded elites and lower-level factions of ruling coalitions has played a central role in undermining the effective enforcement of ASM laws. In a country where over one million people earn their livelihoods from small-scale gold mining, and where presidential elections are sometimes won by less than 50,000 votes, it is easy to understand the political relevance of *galamsey* operators to ruling political elites and in shaping the political settlement around mining sector governance more broadly.

Unemployment is extremely high in rural mining areas, and ASM operations 'offer far more benefits to local residents than does the Government of Ghana's disbursement of mining royalties or employment opportunities offered by the large-scale mines' (Bush, 2009: 57). Young men are disproportionately involved in small-scale mining and are exceptionally influential because they are prone to violent demonstrations which attract the attention of large-scale companies, government officials, and traditional leaders. Supporting small-scale mining is thus one simple way for politicians to appear sympathetic to the rural, unemployed youth and the families they financially support (Teschner, 2012).

Aubynn (2009: 66) notes that 'The lack of political will to control illicit mining in the country has become even more evident since the inception of constitutional rule in 1993.' Having worked as chief executive officer (CEO) at the Ghana Chamber of Mines, and in his present position as CEO of the Ghana Minerals Commission, Aubynn draws attention to the relative success in curbing *galamsey* operations under the dominant leader political settlement in the 1980s, during which time it became 'common to witness police raids on *galamsey* operations... which occasionally culminated in arrests and prosecutions' (Aubynn, 2009).

However, under the new democratic dispensation, the fight against *galamsey* has taken a more 'politically sensitive dimension', as both the NPP and NDC fear that 'any attempt to stop *galamsey* operations... risked putting more people out of a job, with suicidal political consequences' (ibid.). For Aubynn, this explains why most demonstrations by ASM operators, and the serious conflicts between mining companies and *galamsey* operators, have, since 1996, often occurred in the few months leading up to elections (ibid.). Although these observations were made with direct reference to the 1996, 2000, and 2004 elections, the escalation in *galamsey* activities in the few months prior to the December 2016 presidential election suggests a similar situation. For example, following a quit order by the Minerals Commission requiring ASM operators to stop mining in the Obuasi concession of AngloGold Ashanti, *galamsey* miners set off to vandalize the offices of political parties amid chants of 'no *galamsey*, no votes' (see *Daily Graphic*, 2016; Silver News Online, 2016).

Any possibility of curbing illegal mining will flow directly from the nature of the ruling coalition, the degree to which ruling elites are sufficiently insulated from 'pressures from below', and an agreement among elites from different parties that it is needed. Such conditions have not been in place. Part of the reason for the failure of the anti-*galamsey* task force of the 2012–16 government was the lack of an interparty agreement regarding its operations. At the outset, opposition party elements accused the task force of selectively targeting mining concessions belonging to NPP supporters, while *galamsey* operators who were known NDC members were being left off the hook (*Daily Guide*, 2013). Like the NDC in 2008, the NPP's campaign strategy for the 2016 elections was couched in a language that pointed to its support for small-scale mining youth, with its presidential candidate repeatedly drawing attention to how the Mahama-led NDC government 'directed Soldiers to come and drive out all persons involved in *galamsey*' (Starr FM, 2016). Competitive clientelism has thus played a central role in undermining prospects for an interparty consensus in enforcing laws within the ASM sector—a point made by Dickens (2010) following his recent visit to Obuasi:

> Looking at... the overall costs of *galamsey*, it is quite incredible to see politicians adding it to their catalogue of electioneering promises on campaign platforms... Politics is all about winning power at all costs; just promise anything that will bring power... [I]f a politician goes to a community which has gained notoriety for anything criminal, all that he has to do is to promise to legalise it to win the votes of that community... Obviously due to the immoral talks engendered by election fever, 'legalised' *galamsey* was being practised in the full glare of Ghanaians. *Galamsy*... which used to be a covert operation was being practised in broad daylight! (Dickens, 2010).

Indeed, even at the local level, *galamsey* operators tend to be 'divided along party-political lines' (Aubynn, 2009: 66), exacerbating the partisan character of the *galamsey* discourse in the country.

6 Conclusions

This chapter has explored the interplay between politics and mining in Ghana through a political settlements lens which draws attention to the ways in which relations of power and ideas shape the levels of elite commitment to allocating mineral resources towards inclusive development. Our analysis suggests that although there is an overall elite consensus among politicians that mining rents be centralized, the lack of a long-term development vision for the mining industry has enabled ruling elites to skew public spending towards short-term objectives of political survival, rather than long-term investments that are required to structurally transform the economy and promote more inclusive forms of development. This lack of a longer-term vision for the mining sector has itself been a product of the prevailing competitive clientelist political settlement in Ghana, which incentivizes political elites to prioritize policies that enhance prospects for their political survival in the short term.

It is this form of political calculus that shapes the manner in which mining resources are distributed, and the way in which this in turn shapes the impact of mining on national and local development. Notably, allocation of rents to traditional authorities and chiefs does not seem to be driven by socio-economic development concerns but is more of a co-optation strategy driven by: (1) the logic of maintaining social orders, due to the significant leverage of traditional authorities over mineral-rich lands; (2) the desire of ruling elites to win and maintain political power through the support of chiefs, who wield substantial leverage over rural voters. Traditional authorities receive a significant share of mineral rents, mainly because ruling political elites want to avoid provoking resistance from a group in society that brokers land and votes in the rural areas.

These findings have important implications for both theory and policy, especially with regards to the current debates on inclusive political settlements. Although scholars have increasingly highlighted the importance of inclusive political settlements for sustained peace and development, there is often little reflection on the 'how' and 'why' of inclusion (Abdulai, 2017). For example, with specific reference to natural resource governance, di John and Putzel (2009: 20) highlight the importance of inclusive political settlements, stating that 'Broad-based elite inclusion within a political settlement is central for managing mineral rents effectively.' The Ghanaian case suggests that, whereas elite inclusion in the distribution of mining rents can be helpful in facilitating the stability of ruling political coalitions, it can also carry the danger of undermining the effective management of rents for long-term development if mineral rents are deployed with the objective of 'buying-off' elites who can potentially undermine the stability of ruling coalitions. Under such circumstances, broad-based elite inclusion may at best result in 'unproductive peace' (Lindemann, 2011), as substantial mineral resources are shared for consumption rather than development.

Endnotes

1. During this period, the only notable exception was in 2004, when mining was overtaken by the cocoa sector.
2. She highlights Botswana's vulnerability to South Africa, and its membership of the Southern African Customs Union, as having also played important roles in shaping its politics of natural resource governance.
3. Fantis are primarily located in the coastal part of Southern Ghana, specifically the Central region.
4. Kumasi is the capital of the Ashanti region.
5. This was also due in part to Rawlings's perceived weakening control over the military and pressure from foreign aid donors for democratization.
6. According to interviews in the Office of the Administrator of Stool Lands, Ministry of Justice, and Attorney General. See also Carson et al., 2005.
7. There is some similarity here to the forced labour arrangements of *pongeaje* and *mitaje* in colonial and post-colonial Bolivia (see Chapter 3, n. 5).
8. The first official European gold mining company established in the Gold Coast Colony was the African Gold Coast Company in 1878 (Hilson, 2002).
9. At that time, the proliferation of capitalist concessionaire activity derived not only from the impetus of gold mining, but also from the burgeoning commercial timber industry (Dumett, 1998: 274).
10. For details on the nature and extent of these demands and pressures from expatriate companies, see Dumett (1998), particularly Chapter 6, entitled 'The colonial government and the expanding miners' frontier: Pressures for mining district administration, health services, and transport improvements' (1998: 163–204).

11. According to an interview with a former PNDC member, and an activist in the Ghanaian mining sector.
12. These observations are based on an interview with a mining activist.
13. Note that until this period, small-scale mining in Ghana was considered entirely illegal by the state.
14. Essentially a windfall tax.
15. According to interviews with a senior bureaucrat at the Ministry of Lands and Natural Resources and a member of the Mining Review Committee, and at the Office of the Administrator of Stool Lands, Ministry of Justice, and Attorney General.
16. According to an interview with a senior bureaucrat at the Ministry of Lands and Natural Resources and a member of the Mining Review Committee.
17. See also Reuters (25 October 2011). 'Ghana should seek more revenues from mining sector: IMF'. http://www.theafricareport.com/Reuters-Feed/Ghana-should-seek-more-revenues-from-mining-sector-IMF.html, accessed 25 May 2017.
18. These pledges were again repeated in the party's 2012 election manifesto: 'The long-held position of the NDC is that the mining sector has to be re-organized to allow the nation and mining communities specifically to benefit more from their resources' (NDC, 2012: 40).
19. According to an interview with a mining activist and university lecturer.
20. Interview in the Ministry of Lands and Natural Resources.
21. See UNDP (n.d.). 'UNDP in Ghana. Eradicate extreme hunger and poverty. MDG 1'. http://www.gh.undp.org/content/ghana/en/home/post-2015/mdgoverview/overview/mdg1.html, accessed 25 May 2017.
22. Interview with mining sector activist and co-chair for the Ghana Extractive Industry Transparency Initiative.
23. These terms have been recently renegotiated, but the terms of the new agreements are still not in the public domain.
24. The Native Authority/Indirectly rule system in the Gold Coast is often traced back to 1847—the official year of the commencement of British colonialism.
25. The MDF was established to: (1) promote development in local mining communities through the redistribution of mining royalties to mining-affected communities; (2) compensate the same communities for the costs associated with mining; (3) support the operating budget of mining sector institutions (Republic of Ghana, 2013).
26. It dates back to the first post-colonial government in the 1950s and 1960s (see Aryee, 2001).
27. According to an interview with an official of the Ghana Extractive Industry Transparency Initiative (EITI), 20 January 2017.
28. According to an interview with an official of the Ghana EITI.
29. Interview with a mining sector activist and university lecturer.
30. Ibid.
31. In one specific example, barely two weeks before the 2012 presidential elections, President Mahama donated twelve Toyota Land Cruisers to chiefs across the country, in what was widely interpreted as a vote-buying strategy.
32. Interview with a GHEITI official in the Ministry of Finance.

33. The relevance of these observations goes well beyond the Ghanaian context, as suggested by evidence from a recent study on the relationship between politicians and traditional leaders in some nineteen African countries (Baldwin, 2014). The study draws attention to the growing tendency of politicians in Africa to cede power over the control of land to chiefs and explains this phenomenon as part of an elite 'bargain' through which chiefs help politicians in mobilizing electoral support in increasingly competitive electoral environments. It is the 'prospect of competitive elections' that 'triggers decisions to cede power to chiefs', often as a way of overcoming 'the challenge of building winning electoral coalitions' (Baldwin, 2014: 256).
34. These companies are AngloGold Obuasi, Goldfields Tarkwa, and Newmont Ghana Limited. AngloGold contributed 6 per cent of gold exports in 2013, Newmont had 13 per cent, and Goldfields Tarkwa accounted for 15 per cent, equalling 34 per cent—the same as the contribution of small-scale miners.
35. *Galamsey* is an adulterated English phrase for 'gather them and sell' (Aubynn, 2009).

6

Conclusions

Interpreting the Politics of Natural Resource Extraction

As we were in the final stages of preparing this manuscript, Global Witness released its report 'Defenders of the Earth: Global Killings of Land and Environmental Defenders' (Global Witness, 2017). The report records 200 documented killings in 2016, a new record, up from 185 murders in 2015, which had also been a record. In the view of the non-governmental organization (NGO): 'This tide of violence is driven by an intensifying fight for land and natural resources, as mining, logging, hydro-electric and agricultural companies trample on people and the environment in their pursuit of profit.' If one needed a reminder that the drivers of natural resource governance are deeply political, this is an especially poignant one.

Appalling realities such as those described in the Global Witness report demand that discussions of natural resource governance have a substantial political component. This does not mean that resource governance has to be analysed in political terms alone, but it cannot be analysed apolitically. In Chapter 1, we noted that some of the calls for 'better' institutions in extractive industry governance elide discussion of the political processes through which existing institutions have become dominant, or through which they would need to be contested if new arrangements were to emerge. We also noted, though, that there is a significant body of literature that does read extractive industries through a political lens. One of the tasks of this book has been to show what, if anything, a political settlements approach might add to this work.

This existing literature on the politics of extractive industry has followed different lines. Terry Karl's work (1987, 1997), for instance, explored the relationships between extractive industries and the possibilities of democracy. Karl analysed how political pact making related to oil development created incentives to keep democratic institutions weak, with pacts in one period constraining political options in subsequent moments. This interest in the implications of extractives for democracy has also characterized the methodologically varied interventions of authors such as Michael Ross (2012) and James Robinson et al. (2006). At their core, these approaches have explored how subsoil natural resources affect the incentives encountered by political elites and their subsequent behaviour. Much of this work has been focused at a national level, though a number of authors have addressed the same concerns in analyses of the implications of resource extraction for subnational political dynamics and the responses of subnational governments (Arellano-Yanguas, 2011; Asante, 2016).

Research on social mobilization and resistance to extractive industry investment constitutes a distinct approach to the politics of resource governance. Here the emphasis has been on understanding why, and how, affected populations and activists respond to the presence or expectation of extractive industry. The bulk of this research has been at a quite local scale, examining particular community-level conflicts (Bebbington and Bury, 2013; Gilberthorpe and Hilson, 2014; Kirsch, 2014). What this research has done less well is understand the operations of national political and economic elites, both within the state (Kirsch, 2012) and within corporations (Kemp, 2014).

Work such as Karl's and Ross's operate primarily at a national scale, while work on forms of popular agency and resistance tends to have a territorial and local focus. Just as these approaches to resource politics prioritize differing scales of analysis, they also focus on different types of actor. While some authors are primarily concerned with political and economic elites, others are more interested in the actions and motivations of indigenous, non-governmental, community-based, and civic actors who mobilize precisely because they feel excluded from the national and strategic decision making fora that the elites dominate. Another difference among these approaches is that some implicitly take a notion of development for granted, while others question dominant models of development. For some analysts, what is primarily at stake is a politics of interests, while others are more concerned with the contentious politics of ideas that inform natural resource governance.

In some sense, the Global Witness document occupies the space at which the concerns of these different analytical traditions could articulate. The tragic material on which it reports demands an understanding of how the incentives to those who stand to gain from resource extraction drive decisions that ripple out through political and social networks, ultimately leading people to kill those who resist. At the same time, targeted killings and civil conflict are not the only outcome when elite politics and pact making collide with grassroots interpretations of resource extraction. These diverse outcomes demand an explanation of why this articulation sometimes produces violence and at other times produces compromise and institutional innovation. Put in the language of 'good' natural resource governance, the question is, how can the conditions under which more 'effective' and 'inclusive' institutions emerge be understood, anticipated, and facilitated? Political settlements approaches are no panacea in the face of this analytical and political question. However, they may go some way towards helping bridge these different ways of framing natural resource politics, and in bringing elite politics, different forms of political agency, and grassroots contention within the same analytical frame.

Our discussions of Bolivia, Ghana, Peru, and Zambia have offered accounts of the long historical sweep of the politics surrounding extractive industry governance. They have tried to account for the shifting pacts among elites as well as their interactions with grassroots responses to extractive industry investment, and to explain resource governance institutions in terms of these pacts and interactions. At the same time, they have sought pattern in these interactions. The goal has been to show that while there is always negotiation and agency, the politics of resource governance is not one of perpetual change. Instead, this governance is characterized by periods of stability (settlement) punctuated by transitions of instability and contingency. Discussing each country's resource governance history through a shared and integrative conceptual lens helps, we hope, to identify both similarities and differences in ways that push forward conceptual discussions. In this chapter, we focus on those comparisons and contrasts, and use them to revisit a discussion of political settlements and the broader politics of resource governance.

1 Restating the Endeavour

The work underlying this book was predicated on two main claims. First, political settlements theory can help explain how mineral and hydrocarbon resources are governed over time in ways that complement other approaches to the politics of extractive industries governance. Second, a focus on natural resources can bring to the fore important ways in which materiality, scale, and ideas affect relationships among the elites and other social actors in natural resource governance and play a causal role in the constitution of political settlements. In this final chapter, we summarize what the Peruvian, Bolivian, Zambian, and Ghanaian analyses have contributed to these claims. We do this by developing answers to the following three themes that have run through the book: (1) How have transnational factors affected the politics of extractive industry governance and the relationships between the mineral economy and political settlements? (2) How have the circulation of ideas and the materiality of the resources in question affected natural resource politics and the relationships between political settlements and natural resource governance? (3) How has the nature of political settlements affected the governance of the extractive industries sector and relationships between the sector and patterns of social inclusion; and how have the dynamics surrounding resource extraction in turn influenced features of these political settlements? We close with a summary discussion of the ways in which a focus on natural resources can bring new insights to political settlements thinking.

2 Transnational Factors in the Politics of Natural Resource Extraction

In the course of discussing our conclusions with colleagues, we were cautioned against seeing too much convergence across our cases. While this is a fair warning, there is no doubt that a series of transnational processes and shared global histories link resource extraction in the four countries analysed (cf. Cooper et al., 1993). Some of these global histories are more general, some more specific, but each of them cautions against prioritizing the country level in the analysis of political settlements. Key elements of these transnational couplings hinge around: colonialism and post-colonialism; global commodity prices and domestic political and economic dynamics; state capitalism and neoliberalism; and corporate strategy and new investors.

2.1 *Colonialism and Post-Colonialism*

While there are obvious differences among the four countries as regards the specific colonial powers associated with resource extraction and the periods in which those powers exercised direct rule, the association of mining with both colonial rule and truncated post-colonial transitions remains an important element of the contemporary politics of resource governance. In all four countries, resource extraction is still associated with the exercise of colonial power, and some actors relate the inability to become fully 'post-colonial' to the ways in which subsoil resources continue to be governed. This narrative circulates in popular and journalistic[1] texts (Galeano, 1971), academic analysis (Ferguson, 2006), and UN reports (Mbeki Panel, 2015). As a consequence, discussions around extractive industry are simultaneously discussions around sovereignty and dependence, meaning that moves to deregulate and re-regulate resource extraction are interpreted through such languages, as well as in technical terms. As noted in Chapter 5 on Ghana, President John Mahama invoked precisely this sense of continuing dependency when he lamented at the annual World Economic Forum meeting in Davos in 2014, that: '[The mining companies] threatened to lay off workers if we implemented the windfall tax and because we needed the jobs and you don't want workers laid off you are coerced to go along.'

Such histories of truncated transitions in the post-colonial era continue to influence ideas about resource governance in Zambia and Bolivia also. Furthermore, and as the experience of Peru shows, perceived national elite control of mineral resources can be viewed by subnational actors as a continuing form of 'internal colonialism', itself a legacy of racialized, colonial power and the centralization of political authority.

2.2 *Global Commodity Prices and Domestic Political and Economic Dynamics*

Global commodity markets bind these countries' resource sectors together in important ways. Most importantly, all countries are price takers in these markets. While at one level this dependence on global prices is the case everywhere, the implications are more significant when internal demand is limited and economies poorly diversified. The effect is that the policy space open to national elites varies as global prices move. The options open to all four countries to address poverty over the first fifteen years of this century were a direct function of the commodity boom, and in particular of significant increases in gold, copper, gas, oil, and silver prices. By the same token, by the mid-2010s each country was reappraising poverty reduction financing in light of the end of the commodity super-cycle. Other income stream options, absent from government, range from cutbacks in social policy expenditure through to policies favouring the expansion of extraction in an effort to offset declining prices with increasing production, as in Bolivia's approach to expanding its natural gas frontier.[2]

Global commodity markets have also been implicated in the constitution and unravelling of national political actors in each country, as well as in their relative levels of holding power and inclusion in prevailing settlements. This is particularly clear for the cases of organized labour and small-scale miners. In Zambia and Bolivia, unionized mine workers became a critical part of the political landscape up to the late and mid-1980s, respectively, their initial emergence as political actors having been made possible by the combination of nationalized industry and reasonable prices for copper and tin. Their emergence as powerful forces meant that they were very much included within their respective national settlements and able to channel significant benefits in the form of social services and wages towards mining areas and union members. This in turn led to geographically and sectorally concentrated impacts on poverty and inclusion. As noted in the Zambia chapter, during these periods of union strength, '[t]he Copperbelt, in many ways, resembled a mini-developmental state'. The cohesion of these actors and the associated mechanisms of inclusion unravelled quickly when prices collapsed, labour was dismissed, and industry was privatized.

Conversely, as commodity prices began to rise again during the 2000s, a new set of political actors emerged related to artisanal and small-scale mining (ASM). This phenomenon is especially dramatic in Ghana and Bolivia, though it is also significant in Peru. In each case, ASM has become a far more important source of employment than large-scale mining (see, for instance, Cano, 2015a, for Peru, and Hilson, 2009, and Hilson and Garforth, 2013, for Ghana). In addition, ASM organizations and networks have become vehicles for political inclusion expressed through street protest and violence (Bolivia), subnational electoral success (Peru), lobbying (all three countries), and direct representation in debates on national mining policy (Bolivia). While national factors may have helped trigger the initial emergence of ASM through conscious policy to promote it, as in Bolivia in the 1980s and Peru in the 1970s,[3] it is only because of transnational processes of price formation that these sectors have emerged as significant modes of economic inclusion in the mineral economy. These processes also contributed to ASM operators becoming nationally important political actors able to exercise direct influence on legislation and force themselves into the national political settlement, above all in Bolivia.

2.3 *State Capitalism and Neoliberalism*

Another shared experience in all four countries has been the transition to and fro between state-owned and privatized industry. The extent of this oscillation varies among countries, though it has been clearest in the case of hydrocarbons governance in Bolivia, which has been nationalized three times over the last century. The oscillation between different forms of ownership is partly explained by changes in national settlements, while also influencing subsequent settlements because of the effects that nationalization and privatization have on the relative power of different actors. However, there is also a shared transnational dimension to what has happened across Bolivia, Ghana, Peru, and Zambia. Changes in ownership have reflected global shifts in prices, changes in global thinking regarding the merits of state-led investment, the inability of state companies to access leading technology and information (thus reducing their competitiveness), and the influence of international financial institutions, especially the World Bank. It is clearly no coincidence that from the mid-1980s to the late 1990s, each of the four countries moved from state-owned industry to one dominated by the private sector—above all in mining. Thus, the Bolivian Mining Corporation (*Corporación Minera de Bolivia,* COMIBOL), the state-owned mining company, was to all intents and purposes wound down in 1986, Ghana's State Gold Mining Corporation

(SGMC) in the mid-1980s, Peru's various state-owned mining assets in the first half of the 1990s, and Zambia's Consolidated Copper Mines (ZCCM) in 2000. Since these periods, the mining sector in each country has been dominated by private investment,[4] almost entirely international in character.[5] This private investment has been explicitly encouraged by broadly neoliberal policies promoted by international financial institutions and many domestic elites.

The relative coincidence in 'global time' of these transitions attests to the importance of globally circulating ideas regarding state-led management of the economy, such as those emanating from the United Nation's influential Economic Commission for Latin America and the Caribbean (ECLAC) in the mid-twentieth century (Finnemore, 1997) and, later, state withdrawal from the economy based on ideas emanating from Chicago School economists and subsequently distributed globally via iconic cases in the 1970s and 1980s, such as Chile, New Zealand, and the United Kingdom (Maxwell and Stone, 2004; Stone, 2004). However, the nature of the national polity is also important. In each country, resource nationalism has only been institutionalized in the form of state ownership or elevated taxation under dominant party/dominant leader settlements. This suggests (as Soifer, 2015, argues for nineteenth-century Latin America) that state-centric, developmentalist ideas tend to take root when there are high levels of political elite cohesion, and that these elites look to the state as the instrument for implementing their vision of development. Conversely, under conditions of competing elites, there is a preference for a weaker state, lest it be captured by one or another group (Soifer, 2015; vom Hau and Hickey, 2016).

2.4 *Corporate Strategy and New Investors*

As the mineral and hydrocarbon sectors of each country have become dominated by transnational capital investment, they are also affected by global dynamics within that corporate community. Thus, investment and portfolio decisions by corporations in any given country are not independent of the decisions they make in other countries. In addition, even though companies clearly adapt elements of their practices and demands to a particular country, the disciplining effect of global commodity and capital markets together with the club effects of corporate information sharing and self-organizing—for instance, in the form of the International Council of Mining and Metals (ICMM)—mean that ideas and practices circulate transnationally. The rise of corporate social responsibility (CSR) is a case in point. Though the ways in which CSR rolls out in each country are affected by levels of conflict, fiscal policy, and forms of government decentralization, core sets of practices travel the globe, affecting localized forms of patrimonialism and elite capture, as well as local development (Frederiksen, 2017).

A second pattern across all four countries has been the changing composition of investment in extractive industry. Chinese capital has become increasingly important, especially in the mining sector in Peru and Zambia, but also in hydrocarbons in Bolivia (see also Sanborn and Torres, 2009; Mohan et al., 2012; Brautigam and Gallagher, 2014; Gallagher, 2016). However, unlike in the case of resource nationalism, the engagement with Chinese and other 'non-traditional' sources of investment seems to occur across quite different political settlements. While not all Chinese companies have similar practices, the implications for development may be significant and, at the very least, their generalized presence does imply the insertion of the Chinese Embassy, Chinese foreign policy, and new corporate actors into discussions of extractive industry policy in ways that challenge national elites (corporate, public, and civic) who have a relative lack of experience in negotiating with Chinese capital. Commenting on the mining sector in Peru, Sanborn and Chonn (2015) note that by 2015, Chinese state-owned enterprises had come to hold more than a third of the country's projected investment portfolio, and, in the authors' view, appeared less willing than their western and Peruvian counterparts to communicate with diverse actors or engage in local power struggles. This increased presence of new forms of capital in each country is also affected by domestic elites' efforts to seek sources of investment that establish less political conditionalities.

From the colonial era to the present, therefore, transnational factors ranging from global prices to the practices of international corporations have affected the nature of political settlements and the governance of natural resources. National dynamics thus cannot be considered in isolation from the broader context in which they are situated. These transnational factors are, in turn, the result of the global circulation of ideas, a topic we turn to in the following section.

3 Materiality, Ideas, and the Politics of Extractive Industry Governance

The histories of natural resource politics in Bolivia, Ghana, Peru, and Zambia have suggested that these politics are best understood not just in terms of the interests of different parties negotiating resource use and control, but also in terms of the very nature of the resource itself and of ideas about that resource. While those ideas might be mobilized in pursuit of particular interests, they exist separate from those interests, often emanate from other locations and scales, and have had effects that cannot be explained solely in terms of interest-based politics. The nature of the resource in question—its location, its quality, its ease of extraction and so on—has also had political effects.

In this sense, both ideas about, and the materiality of, resources have affected resource governance and the formation of political settlements.

3.1 *Materiality*

Mineral and hydrocarbon resources have patchy geographies that overlap with geographies of political authority, race and ethnicity, land and territorial claims, and other natural resources. In each of the countries studied, relatively long-standing, historically stable geographies of resource extraction have been disrupted in recent decades in ways that influence the politics of extractive industry governance. In Zambia, the notion that mining is primarily a feature of the Copperbelt has now been upset as copper mining moves into North-Western Province. In Ghana, the association of resource extraction with Ashanti and Western regions has now been overturned by the spread of mineral concessions into other areas, as well as by offshore oil (Cuba et al., 2014). In Bolivia, the notion that the eastern lowland department of Santa Cruz was the centre of the hydrocarbon economy was rapidly upended by the post-1990s discoveries of remarkable gas reserves in Tarija (Humphreys Bebbington, 2010). And in Peru, the opening of new mining frontiers in the north of the country has challenged the traditional association of hard-rock mining with the Central Andes and Southern Coast.

These new frontiers are not just geographical phenomena driven by a mix of global changes in prices and demand and national policy incentives (Bridge, 2004)—they also produce political change. The expansion of mining into northern Peru has created political actors with considerable power. These actors include the owners of new and extremely profitable mines, as well as the regional political and civic actors contesting the forms taken by this mining.[6] The growth of the gas economy in Tarija and the capture of revenue from it helped produce regional political elites with the capacity to make themselves essential ideological allies of the national elites with whom they converged, or powerful opponents of other elites with whom they disagreed. Gas also provided new sources of political leverage for traditionally marginalized Guaraní communities under whose land the newly found deposits lay (Ospina et al., 2015). In other instances, this expanding frontier has led ASM miners to gain political influence. This has tended to occur in areas where minerals are accessible with relatively low-tech practices, as in the case of alluvial gold in Madre de Dios, Peru; near-surface gold in parts of Ghana; or abandoned subsurface mines in highland Bolivia.

While the expansion of copper into Zambia's North-Western Province has not yet created regionally based political actors with the capacity to break into the national settlement, it may well do so in the future, and it has at least increased the leverage of local chiefs who have influence over land and access to the subsoil. The expansion of mining and oil into non-traditional regions of Ghana has brought into being subnational political actors (chiefs and otherwise) with capacity to engage the central government directly (see also Asante, 2016). At the same time as they strengthen new actors, these processes weaken the relative power of actors in traditional areas of extraction—as in the case of political authorities and labour in the Zambian Copperbelt. This intersection of the materiality of subsoil resources with frontier expansion due to global demand and prices thus becomes part of an explanation of how actors once excluded from national settlements gain holding power that can enable them to influence national debates on resource governance. These processes also help explain how factions that were at one time vertically included in the political settlement—perhaps especially organized labour in areas of traditional production—slowly lose leverage within the dominant coalition.

Furthermore, these processes and shifts in the balance of power are part of an explanation for the emergence of and struggles over new rules governing the distribution and spending of resource rents. Across all four countries, though perhaps in ways that are more pronounced in Peru and Bolivia, the expansion of the extractive frontier into areas without a tradition of mining or hydrocarbon production has been characterized by conflict and resistance. This has generated a broad literature suggesting that such conflict has sometimes reflected efforts to protect or claim rights (to territory, water, self-governance, etc.) and at other times has been used as a tool to gain access to employment, rents, subcontracts, and other benefits or compensations (Arellano-Yanguas, 2011; Bebbington, 2012). Regardless of these different drivers of protest (some of which are interest-based, others of which are idea-based), a common response across all four countries has been for the national elites to share resource rents with subnational and local authorities in the hope that this will dissipate conflict, buy off resistance, and create conditions allowing access to subsoil resources.

One such mechanism in each of the countries has been the use of CSR as a way of co-opting local elites (Frederiksen, 2017). In three of the countries (Peru, Bolivia, and Ghana), a second, and financially much more important, mechanism has been to institute systems for the transfer of taxes and royalties to the regions in which resource extraction occurs. The most generous of these transfers has been the so-called *canon minero* in Peru, which returns 50 per cent of all taxes on mining companies to authorities in the regions of extraction. The least generous is that in Ghana, which sends just 10 per cent of royalties back to a mix of district assemblies, traditional authorities, and stools.[7] Bolivia sits in between, with more substantial transfers of hydrocarbon taxes back to gas- and oil-producing areas, and much smaller transfers of mining taxes to mining regions. Peru appears to have been particularly generous because of the level of local conflict surrounding resource extraction. Government and corporate elites believed, incorrectly as it turned out, that transferring resources to these regions would reduce conflict (Arellano-Yanguas, 2011; Ponce and McClintock, 2014). In both Peru and Bolivia, when central authorities have subsequently sought to reduce such transfers, they have been largely unable to do so because of the level of local resistance. Such resistance, driven by actors who have become accustomed to the receipt of these transfers, reflects a further sense in which the geography of resource extraction contributes to the emergence of subnational constituencies with holding power.

It is not just the physical location of resources that can have such political effects. The quality of the resource helps determine whether it becomes viable or not, how it will be mined, how much water will be used in the extraction process and so forth. Just as one example, the concentration of deposits determines whether they will be mined using open-pit or underground mining techniques. Open-pit techniques involve far more movement of earth, affect more surface property rights, and demand more water use. Such techniques have typically been much more conflictive than underground mining. The high levels of conflict in northern Peru which have had significant consequences for regional and national politics, owe much to the fact that deposits have demanded open-pit mining.

3.2 *Ideas: Resource Nationalism, the Nation, and Technopols*

Different ideas related to resource extraction have influenced the constitution of national political settlements and governance arrangements. Ideas surrounding territory, rights, environmental impacts, and ethnic–racial identity have been important in the emergence of subnational actors that contest resource extraction and the distribution of rents generated from minerals and hydrocarbons. While the experiences in Bolivia, Ghana, Peru, and Zambia suggest many ways in which ideas are important, here we focus specifically on the influence of ideas of resource populism, national unity and the nation, and the idea that technocrats are objective and above special interests, and so are able to govern more effectively than politicians.

Resource nationalism is the notion that natural resources should be managed above all for the needs of 'the nation', and therefore should be controlled by the state for 'the people'. This idea is closely related to historical experiences of colonialism, dependent development, and the capture of resource rents by foreign capital. It also has a constitutional basis in many countries, insofar as national constitutions define the state as the owner of subsoil mineral resources. This observation is important because the global industry typically talks of resource nationalism in negative terms, as an unauthorized and inefficient exercise of state power that puts a break on market functioning. This framing understates the constitutional obligation of many states to administer their countries' subsoil resource wealth, as well as the resonance that this idea has with broad parts of national populations.

Such national-populist renderings of resource governance have been important in all four countries. They have emerged at different historical moments and have typically been associated with dominant party/dominant leader settlements. In Zambia, such ideas informed the nationalizations effected by the United National Independence Party (UNIP) of Kenneth Kaunda, the first president after independence, during the late 1960s and early 1970s. They were also present in the approach to natural resource governance of Kwame Nkrumah, the first president and prime minister of Ghana following independence in 1957. In Peru, they were especially strong during the period of the nationalist Revolutionary Government of the Armed Forces (*Gobierno Revolucionario de las Fuerzas Armadas*, GRFA) from 1969 to 1974. In Bolivia, they were at the core of the agenda of the post-1952 government of the National Revolutionary Movement (*Movimiento Nacionalista Revolucionario*, MNR) and then again, more recently, since the 2006 election of the indigenist–socialist government of Evo Morales' Movement to Socialism (*Movimiento al Socialismo*, MAS).

In each of these cases, ideas of resource nationalism grounded in organized labour in the mining and oil sectors, party intellectuals, and other factions provided ideological support for notions of state ownership of extractive industry. While in more recent periods such ideas have been most forcefully mobilized in Bolivia, they have also been apparent in mineral taxation debates in the three other countries, in each instance informing (usually short-lived) efforts to introduce tax increases during periods of commodity boom.[8] Interestingly, there is some indication that the Bolivian example has served as a point of reference for some African countries pursuing such options. One prominent example has been the concept that anti-poverty policy instruments could be directly funded by taxes on the mineral and hydrocarbon sectors (Mosley, 2017). What is important here is to recognize that these sets of ideas only come into being because of the long-standing couplings of resource extraction with colonial and post-colonial exploitation. How history is remembered and interpreted thus matters. The ideological significance of natural resources in these histories creates ideational space for ideas of resource nationalism.

Ideas of the nation, national unity, and sovereignty influence the governance of extractive industries in additional ways. To the extent that the localized nature of resource extraction can elicit subnational movements demanding either greater autonomy in the governance of natural resources, or greater claims over the revenue streams made possible by royalties and the taxation of extractive industry, there is always a sense in which the political dynamics surrounding extraction can challenge national integration. Indeed, while transferring revenue to mineral- and hydrocarbon-producing regions, Ghanaian and Bolivian national authorities have also mobilized ideas of national unity (Ghana) and national equity/harmony (Bolivia) as rationales for increasing the proportion of resource rents that are centrally controlled, with a view to spending them in line with national policies and in a way that does not concentrate fiscal transfers in the regions in which extraction occurs. In Ghana, there has been a recurring commitment to distribute rents without regard for regions of extraction. Even resources from the Mineral Development Fund, which are theoretically meant to mitigate the environmental and social costs in the communities where mining occurs, are distributed to benefit non-mining communities in the name of 'unity'. In Bolivia, the MAS government has deployed ideas of the nation as a justification for changes to fiscal policy that seek to reduce the proportion of rents going to departments in the eastern lowlands that have been critical of the MAS government. Though these moves have also been part of conscious efforts to reduce the power of subnational factions that had been empowered by previously more generous fiscal transfers, they have been crafted in terms of 'the nation' and 'the people'.

Peru offers further insight into the importance of ideas. This is a case in which the idea of technocracy as legitimate government has been important in influencing the governance of extractives and development. The relative stability of macroeconomic policy, and the suite of incentives to encourage extractive industry investment across the country, even in the face of relatively unstable governments and sustained social conflict over resource extraction, is taken by some scholars to reflect the relative power of technocrats within key ministries in defining national policy (Dargent, 2015). These technocrats have, over the last twenty years, been committed to ideas that place value on free markets, are suspicious of planning, and deeply doubt the capacity of the state to be an efficient and effective economic actor. This relationship between ideas and pockets of bureaucratic and technocratic competence has also been visible in other parts of the Peruvian state, where over the last two decades, a strong, rights-oriented legal technocracy has been consolidated in the Human Rights Ombudsman's office and, with somewhat less autonomy (and more recently), in the Ministry of Environment and Vice-Ministry for Intercultural Affairs.[9] Together, these different concentrations of technocratic strength have played important roles in determining how resource governance institutions are designed to manage the trade-offs between the promotion of investment and the protection of citizenship rights in relation to natural resource governance.

Quoting from Chapter 2, the argument here is that in a 'context of "fractured politics" (Crabtree, 2011), technocrats have remained fundamental to operating the central state in Peru, and this has contributed to a higher degree of stability and responsibility in macroeconomic policymaking than in past eras (Dargent, 2015)'. Of course, this is also possible because of a certain alignment between the thinking of technocrats and that of national business elites, but it also appears that the very *idea* of being technical rather than political is mobilized in ways that protect space for such so-called 'techno-pols'.

The ideas embodied in technocracy or resource nationalism as forms of governing, as well as ideas that have motivated mobilization and protest, have interacted with the material qualities of subsoil resources in ways that have had clear implications for resource politics and national politics more generally. Though these ideas and materialities cannot be explained away as mere artefacts of a politics of interests and incentives, the effects that they have derive from the particular ways in which they interact with such interests. We now turn to a closing discussion of these interests and their implications for mineral governance.

4 Political Settlements, Extractive Industry, and Inclusive Development

Terry Karl once commented that 'the "resource curse" is primarily a political and not an economic phenomenon', and that the institutional distortions that prevent economic diversification and inclusive development 'cannot be undone without a huge coordinated effort by all stakeholders involved' (Karl, 2007: 256, 258). Introducing this chapter, we noted that scholarly and activist work alike have highlighted the importance of politics and power in resource extraction. The question, however, is how to talk about such power in a formal, analytical way that combines both elite and grassroots politics. Our argument has been that political settlements approaches offer a fruitful response to this task.

Political settlement frameworks focus attention on relationships of *vertical* power between elites and bases within a dominant coalition, and *horizontal* power between elites of a dominant coalition and excluded factions who are not party to the benefits bestowed by the coalition (Khan, 2010). Levy and Walton (2013) and Levy (2014) complement this framework by arguing that how elites within a dominant coalition manage these relationships and approach development depends on whether the broader political system is characterized by competition among leaders and parties or the dominance of a particular leader or party. Political competition would lead elites to recruit clients into the coalition as a means of holding on to power (a form of political settlement they refer to as 'competitive clientelism') and would tend therefore to operate with shorter-term time horizons oriented towards recruitment of clients ahead of electoral cycles. Conversely, dominant leaders and parties are able to worry less about client recruitment and to use resources for longer-term political projects based on particular ideas of development or personal gain, a form of settlement referred to as a dominant leader/dominant party settlement. Such forms of dominant party/dominant leader settlement can range from the authoritarian modernization project of a developmental state through to a personalized kleptocratic project, and can involve leadership that is autocratic or elected, but in either instance, dominant.

How far do these frameworks help explain how extractive industries have been governed across Bolivia, Ghana, Peru, and Zambia? In turn, how far does the prominence of extractive industries in these economies help explain these vertical and horizontal relationships and the extent to which political arrangements are characterized by competition or authoritarianism? Several themes emerge in the country analyses, which we address in this section. The first two themes relate to the relationships between the nature of the broader political system, extractive industry governance, and modes of inclusion. The second two themes have to do with the relationships between horizontal and vertical distribution of power among elites, excluded factions and 'lower-level groups', and institutional change. The final issue relates to the particular insights to be gained from a long-term view of these relationships.

4.1 *Competitive Clientelism, Economic Transformation, and Modes of Inclusion*

It has been argued in some of the political settlements literature that competitive clientelist systems tend to be associated with weaker commitment to investment of resources in structural transformation of the economy because leaders' primary concern is to use resources to recruit electoral support in order to remain in power (Hickey et al., 2015; Whitfield et al., 2015). As noted in Chapter 1, the notion of clientelism in this concept is not one of the traditional patron–client relationship of dominance and dependence, but rather of the elites who, in competing for political power, need to recruit and sustain supporters both to assume, and then retain, governing power. The 'clients' in 'competitive clientelism' thus have significant power themselves, which they can use to trade their support for governing elites in return for benefits of different types. This creates incentives for elites to channel resources to different constituencies rather than to invest those resources in one or other development strategy. This claim that competitive political systems can lead to dissipation of resources has led to arguments for the developmental state, and the notion that a combination of authoritarian rule with bureaucratic competence can allow states to introduce coordinated programmes of economic and institutional modernization without having to dilute reforms to accommodate the electoral and political claims made by those who lose out in such processes (O'Donnell, 1973, 1988; Evans, 1995; Golooba-Mutebi, 2013).

At one read, the case for the limited developmental efficacy of competitive clientelism seems to be borne out by the four country histories. The argument is made most forcefully through the discussion of mining governance in Ghana in Chapter 5, which argues that a competitive clientelist system has created incentives for the political party in power to use rents from extractives primarily as a means of cultivating clients with a view to securing allegiance ahead of the next electoral campaign. It is worth repeating the text of that chapter:

> It is this form of political calculus that shapes the manner in which mining resources are distributed, and the way in which this in turn shapes the impact of mining on national and local development. Notably, allocation of rents to traditional authorities and chiefs does not seem to be driven by socio-economic development concerns but is more of a co-optation strategy driven by: (1) the logic of maintaining social orders, due to the significant leverage of traditional authorities over mineral-rich lands; (2) the desire of ruling elites to win and maintain political power through the political support of chiefs, who wield substantial leverage over rural voters. Traditional authorities receive a significant share of mineral rents, mainly because ruling political elites want to avoid provoking resistance from a group in society that brokers land and votes in the rural areas.

We make a similar argument in Chapter 3 on Bolivia, though in that instance, the emphasis is less on using resource rents to cultivate clients, and more on building political alliances:

> [T]he incentive for elites has consistently been to control revenue streams from resources in order to spend on managing political alliances, rather than to invest in economic and social development.

However, a closer look at the extractives sector suggests that while competitive clientelist systems might underinvest in forceful state-directed approaches to economic diversification and transformation, they *have* nonetheless been associated with transformational policy in the extractives sector and the economy as a whole. The introduction of thoroughgoing neoliberal reforms to break up state-owned extractive industry enterprises and encourage foreign direct investment has occurred during periods of democracy characterized by competitive clientelist practices. This is particularly clear for the periods from the latter 1980s to mid-1990s in Bolivia and Zambia, and to some degree also in Peru.[10]

Across the four countries, periods of competitive clientelist rule have not succeeded in using resource rents to foster any substantial diversification of the economy. In Peru, the commitment of 50 per cent of taxes paid by mining companies to the *canon minero*, the return of all royalties to the producing regions, and the use of part of those rents that *do* accrue to central government for the financing of national social programmes, has the knock-on effect of reducing resource availability for investment in structural transformation of the economy, even when policymakers have identified this to be a critical need (Ghezzi and Gallardo, 2013). In the Andean region, the argument is made that, for obvious political reasons, governments systematically underinvest in research and development relative to what they spend on transfers, and this lack of spending on innovation holds back economic change. Chapter 5, on Ghana, argues that the emphasis on channelling rents to clients has meant that they are not available for investment in alternative forms of economic development and has contributed to the creation of a more broadly based national capitalist class. It is also possible that the combination of Dutch disease effects, global competition, and free trade agreements that hinder preferential treatment of domestic industry together made such diversification unlikely, with or without targeted investment.

One consequence of this is that under these regimes, large-scale extractive industry has fostered social inclusion at least as much through contributing taxes and royalties that have then been spent on targeted social protection and other transfer programmes, as it has through the labour market. This pattern varies across the countries, with the more significant successes in poverty reduction in Peru and Bolivia arguably reflecting the combination of transfer programmes and the trickle-down effect of rapid economic growth fuelled by the mining and hydrocarbon sectors (Mosley, 2017). It remains an open question as to how durable such poverty reduction will be if commodity prices continue to fall, or if investors choose not to proceed with new projects, which would result in a reduction in the tax and royalty payments that form the fiscal base of social protection programmes.

Finally, the fact that both Peru and Bolivia have had significant success in poverty reduction over the last decade presents a challenge to arguments about the relations between political settlements and inclusive development. While both contexts are characterized by a broadly competitive clientelist political logic, Bolivia's MAS government has been in power for a decade and is beginning to display features that are more characteristic of dominant party contexts. It also espouses an ideological commitment to socialism. Peru looks very different. The same period has seen regular turnover of governing parties, with swings from the right to centre-right and a more or less sustained ideological commitment to the market as the most effective allocator of resources and investments. Moreover, these two quite distinct cases share similar patterns of inclusion in terms of both poverty reduction and the forms taken for consultation over resource extraction, with evidence in each country of significant limits on community-level voice regarding the viability, design, and governance of mining and hydrocarbons (Humphreys Bebbington and Bebbington, 2012; Gustafsson, 2017; Schilling-Vacaflor, 2017). The implication is that the relations between inclusive development and natural resource extraction can be similar under differently structured settlements. This may suggest equifinality, in which the workings of different types of political settlements end up achieving similar outcomes by different means, or it may suggest different settlements following ultimately similar strategies: the promotion of rapid growth of extractive investment, coupled with concerted efforts to redistribute the benefits of this growth.

4.2 *Dominance and Modes of Inclusion*

Over the *longue durée* considered in the four country studies, there have been several periods of more or less authoritarian and personalized dominant leader/dominant party rule. The most obvious of these are the military government of Peru from 1968 to 1980 and the period of Kenneth Kaunda's rule in Zambia from 1964 to 1991.[11] As just noted, Evo Morales' MAS government in Bolivia may also be easing into a dominant leader/party mode of rule. These periods have been associated with state ownership of extractive industries (the MAS government has re-floated/re-strengthened state mining and oil companies)[12] and a unionized workforce, with benefits channelled primarily to unions and to human settlements around mine sites.

The Kaunda and Peruvian military regimes did seek state-led modes of economic transformation, but ultimately with little success—neither in economic diversification nor in sustained poverty reduction. Efforts to foster inclusion through employment or unions (but not political participation) also unravelled. Thus, while a case could be made that these authoritarian/dominant party systems did encourage development policy that looked beyond the short-term need to recruit clients for electoral success (MAS being an exception, as it is still subject to electoral disciplining), they were not successful in converting these visions into sustainable forms of social inclusion. This is so because of limited governing and technical capacity and (in Zambia's case) because of falling commodity prices. So, while the Levy and Walton (2013) framework might go some way in explaining how and why certain ideas about development and inclusion emerged under these authoritarian systems, it remains the case that these ideas failed on their own terms.

4.3 *Horizontal and Vertical Power Relations and Piecemeal Institutional Reform*

In each of the four countries, a significant part of the post-1995 expansion of large-scale extractive industry has occurred in non-traditional areas for mining and hydrocarbons.[13] In most instances, these have also been areas occupied by resource-poor and politically excluded populations. Examples include: the ethnically diverse communities of North-Western Province in Zambia long excluded from the Copperbelt–Lusaka axis of power; the resource-poor municipalities and historically marginalized Guaraní and Weenhayek peoples of the sparsely populated dry Chaco of Bolivia; chronically poor peasant and indigenous communities of the Peruvian Andes; and resource-poor communities in Ghana. In Khan's (2010) terms, expansion has largely occurred in areas occupied by lower-level factions, some of them ostensibly within the dominant coalition, others not—but in all cases, these have been groups in positions of relative exclusion from centres of power.

However, as noted in Subsection 3.1, this self-same expansion has increased the potential political leverage of these excluded groups insofar as they can complicate company access to the subsoil. This leverage has increased further as transnational and national urban actors concerned with rights, environmental impacts, and justice have reached out to these factions. Often the response of the elites within the dominant coalition has been to try and co-opt these newly empowered actors, and this has sometimes been successful. However, at the same time, the mobilization (or threat of mobilization) on the part of these factions has also induced a series of institutional reforms. This has perhaps been most evident in Peru, where, in the face of conflict, governments have introduced new laws and regulations on environmental impact, prior consultation, revenue sharing and local land-use planning, among others. These regulations have, however, been introduced in response to horizontal pressures, rather than because of fundamental changes in development thinking among the elites and within the dominant coalition. As a result, these reforms have also been introduced in a piecemeal fashion and are fragile and subject to reversal. This use of institutional change in response to specific claims and perceived urgencies has tended to produce governance arrangements that lack strategic coherence.

4.4 *ASM as a Constraining Form of Horizontal Power*

In Bolivia, Ghana, and Peru, though to a lesser extent in Zambia, the last three decades have been associated with the continuing and substantial growth of an artisanal, small- and medium-scale mining sector. This sector, which is composed largely of poor un- or under-employed parts of the rural and urban population, has emerged from factions long excluded from the formal economy, as in the case of communities affected by the expansion of the extractive frontier, noted above. There are two significant exceptions to this trend. First, the sector also incorporates relatively significant owners of capital. These are the entrepreneurs who provide the larger-scale machinery to miners, organize work gangs, control marketing, and, in some instances, participate in laundering illegally sourced investment capital and/or the illegally extracted gold. Second, in the specific case of Bolivia, a number of these miners were previously members of the miners' union of the pre-1985 period. When union workers were laid off as part of structural adjustment programmes, some were given mining licences as compensation. These rights have become part of the basis for the growing informal sector. Importantly, such resource rights are also a key asset with which these miners have sought to negotiate with larger-scale companies interested in mining the areas to which the formerly laid-off miners now hold mineral rights.

For these different reasons, the ASM sector has emerged as a particularly powerful faction. Its influence resides in the fact that it not only controls access to the same subsoil often sought by expanding large-scale mining operations, but, in Ghana, Peru, and Bolivia, is also responsible for a substantial percentage of all gold leaving the country. In addition, the low-tech, labour-intensive nature of ASM means that the sector generates many more jobs than does large-scale mining. This combination of factors has meant that these sectors have had the potential to influence dominant coalitions in more significant ways than do dispersed communities, municipalities, environmentalists, and others with their more specific claims. In Bolivia, the mobilizing power of the cooperatives has meant that they were able to exercise significant influence over new mining legislation in 2014. In Peru and Bolivia, there is evidence to suggest that the sector (or at least important actors within the sector) has been able to use its resources to influence the election of subnational and national representatives. In Ghana, the ASM sector provides livelihoods to over 1 million people and produces around one-third of gold exports. This sheer scale, coupled with the sector's links to local chiefs and business elites, gives it power. As we note in Chapter 5 on Ghana, '[s]upporting small-scale mining is... one simple way for politicians to appear sympathetic to the rural, unemployed youth and the families they financially support, (Teschner, 2012); and '[i]n a country where... presidential elections are sometimes won by less than 50,000 votes, it is easy to understand the political relevance of *galamsey* operators to ruling political elites and in shaping the political settlement around mining sector governance more broadly'.

4.5 *Cautionary Insights From the* Longue Durée

The *longue durée* perspective taken in our country studies has been sobering. Notwithstanding the many specific regulatory changes documented, and the many shifts to and fro in dominant political coalitions, the impression is that underlying productive structures have been relatively immutable. At the beginning of the periods under analysis, these four economies were dependent on resource extraction (at least for foreign direct investment (FDI), fiscal revenue, and export earnings), and by 2015 they were still dependent on resource extraction, albeit sometimes of different natural resources. Notwithstanding the emergence of more complex urban service and informal economies over time, or of a moderately diversified export agriculture and agro-industry, these four countries have not moved far beyond economies that are dependent on the primary sector. They have seen no real success in developing and diversifying a secondary sector and continue to have public budgets that are dependent on the rise and fall of commodity prices. Put another way, they have not been terribly successful in developing stable, durable, and diverse channels of inclusion through either the labour market or public expenditure.

This presents the slightly perplexing dilemma of how to relate a picture of political settlements that change, but a productive structure that changes very little. Even if taking a longer historical view allowed us to see beyond the short-term political volatility that occupies the minds of many commentators, we did still identify a number of changes between political settlements over the last century in each of the countries studied. If, put very crudely, our independent variable was changing but our dependent variable was stable, does this mean that there is no relationship between the two?

Our resolution of this dilemma has been to talk of 'meta-settlements'. This idea initially emerged from our analysis of Zambia, in an effort to tie together five distinct political settlements running from the colonial era to the present. Ultimately, we identified two key phenomena that have persisted across different settlements: authoritarianism and a narrow (vulnerable) elite. To quote from Chapter 4, the first is manifest in a 'concentration of power in the hands of the executive branch and a weakening of institutions of accountability, including parliament and the judiciary'. This authoritarianism persists even after the emergence of multiparty elections. With regard to the second, Zambian leadership has tended to pass between relatively few hands, even if this change of power occurs often, as in recent years. This notion of 'meta-settlement' became useful for seeing enduring trends in political relationships across all four countries. Examples of such durable phenomena include: the long historical tug-of-war over control of natural resources between chiefs and central government in Ghana; the recurring struggle over political control among Bolivia's regional elites, funded by the most lucrative subsoil resource of the moment; or the persistent centralized control of resource rents in Peru, until the last decade.

This observation raises a follow-on question: if certain features have been so resilient to change, why is this so? The experiences of Bolivia, Ghana, Peru, and Zambia suggest that part of the answer to this question may have to do with natural resource dependence itself. First, through creating the reality, or the prospect, of significant rents, the very imaginary of subsoil wealth creates incentives that encourage political and economic elites to focus on capturing these rents, rather than seeking economic and political innovations that might create new value. Second, by producing highly uneven geographies of accumulation and dispossession, and creating incentives to particular regions to increase their capture of rents, the natural resource economy creates serious obstacles to the building of broad-based coalitions that share a national development imaginary (Watts, 2004a, 2004b). Natural resource-dependent economies may tend to foster political splintering more than alliance.

Having said this, it is important not to overstate the idea of underlying continuity and limited change. The emergence of powerful actors, along with changes in foundational ideas, *have* modified elements of the political settlements in each of the four countries in ways that *have* enhanced inclusion: colonial subjects *have* become citizens with rights and voting power in all four countries; access to rule *has* become somewhat less determined by race or family; and degrees of competition among economic elites *have* increased. In general, competitive clientelist settlements have been associated with a sustained widening of citizenship rights more than dominant party/dominant leader settlements. Competitive clientelist settlements, while certainly not free of corruption, have been characterized by relatively greater degrees of political accountability in the use of resource rents. The nature of settlements has, therefore, had important implications for the relationships between resource-dependent economies and the nature and degree of social inclusion. Where the nature of settlements appears to have had less effect has been in the successful fostering of economic diversification and reduction of the weight of resource rents within the national economy.

5 A Long-Term Natural Resource Governance Lens on Political Settlements

Mineral and hydrocarbon resources are intensely local. Even when it can seem that the extractive frontier is everywhere (especially when represented through maps of exploration licences), it remains the case that commercial quantities of these resources are located in relatively few places, and many of the environmental and social consequences of their extraction are relatively concentrated in space.[14] At the same time, mineral resources have been part of international value chains that have become increasingly globalized and integrated, at least since the Iberian pillage of Latin America. Over the last century, these commodity markets have been further internationalized, with prices set globally, and an increasingly wide range of transnational actors interested in securing access to the resources. In between these two scales, subsoil resources are also deeply national. Their commodification has often been one of the principal pillars (if not *the* pillar) of national economies, serving as an important source of fiscal revenue and foreign exchange, and a driver of national investment and elite formation through the capture of rents. Subsoil resources have also often become national icons. Histories of Andean identities cannot be told without reference to gold and silver, the centrality of mining and now natural gas to Bolivian nationalism is clear, and Zambian 'expectations of modernity' (Ferguson, 1999) continue to pass through copper. And beyond the countries in which we worked, oil is part of national and subnational identities in Nigeria (Watts, 2004a), while in the UK, the miners' strike of 1984–85 was profound not just because coal was a valuable commodity that created jobs, but also because it was part of national and class identities.

These qualities of subsoil resources have implications for themes within any discussion of the politics of extractive industry governance and of political settlements in natural resource-dependent economies. We summarize the key arguments we have made in this chapter and throughout our country chapters with six themes of special significance: (1) the distinction between national settlements and policy domain settlements; (2) scalar relations within political settlements; (3) the implications of natural resource rents for settlements; (4) the scale of investment required to develop mineral and hydrocarbon deposits; (5) the symbolic power of subsoil resources; (6) the *longue durée* of resource extraction. In the following paragraphs, we elaborate on each of these.

While some approaches (Hickey and Sen, 2016; Levy and Kelsall, 2016) distinguish between the overall national political settlement and more specific settlements in particular policy domains (such as education, health, or social protection), this distinction may not always be relevant for natural resource extraction. In those instances in which the mining, oil, and gas sectors are central to the national political economy, identity formation, and the constitution of national political actors, it may be unhelpful to imply a sharp distinction between the overall political settlement and the natural resource policy domain. Instead, these two 'spaces' may be mutually constitutive. The historical experiences of Bolivia, Ghana, Peru, and Zambia show just how central mining and hydrocarbons have been to national political debates. Over extended periods in each country, the mining and hydrocarbons 'policy domain' has been *the* key national political domain.

Second, the local, national, and global dimensions of resource extraction also imply that an analysis of the politics of extractive industry governance and of the constitution of political settlements must work across scales. The transnational enters in the form of global investment capital and practices, multinational companies, regulation of global commodity markets, global price trends, international financial institutions, transnational civil society, and global environmental and human rights frameworks. By the same token, the localized nature of minerals and hydrocarbons means that their extraction consistently brings subnational actors into national and international dynamics. Because local actors have significant influence over the ability of companies and states to secure access to these natural resources, national and international elites often have to negotiate with them and at times have to enrol them into broader political settlements in order to be able to extract minerals and hydrocarbons. In this sense, the geographically specific location of resources can frequently produce new subnational elites with substantial power to influence the course of extractive industry development.

A third special feature of subsoil resources derives from their ability to produce significant rents, especially during periods of commodity boom. The combination of relatively easy-to-capture 'super-rents' and the potential power of local actors to restrict access to the subsoil means that the politics surrounding resource extraction can be particularly prone to violence and corruption. In addition, the potential to capture such rents can make these resources singularly attractive to actors seeking to realize and finance a broad range of other political projects. We see diverse projects financed by these resources across Chapters 2 to 5. In Bolivia, MAS increased central government capture of hydrocarbon rents to finance broad-based social redistribution. Chiefs in Ghana sought the means to consolidate territorial and political authority through natural resource rents. Copper revenues were central to the nationalist post-colonial project in Zambia, while in Peru the development of the mining sector was crucial to the effort of different post-internal conflict governments to establish political order in the highlands. The politics of extractive industry governance are thus also the politics of core financing mechanisms for the explicitly political and ideological strategies of elites of diverse types. Political settlements analysis, with its focus on elite strategy in relation to 'excluded factions', is particularly useful for drawing attention to these types of relationship.

Fourth, and related to the prior point, large-scale natural resource extraction projects typically require substantial up-front investments, which then become immobile capital. The same would apply for many infrastructural projects that often accompany resource extraction, such as dams, ports, trunk roads, and rail lines. Such investments require significant 'credible commitment' from government (Sen, 2013) to provide investors with the financial, legal, and physical security they demand in order to proceed with these projects. In order to commit to investments on such a scale, companies seek sizeable tax holidays or reductions, as well as legal and contract security. Because the fixity of investments makes them more vulnerable to expropriation and the demands of localized protest and social conflict, investors also seek physical and juridical security from the state, which can translate into assurances that public force will be used against protest and demands for legal exceptions and guarantees. In the case of hydrocarbons, the scale of necessary investment also makes this a sector dominated by large-scale capital ownership. Consequently, the sector is characterized by asymmetries of power, knowledge, and expertise which often can only be offset (albeit partially) by social conflict, public debate, or relatively autonomous countervailing regulatory bodies within the state. The exception to this pattern is the case of ASM—an activity whose geography is itself related to the nature of mineral deposits, only some of which are accessible to ASM. In these different ways, the materialities of the mine, well, pipeline or resource deposit have implications for resource politics and lead economic and political elites to establish agreements that can be resilient in the face of popular protest. Insofar as it situates civic movements' holding power in relation to these other players in the settlement and in relation to the ruling coalition, political settlements analysis is useful in qualifying some of the more hopeful and populist sentiments that can inform studies that focus only on grassroots resistance.

Fifth the symbolic significance of subsoil resources means that 'ideas' take on potentially causal power. The implication is that the nature of the political settlement has to be understood not just in terms of interests, but also of the politics of ideas, some of which have considerable political valence and a capacity to mobilize resistance (Hall, 2010; Hickey, 2012; Hickey et al., 2015). Across all four countries, 'resource populism' and 'justice' have been and continue to be important ideas that have affected natural resource governance and social mobilization. In the specific cases of Peru and Bolivia, ideas surrounding indigenous peoples' rights of consultation have also influenced negotiations around mining and hydrocarbon investments. The cultural significance and historical resonance of these ideas—and the extent to which they are mobilized by actors who draw no obvious gain from them—suggests that this is clearly an instance in which ideas cannot be collapsed into interests, and that they have a causal effect on the constitution of settlements and the governance arrangements pursued under those settlements. The politics of extractive industry governance is a clear illustration of Hall's claim that 'the politics of ideas is intrinsic, rather than epiphenomenal, to the processes of coalition formation that underpin institutional change' (2010: 212).

Finally, the *longue durée* view taken in this project complicates some of the categorical frameworks used in political settlements thinking. In particular, the distinction between competitive clientelist/dominant leader-party forms of settlement loses some of its cogency (cf. Khan, 2010; Levy and Walton, 2013). Competitive clientelism refers to systems in which the elites need to compete with supporters in order to gain or maintain power, in contrast to a dominant leader/party system, in which the elites are able to wield power relatively uncontested (Levy and Walton, 2013; Levy, 2014). At the very least, our analysis makes the distinction between these two types of settlements appear descriptive, rather than explanatory, insofar as it begs the question of why more dominant or competitive modes of rule emerge in the first place. While some argue that the purpose of political settlements theory is precisely to understand how particular forms of 'settled' relationships affect development processes and outcomes, looking at politics over the *longue durée* demands explanation of how and why settlements change, and how far these changes are related to the dynamics of development.

In the country analyses in Chapters 2 to 5, a view of the *longue durée* also allowed us to map more explicitly the rise and demise of different political actors as a means of explaining how certain periods of rule emerged. In this regard, the long-term historical approach of this research has made more use of Khan's (2010) emphasis on understanding how boundaries of horizontal and vertical exclusion are negotiated, and the implications of these boundaries for the ways in which dominant coalitions form and unravel and how resources are governed. The country analyses have also made clear the importance of understanding the causal processes that explain how certain actors acquire or lose holding power[15] in ways that influence their position within a political settlement. In particular the materiality of the resource, transnational linkages, and certain ideas were each often central to these relationships of relative power as were the patterns of accumulation and dispossession unleashed by prior political settlements.

Taking a longer-term view has helped guard against associating settlements with regimes. Put another way, settlements for the most part last much longer than governments. In the case of Peru, for instance, just three periods of settlement are identified between 1895 and 2016, even though, as we noted in the introduction to Chapter 2, 'the country has had twelve constitutions and over 100 governments [since independence in 1821], while its economic system has run the gamut from extreme liberalism to statism and back again'. These settlements are associated, chronologically, with periods of: oligarchic rule and foreign capital domination; statism and accelerated social change; and neoliberalism characterized by both competitive authoritarianism and multiparty democracy. These longer-term readings of settlements make clear that certain elite pacts associated with key organizing ideas (e.g. foreign capital dominance; neoliberalism; curtailment of citizenship rights) endure well beyond specific governments. Thus, while things may appear to change from government to government, this should not divert attention from the persistence of 'meta-settlements' that are much more stable over time and involve similar elites and foundational ideas.

6 Final Words

Political settlements and natural resource extraction exist in a relationship of mutual constitution from which there is no escape. The nature of the political settlement has significant influence on how extractive industries are governed, and how their role in national and local development is understood. The settlement defines those elites whose interests will have most influence on resource extraction, but also the relationships of incorporation and clientelism that elites must finance through the use of resource rents if they are to sustain the settlement. Conversely, the existence of significant subsoil resources that are capable of generating large rents defines the terrain on which settlements are constituted, negotiated, and contested. In some sense, these resource rents become one of the main stories in town, a narrative axis around which political actors revolve in their attempts to capture those rents, whether for personal gain or to finance particular visions of society. This does not mean that natural resources or resource rents define the actual nature of the settlement—there is much room for creativity and change; it *does* mean, however, that whatever the political innovations that might emerge in such processes of change, these innovations will never escape the incentives and ideas brought into being by natural resource wealth.

Ideas and materiality are critically important in bringing new political actors into being. In natural resource politics, much mobilization and aggregation of interests and motivations hinges upon shared ideas that articulate movements, and also upon the shared opportunities and losses, both real and perceived, which derive from the material nature and geographical location of the resource in question. Ideas are also critical because they frame debates and bound the limits of the thinkable: they can therefore restrict political action and imagination while also becoming the targets of actions that aim to challenge and reframe these dominant ideas.

And finally, for the four countries in which we have worked, transnational factors have been central to the politics of natural resource governance since colonial times. Global valuation of gold, copper, tin, silver, and hydrocarbons (the main resources that we have discussed) has been the primary factor bringing the subsoils of these four countries into global circuits of finance. With these valuations have come transnational demands, explorers, and interests, as much in colonial times as in the present. It is impossible to understand the nature of national resource politics absent an attention to these global actors and factors.

Regardless of whether one finds the language of political settlements useful, the long histories of Bolivia, Ghana, Peru, and Zambia make palpably clear that pact making, contestation, negotiation, and violence have been part and parcel of the governance of natural resource extraction. There has never been, nor will there ever be, a national collective meeting of minds on what constitutes 'good' natural resource governance: there is only ever some degree of balance ('settlement') among consent, dissent, and imposition. By the same token, there is rarely, if ever, a fully collective agreement on the sort of 'inclusive development' towards which this 'good' resource governance should be oriented. Some voices, some interests, and some ideas are always more excluded and less powerful than others. Analytically, what matters is to understand how certain voices, interests, and ideas become ascendant in resource governance and how they are able to stabilize this ascendancy. Politically, what matters is to use such an analysis to pursue the balance of power, interests, and ideas that the actor in question is seeking. At least in the countries studied here, resource governance was never just a question of getting the institutions right. It has only ever been part of a political strategy that in turn has its own political effects.

Endnotes

1. This term is not used in a pejorative sense, but rather to refer to the style and the wider circulation and recognition of the text.
2. Another example of this route is the Temer government of Brazil, which is seeking aggressively to increase mining and other forms of resource extraction in order to help fill budget gaps produced by crises in other sectors and in the macroeconomy.
3. The absence or failure of policies to offset the stagnation of small-scale farming was another factor in the movement of younger, mostly male, adults into ASM.
4. After 2006, Bolivia diverges from this pattern somewhat. That said, though the MAS government has relaunched COMIBOL as part of its resource populist endeavours, investment in large-scale mining is still dominated by international companies. Note that investment in small-scale mining, which responds to very different economic and social dynamics and is less formalized, is dominated by the domestic licit and illicit private sector.
5. Peru is a partial exception in that, while dominated by international investors, there is also a national mining capitalist class invested mostly in medium-scale mines.
6. Two of these actors were, for instance, important figures in the 2016 national presidential and congressional elections.
7. Stools are a form of local authority in Ghana. Note also that a tenth of this 10 per cent can be retained by the Office of Administration of Stool Lands for administrative costs.
8. In Ghana in 2009; Peru in 2011; and Zambia in 2008.
9. Though these offices have, since late 2016, become somewhat more fragile.
10. The precise timing varies slightly among the three countries. Peru is a partial exception, because the authoritarian Fujimori regime (1990–2000) introduced many such reforms. However, early shock and neoliberalizing reforms (albeit not related to the mining sector) *were* introduced under the preceding competitive

regimes from 1981–85 and 1985–90. Also, after 2000, elected governments have maintained the Fujimori reforms.

11. In particular, during his period of one-party rule from 1973 onwards.
12. In Peru, one US mining company survived nationalization.
13. There has also been expanded investment in traditional areas.
14. Many other consequences reach much further of course: the downstream effects of oil spills or tailing dam failures; the climate effects of hydrocarbon burning; the national governance effects of severe subnational conflict over resources; etc.
15. Khan's notion of 'holding power' refers to the power of actors to hold their position and push back on the ability of other actors to impose their interests.

References

Abdulai, A.-G. 2012. 'State Elites and the Politics of Regional Inequality in Ghana'. Unpublished PhD thesis, University of Manchester, Manchester.

Abdulai, A.-G. 2017. 'The political economy of regional inequality in Ghana: Do political settlements matter?'. *European Journal of Development Research* 29(1): 213–29.

Abdulai, A.-G. and S. Hickey. 2016. 'The politics of development under competitive clientelism: Insights from Ghana's education sector'. *African Affairs* 115(458): 44–72.

Abdulai, A.-G. and D. Hulme. 2015. 'The politics of regional inequality in Ghana: State elites, donors and PRSPs'. *Development Policy Review* 33(5): 529–53.

Abusada, R., F. Du Bois, E. Morón, and J. Valderrama. 2000. *La Reforma Incompleta.* Lima: Instituto Peruano de Economía, Universidad del Pacífico.

Acemoglu, D. and J. A. Robinson. 2012. *Why Nations Fail: The Origins of Power, Prosperity and Poverty*. New York: Crown.

Acemoglu, D., S. Johnson, and J. A. Robinson. 2001. 'The colonial origins of comparative development: An empirical investigation'. *American Economic Review* 91: 1369–401.

Acemoglu, D., S. Johnson, and J. A. Robinson. 2002. 'Reversal of fortune: Geography and institutions in the making of the modern world income distribution'. *Quarterly Journal of Economics* 117: 1231–94.

Acheampong, J. 2015. 'Small-scale gold exports on the rise'. Graphic online, 14 April. Available at http://www.graphic.com.gh/business/business-news/small-scale-goldexports-on-the-rise.html, accessed 26 May 2017.

Addy, S. N. 1998. 'Ghana: Revival of the mineral sector'. *Resources Policy* 24(4): 229–39.

Afryie, K., J. K. Ganle, and A. A. Adomako. 2016. 'The good in evil: A discourse analysis of the galamsey industry in Ghana'. *Oxford Development Studies* 44(4): 493–508.

Akabzaa, T. 2009. 'Mining in Ghana: Implications for national economic development and poverty reduction'. In *Mining and Development in Africa*, edited by B. Campbell, pp. 25–65. Montreal: Pluto Publishers.

Akabzaa, T. and A. Darimani. 2001. 'A study of impacts of mining sector investment in Ghana on mining communities'. Report prepared for the Technical Committee on Structural Adjustment Participatory Review Initiative (SAPRI) on Ghana.

Amanor, K. S. 2008. 'The changing face of customary land tenure'. In *Contesting Land and Custom in Ghana: State, Chief and the Citizen*, edited by J. M. Ubink and K. S. Amanor, pp. 55–81. Amsterdam: Leiden University Press.

Amanor, K. S. 2009. 'Securing land rights in Ghana'. In *Legalising Land Rights Local Practices, State Responses and Tenure Security in Africa, Asia and Latin America*, edited by

J. M. Ubink, A. J. Hoekema and W. J. Assies, pp. 97–131. Leiden: Leiden University Press.

Amnesty International. 2014. *Peru: Five Years on from Bagua Violence and Still No Justice for Victims*. Lima: Amnesty International.

Anin, T. E. 1994. *Gold in Ghana*. 4th Edn. Accra: Selwyn Publishers.

Arellano-Yanguas, J. 2008. A thoroughly modern resource curse?: The new natural resource policy agenda and the mining revival in Peru. Working paper series, 300. Brighton: IDS.

Arellano-Yanguas, J. 2011. *¿Minería sin fronteras? Conflicto y desarrollo en regiones mineras del Perú*. Lima: Instituto de Estudios Peruanos.

Arellano-Yanguas, J. 2014. 'Industrias extractivas, descentralización y desarrollo local: Economía política de políticas fiscales y redistributivas en Perú y Bolivia'. Reporte Anual de Industrias Extractivas II. La Paz, Bolivia: CEDLA.

Arellano-Yanguas, J. 2016. 'Mining policies in Humala's Peru. A patchwork of improvised nationalism and corporate interests'. In *The Political Economy of Natural Resources and Development: From Neoliberalism to Resource Nationalism*, edited by Paul A. Haslam and Pablo Heidrich, pp. 174–90. New York: Routledge.

Arhin, K. 1967. 'The financing of the Ashanti expansion (1700–1820)'. *Africa* 37(3): 283–91.

Arhin, K. 1978. 'Gold-mining and trading among the Ashanti of Ghana'. *Journal desafricanistes* 48(1): 89–100.

Armstrong, A. T. 2008. 'Gold strike in the bread basket: Indigenous livelihoods, the World Bank, and territorial restructuring in Western Ghana'. Development Report No.18, Institute for Food and Development Policy, Oakland, CA.

Aryee, B. N. A. 2001. 'Ghana's mining sector: Its contribution to the national economy'. *Resources Policy* 27: 61–75.

Aryee, B. N. A. 2014. 'Recent trends and developments in Ghana's mining fiscal regime'. PowerPoint presentation at the workshop for ECOWAS public officials on the implementation of the African Mining Vision (AMV) and the ECOWAS Minerals Development Policy (EMDP), 3–4 November, Accra.

Aryeetey, E. and A. McKay. 2007. 'Ghana: The challenge of translating sustained growth into poverty reduction'. In *Delivering on the Promise of Pro-poor Growth: Insights and Lessons from Country Experiences*, edited by T. Besley and L. J. Cord, pp. 147–68. New York and Washington, DC: Palgrave Macmillan and World Bank.

Asante, E. P. 2016. 'Pathway/s to Inclusive Development in Ghana: Oil, Subnational–National Power Relations and Ideas'. DPhil thesis Faculty of Humanities. Manchester: University of Manchester.

Assies, W. 2004. 'Bolivia: A gasified democracy'. *Revista Europea de Estudios Latinoamericanos del Caribe* 76: 25–43.

Aste, J. 1986. *Minería Peruana: Empresas Estatales y Generación de Divisas, 1970–1984*. Lima: Fundación Friedrich Ebert.

Aterkyi II, O. K. 2007. 'Statement on behalf of the Traditional Authorities in Ghana through the National House of Chiefs for Successful Implementation of the EITI'. Accra, Ghana, 15 January. Available at http://www.gheiti.gov.gh/site/index.php?option=com_phocadownload&view=category&download=16:statement-of-behalf-

of-traditional-authories-in-ghana-through-national-house-of-chiefs&id=11:speeches&Itemid=54&start=40, accessed 25 May 2017.

Atta-Quayson, A. 2012. 'Analysis: Can government of Ghana implement proposed mining taxes?' Available at https://www.ghanabusinessnews.com/2012/01/31/cangovernment-of-ghana-implement-proposed-mining-taxes/, accessed 26 May 2017.

Aubynn, A. 2009. 'Sustainable solution or a marriage of inconvenience? The coexistence of large-scale mining and artisanal and small-scale mining on the Abosso Goldfields concession in Western Ghana'. *Resources Policy* 34(1): 64–70.

Austin, D. 1964. *Politics in Ghana, 1946–1960*. London: Oxford University Press.

Auty, R. 1993. *Sustaining Development in Mineral Economies: The Resource Curse Thesis*. London: Routledge.

Ayee, J., T. Søreide, G. P. Shukla, and T. M. Le. 2011. 'Political economy of the mining sector in Ghana', Policy Research Working Paper 5730. Washington DC: The World Bank.

Bakker, K. and G. Bridge. 2006. 'Material worlds? Resource geographies and the matter of nature'. *Progress in Human Geography* 30(1): 5–27.

Baldwin, K. 2014. 'When politicians cede control of resources: Land, chiefs and coalition-building in Africa'. *Comparative Politics* 46(3): 253–71.

Ballantyne, Janet (1976) 'The Political Economy of Peruvian Gran Minería'. Doctoral dissertation, Cornell University, USA, Ann Arbor, MI: University Microfilm.

Bansah, K. J., A. B. Yalley, and N. Dumakor-Dupey. 2016. 'The hazardous nature of small-scale underground mining in Ghana'. *Journal of Sustainable Mining* 15(1): 8–25.

Barandiarán Gomez, A. 2008. *Análisis de la Institucionalidad Ambiental en los Decretos Legislativos de la Implementación del TLC Perú—EE.UU.* Lima: CEPES, Cooperacción.

Barragán, R. 2008. 'Oppressed or privileged regions? Some historical reflections on the use of state resources'. In *Unresolved Tensions: Bolivia Past and Present*, edited by J. Crabtree and and L. Whitehead, pp. 83–104. Pittsburgh, PA: University of Pittsburgh Press.

Barrera-Hernández, L. 2009. 'Peruvian indigenous land conflict explained'. *Americas Quarterly* 12 June.

BCRP (Banco Central de Reserva del Perú). 2016. 'Series Estadísticas'. Available at https://estadisticas.bcrp.gob.pe/estadisticas/series/, accessed 20 February 2018.

BCRP (Banco Central de Reserva del Perú). 2017. 'Series Estadísticas'. Available at https://estadisticas.bcrp.gob.pe/estadisticas/series/buscador, accessed 20 February 2018.

Bebbington, A. (ed.) 2012. *Social Conflict, Economic Development and Extractive Industry: Evidence from South America*. London: Routledge.

Bebbington, A. 2013a. *Industrias extractivas, conflicto social y dinámicas institucionales en la región andina*. Lima: Instituto de Estudios Peruanos.

Bebbington, A. 2013b. 'Natural resource extraction and the possibilities of inclusive development: Politics across space and time'. ESID Working Paper No. 21. Manchester: Effective States and Inclusive Development Research Centre, University of Manchester.

Bebbington, A. 2015. 'Governing natural resources for inclusive development'. In *The Politics of Inclusive Development: Interrogating the Evidence*, edited by S. Hickey, K. Sen, and B. Bukenya, pp. 86–115. Oxford: Oxford University Press.

Bebbington, A. and J. Bury. (eds). 2013. *Subterranean Struggles: New Dynamics of Mining, Oil and Gas in Latin America*. Austin, TX: University of Texas Press.

Bebbington, A., L. Hinojosa, D. Humphreys Bebbington, M. L. Burneo, and X. Warnaars. 2008. 'Contention and ambiguity: Mining and the possibilities of development'. *Development and Change* 39(6): 887–914.

Bebbington, A., D. Humphreys Bebbington, J. Bury, J. Lingan, J. P. Muñoz, and M. Scurrah. 2008. 'Mining and social movements: Struggles over livelihood and rural territorial development in the Andes'. *World Development* 36(12): 2888–905.

Bebbington, A., M. Scurrah, and A. Chaparro. 2014. 'El Estado Compensador peruano y la persistencia del modelo neo-extractivista: seis hipótesis sobre el (no-) cambio institucional'. *Debate Agrario* 46: 29–50.

Bebbington, A., E. Arond, and J. Dammert. 2017. 'Explaining diverse national responses to the extractive industries transparency initiative in the Andes: What sort of politics matters?' *Extractive Industries and Society* 4(4): 833–41.

Becker, D. 1983. *The New Bourgeoisie and the Limits of Dependency: Mining, Class and Power in 'Revolutionary' Peru*. Princeton, NJ: Princeton University Press.

Berdegué, J., A. Bebbington, and A., Escobar, J. 2015. 'Conceptualizing spatial diversity in Latin American rural development: Structures, institutions and coalitions'. *World Development* 73: 1–10.

Berry, S. 2008. 'Ancestral property: Land, politics and "the deeds of the ancestors" in Ghana and Côte d'Ivoire'. In *Contesting Land and Custom in Ghana: State, Chief and the Citizen*, edited by J. M. Ubink and K. S. Amanor, pp. 27–53. Leiden: Leiden University Press.

Bielich, C. 2009. *La guerra del centavo. Una mirada actual al transporte público en Lima Metropolitana*. Lima: CIES, IEP. Available at http://archivo.iep.pe/textos/DDT/ddt155.pdf, accessed 20 February 2018.

Blaser, M. 2010. *Storytelling Globalization from the Chaco and Beyond*. Durham, NC: Duke University Press.

Bloch, R. and G. Owusu. 2012. 'Linkages in Ghana's gold mining industry: Challenging the enclave thesis'. *Resources Policy* 37(4): 434–42.

Boakye, D., S. Dessus, Y. Foday, and F. Oppong. 2012. 'Investing the mineral wealth in development assets: Ghana, Liberia and Sierra Leone'. Policy Research Working Paper. Washington, DC: World Bank.

Boampong, O. 2012. 'Ghana's golden opportunity: A district struggles with striking it rich'. Revenue Watch Institute, New York.

Bob-Milliar, G. M. 2012. 'Political party activism in Ghana: Factors influencing the decision of the politically active to join a political party'. *Democratization* 19(4): 668–8.

Boix, C. 2008. 'Spain: Development, democracy, and equity'. In *Institutional Pathways to Equity: Addressing Inequality Traps*, edited by A. Bebbington, A. Dani, A. de Haan, and M. Walton, pp. 217–44. Washington, DC: World Bank.

Booth, D. 2015. 'What next for political settlements theory and African development?' Paper submitted to the ESID Synthesis workshop, Dunford House, Midford, UK, 8–11 November.

Bornschlegl, T. 2017. 'Three Snapshots into Complexity. A Political Ecological Analysis of the Regulatory Enforcement of Environmental Laws in the Oil and Gas Sector in

Ecuador'. PhD thesis, Worcester, MA: Graduate School of Geography, Clark University.

Brautigam, D. and K. Gallagher. 2014. 'Bartering globalization: China's commodity-backed finance in Africa and Latin America'. *Global Policy* 5(3): 346–52.

Bridge, G. 2004. 'Contested terrain: Mining and the environment'. *Annual Review of Environment and Resources* 29: 205–59.

Brown, K. 2012. *A History of Mining in Latin America: From the Colonial Era to the Present.* Albuquerque, NM: University of New Mexico Press.

Brunnschweiler, C. and E. Bulte. 2008. 'Linking natural resources to slow growth and more conflict.' *Science* 320 (2 May): 616–17.

Burga, M. and A. F. Galindo. 1979. *Apogeo y crisis de la República Aristocrática: oligarquía, aprismo y comunismo en el Perú 1895–1932.* Lima: Rikchay Perú.

Bury, J. 2005. 'Mining mountains: Neoliberalism, land tenure, livelihoods and the new Peruvian mining industry in Cajamarca'. *Environment and Planning* A 37(2): 221–39.

Bury, J. 2011. 'Neoliberalismo, minería y cambios rurales en Cajamarca'. In *Minería, Movimientos Sociales y Respuestas Campesinas: Una Ecología Política de las Transformaciones Territoriales*, edited by Anthony Bebbington. Lima: Instituto de Estudios Peruanos.

Bush, R. 2009. '"Soon there will be no-one left to take the corpses to the morgue": Accumulation and abjection in Ghana's mining communities'. *Resources Policy* 34: 57–63.

Bush, R. 2010. 'Mining and improvement: Beyond foreign direct investment?' In *Enclaves of Wealth and Hinterlands of Discontent: Foreign Mining Companies in Africa's Development*, edited by G. Hilson, pp. 102–16. Accra: TWN-Africa.

Cameron, M. 1997. 'Political and economic origins of regime change: The eighteenth brumaire of Alberto Fujimori'. In *The Peruvian Labyrinth: Polity, Society, Economy*, edited by Maxwell Cameron and Philip Mauceri, pp. 37–69. University Park, PA: Pennsylvania State University Press.

Campbell, B. 1998. 'Liberalisation, deregulation, state promoted investment: Canadian mining interests in Africa'. *Minerals and Energy-Raw Materials Report*, 13 (4):14–34.

Cano, Á. 2015a. 'Minería artesanal y en pequeña escala: Explorando los vínculos entre la política nacional y el desarrollo inclusivo'. Lima, CIUP Draft Working Paper.

Cano, A. 2015b. *Small-scale Curse or Possibility of Inclusive Development? Researching the Politics of Artisanal, Informal and Illegal Mining in Peru (1930–2015).* Mimeo, Universidad del Pacífico, Lima.

Capriles Villazon, O. 1977. *Historía de la Minería Boliviana.* La Paz: Banco Minero de Bolivia.

Carson, M., S. Cottrell, J. Dickman, E. Gummerson, T. L. Yanliang, M. Noriko, T. Catarina, and T. C. Uregian. 2005. *Managing Mineral Resources through Public–Private Partnerships: Mitigating Conflict in Ghanaian Gold Mining.* Princeton, NJ: Woodrow Wilson School of Public and International Affairs, Princeton University.

Castro, J. F., G. Yamada, and N. Oviedo. 2016. 'Revisitando el coeficiente de Gini en el Perú: el rol de las políticas públicas en la evolución de la desigualdad'. Lima: Documento de Trabajo, CIUP.

CEDIB (Centro de Documentación e Información Bolivia). 2013. 'Minería en Bolivia' (PowerPoint slides). Available at http://www.somossur.net/documentos/Mineria_Bolivia_CEDIB2013.pdf, accessed 20 February 2018.

CEDLA (Centro de Estudios de Desarrollo Laboral). 2014. *Reporte Anual de Industrias Extractivas II*. La Paz: CEDLA.

Charpentier, S. and J. Hidalgo. 1999. *Las Políticas Ambientales en el Perú*. Lima: AGENDA PERU.

Chazan, N. 1982. 'Ethnicity and politics in Ghana'. *Political Science Quarterly* 97(3): 461–85.

Cheelo, K. H. 2008. 'Behind the Economic Figures: Large-Scale Mining and Rural Poverty Reduction in Zambia, the Case of Kansanshi Copper Mine in Solwezi'. MA dissertation, Massey University, Palmerston North, New Zealand.

Chong, A., J. Galdo, and J. Saavedra. 2007. 'Informality and productivity in the labor market: Peru 1986–2001'. Research Department Working Paper Series. Washington: Inter-American Development Bank.

Cleaves, P. and M. Scurrah. 1980. *Agriculture, Bureaucracy, and Military Government in Peru*. Ithaca, NY: Cornell University Press.

Coffey International Development. 2011. 'Political economy of Ghana and thematic strategy development for STAR-Ghana'. Inception Report for DFID STAR-Ghana, DfIDGhana, Accra.

Collier, D. et al. 1979. *The New Authoritarianism in Latin America*. Princeton, NJ: Princeton University Press.

Collier, P., A. Hoeffler, and D. Rohner. 2009. 'Beyond greed and grievance: Feasibility and civil war'. *Oxford Economic Papers* 61: 1–27.

Conaghan, Catherine and James Malloy. 1994. *Unsettling Statecraft: Democracy and Neoliberalism in the Central Andes*. Pitt Latin American Series. Pittsburgh, PA: University of Pittsburgh Press.

Concytec. 2017. 'Primer Censo revela baja inversión en investigación y desarrollo en el Perú', Consejo Nacional de Ciencia y Tecnologia, May 19, 2017. Available at https://portal.concytec.gob.pe/index.php/noticias/1051-primer-censo-revela-baja-inversion-en-investigacion-y-desarrollo-en-el-peru, accessed 20 February 2018.

Conrad, R. F. 2014. 'Mineral taxation in Zambia'. In *Zambia: Building Prosperity from Mineral Wealth*, edited by C. S. Adam, P. Collier, and M. Gondwe, pp. 82–109. Oxford: Oxford University Press.

Contreras, C. and M. Cueto. 2009. *Historia del Perú Contemporáneo*. Lima: Instituto de Estudios Peruanos.

Contreras, M. 1993. 'The Bolivian tin mining industry in the first half of the twentieth century'. In *Institute of Latin American Studies (ILAS) Research Papers*, p. 32. London: University of London.

Cooper, F., A. Isaacman, F. Mallon, W. Roseberry, and S. Stern. 1993. *Confronting Historical Paradigms: Peasants, Labor, and the Capitalist World System in Africa and Latin America*. Madison, WI: University of Wisconsin Press.

Cord, L., M. E. Genoni, and C. R. Castelan. 2015. *Shared Prosperity and Poverty Eradication in Latin America and the Caribbean*. Washington, DC: World Bank.

Cotler, J. 1995. 'Political parties and the problems of democratic consolidation in Peru'. In *Building Democratic Institutions: Party Systems in Latin America*, edited by

Scott Mainwaring and Timothy R. Scully, pp. 323—53. Stanford, CA: Stanford University Press.

Coumans, C. 2011. 'Occupying spaces created by conflict: Anthropologists, development NGOs, responsible investment, and mining'. *Current Anthropology* 52: S29–S40.

Crabtree, J. (ed.). 2011. *Fractured Politics: Peruvian Democracy Past and Present.* London: Institute of Latin American Studies.

Crabtree, J. and L. Whitehead. (eds). 2008. *Unresolved Tensions: Bolivia Past and Present.* Pittsburgh, PA: University of Pittsburgh Press.

Craig, J. R. 1999. 'State Enterprise and Privatisation in Zambia, 1968–1998'. PhD dissertation, University of Leeds.

Crawford, G. and G. Botchwey. 2017. 'Conflict, collusion and corruption in small-scale gold mining: Chinese miners and the state in Ghana'. *Commonwealth and Comparative Politics* February 9: 1–28. doi: 10.1080/14662043.2017.1283479.

Crook, R. 2005. 'The role of traditional institutions in political change and development', CDD/ODI Policy Brief No. 4, November.

Cuba, N., A. Bebbington, J. Rogan, and M. Millones. 2014. 'Extractive industries, livelihoods and natural resource competition: Mapping overlapping claims in Peru and Ghana'. *Applied Geography* 54: 250–61.

CVR (Comisión de la Verdad y Reconciliación). 2003. *Informe final.* Lima: CVR.

Daily Express. (2013, March 21). 'Review of mining stability agreements on course'. Available at http://dailyexpressonline.com/review-of-mining-stability-agreements-on-course-2013-03-21/, accessed 2 January 2015.

Daily Graphic. 2016. 'Obuasi: Galamsey operators on rampage'. 19 October. Available at http://www.graphic.com.gh/news/general-news/obuasi-galamsey-operators-onrampage. html, accessed 11 May 2017.

Daily Guide. 2013. 'NPP scribe blasts Mahama over galamsey'. 7 June. Available at https://www.modernghana.com/news/467577/2122/npp-scribe-blasts-mahama-overgalamsey.html, accessed 11 May 2017.

Dargent, E. 2015. *Technocracy and Democracy in Latin America: The Experts Running Government.* Cambridge: Cambridge University Press.

Dargent, E. and P. Muñoz. 2012. 'Perú 2011: Continuidades y cambios en la política sin partidos'. *Revista de Ciencia Política* 32(1): 245–68.

Dargent, E., J. C. Orihuela, M. Paredes, and E. M. Ulfe (eds). 2017. *Resource Booms and Institutional Pathways: The Case of the Extractive Industry in Peru.* London: Palgrave Macmillan.

Davis, G. A. 1995. 'Learning to love the Dutch disease: Evidence from the mineral economies'. *World Development* 23 (10): 1765–79.

Davis, G. A. 2009. 'Extractive economies, growth and the poor'. In *Mining, Society and a Sustainable World,* edited by J. P. Richards, pp. 37–60. Berlin Heidelberg: Springer–Verlag.

Davis, G. A. and J. Tilton. 2005. 'The resource curse'. *Natural Resources Forum* 29(3): 233–42.

De Echave, J. and A. Diez. 2013. *Más allá de Conga.* Lima: RedGE, Cooperacción.

de la Cadena, M. 2015. *Earth Beings: Ecologies of Practice across Andean Worlds.* Durham, NC: Duke University Press.

Debrah, E. 2013. 'Alleviating poverty in Ghana: The case of Livelihood Empowerment against Poverty (LEAP)'. *Africa Today* 59(4): 41–67.

Defensoría del Pueblo. 2017. Reportes mensuales conflictos sociales, 2005–2016. Available at https://www.defensoria.gob.pe/temas.php?des=3#r, accessed 20 February 2018.

Dell, M. 2010. 'The persistent effects of Mita'. *Econometrica* 78: 1863–903.

Descola, P. 1996. *La Selva Culta: Simbolismo y Praxis en la Ecología de los Achuar*. Quito: Abya Yala.

Deustua, J. 1995. '"¡Campesino, el patrón no comerá más de tu pobreza!" Economía, mercado y campesinos en los Andes: el caso de la minería peruana en el siglo XIX'. Documento de Trabajo 70, Serie Historia 13. Lima: Instituto de Estudios Peruanos.

Di John, J. 2010. 'The political economy of taxation and state resilience in Zambia since 1990'. Available at http://www.lse.ac.uk/internationalDevelopment/research/crisisStates/download/wp/wpSeries2/WP842.pdf, accessed 25 March 2017.

Di John, J. and J. Putzel. 2009. 'Political settlements'. Issues paper, June. Governance and Social Development Resource Centre, Birmingham. Available at http://core.ac.uk/download/files/119/103642.pdf, accessed 20 February 2018.

Dickens, T. 2010. 'Legalising "galamsey" in Ghana'. Feature Article. *Ghana Web*. Available at http://www.ghanaweb.com/GhanaHomePage/NewsArchive/Legalising-Galamsey-in Ghana-180922, accessed 20 February 2018.

Donkor, K. 1997. *Structural Adjustment and Mass Poverty in Ghana*. London: Ashgate.

Dore, Elizabeth. 1986. *Acumulación y Crisis en la Minería Peruana, 1900–1977*. Lima: UNMSM.

Dumett, R. E. 1998. *El Dorado in West Africa: The Gold-Mining Frontier, African Labor, and Colonial Capitalism on the Gold Coast, 1875–1900*. Athens, OH: Heinemann.

Dunkerley, J. 2007. 'Evo Morales, the "two Bolivias" and the third Bolivian revolution'. *Journal of Latin American Studies* 39(1): 133–66.

Eifert, B., A. Gelb, and N. Tallroth. 2003. 'The political economy of fiscal policy and economic management in oil-exporting countries'. In *Fiscal Policy Formulation and Implementation in Oil Producing Countries*, edited by J. M. Davis, R. Ossowski, and A. Fedelino, pp. 82–122. Washington, DC: IMF.

Englund, H. (ed.). 2002. *A Democracy of Chameleons: Politics and Culture in the New Malawi*. Zomba: Kachere Books.

Espinoza Morales, J. 2010. *Minería Boliviana: Su Realidad*. La Paz, Bolivia: Plural.

Evans, P. 1995. *Embedded Autonomy: States and Industrial Transformation*. Princeton, NJ: Princeton University Press.

EY. 2014. *Peru's Mining and Metals Investment Guide 2014/2015*. Lima: EY.

EY. 2017. *Peru's Mining and Metals Investment Guide 2017/2018*. Lima: EY.

Faguet, J.-P. 2012. *Decentralization and Popular Democracy: Governance from below in Bolivia*. Ann Arbor, MI: University of Michigan Press.

Farthing, L. and B. Kohl. 2005. 'Conflicting agendas: The politics of development aid in drug-producing areas'. *Development Policy Review* 23: 183–98.

Farthing, L. and B. Kohl. 2014. *Evo's Bolivia: Continuity and Change*. Austin, TX: University of Texas Press.

Ferguson, J. 1999. *Expectations of Modernity: Myths and Meanings of Urban Life on the Zambian Copperbelt*. Berkeley, CA: University of California Press.

Ferguson, J. 2006. *Global Shadows: Africa in the Neoliberal Order*. Durham, NC: Duke University Press.

Finnemore, M. 1997. 'Redefining development at the World Bank'. In *International Development and the Social Sciences*, edited by F. Cooper and R. Packard, pp. 203–27. Berkeley, CA: University of California Press.

Fitzgerald, E. V. K. 1979. *La Economía Política del Perú. 1956–1978. Desarrollo Económico y Reestructuración del Capital*. Lima: Instituto de Estudios Peruanos.

Fort, Ricardo, María Isabel Remy, and Héctor Paredes (2015). *Es Necesaria una Estrategia Nacional de Desarrollo Rural en el Perú? Aportes Para el Debate y Propuesta de Implementación*. Lima: GRADE.

Fox, L., B. Hoffman, A. Anyimadu, and M. Keshishian. 2011. 'Ghana democracy and governance assessment'. Report submitted to USAID/Ghana. Final report, August.

Francescone, K. 2015. 'Cooperative miners and the politics of abandonment in Bolivia'. *Extractive Industries and Society* 2: 746–55.

Francescone, K. and V. Díaz. 2014. 'Cooperativas mineras bolivianas: Entre socios, patrones y peones'. CEDIB. Available at http://www.cedib.org/petropress/cooperativas-mineras-entre-socias-patrones-y-peones-petropress-30-1-13/, accessed 29 May 2014.

Fraser, A. 2010. 'Prefab Politics: Poverty Reduction Strategies and the Limits of Donor-Built Civil Society in Zambia, 1999–2009'. PhD thesis, Oxford University.

Fraser, A. and M. Larmer. (eds). 2011. *Zambia, Mining and Neoliberalism: Boom and Bust on the Globalized Copperbelt*. New York: Palgrave Macmillan.

Fraser, A. and J. Lungu. 2007. *For Whom the Windfalls? Winners and Losers in the Privatization of Zambia's Copper Mines*. Lusaka: Minewatch Zambia. Available at https://www.researchgate.net/publication/237428939_FOR_WHOM_THE_WIND FALLS_Winners_losers_in_the_privatisation_of_Zambia%27s_copper_mines, accessed 20 February 2018.

Frederiksen, T. 2017. 'Corporate Social Responsibility and Political Settlements in the Mining Sector in Ghana, Peru and Zambia'. ESID Working Paper 74. Manchester: Effective States and Inclusive Development Centre.

Fundación Unir. 2014. *La Veta del Conflicto. Ocho Miradas Sobre Conflictividad Minera en Bolivia (2010–2014)*. Santa Cruz: Fundación Unir.

Galeano, E. 1971. *The Open Veins of Latin America. Five Centuries of the Pillage of a Continent*. New York: Monthly Review Press.

Gallagher, K. 2016. *The China Triangle: Latin America's China Boom and the Fate of the Washington Consensus*. New York: Oxford University Press.

Gallo, C. 1991. *Taxes and State Power: Political Instability in Bolivia, 1900–1950*. Philadelphia, PA: Temple University Press.

García Linera, A. 2008. 'Empate catastrófico y su punto de bifurcación'. *Crítica y Emancipación* 1(1): 23–33.

García Linera, A. n.d. 'El nuevo modelo económico nacional productivo'. *Revista de Análisis*. Presidencia del H. Congreso Nacional Vicepresidencia del Estado Plurinacional, Año 2, número 2. Available at https://www.vicepresidencia.gob.bo/IMG/pdf/revista_analisis_2.pdf, accessed 20 February 2018.

Gelb, A. 1988. *Oil Windfalls: Blessing or Curse?* New York: Oxford University Press.

Ghana Chamber of Mines. 2013. *Performance of the Mining Industry in 2012*. Accra: Ghana Chamber of Mines.

Ghana Chamber of Mines. 2016. *The Ghana Chamber of Mines Factoid 2015*. Accra: Ghana Chamber of Mines.

Ghana Chamber of Mines and ICMM. 2015. *Mining in Ghana – What Future Can We Expect?* Accra: Ghana Chamber of Mines.

Ghana News Agency. 2015. 'Current mining royalties not enough – Chamber of Mines'. 21 September. Available at https://www.ghanabusinessnews.com/2015/09/21/currentmining-royalties-not-enough-chamber-of-mines/, accessed 11 May 2017.

Ghana Statistical Service. 2007. *Pattern and Trends of Poverty in Ghana 1991–2006*. Accra: Ghana Statistical Service.

Ghana Statistical Service. 2014. *Poverty Profile in Ghana: 2005–2013*. Accra: Ghana Statistical Service.

Ghanaian Chronicle. 2014, 24 January, 2014. 'Presidency succumbs to mining blackmail?' Available at: http://www.modernghana.com/news/517845/1/presidency-succumbs-to-mining-blackmail.html, accessed 20 February 2018.

Ghezzi, P. 2015, October 29. 'La falsa dicotomía'. Lima: El Comercio. Available at http://elcomercio.pe/opinion/colaboradores/falsa-dicotomia-piero-ghezzi-solis-noticia-1851717, accessed 20 February 2018.

Ghezzi, P. and J. Gallardo. 2013. *Que se puede hacer con el Perú? Ideas para sostener el crecimiento en el largo plazo*. Lima: Fondo Editorial de la Universidad del Pacífico.

Gilberthorpe, E. and G. Hilson. (eds). 2014. *Natural Resource Extraction and Indigenous Livelihoods*. London: Routledge.

Glave, M. and J. Kuramoto. 2007. *La Minería Peruana: Lo que Sabemos y lo que Aún nos Falta por Saber*. Lima: GRADE.

Global Witness. 2017. *Defenders of the Earth: Global Killings of Land and Environmental Defenders in 2016*. London: Global Witness.

Golooba-Mutebi, F. 2013. 'Politics, political settlements and social change in postcolonial Rwanda'. ESID Working Paper No. 24. Manchester: Effective States and Inclusive Development Research Centre, The University of Manchester.

Gonzales de Olarte, E. and L. Samamé. 1991. *El Péndulo Peruano: Políticas Económicas, Gobernabilidad y Subdesarrollo, 1963–1990*. Lima: Instituto de Estudios Peruanos.

Gotkowitz, L. 2008. *A Revolution for Our Rights: Indigenous Struggles for Land and Justice in Bolivia, 1880–1952*. Durham, NC: Duke University Press.

Gould, J. 2010. *Left Behind: Rural Zambia in the Third Republic*. Lusaka: The Lembani Trust.

Government of Ghana. 2010. *The Savannah Accelerated Development Authority (SADA): Synopsis of Development Strategy (2010–2030)*. Accra: Policy Unit, Office of the Vice-President.

Government of Ghana. 2012. *Ghana National Social Protection Strategy*. Accra: Ministry of Gender, Children and Social Protection.

Government of Ghana. 2014. *Ghana Shared Growth and Development Agenda (GSGDA) II*. Accra: National Development Planning Commission.

Granados, O. 2015. 'Bankers, entrepreneurs and Bolivian tin in international economy, 1900–1932'. In *Tin and Global Capitalism, A History of the Devil's Metal*, edited by M. Ingusltad, A. Perchard, and E. Storli, pp. 46–73. New York: Routledge.

Guasti, L. 1985. 'El Gobierno Militar Peruano y las corporaciones internacionales'. In *El Gobierno Militar: Una Experiencia Peruana 1968–1980*. Lima: Instituto de Estudios Peruanos.

Gudynas, E. 2012. 'Estado compensador y nuevos extractivismos. Las ambivalencias del progresismo sudamericano'. *Nueva Sociedad* 237: 128–46.

Gudynas, E. 2014. *Derechos de la Naturaleza. Etica Biocéntrica y Políticas Ambientales*. La Paz (Bolivia): Plural.

Gustafsson, M.-T. 2017. 'The struggles surrounding ecological and economic zoning in Peru'. *Third World Quarterly* 38(5): 1146–63.

Gyimah-Boadi, E. and H. K. Prempeh. 2012. 'Oil, politics, and Ghana's democracy'. *Journal of Democracy* 23(3): 94–107.

Haas, P. 1992. *Epistemic Communities and International Policy Coordination*. Cambridge, MA: MIT Press.

Hall, P. 2010. 'Historical institutionalism in rationalist and sociological perspective'. In *Explaining Institutional Change: Ambiguity, Agency, and Power*, edited by J. Mahoney and K. Thelen, pp. 204–24. Cambridge: Cambridge University Press.

Hern, E. and J. Achberger. 2014. 'Imagining development, confronting reality: Domestic and international constraints on Zambia's First and Second National Development Plans'. SAIPAR Working Paper.

Hickey, S. 2013. 'Thinking about the politics of inclusive development: Towards a relational approach'. ESID Working Paper No. 1. Manchester: Effective States and Inclusive Development Research Centre, University of Manchester.

Hickey, S. and A. Izama. 2017. 'The politics of governing oil in Uganda: Going against the grain?' *African Affairs* 116(463): 163–85.

Hickey, S. and K. Sen. 2016. 'ESID overview paper for Bellagio'. Unpublished paper prepared for the Effective States and Inclusive Development (ESID) Research Centre. Manchester: ESID, University of Manchester.

Hickey, S., K. Sen, and B. Bukenya. 2015a. 'Introduction: The politics of inclusive development'. In *The Politics of Inclusive Development: Interrogating the Evidence*, edited by S. Hickey, K. Sen, and B. Bukenya, pp. 1–39. Oxford: Oxford University Press.

Hickey, S., A.-G. Abdulai, A. Izama, and G. Mohan. 2015b. 'The politics of governing oil effectively: A comparative study of two new oil-rich states in Africa'. ESID Working Paper No. 54. Manchester: Effective States and Inclusive Development Research Centre, University of Manchester.

Hilson, G. 2002. 'Harvesting mineral riches: 1000 years of gold mining in Ghana'. *Resources Policy* 28(1): 13–26.

Hilson, G. 2009. 'Small-Scale mining, poverty and economic development in Sub-Saharan Africa: An overview'. *Resources Policy* 34 (1–2): 1–5.

Hilson G. and C. Garforth. 2013. '"Everyone now is concentrating on the mining": Drivers and implications of rural economic transition in the Eastern Region of Ghana'. *Journal of Development Studies* 49(3): 348–64.

Hilson, G., A. Hilson, and E. Adu-Darko. 2014. 'Chinese participation in Ghana's informal gold mining economy: Drivers, implications and clarifications'. *Journal of Rural Studies* 34: 292–303.

Hilson, G. and C. Potter. 2003. 'Why is illegal gold mining activity so ubiquitous in rural Ghana?' *African Development Review* 15(2): 237–70.

Hindery, D. 2013a. *From Enron to Evo: Pipeline Politics, Global Environmentalism and Indigenous Rights in Bolivia*. Tucson, AZ: University of Arizona Press.

Hindery, D. 2013b. 'Synergistic impacts of gas and mining development in Bolivia's Chiquitanía: The significance of analytical scale'. In *Subterranean Struggles New Dynamics of Mining, Oil and Gas in Latin America*, edited by A. Bebbington and J. Bury, pp. 197–222. Austin, TX: University of Texas Press.

Holloway, J. 2010. *Crack Capitalism*. London: Pluto Press.

Humphreys, M., J. Sachs, and J. Stiglitz. (eds). 2007. *Escaping the Resource Curse*. New York: Initiative for Policy Dialogue, Columbia University Press.

Humphreys Bebbington, D. 2010. 'The Political Ecology of Natural Gas Extraction in Southern Bolivia'. PhD thesis, University of Manchester.

Humphreys Bebbington, D. and A. Bebbington. 2010. 'Extraction, territory and inequalities: Gas in the Bolivian Chaco'. *Canadian Journal of Development Studies* 30(1–2): 259–80.

Humphreys Bebbington, D. and A. Bebbington. 2012. 'Post-what? Extractive industries, narratives of development and socio-environmental disputes across the (ostensibly changing) Andean region'. In *New Political Spaces in Latin American Natural Resource Governance*, edited by H. Haarstad, pp. 17–37. Oxford: Palgrave Macmillan.

Hunt, S. 2011. *La Formación de la Economía Peruana: Distribución y Crecimiento en la Historia Económica del Perú y América Latina*. Lima: BCRP, IEP, PUCP.

Hutchful, E. 2002. *Ghana's Adjustment Experience: The Paradox of Reform*. Geneva and Oxford: UNRISD and James Currey.

Hylton, F. and S. Thomson. 2005. 'The chequered rainbow'. *New Left Review* 35: 40–64.

ICMM (International Council on Mining and Metals). 2007. *Ghana Country Case Study – The Challenge of Mineral Wealth: Using Resource Endowments to Foster Sustainable Development'*. London: ICMM.

ICMM (International Council on Mining and Metals). 2014. Press information sheet 1. 'ICMM assesses mining's contribution to Zambia's national and local economy'. Available at http://www.eisourcebook.org/cms/April%202014/Zambia,%20macroeconomic%20contributions%20of%20mining.pdf, accessed 23 March 2017.

ILO (International Labor Organization)., 2017. Labor Overview: Latin America and the Caribbean, 18 December 2017. Available at http://www.ilo.org/wcmsp5/groups/public/—americas/—ro-lima/—sro-port_of_spain/documents/publication/wcms_614132.pdf, accessed 20 February 2018.

Inchauste, G., J. Azevedo, S. Olivieri, J. Saavedra, and H. Winkler. 2012. *When Job Earnings Are Behind Poverty Reduction*. Economic Premise, 97. Washington, DC: World Bank.

INEI (Instituto Nacional de Estadística e Informática). 2007. *XI Censo Nacional de Población y VI de Vivienda. Sistema de Consulta de Datos*. Lima: INEI. Available at http://censos.inei.gob.pe/Censos2007/redatam/#, accessed 20 February 2018.

INEI (Instituto Nacional de Estadística e Informática). 2016. *Producción y Empleo Informal en el Perú. Cuenta Satélite de la Economía Informal 2007–2012*. Lima: INEI.

INGEMMET. 2017. 'Estadísticas de Gestión Mensual y Anual. Totalidad de Derechos Mineros Vigentes a Nivel Nacional'. Available at http://ecatastro.ingemmet.gob.pe:83/PresentacionDatos/ReporteDMTodos.aspx, accessed 20 February 2018.

IPE (Instituto Peruano de Economía). 2013. *Efecto de la Minería Sobre el Empleo, el Producto y la Recaudación en el Perú*. Lima: SNMPE.

Jones, N., W. Ahadzie, and D. Doh. 2009. *Social Protection and Children: Opportunities and Challenges in Ghana*. Accra: UNICEF.

Jordan, R. 2012. 'Análisis y visiones del cooperativismo minero boliviano, un poder politico y social intocable'. *La Razon*, 2 July. Available at http://www.plataformaenergetica.org/content/29693, accessed 7 July 2012.

Joy Online. 2015, August 10. '40-year dev't plan will be legally binding but flexible – Kwesi Botchwey'. Available at http://www.myjoyonline.com/news/2015/August-10th/40-year-devt-plan-will-be-legally-binding-but-flexible-kwesi-botchwey.php, accessed 25 May 2017.

Joy Online. 2017, March 22. 'World Water Day: Ghana risks importing water – experts'. Available at http://www.myjoyonline.com/news/2017/March-22nd/world-water-day-ghana-risks-importing-water-experts.php, accessed 25 May 2017.

Kapstein, E. B. and R. Kim. 2011. *The Socio-Economic Impact of Newmont Ghana Gold Limited*. Haarlem: Stratcomm Africa.

Karl, T. 1986. 'Petroleum and political pacts: The transition to democracy in Venezuela'. In *Transitions from Authoritarian Rule*, edited by Guillermo O'Donnell, Philippe C. Schmitter, and Laurence Whitehead, pp. 196–219. Baltimore, MD: Johns Hopkins Press.

Karl, T. 1987. 'Petroleum and political pacts: the transition to democracy in Venezuela'. *Latin American Research Review* 22(1): 63–94.

Karl, T. 1997. *The Paradox of Plenty: Oil Booms and Petro States*. Oakland, CA: University of California University Press.

Karl, T. 2007. 'Ensuring fairness: The case for a transparent fiscal contract'. In *Escaping the Resource Curse*, edited by M. Humphreys, J. Sachs, and J. Stiglitz, pp. 256–85. New York: Columbia University Press.

Kaup, B. 2013. *Market Justice: Political Economic Struggle in Bolivia*. New York: Cambridge University Press.

Kemp, D. 2014. Review of 'Subterranean struggles: New dynamics of mining, oil and gas in Latin America, by Anthony Bebbington and Jeffrey Bury'. *Journal of Development Studies* 50(5): 770–1.

Khan, M. 2010. 'Political settlements and the governance of growth-enhancing institutions'. *Mimeo*. London: School of Oriental and African Studies, University of London.

Kirsch, S. 2012. 'Afterword: Extractive conflicts compared'. In *Social Conflict, Economic Development and Extractive Industries: Evidence from South America*, edited by A. Bebbington, pp. 201–13. London: Routledge.

Kirsch, S. 2014. *Mining Capitalism: The Relationship between Corporations and their Critics*. Berkeley, CA: University of California Press.

Klarén, P. 2004. *Nación y Sociedad en la Historia del Perú*. Lima: Instituto de Estudios Peruanos.

Klein, H. 2011. *A Concise History of Bolivia*. Cambridge: Cambridge University Press.

Klein, H. and J. Peres Cajías. 2014. 'Bolivian oil and natural gas under state and private control, 1910–2010'. *Bolivian Studies Journal* 20: 141–64.

Kohl, B. 2002. 'Stabilising neoliberalism in Bolivia: Popular participation and privatization'. *Political Geography* 21(4): 449–72.

Kruijt, M. and D. Vellinga. 1983. *Estado, Clase Obrera y Empresa Transnacional. El Caso de la Mineria Peruana, 1900–1980*. México: Siglo XXI Editores.

Kuma, J. S. and J. A. Yendaw. 2010. 'The need to regularise activities of illegal small-scale mining in Ghana: A focus on the Tarkwa–Dunkwa Highway'. *International Journal of Geosciences* 1(3): 113–20.

Ladouceur, P. A. 1979. *Chiefs and Politicians: The Politics of Regionalism in Northern Ghana*. London and New York: Longman Group.

Lanegra, I. 2015, March 22. 'El largo nacimiento de Senace', *OjoPúblico*, Opinion. Available at http://ojo-publico.com/41/el-largo-nacimiento-del-senace, accessed 20 February 2018.

Larmer, M. 2006. '"The hour has come at the pit": The Mineworkers' Union of Zambia and the Movement for Multiparty Democracy, 1982–1991', *Journal of Southern African Studies* (32)2: 293–312.

Larmer, M. (ed.). 2010. *The Musakanya Papers. The Autobiographical Writings of Valentine Musakanya*. Lusaka: Lembani Trust.

Larmer, M. 2011. 'Historical perspectives on Zambia's mining booms and busts'. In *Zambia, Mining and Neoliberalism: Boom and Bust on the Globalized Copperbelt*, edited by A. Fraser and M. Larmer, pp. 31–58. New York: Palgrave Macmillan.

Larmer, M. and Macola, G. 2007. 'The origins, context and political significance of the Mushala Rebellion against the Zambian one-party state'. *International Journal of African Historical Studies* 40(3): 471–96.

Laws, E. 2012. 'Political Settlements, Elite Pacts, and Governments of National Unity. A Conceptual Study'. Background Paper 10. Birmingham: Developmental Leadership Program.

Le Billon, P. 2005. *Fuelling War: Natural Resources and Armed Conflicts*. New York: Routledge.

Lee, C. K. 2014. 'China on the Copperbelt'. *New Left Review* (89) (Sep./Oct.): 29–66.

Lee, C. K. 2017. *The Specter of Global China: Politics, Labor, and Foreign Investment in Africa*. Chicago, IL: University of Chicago Press.

Leith, D. 2003. *The Politics of Power: Freeport in Suharto's Indonesia*. Honolulu: University of Hawai'i Press.

Levitsky, S. and L. A. Way. 2010. *Competitive Authoritarianism: Hybrid Regimes after the Cold War*. Cambridge: Cambridge University Press.

Levy, B. 2014. *Working with the Grain: Integrating Governance and Growth in Development Strategies*. Oxford: Oxford University Press.

Levy, B. and T. Kelsall, T. 2016. 'Working contextually: What works in different types of political settlement'. Unpublished paper prepared for ESID. Manchester: Effective States and Inclusive Development Research Centre, University of Manchester.

Levy, B. and M. Walton. 2013. 'Institutions, incentives and service provision: Bringing politics back in'. ESID Working Paper No. 18. Manchester: Effective States and Inclusive Development Research Centre, University of Manchester.

Li, F. 2015. *Unearthing Conflict: Corporate Mining, Activism and Expertise in Peru*. Durham, NC: Duke University Press.

Lindemann, S. 2011. 'Inclusive elite bargains and the dilemma of unproductive peace: A Zambian case study'. *Third World Quarterly* 32(10): 1843–69.

Loayza, N. 2007. 'The causes and consequences of informality in Peru'. Working Paper series. DT. Nº 2007-018. Washington, DC: World Bank.

McClintock, C. and A. Lowenthal. 1983. *The Peruvian Experiment Reconsidered*. Princeton, NJ: Princeton University Press.

McKinsey & Company. 2013. An assessment of the competitiveness and health of Peru's mining industry. Available at http://www.mckinsey.com/~/media/mckinsey/dotcom/client_service/Metals%20and%20Mining/PDFs/Competitiveness%20and%20health%20of%20the%20Peruvian%20Mining%20Sector-vf.ashx, accessed 20 February 2018.

Macola, G. 2006. '"It means as if we are excluded from the good freedom": Thwarted expectations of independence in the Luapula Province of Zambia, 1964–6'. *The Journal of African History* 47(1): 43–56.

Macola, G. 2008. 'Harry Mwaanga Nkumbula, UNIP and the roots of authoritarianism in nationalist Zambia'. In *One Zambia, Many Histories. Towards a History of Post-colonial Zambia*, edited by J. B. Gewald, M. Hinfelaar, and G. Macola, pp. 17–44. Leiden: Brill.

Macola, G. 2010. *Liberal Nationalism in Central Africa: A Biography of Harry Mwaanga Nkumbula*. New York: Palgrave Macmillan.

Maconachie, R., R. Srinivasan, and N. Menzies. 2015. *Responding To The Challenge Of Fragility And Security In West Africa: Natural Resources, Extractive Industry Investment, And Social Conflict*. Washington, DC: World Bank.

Mahoney, J. and K. Thelen. (eds). 2010. *Explaining Institutional Change: Ambiguity, Agency, and Power*. Cambridge: Cambridge University Press.

Mann, M. 2007 (1986). 'El poder autónomo del Estado: sus orígenes, mecanismos y resultados'. *Revista Académica de Relaciones Internacionales* 5 (November 2007). Available at http://www.relacionesinternacionales.info/ojs/article/view/49.html, accessed 20 February 2018.

Manrique, N. 2009. *Usted fue Aprista! Bases para una historia crítica del APRA*. Lima: CLACSO, Pontificia Universidad Católica del Perú.

Maplecroft. 2013. Maplecroft Risk Index, Bolivia 2013. Available at http://maplecroft.com/about/news/pra_2013.html, accessed 13 August 2013.

Maxwell, S. and D. Stone (eds). 2004. *Global Knowledge Networks and International Development: Bridge across Boundaries*. London: Routledge.

Mbeki Panel. 2015. 'Illicit Financial Flow. Report of the High Level Panel on Illicit Financial Flows from Africa'. Commissioned by the AU/ECA Conference of Ministers of Finance, Planning and Economic Development.

Medina, G. 2014. *Formalización de la Minería en Pequeña Escala ¿por qué?...Y cómo*. Lima: Better Gold Initiative.

MEF (Ministry of Economy and Finance). 2016a. Consulta Amigable. Consulta de Ejecución del Gasto.

MEF (Ministry of Economy and Finance). 2016b. 'Estadísticas: Política Económica y Social'. Available at https://www.mef.gob.pe/es/sistema-nacional-de-contabilidad-sp-9060/politica-economica-y-social, accessed 20 February 2018.

Mesa, J., T. Gisbert, and C. D. Mesa. 1998. *Historia de Bolivia*. La Paz, Bolivia: Editorial Gisbert.

Migdal, J. S. 1988. *Strong Societies and Weak States: State–Society Relations and State Capabilities in the Third World*. Princeton, NJ: Princeton University Press.

Miller, R. 2011. *Empresas Británicas, Economía y Política en el Perú, 1850–1934*. Lima: BCRP, IEP.

MINEM (Ministry of Energy and Mines). 2011. 'Programa Minero de Solidaridad con el Pueblo Informe N° 040'. Lima: MINEM.

MINEM (Ministry of Energy and Mines). 2016. Anuario Minero 2015. Available at http://www.minem.gob.pe/_publicacion.php?idSector=1&idPublicacion=524, accessed 20 February 2018.

Minerals and Mining Act. 2006. Act 703, Parliament of the Republic of Ghana.

Ministry of Culture, 2017. 'Procesos de Consulta Previa'. Available at http://consultaprevia.cultura.gob.pe/proceso/, accessed 11 January 2018.

Ministry of Environment (2015). 'Zonas con Minería Ilegal e Informal'. Source: Ministry of Environment, National Institute of Statistics and Informatics, Centros Poblados (IGN). Available at http://geoservidor.minam.gob.pe/monitoreo-y-evaluacion/cambios-por-mineria-ilegal-e-informal/, accessed 20 February 2018.

Ministry of Lands and Natural Resources. 2011. 'Land Administration Project Phase Two: Project implementation manual'. Accra.

Ministry of Lands and Natural Resources. 2013. 'Statement by the Hon. Minister of Lands and Natural Resources Relating to Gov'ts Position on Small Scale Mining (SSM)'. Accra.

Mitchell, T. 2012. *Carbon Democracy: Political Power in the Age of Oil*. New York: Verso.

Mkandawire, T. 2006. 'Disempowering new democracies and the persistence of poverty'. UNSRID Democracy, Governance and Human Rights Programme Paper No. 21, January. Available at http://www.unrisd.org/unrisd/website/document.nsf/(httpPublications)/6602342%2031C9D6710C125717800248890?OpenDocument, accessed 25 March 2017.

MOFEP. 2017. 'Budget Statements'. *Ministry of Finance*. Available at http://www.mofep.gov.gh/?q=budget-statements, accessed 20 February 2018.

Mohan, G. and K. P. Asante. 2015. 'Transnational capital and the political settlement of Ghana's oil economy'. ESID Working Paper No. 49. Manchester: Effective States and Inclusive Development Research Centre, University of Manchester.

Mohan, G., M. Power, and M. Tan-Mullins, 2012. *China's Resource Diplomacy in Africa: Powering Development?* London: Palgrave Macmillan.

Mohan, G., K. P. Asante, and A.-G. Abdulai. 2017. 'Party politics and the political economy of Ghana's oil'. *New Political Economy*. Available at www.tandfonline.com/doi/full/10.1080/13563467.2017.1349087, accessed 20 February 2018.

Molina, F. 2008. 'Bolivia: La geografía de un conflicto'. *Nueva Sociedad* 218: 4–13.

Molina, F. 2011. *El Pensamiento Boliviano Sobre los Recursos Nacionales*. 2nd Edn. La Paz: Fundación Vicente Pazos Kanki.

Morales, J. A. 1992. 'Bolivia's tin and natural gas crises of 1985–1989'. Instituto de Investigaciones Socio-Economicas Working Paper No. 04/92. La Paz: Universidad Catolica Boliviana.

Morón, E. A. and C. Sanborn. 2007. *Los Desafíos del Policymaking en Perú: Actores, Instituciones y Reglas de Juego*. Lima: CIUP, Documento de Trabajo 77.

Mosquera, César. (2006). 'El desafío de la formalizacíon de la minería artesanal y de pequeña escala'. Available at https://idl-bnc-idrc.dspacedirect.org/bitstream/handle/10625/26183/123847.pdf?sequence=1, accessed 20 February 2018.

Munck, G. L. and R. Snyder. 2007. *Passion, Craft, and Method in Comparative Politics*. Baltimore, MD: The Johns Hopkins University Press.

Muñoz, I. and M. Vega. 2000. 'El fomento de la inversión privada'. In *La Reforma Incompleta*, edited by Roberto Abusada, Fritz Du Bois, Eduardo Morón, and José Valderrama, pp. 13–62. Lima: Instituto Peruano de Economía, Universidad del Pacífico.

Muñoz Chirinos, P. 2010. 'Consistencia política regional o frágiles alianzas electorales? El escenario electoral cuzqueño actual'. *Revista Argumentos* 4(3).

Nash, J. C. 1993. *We Eat the Mines and the Mines Eat Us: Dependency and Exploitation in Bolivian Tin Mines*. New York: Columbia University Press.

NCOM (National Coalition on Mining). 2011. 'Statement by National Coalition on Mining on 2012 Budget: Proceed with further reforms in the mining sector'. 21 November. Accra.

NDC (National Democratic Congress). 2004. 'National Democratic Congress Manifesto 2004: A better Ghana'. Accra.

NDC (National Democratic Congress). 2008. 'Manifesto for a Better Ghana 2008'. Accra.

NDC (National Democratic Congress). 2012. '2012 Manifesto: Advancing the Better Ghana Agenda'. Accra.

NDPC. 2017. 'Budgets (National)'. *National Development Planning Commission*. Available at http://www.ndpc.gov.gh/downloads/8/, accessed 20 February 2018.

Negi, R. 2011. 'The micropolitics of mining and development in Zambia: Insights from the Northwestern Province'. *African Studies Quarterly* 12(2): 27–44.

Negi, R. 2014. '"Solwezi Mabanga": Ambivalent developments on Zambia's new mining frontier'. *Journal of Southern African Studies* 40(5): 999–1013.

North, D. C., J. J. Wallis, S. B. Webb, and B. R. Weingast. 2007. 'Limited access orders in the developing world: A new approach to the problems of development', Policy Research Working Paper 4359. Washington, DC: World Bank.

North, D. C., J. J. Wallis, and B. R. Weingast. 2009. *Violence and Social Orders: A Conceptual Framework for Interpreting Recorded Human History*. Cambridge and New York: Cambridge University Press.

NPP (New Patriotic Party). 2008. 'New Patriotic Party manifesto 2008'. Accra.

NPP (New Patriotic Party). 2012. 'Transforming lives, transforming Ghana: Building a free, fair and prosperous society'. Manifesto for election 2012. Accra.

NRGI (National Resource Governance Institute). 2017. '2017 Resource Governance Index'. Available at https://resourcegovernance.org/analysis-tools/publications/2017-resource-governance-index, accessed 20 February 2018.

Nyame, F. K. and J. Blocher. 2010. 'Influence of land tenure practices on artisanal mining activity in Ghana'. *Resources Policy* 35(1): 47–53.

O'Donnell, G. 1973. *Modernization and Bureaucratic-Authoritarianism: Studies in South American Politics*. Berkeley, CA: Institute of International Studies, University of California.

O'Donnell, G. 1988. *Bureaucratic Authoritarianism: Argentina (1966–73) in Comparative Perspective*. Berkeley, CA: University of California Press.

Oduro, F., M. Awal, and M. A. Ashon. 2014. 'A dynamic mapping of the political settlement in Ghana'. ESID Working Paper No. 28. Manchester: Effective States and Inclusive Development Research Centre, University of Manchester.

Oelbaum, J. 2007. 'Liberalisation or liberation? Economic reform, spatial poverty, and the irony of conflict in Ghana's Northern Region'. A paper prepared for the international workshop 'Understanding and addressing spatial poverty traps: An international workshop', 29 March, Stellenbosch, South Africa. Chronic Poverty Research Centre and the Overseas Development Institute.

Ofosu-Mensah, E. A. 2016. 'Mining in colonial Ghana: Extractive capitalism and its social benefits in Akyem Abuakwa under Nana Ofori Atta I'. *Africa Today* 63(1): 23–55.

Omosini, O. 1972. 'The Gold Coast land question, 1894–1900: Some issues raised on West Africa's economic development'. *International Journal of African Historical Studies* 5(3): 453–69.

ONAMIAP. 2014. 'Lideresas indígenas de ONAMIAP se pronuncian sobre la cuota indígena'. Lima, Peru. Available at http://www.onamiap.org/2014/05/lideresas-indigenas-de-onamiap-se.html, accessed 20 February 2018.

Oporto, H. 2012. *Los Dilemas de la Minería*. La Paz: Fundación Vicente Pazos Kanki.

Orihuela, J. C. 2013. 'Instituciones y cambio institucional: Repensando la maldición de los recursos desde los nuevos institucionalismos y la experiencia peruana'. *Revista Politai* 6: 47–62.

Orihuela, J. C. and R. Thorp. 2012. 'Political economy of extractive industries in Bolivia, Ecuador and Peru'. In *Social Conflict, Economic Development and the Extractive Industry: Evidence from South America*, edited by A. Bebbington, pp. 27–45. London: Routledge.

Orrego, J. L. 2012. 'Breve historia de la banca en Lima hasta 1950.' Lima: Blog de Juan Luis Orrego Penagos, Historia del Perú, América y el Mundo, Siglos XIX y XX. Available at http://blog.pucp.edu.pe/blog/juanluisorrego/2012/01/01/breve-historia-de-la-banca-en-lima-hasta-1950/, accessed 20 February 2018.

Osei-Hwedie, B. 2003. 'Development policy and economic change in Zambia: A reassessment'. *DPMN Bulletin* X(2), April.

Ospina, A., A. J. Bebbington, P. Hollenstein, I. Nussbaum, and E. Ramírez. 2015. 'Extraterritorial investments, environmental crisis and collective action in Latin America'. *World Development* 73: 32–43.

Oxfam America. 2014. 'Geographies of conflict. Mapping overlaps between extractive industries and agricultural land uses in Ghana and Peru'. Washington: Oxfam America.

Pachas, V. 2012. *El Sueño del Corredor Minero. Cómo Aprender a Vivir Contigo y Sin ti*. Lima: CBC, GOMIAN.

Página Siete. 2013. 'Investigación indaga sobre los préstamos de Patiño al Estado'. *Página Siete* 16 (October). Available at http://www.paginasiete.bo/cultura/2013/10/16/investigacion-indaga-sobre-prestamos-patino-estado-3308.html, accessed 16 October 2013.

Página Siete. 2016. 'Campamento petrolero de Lliquimuni en retira, pozo de hidrocarburos dio negativo', 21 March. Available at http://www.paginasiete.bo/economia/2016/3/21/campamento-petrolero-lliquimuni-retirada-pozo-hidrocarburos-negativo-90558.html, accessed 30 March 2016.

Panfichi, A. 2011. 'Contentious representation and its impact in contemporary Peru'. In *Fractured Politics: Peruvian Democracy Past and Present*, edited by J. Crabtree. London: Institute for the Study of the Americas, University of London.

Paredes, M. 2013. *Shaping State Capacity: A Comparative Historical Analysis of Mining Dependence in the Andes, 1840–1920*. Unpublished Ph.D. thesis, Oxford, UK: University of Oxford.

Paredes, M., J. C. Orihuela, and C. Huaroto. 2013. *Escapando de la maldición de los recursos local: conflictos socioambientales y salidas institucionales*. Lima: CIES, PUCP.

Parks, T. and W. Cole. 2010. 'Political settlements: Implications for international development policy and practice'. The Asia Foundation. Occasional Paper, No. 2, July 2010.

Parodi, C. 2002. *Perú 1960–2000: Política Económica y Entornos Cambiantes*. Lima: Universidad del Pacífico.

Pascó-Font, A. 2000. *The Social Impact of Privatization and Regulation of Utilities in Urban Peru*. Helsinki: World Bank.

Pasco Font, A. and Maximo Torero. 2001. 'El impacto social de la privatización y la regulación de los servicios públicos en el Perú'. Lima: Grade (Documento de Trabajo, 35). Available at http://ageconsearch.umn.edu/bitstream/37758/2/ddt35.pdf, accessed 20 February 2018.

Peet, R. and E. Hartwick. 2015. *Theories of Development. Contentions, Arguments, Alternatives*. New York: Guilford Press.

Peet, R. and M. Watts. (eds). 1996. *Liberation Ecologies: Environment, Development, Social Movements*. London: Routledge.

Peres Cajías, J. 2011. 'Repensando el desarrollo desde la historia económica: crecimiento y lucha de débiles'. In *Desarrollo en Cuestión: reflexiones desde América Latina*, edited by F. Wanderley, pp. 99–131. La Paz: CIDES-UMSA and Plural.

Peres Cajías, J. 2014. 'Bolivian public finances, 1882–2010: The challenge to make social spending sustainable'. *Journal of Iberian and Latin American Economic History* 32(1): 77–117.

Perla, C. 2012. 'Extracting from the Extractors: The Politics of Private Welfare in the Peruvian Mining Industry'. Unpublished PhD thesis, Providence, RI: Brown University.

Perreault, T. 2006. 'From the Guerra del Agua to the Guerra del Gas: Resource governance, neoliberalism and popular protest in Bolivia'. *Antipode* 38(1): 150–72.

Perreault, T. 2013. 'Nature and nation: Hydrocarbons, governance, and the territorial logics of resource nationalism in Bolivia'. In *Subterranean Struggles: New Geographies of Extractive Industries in Latin America*, edited by A. Bebbington and J. Bury, pp. 67–90. Austin, TX: University of Texas Press.

Pesa, I. 2014. 'Moving along the Roadside. A Social History of Mwinilunga District, 1870s–1970s'. PhD thesis, University of Leiden.

Phillips, J., E. Hailwood, and A. Brooks. 2016. 'Sovereignty, the "resource curse" and the limits of good governance: A political economy of oil in Ghana'. *Review of African Political Economy* 43(47): 26–42.

Phimister, I. 2011. 'Proletarians in paradise: The historiography and historical sociology of white miners on the Copperbelt'. In *Living the End of Empire. Politics and Society in Late Colonial Zambia*, edited by J. B. Gewald, M. Hinfelaar, and G. Macola, pp. 141–60. Leiden: Brill.

Plange, Nii-K. 1979. 'Underdevelopment in Northern Ghana: Natural causes or colonial capitalism?' *Review of African Political Economy* 6(15–16): 4–14.

Ponce, A. and C. McClintock. 2014. 'The explosive combination of inefficient local bureaucracies and mining production: Evidence from localized societal protests in Peru'. *Latin American Politics and Society* 56(3): 118–40.

Portocarrero M., Gonzalo. 1983. 'Ideologías, funciones del estado y políticas económicas Perú: 1900–1980.' *Debates en Sociología* 9: 7–30. Lima: Pontificia Universidad Católica del Perú.

Portocarrero S., Felipe. 2013. *Grandes Fortunas en el Perú: 1916–1960*. Lima: Fondo Editorial de la Universidad del Pacífico.

Portocarrero S., Felipe, Cynthia Sanborn, and Luis Antonio Camacho. (2007). *Moviendo Montañas: Empresas, Comunidades y ONG en las Industrias Extractivas*. Lima: Fondo Editorial de la Universidad del Pacífico.

Poteete, A. 2009. 'Is development path dependent or political? A reinterpretation of mineral-dependent development in Botswana'. *Journal of Development Studies* 45(4): 544–71.

Poveda, R. 2007. 'Minería'. In *Perú: La Oportunidad de un País en Diferente. Próspero, Equitativo y Gobernable*, edited by Marcelo Giugale, Vicente Fretes-Cibilis, and John Newman, chap. 20, pp. 445–66. Lima: World Bank.

Poveda, P. 2012. *Diagnóstico del Sector Minero*. La Paz: Fundación Jublileo.

PRODUCE (Ministerio de la Producción). 2014. 'Plan nacional de diversificación productiva'. Available at http://sinia.minam.gob.pe/documentos/plan-nacional-diversificacion-productiva, accessed 20 February 2018.

Pulgar-Vidal, M. 2008. 'Ministerio del ambiente: un largo proceso de construcción de la institucionalidad ambiental en el Perú' THEMIS 56.

Quandzie, E. 2011, 17 November. 'Ghana bows to IMF by hiking mining taxes to 35% from 25%'. *Ghana Business News*. Available at https://www.ghanabusinessnews.com/2011/11/17/ghana-bows-to-imf-by-hiking-mining-taxes-to-35-from-25/, accessed 25 May 2017.

Quarshie, A. N. K. 2015. 'Mining and Development in Ghana: A Case Study of the Mineral Development Fund in the Obuasi Municipal Assembly'. Unpublished MA dissertion, University of Ghana.

Rajan, S. C. 2011. 'Poor little rich countries: Another look at the "resource curse"'. *Environmental Politics* 20(5): 617–32.

Rakner, L. 2003. *Political and Economic Liberalisation in Zambia 1991–2001*. Uppsala: Nordic Africa Institute.

Remy, M. I. 2005. *Los Múltiples Campos de la Participación Ciudadana en el Perú: Un Reconocimiento del Terreno y Algunas Reflexiones*. Lima: Instituto de Estudios Peruanos.

Republic of Ghana. 1992. *Constitution of the Republic of Ghana, 1992*. Tema: Ghana Publishing Corporation.

Republic of Ghana. 2009. 'Budget statement and economic policy of the Government of Ghana for the 2010 financial year's budget speech'. Presented to parliament, 18 November. 2009 financial year budget speech.

Republic of Ghana. 2011. 'Budget statement and economic policy of the Government of Ghana for the 2012 financial year's budget speech'. Presented to parliament, 18 November. 2011 financial year budget speech.

Republic of Ghana. 2013. 'Performance audit report of the Auditor General Utilisation of Mining Development Fund by metropolitan, municipal and district assemblies'. Accra.

Republic of Ghana. 2014. 'Minerals and mining policy of Ghana: Ensuring mining contributes to sustainable development'. Accra: Ministry of Lands and Natural Resources.

Roberts, A. 2011. 'Northern-Rhodesia: The post-war background 1945–1953'. In *Living the End of Empire: Politics and Society in late Colonial Zambia*, edited by J. B. Gewald, M. Hinfelaar, and G. Macola, pp. 18–28. Leiden: Brill.

Robertson, G. A. 1819. *Notes on Africa*. London.

Robinson, J., R. Torvik, and T. Verdier. 2006. 'Political foundations of the resource curse'. *Journal of Development Economics* 79: 447–68.

Roca, J. L. 2008. 'Regionalism revisited'. In *Unresolved Tensions: Bolivia Past and Present*, edited by J. Crabtree and L. Whitehead, pp. 65–82. Pittsburgh, PA: University of Pittsburgh Press.

Rodríguez, G. 1994. *Élites, Mercado y Cuestión Regional en Bolivia*. La Paz: ILDIS.

Ross, M. 1999. 'The political economy of the Resource Curse'. *World Politics* 15 (January): 297–322.

Ross, M. 2001a. 'Does oil hinder democracy?' *World Politics* 53(3): 325–61.

Ross, M. 2001b. *Extractive Sectors and the Poor: An Oxfam America Report*. Boston, MA: Oxfam America.

Ross, M. 2012. *The Oil Curse: How Petroleum Wealth Shapes the Development of Nations*. Princeton, NJ: Princeton University Press.

Ross, M. 2015. 'What have we learned about the Resource Curse?'. *Annual Review of Political Science* 18: 239–59.

Ruiz Caro, A. 2002. *El Proceso de Privatizaciones en el Perú Durante el Período 1991–2002*. Santiago de Chile: CEPAL-ILPES.

Sachs, J. and A. Warner. 1995. 'Natural resource abundance and economic growth'. National Bureau of Economic Research Working Paper Series, No. 539. Cambridge, MA: National Bureau of Economic Research, pp. 1–46.

Sanborn, C. 1991. 'The Democratic Left and the Persistence of Populism in Peru, 1975–1985'. Unpublished PhD thesis, Harvard University Department of Government.

Sanborn, C. 2008. 'Del dicho al hecho: Empresarios y responsabilidad social en el Perú'. *Revista Brújula*, PUCP, Abril–Julio.

Sanborn, C. and V. Chonn. 2015. 'Chinese Investment in Peru's Mining Industry: Blessing or Curse?' Boston: Global Economic Governance Initiative, Discussion Paper 2015–8.

Sanborn, C. and J. L. Dammert. 2013. 'Extracción de recursos naturales, desarrollo económico e inclusión social en el Perú'. *Americas Quarterly*, June 19.

Sanborn, C., V. Hurtado, and T. Ramírez. 2016. 'La consulta previa en el Perú: avances y retos'. Lima: Universidad del Pacífico, Documento de Investigación 6. Available at http://www.up.edu.pe/investigacion-centros/fondo-editorial/catalogo/la-consulta-previa-en-peru, accessed 20 February 2018.

Sanborn, C. and A. Paredes. 2015. *Getting it Right? Challenges to Prior Consultation in Peru*. Centre for Social Responsibility in Mining Sustainable Minerals Institute. St Lucia, QLD: University of Queensland, Australia.

Sanborn, C., T. Ramírez, and V. Hurtado. 2017. 'Mining, political settlements and inclusive development in Peru'. ESID Working Paper No. 79. Manchester: Effective States and Inclusive Development Research Centre, University of Manchester.

Sanborn, C. and V. Torres. 2009. *La economía china y las industrias extractivas: desafíos para el Perú*. Lima: Fondo Editorial de la Universidad del Pacífico, CooperAcción.

Sánchez Albavera, F. 1981. *Minería, Capital Transnacional y Poder en el Perú*. Lima: DESCO.

Santiago, M. L. 2006. *The Ecology of Oil: Environment, Labor, and the Mexican Revolution, 1900–1938*. New York: Cambridge University Press.

Schilling-Vacaflor, A. 2017. 'Who controls the territory and the resources? Free, prior and informed consent (FPIC) as a contested human rights practice in Bolivia'. *Third World Quarterly* 38(5): 1058–74.

Schmidt, G. D. 2008. *Peru: The Politics of Surprise*. 2nd Edn. London: Mcgraw-Hill.

Schmitter, P. and T. Karl. 1991. 'What Democracy is ... and is not'. *Journal of Democracy* 2(3): 75–88.

Schmitter, Philippe C. (1992). 'The consolidation of democracy and the representation of social groups'. *American Behavioral Scientist* 35(4–5): 422–49.

Schuldt, J. 2013. 'Futurología de la economía política Peruana'. In *Cuando despertemos en el 2062: visiones del Perú en 50 años*, edited by Bruno Seminario, Cynthia A. Sanborn, and Nikolai Alva, pp. 73–116. Lima: Fondo Editorial de la Universidad del Pacifico.

Schünemann, J. and A. Lucey. 2015. 'Success and failure of political settlements: defining and measuring transformation'. Working Paper 2, Political Settlements Research Programme. Edinburgh: University of Edinburgh.

Seminario, B. 2014. *Breve historia de los precios, población y actividad económica del Perú: reconstrucción de las cuentas nacionales, 1700–2013*. Lima: PUCP.

Seminario, B. 2015. *El desarrollo de la economía peruana en la era moderna. Precios, población, demanda y producción desde 1700*. Lima: Universidad del Pacífico.

Sen, K. 2013. 'The political dynamics of economic growth'. *World Development* 47: 71–86.

Silver News Online. 2016. 'Obuasi galamsey: Irrate illegal miners destroy MCE, NDC offices, billboards'. 19 March.

Simuntanyi, N. 2015. 'Political economy analysis'. Unpublished. Internal PEA analysis, Center for Policy Dialogue.

Slater, D. and H. Soifer. 2010. *Ordering Power: Contentious Politics and Authoritarian Leviathans in Southeast Asia*. Cambridge: Cambridge University Press.

Smock, D. R. and A. Smock. 1975. *The Politics of Pluralism: A Comparative Study of Lebanon and Ghana*. New York and Amsterdam: Elsevier.

SNMPE. 2012. *Impacto Económico de la Actividad Minera en el Perú*. Lima: SNMPE.

Soifer, H. 2012. 'Midiendo la capacidad estatal en la América Latina contemporánea'. *Revista de Ciencia Política* 32(3): 585–98 (Santiago).

Soifer, H. 2015. *State Building in Latin America*. Cambridge: Cambridge University Press.

Songsore, J., A. Denkabe, C. D. Jebuni, and S. Ayidiya. 2001. 'Challenges of education in Northern Ghana: A case for Northern Ghana Education Trust Fund (NETFUND)'. In *Regionalism and Public Policy in Northern Ghana*, edited by Y. Saaka, pp. 222–39. New York: Peter Lang.

Stallings, B. 1992. 'International influence on economic policy: Debt, stabilization, and structural reform'. In *The Politics of Economic Adjustment: International Constraints, Distributive Conflicts and the State*, edited by Stephan Haggard and Robert R. Kaufman, pp. 41–88. Princeton, NJ: Princeton University Press.

Standing, A. 2014. 'Ghana's extractive industries and community benefit sharing: The case for cash transfers'. *Resources Policy* 40: 74–82.

Starr FM. 2016. 'NPP will regularize "galamsey" - Akufo-Addo'. 15 July. Available at http://www.ghanaweb.com/GhanaHomePage/NewsArchive/NPP-will-regularizegalamsey-Akufo-Addo-455652, accessed 11 May 2017.

Stein, F. 2010. 'Bolivian tin miners reconciled'. *Americas Quarterly*, Fall. Available at http://americasquarterly.org/node/1922, accessed 1 June 2017.

Stepan, A. 1978. *The State and Society: Peru in Comparative Perspective*. Princeton, NJ: Princeton Legacy Library.

Stern, S. J. 1993. *Peru's Indian peoples and the Challenge of Spanish Conquest: Huamanga to 1640*. Madison, WI: University of Wisconsin Press.

Stone, D. 2004. *Think Tank Traditions: Policy Research and the Politics of Ideas*. Manchester: University of Manchester Press.

Sulmont, D. 1980. 'Situación y perspectiva del movimiento sindical'. Cuadernos Laborales N°1. Lima: PUCP.

Sulmont, D. 2012. 'Raza y etnicidad desde las encuestas sociales y de opinión: dime cuántos quieres encontrar y te diré qué preguntar'. In *La discriminación en el Perú: balance y desafíos*, pp. 51—74. Lima: Universidad del Pacífico.

SUNAT. 2017. 'Estadística y Estudios; Ingresos Tributarios Recaudados por la Sunat - Tributos Internos según Actividad Económica, 1998- 2016 (Millones de soles)'. Available at http://www.sunat.gob.pe/estadisticasestudios/busqueda_actividad_economica.html, accessed 20 February 2018.

Sutton, J. and Langmead, G. 2013. *Enterprise Map of Zambia*. Lusaka: International Growth Centre.

Swanzy, S. A. 2016. '"Pay us all our royalties" – Chiefs cry out to finance ministry'. 16 August. Available at http://pulse.com.gh/business/mining-pay-us-all-our-royaltieschiefs-cry-out-to-finance-ministry-id5384719.html, accessed 11 May 2017.

Szablowski, D. 2002. 'Mining, displacement and the World Bank: A case analysis of Compañia Minera Antamina's operations in Peru'. *Journal of Business Ethics* 39(3): 247–73.

Szeftel, M. 1982. 'Political graft and the spoils system in Zambia – the state as a resource in itself'. *Review of African Political Economy* (9)24: 4–21.

Tanaka, M. 1998. *Los Espejismos de la Democracia: El Colapso del Sistema de Partidos en el Perú*. Lima: Instituto de Estudios Peruanos.

Teschner, B. A. 2012. 'Small-scale mining in Ghana: The government and the galamsey'. *Resources Policy* 37(3): 308–14.

Thorp, R. and G. Bertram. 2013. *Perú 1890–1977: Crecimiento y Políticas en una Economía Abierta*. Lima: Universidad del Pacífico.

Thorp, R., S. Battistelli, Y. Guichaoua, J. Orihuela, and M. Paredes. 2012. *The Developmental Challenges of Mining and Oil: Lessons from Africa and Latin America*. Oxford: Palgrave MacMillan.

Tilly, C. 1978. *From Mobilization to Revolution*. Boston, MA: Addison-Wesley.

Tilly, C. 2004. *Contention and Democracy in Europe, 1650–2000*. Cambridge: Cambridge University Press.

Toranzo Roca, C. 2009. 'Economía Política de los hidrocarburos en Bolivia'. DRAFT. pp. 3–5. Available at http://siteresources.worldbank.org/EXTLACOFFICEOFCE/Resources/870892-1253047679843/CarlosToranzo2009.pdf, accessed 20 February 2018.

Torres, V. 2013. *Grupos Económicos y Bonanza Minera en el Perú: el Caso de Cinco Grupos Mineros Nacionales*. Lima: Cooperacción.

Tsikata, F. S. 1997. 'The vicissitudes of mineral policy in Ghana', *Resources Policy* 23(1): 9–14.

Tsuma, W. 2010. 'Gold Mining in Ghana: Actors, Alliances and Power'. ZEF Development Studies, University of Bonn.

Tuesta, F. 1996. *Los Enigmas del Poder. Fujimori 1990–1996*. Lima: Fundación Frederich Ebert.

TWN-Africa. 2016. 'Ghana government's development agreements with Goldfields illegal – TWN-Africa'. Available at http://twnafrica.org/Goldfields%20development%20agreement%20with%20Ghana%2%20illegal-pr-2016.pdf, accessed 11 May 2017.

UNCTADSTAT. 2017. 'Free market commodity prices, annual, 1960–2016'. Available at http://unctadstat.unctad.org/wds/TableViewer/tableView.aspx?ReportId=30727, accessed 20 February 2018.

Valencia, L. 2014. *Madre de Dios: ¿Podemos Evitar la Tragedia? Políticas de Ordenamiento de la Minería Aurífera*. Lima: Sociedad Peruana de Derecho Ambiental.

Van Cott, D. L. 2007. *From Movements to Parties in Latin America: The Evolution of Ethnic Politics*. Cambridge: Cambridge University Press.

Vásquez, E. 2016. 'Pobreza e inversión social en Perú al 2011'. In *Metas del Perú al Bicentenario*, pp. 110–24. Lima: Consorcio de Universidades.

Vergara, A. and D. Encinas. 2016. 'Continuity by surprise. Explaining institutional stability in contemporary Peru'. *Latin American Research Review* 51(1): 159–80.

Villavicencio, A. 2015. 'La negociación colectiva en el Perú: la hiperdescentralización y sus múltiples inconvenientes'. Derecho PUCP, N° 75, pp. 333–53. Lima: PUCP.

Vom Hau, M. and S. Hickey. 2016. 'Power relations, political settlements, and the deployment of state capacity in the developing world'. *Mimeo*. Paper prepared for

ESID. Manchester: Effective States and Inclusive Development Research Centre, University of Manchester.

Wainwright, J. and M. Robertson. 2003. 'Territorialization, science and the colonial state: The case of Highway 55 in Minnesota'. *Cultural Geographies* 10: 196–217.

Wardell, D. A. 2006. 'Collision, collusion and muted resistance—contrasting early and later encounters with Empire forestry in the Gold Coast, 1874–1957'. In *Collisions of Cultures and Identifies: Settlers and Indigenous Peoples*, edited by P. Grimshaw and R. McGregor, pp. 79–103. Melbourne, VIC: University of Melbourne.

Watts, M. J. 2004a. 'Antinomies of community: Some thoughts on geography, resources and Empire'. *Transactions of the Institute of British Geographers* 29(2): 195–216.

Watts, M. J. 2004b. 'Resource Curse? Governmentality, oil and power in the Niger Delta, Nigeria'. *Geopolitics* 9(1): 50–80.

Watts, M. J. with E. Kashi (photographer). 2008. *The Curse of the Black Gold*. New York: Powerhouse Press.

Weber-Fahr, M. 2002. *Treasure or Trouble? Mining in Developing Countries*. Washington, DC: World Bank and International Finance Corporation.

Whitehead, L. 1972. 'El impacto de la Gran Depresión en Bolivia'. *Desarrollo Económico* 12 (45): 49–80.

Whitfield, L. 2011a. 'Competitive clientelism, easy financing and weak capitalists: The contemporary political settlement in Ghana'. DIIS Working Paper 27. Copenhagen: Danish Institute for International Studies.

Whitfield, L. 2011b. 'Growth without economic transformation: Economic impacts of Ghana's political settlement'. DIIS Working Paper 28. Copenhagen: Danish Institute for International Studies.

Whitfield, L. 2018. *Economies after Colonialism: Ghana and the Struggle for Power*. Cambridge: Cambridge University Press.

Whitfield, L., O. Therkildsen, L. Buur, and A. M. Kjær. 2015. *The Politics of African Industrial Policy: A Comparative Perspective*. Cambridge: Cambridge University Press.

Wilson, F. 2004. 'Towards a political economy of roads: Experiences from Peru'. *Development and Change* 35(3): 525–46.

Wise, C. 2003. *Reinventando el Estado: Estrategia Económica y Cambio Institucional en el Perú*. Lima: Universidad del Pacífico.

Wodon, Q. 2012. *Improving the Targeting of Social Programs in Ghana*. Washington DC: World Bank.

Wood Mackenzie. 2012. *Ghana's Upstream Sector: Country Overview Slides*. London: Wood Mackenzie.

World Bank. 1992. 'Strategy for African mining', World Bank Technical Paper No. 181. Washington, DC: World Bank.

World Bank. 2003. *Project Performance Assessment Report, Ghana: Mining Sector Rehabilitation Project (Credit 1921-GH) and Mining Sector Development and Environment Project (Credit 2743-GH)*. Washington, DC: World Bank.

World Bank. 2005. 'Riqueza y Sostenibilidad: Dimensiones Sociales y Ambientales de la Minería en el Perú. Unidad de Gestión del País-Perú Desarrollo Ambiental y Social Sostenible Región Latinoamérica y El Caribe.' Washington, DC: World Bank.

World Bank. 2008. 'International Development Association programme document for a proposed credit in the amount of SDR8.2 Million (SS$13 million equivalent) to the Republic of Ghana for a natural resources and environmental governance first development policy operation. Report No. 42787-GH'. Washington, DC: World Bank.

World Bank. 2009. 'Economy-wide impact of oil discovery in Ghana'. 30 November, Report No. 47321-GH.

World Bank. 2013. 'Project performance assessment report: Ghana Land Administration Project'. Report No. 75084. Washington, DC: The World Bank.

World Bank. 2016a. 'Gasto público en educación, total (% del PIB)'. Available at http://datos.bancomundial.org/indicador/SE.XPD.TOTL.GD.ZS, accessed 20 February 2018.

World Bank. 2016b. 'World development indicators: Peru'. Available at http://data.worldbank.org/country/peru, accessed 20 February 2018.

World Bank. 2017. 'The World Bank in Peru: Overview'. Available at http://www.worldbank.org/en/country/peru/overview, accessed 15 July 2017.

Yampara, S. 2011. 'Cosmovivencia Andina. Vivir y Convivir en Armonía Integral — Suma Qamaña.' *Bolivian Studies Journal* 18: 1–22.

Yashar, D. 2005. *Contesting Citizenship in Latin America: The Rise of Indigenous Movements and the Postliberal Challenge*. Cambridge: Cambridge University Press.

Zegarra, E., J. C. Orihuela and M. Paredes. 2007. 'Minería y economía de los hogares en la sierra peruana: impactos y espacios de conflicto'. Lima: GRADE; CIES. Documento de Trabajo, No. 51.

Index

Note: bold = extended treatment or term highlighted in text, f = figure, m = map, n = footnote, t = table, [-] = intermediate page skipped.

The manufacturer's authorised representative in the EU for product safety is Oxford University Press España S.A. of el Parque Empresarial San Fernando de Henares, Avenida de Castilla, 2 – 28830 Madrid (www.oup.es/en or product.safety@oup.com). OUP España S.A. also acts as importer into Spain of products made by the manufacturer.

www.ingramcontent.com/pod-product-compliance
Lightning Source LLC
LaVergne TN
LVHW011750200926
848484LV00003B/663
* 9 7 8 0 1 9 8 8 2 0 9 3 2 *